THE LOCOMOTIVE
OF WAR

Money, Empire, Power and Guilt

Peter Clarke

BLOOMSBURY

LONDON · OXFORD · NEW YORK · NEW DELHI · SYDNEY

Bloomsbury Paperbacks
An imprint of Bloomsbury Publishing Plc

50 Bedford Square
London
WC1B 3DP
UK

1385 Broadway
New York
NY 10018
USA

www.bloomsbury.com

BLOOMSBURY and the Diana logo are trademarks of Bloomsbury Publishing Plc

First published in Great Britain 2017
This paperback edition first published in 2018

British Library Cataloguing-in-Publication Data
A catalogue record for this book is available from the British Library.

ISBN: HB: 978-1-4088-5165-4
PB: 978-1-4088-5168-5
ePub: 978-1-4088-5164-7

2 4 6 8 10 9 7 5 3 1

Typeset by Newgen Knowledge Works (P) Ltd., Chennai, India
Printed and bound in Great Britain by CPI Group (UK) Ltd, Croydon CR0 4YY

MIX
Paper from
responsible sources
FSC® C020471
www.fsc.org

To find out more about our authors and books visit www.bloomsbury.com.
Here you will find extracts, author interviews, details of forthcoming events and the
option to sign up for our newsletters.

For Emily and Libby

A NOTE ON THE AUTHOR

PETER CLARKE was formerly a professor of modern history and Master of Trinity Hall at Cambridge. His many books include *Keynes: The Twentieth Century's Most Influential Economist,* the acclaimed final volume of *The Penguin History of Britain, Hope and Glory, Britain 1900–2000* and *Mr Churchill's Profession,* a study of Churchill as writer. He is now resident in Cambridge.

CONTENTS

AUTHOR'S NOTE

To keep the narrative as clear and uncluttered as possible for the reader, I have restricted the numbered endnotes in the text. What these specify are only the references to some twenty-odd publications – significant and widely cited sources on which my own history offers a critical commentary. This is specifically what I mean in the Prologue by 'special scrutiny of some texts generated by these events – memoirs, diaries, letters and other published documents, along with some influential polemical tracts'. In length, these vary from the sixty-nine fat volumes of Woodrow Wilson's papers to the spare thirty-nine pages of John Morley's memorandum on the 1914 crisis. But I am humbly conscious of how much this book also relies on the scholarship of other historians: sometimes in the form of my specific quotations but – even more – in the general insights that I have gleaned from their work. All these debts are, I hope, properly acknowledged in my Notes on Sources at the end, where I feel free to reflect more fully on the historiography as shaped by my many distinguished predecessors.

PROLOGUE

A Train of Thought

I FROM TROTSKY TO PIKETTY

'War is the locomotive of history.' Is it? If so, how? And with what results? The phrase is often quoted, with or without attribution to Leon Trotsky. We tend to assume that Trotsky was speaking of Russia. After all, he was well aware of the crucial role of the First World War in giving the Bolsheviks their opportunity to seize power in Russia in 1917. He had been up to his neck in these events, as Lenin's partner and rival; and, undeniably, the creation of the Soviet Union as a Communist state made history on the grand scale. But what if Trotsky's claim about war's catastrophic impact and revolutionary potential did not really have Russia in mind? What if he had been thinking more of Great Britain and, in particular, the United States, when he talked about this locomotive?

We might call that a different train of thought. For Trotsky not only pointed to the motive force of war in making the history that had already happened but also appealed to it, prophetically, in guaranteeing the shape of the future, on the assumption that only one outcome was available, not only in Russia but elsewhere. But our perspective today is inevitably different. Trotsky, who has sometimes been hailed as a prophet, may now appear in a different light: not as a man whose expectations were fulfilled by the Russian revolution but as a man who somehow failed to understand the dynamics of history, especially the relationship between western capitalism and democracy, under conditions of war and peace alike.

I readily acknowledge some irony in appropriating Trotsky's memorable image. For the conclusions that I draw are very different from Trotsky's own claims. He was, of course, a follower of Karl Marx – who was evidently another railway buff, since both men can be quoted deploying their own variations on the graphic image that either revolution or war is the locomotive in driving historical change. The source most commonly cited for Trotsky's preferred formula is a speech that he gave at the end of 1922, and this context is illuminating about his own meaning.

It was only in 1917 that Trotsky had actually become a Bolshevik himself. Previously he had voiced prescient fears about the dictatorial tendencies implicit in Lenin's methods. Yet it was Trotsky who opportunely supplied the idea that a socialist revolution might be instigated in backward Russia – rather than just a bourgeois revolution to overthrow Tsarism. He thought this feasible if an alliance could be forged between the (relatively small) proletariat and the great masses of the peasantry who could thereby be liberated.

Lenin and Trotsky now agreed that the backwardness of Russia could be compensated by forcing the pace of history in this way, given that war had now made all of Europe ripe for revolution. With the Romanovs doomed, and the Habsburgs and the Hohenzollerns trembling, why should Windsor Castle or even the White House, those bastions of modern capitalism, not face a similar fate, sooner or later? Thus Trotsky came to speak of the skein of history unwinding *from the wrong end*. The point was that some temporary abridgment of democratic methods in Russia would be justified once the Bolshevik coup had the desired effect of stimulating proletarian revolution in the advanced capitalist countries – in defeated Germany, of course, but also in Britain and the United States.

Alas for Trotsky, this ambitious scenario was already in need of revision by the time he addressed his comrades in the Communist

International in 1922. By that point he had to acknowledge the rather patchy record of the immediate post-war years – Bolshevik success at a price in the east, but a failure in western Europe that he attributed to poor political strategy. And the United States? Here he succumbed to a sobering sense of realism in acknowledging that a Communist revolution now had even bleaker prospects. It was an admission that the orator softened with a throwaway line, simply offering this parenthetical caveat: '(naturally all sorts of new facts are possible such as, say, a war between America and Japan; and war, Comrades, is a great locomotive of history)'.

A loyal Trotskyite might claim that, twenty years before Pearl Harbor, the prophet at least correctly predicted that particular war. But the bigger point is that the famous phrase about the locomotive was defensively offered, for the obvious reason that Trotsky's own predictions about the imminence of revolution in the advanced economies of the capitalist west were already under challenge from what he saw happening around him. His own assumption remained that, sooner or later, a Communist-led revolution would indeed overthrow and supersede capitalism – by one route or another. Thus once the locomotive reaches the end of any journey, we might then proclaim this as its *destination*, as though it had always been *destined* to get there; but this sort of redefinition of *destiny* is actually little more than a play on words.

Trotsky's critical analysis had an understandable appeal, right across the world, for many revolutionists who could not accept that Soviet Communism embodied Marx's vision. On this reading, the 'actually existing socialism' of Soviet Communism was indeed marred by Stalin's dictatorship – a remediable problem for Trotskyists since it simply required a better kind of Marxist leadership. And once the skein of history unwound, at last, from the right end, bringing revolution in the advanced capitalist west, this historical wrong turning could perhaps be put right.

Such arguments no longer seem plausible. What Trotsky had proclaimed about the locomotive in 1922 inevitably reads rather differently in the world after 1989. So I think he was wrong; but wrong in an interesting and suggestive way. We certainly do not need an alternative triumphalist story of liberal progress.

It is not only Marxists who have been ideologically disconcerted by the actual impact of the locomotive of war. Anglo-American liberals shared many political assumptions in the twentieth century, as I shall hope to bring out in this book; and one of them was that reform of the economic system was possible without abolishing capitalism and the market mechanism itself. The inception of a welfare state in Britain, a project pioneered before the First World War under a Liberal government and largely fulfilled after the Second World War under a Labour government, was a legislative embodiment of this aspiration. And in the United States, there was a somewhat similar ideological affinity between the progressive movement of the early twentieth century and the economic and social reforms of the New Deal era. So by 1945 this strand of liberalism – which we might well term social democratic – seemed to enjoy a similar sort of ascendancy on both sides of the Atlantic.

Yet historically, liberalism and militarism have often been seen as irreconcilable. Both before and after the world wars, those within the big tent of Anglo-American liberalism proclaimed this as axiomatic. It was as a newly minted Liberal (with a capital letter) that the young Winston Churchill, in the years before the First World War, dogmatically affirmed his new party's conventional view. 'The first indispensable condition of democratic progress must be the maintenance of European peace,' he asserted in 1906. 'War is fatal to Liberalism.'[1] Both then and later, similar contentions have often been endorsed, not only in Britain but in the United States. 'War has always been the Nemesis of the liberal tradition in America,' wrote the great historian of the progressive era, Richard Hofstadter, nearly half a century after Churchill's equally sweeping utterance.

Thus many liberals have been manifestly reluctant to acknowledge any positive or constructive role for war. Moreover, their reasoning has not been insubstantial or simply misguided; their misgivings have proved not only understandable but also often well founded. Nonetheless, theirs was a partial view in more senses than one.

With the crucial advantage of hindsight we can profitably reformulate the issue in a less dogmatic form. I think we should now ask: *how* did the locomotive of war transform the role of government and the workings of the economic system? For it surely did so in the twentieth century, and not always by bringing political revolution of the kind that Trotsky envisaged as synonymous with war. Instead, in both western Europe and the United States, democratic regimes recast the political economy of capitalism itself in ways that challenged the assumption that here was a system that structurally enshrined privilege and inequality.

The publication of a seminal work by the French economist Thomas Piketty, *Capital in the Twenty-First Century* (2014), has had an impact that has been little less than sensational. What has largely escaped comment, however, is Piketty's own statement that 'this book is as much a work of history as of economics'.[2] His persuasive account depends less on the logic of economic equations than on an empirical demonstration of how history actually unfolded. Moreover, the outcome was far from predictable – indeed most economists not only failed to foresee what would happen but subsequently failed to recognise what had actually happened because it was so unexpected. The wild card here was war.

What has received most attention is Piketty's meticulous account of the entrenchment of inequality, during a century that was conventionally supposed to have witnessed its inexorable erosion in the western democracies. As an economist, he thus illuminates salient aspects of the world in which we now live; he certainly subverts the assumptions of a previous generation who supposed that a move towards greater equality was virtually irresistible. As a work of history, however, Piketty's *Capital* develops another aspect of the story that is highly relevant here – about that crucially significant half-century beginning in 1914 which actually saw inequality eroded.

In short, he has a lot to tell us about the locomotive of war. 'The history of the distribution of wealth has always been deeply political, and it cannot be reduced to purely economic mechanisms,' he states. 'In particular, the reduction of inequality that took place in most developed countries between 1910 and 1950 was above all a consequence of war and of policies adopted to cope with the shocks of war.'[3] The impact came not so much from the destruction of the infrastructure as through the effects upon budgetary and political mechanisms. 'Briefly, the shocks that buffeted the economy in the period 1914–1945 – World War I, the Bolshevik Revolution of 1917, the Great Depression, World War II, and the consequent advent of new regulatory and tax policies along with controls on capital – reduced capital's share of income to historically low levels in the 1950s.'[4]

So radical was the impact of these changes that it was understandable at the time to suppose that they were irreversible. 'Broadly speaking, it was the wars of the twentieth century that wiped away the past to create the illusion that capitalism had been structurally transformed.'[5] Trotsky, who had used the term 'permanent revolution' to describe the ongoing surge of Communism, might thus have been surprised by a sort of 'permanent reformism' in the capitalist countries of the west. 'People felt', as Piketty puts it, 'that capitalism had been overcome and that inequality and class society had been relegated to the past.'[6] The change may indeed have proved rather less permanent than it seemed at the time; but it was real enough for the two generations that experienced it. Piketty's historical conclusion is confident: 'it was the wars of the twentieth century that, to a large extent, wiped away the past and transformed the structure of inequality.'[7]

We can now see that the relationship between capitalism and democracy, on both sides of the Atlantic, has been complex in the twentieth century; and aspects of it will require closer attention in later chapters. It was a young liberal economist, John Maynard Keynes, who published an influential book called *The Economic Consequences of the Peace* (1919), to which I shall often refer. Perhaps the Keynesian economic agenda that came to legitimise the

Anglo-American economic order from the 1940s ought to be seen as one of the economic consequences of war.

Every book has a viewpoint. The chapters that follow do not purport to offer a bloodlessly dispassionate account of what happened; they seek to capture an understanding of events and causation as viewed at the time through the spectacles of Anglo-American liberalism. Here was a coherent political tradition, as I shall argue, replete with its own distinctive values and language and symbolism. In different ways this informed the careers not only of Keynes but of the four leading political figures whose own words will receive close attention: Woodrow Wilson, David Lloyd George, Winston Churchill and Franklin Roosevelt. I am telling a story that has a wide historical significance – indeed a worldwide significance in some dimensions – but I am telling it from their points of view. Moreover, when we seek to understand this Anglo-American tradition, its common heritage of moralism suggests a further important theme – the concept of guilt. And seen in this perspective, the long-standing historical debate about 'war guilt' may look rather different.

2 EMPIRE

The First World War was a war of empires, in more than one sense; and thus a war of words too. It fostered the ideological use of the terms 'empire' and 'imperialism', generally in a derogatory way. Lenin made his famous analysis of imperialism as the highest stage of capitalism (thus, he argued, signalling the imminent collapse of capitalism in the bourgeois democracies). Conversely, Anglo-American liberals projected the war as one to uphold democratic ideals. These were not the abstract polemical ploys of a debating society but the terms in which a life-and-death struggle was waged.

The war certainly presented fundamental challenges to those belligerent nations that were broadly democratic in government, in particular France as well as Britain from 1914, and the United States from 1917. True, all three countries broadly conformed in practical terms to democratic norms, so there was some justification for their own frequent rhetorical juxtaposition of their system of 'democracy' with the 'autocracy' and 'imperialism' of their principal enemies in Germany, Austria-Hungary and also the Ottoman Empire.

Of course, the presence on the Allied side of the Russian Empire was an ideological embarrassment in making this sort of democratic case. But the initial stage of the Russian revolution at the beginning of 1917, notably the deposition of the Tsar, did much to remove such qualms, especially when quickly reinforced by the American declaration of war against Germany. The liberal prospect was now of a worldwide victory for democracy – the message with which Wilson became identified as American President.

It was never quite so simple as this stereotype, yet the juxtaposition was not without foundation. The fact is that the wartime experience of France, Britain and the United States, as democracies, was more complex and their response more ambiguous than that of an atavistic autocratic regime. Through trial and error, this unprecedented challenge proved their own systems of representative government more flexible and viable; and capitalism too was made to work in new ways, bending rather than breaking. Crucially, in a democracy it is possible to change a (French) ministry, or an (American) administration, or a (British) government *without changing the regime itself*. But in a regime where nobody can say that the emperor has no clothes, he may quickly end up with no throne when things go badly – as they are always liable to do in wartime.

Clearly the war did not turn out well for emperors. The sheer power of the locomotive, once it was geared up to unprecedented levels in twentieth-century warfare, based on new technologies and mass armies, imposed harsh new imperatives on the autocratic empires of Russia, Austria-Hungary and Germany. Yet while other great empires crumbled, ultimately deposing the Romanovs, the Habsburgs and the Hohenzollerns alike, their cousins in the British royal house were better advised. They had adroitly changed their name from Saxe-Coburg-Gotha to Windsor, signalling their identification with British constitutional government and the defence of its liberties. This can be called 'muddling through' of a high order, perhaps even claimed as an example of democratic resilience.

The peculiarity of the British Empire does not need to be celebrated; but it does need to be understood. This worldwide Empire reached its greatest territorial extent after the First World War. For the British, this had been an imperialist war – how could it have been otherwise? Britain had built an empire that controlled a quarter of the world's land space and a quarter of the world's population and was determined to defend it.

It was not, however, the sheer size of the British Empire that made it peculiar – bigger than the Roman Empire, as many classically educated British people often proudly claimed at the time. One thing that was highly unusual about the British Empire was that it was not protectionist. From the mid-nineteenth century it was built on free trade, with a symbiotic relationship between Britain as the hub of a global financial system and the agrarian societies in other continents that increasingly supplied its essential foodstuffs. This relationship enhanced the priority of protecting vulnerable international shipping routes, and hence was underpinned by naval supremacy over any likely rival. Not for nothing did the great patriotic song enjoin: 'Rule, Britannia, Britannia rule the waves.'

It was not a peculiarity of the British Empire that so many of its far-flung citizens happily accepted it at the time. Today, assumptions are different and the moral issue of whether empire is 'a bad thing' is hardly worth debating when an adverse verdict is so clear. Yet the sobering fact remains that, across the long sweep of history, virtually every significant power that could do so has at some time been involved in imperial wars and expansion; the observation that empire has been 'the default mode of state organization' is surely well founded. Virtually the only nationalities that escape the moral opprobrium with which the term is now laden are the unfortunate victims on the receiving end (though many of these peoples had historically been victors, oppressing others when they could do so in earlier eras).

Inveterate Anglo-German antagonism was hardly a peculiarity of the British Empire. It was not Germany, which emerged as a united country only after 1870, that had been Britain's great imperial rival but France. Wars with France, fought across three continents in the eighteenth century, had eventually been won, with two long-lasting implications. First, the British had now seized increasingly effective control of an Indian empire, which itself constituted a huge territory and subject population, and with an army that could be mobilised overseas. Second, the French had likewise been driven out of North America, politically at least – though the continuing francophone identity of Quebec was to endure. This reminds us that the older American empires of Spain and Portugal, which collapsed after the Napoleonic Wars, likewise left a powerful legacy or cultural residue, expressed through the Spanish language in the stubbornly flourishing hispanic presence across the American continent, and through the parallel survival of Portuguese in Brazil.

Such cultural and linguistic residues, long outlasting the bonds of political control, are even more significant in tracing the historic anglophone footprint of the British Empire in the world. Although the United States had triumphantly claimed its independence from Britain (with French assistance), and established its political autonomy on a new federal republican basis, its new citizens continued to speak the language of the old country. The Declaration of Independence was the first, but by no means the last, great American political testament to resonate as a masterpiece of English prose. The phrases of Jefferson and Lincoln became the commonplaces of political discourse throughout the British Empire.

The real peculiarity of the British Empire was thus the phenomenon of an anglophone settler explosion on a worldwide scale. This had peopled significant parts of three continents to create an 'anglo-world' that sustained the United Kingdom – at a price. The origins of the world war that broke out in 1914 need to be understood in this context, as does its outcome and its aftermath. Canada, Newfoundland, Australia, New Zealand and South Africa had come into the war on Britain's coat-tails; but their status as self-governing Dominions was crucially enhanced as a natural result of the pivotal role that they played in the war. A tragic testament to this was apparent in the losses that the Australian and New Zealand (ANZAC) forces sustained at Gallipoli and those that the Canadian and Newfoundland regiments suffered on the western front. None of this was forgotten; some of it not forgiven.

Such wartime experiences fostered a sense of national identity in the Dominions. Their separate representation at the Paris peace conference, albeit within the British Empire delegation, was initially seen by other victors as a ruse to secure Britain more votes at the table (and in the projected League of Nations). In fact, the role played by leaders like Jan Christiaan Smuts of South Africa and W. M. ('Billy') Hughes of Australia proved that they were no mere ciphers. On the key question of reparations, the tail wagged the dog, with profound consequences. One of them was the notorious war-guilt clause in the Versailles Treaty.

The historic cultural residue of the British Empire was to survive its own political eclipse. Just as it is important that Quebec remained francophone despite the severance of its political ties with France, so it is even more significant that the United States remained a part of the anglo-world – indeed an inexorably more dominant part. Moreover, it is far too simple to characterise Americans as either anglophiles or anglophobes; the extent of a shared political culture made for a much more complex form of interaction. The Anglo-American relationship obviously bulked large in diplomatic and military terms, but it also operated at other levels than simply brute power.

Though hard power is hard to ignore, we should also acknowledge the play of softer forms of influence. And if such soft power within the anglo-world was potent in the historical interplay between Britain and the Dominions, it also informed the evolving Anglo-American relationship, with its shifting balance of power between Britain and the United States. The currency of the term 'English-speaking peoples'

gestured towards a cultural dimension within this imagined community. It was hardly a diplomatic or a military term, and in origin at least
was populist rather than elitist in its resonance. Yet, as I shall argue,
the fact that these peoples shared a common vocabulary was a significant facet of their *political* culture in this period. This was notably the
case in propagating an ethically strenuous version of liberalism that
easily crossed the Atlantic – in ways that are still recognisable today.

3 MONEY AND POWER

It has always been part of our fascination with the Great War that it
apparently exploded so suddenly, so unexpectedly, upon a world that
was serenely unconscious of its impending fate. 'Little did they know'
has long been the sentiment, if not the literal phraseology, of many of
the bestselling, well-thumbed chronicles of the end of the sunlit garden
party that was, all too soon, to succumb to tragedy. We are shown the
charming young men in their boaters and blazers, which we know will
abruptly be exchanged for military uniforms; we see the elegant young
women in their elaborate dresses, which we know will soon be put away
as they wait anxiously for news from the trenches of the western front. It
is a world living on borrowed time – and, of course, on rentier incomes.

Until now, however, the sheer scale of the disparities of wealth
before the war has never been so well documented. Readers of Piketty
will be familiar, from the movement to 'Occupy Wall Street', with the
rhetoric of the '1 per cent' of plutocrats in our own era, and through his
research we are confronted with the even greater structural inequality
that prevailed in Europe a century ago. Here was a society with almost
no middle class in the modern sense: not only did the bottom 50 per
cent of the population own virtually no capital, much the same was
true of the next 40 per cent on higher rungs of the social ladder, and it
was just the top 10 per cent who owned nearly everything.[8] In Britain
before the First World War, the '1 per cent' owned over 60 per cent
of all wealth, even more than in France; and this was also more than
in the United States, though the American distribution of wealth was

actually less different from that in Europe than popular mythology suggested. If we take inequality of income before 1914 as the measure, the '1 per cent' took 22 per cent of total income in Britain, over 20 per cent in France and about 18 per cent in the United States.[9]

Money talks. Yet these were the same capitalist countries that, despite their own grossly inegalitarian structure, then proceeded to fight the Great War proclaiming their slogans about democracy. This may seem paradoxical, yet it was not entirely hypocritical. Republican France had always led the way in proclaiming the virtue of not only liberty but equality and fraternity too. With its intermittent revolutionary episodes from 1789 onwards, France had reinstated manhood suffrage from 1848 and restored republican government after the disastrous Franco-Prussian War of 1870. True, the franchise was not actually universal; the female half of the population could not vote in national elections before the Great War, as in Britain and the United States (and in France itself not until 1944). Nonetheless, Piketty is not alone in making ritual references to 'republican France' in contrast to 'monarchical Britain'. Yet this trope sometimes has an ironic edge, sharpened by his own discovery that the two countries actually had rather similar levels of economic inequality.

How can this be? Did the people not have power? Historical research can help unlock this paradox. For the fact is that the system of 'household suffrage' in late nineteenth-century Britain exhibited no crucial bias against the working class in the way that it actually operated. Household suffrage, originally introduced in urban areas in 1867, was extended to the whole country in the mid-1880s, with the result that the electorate now included most married men – of all classes. If there was a democratic deficit in Britain, it was one faced by younger, single men – again, of all classes – and, of course, by women of all ages. In its own way, the British regime of 1900 can indeed stand alongside that of France, in that the franchise already empowered the working-class majority in the electorate.

The United States too had generic similarities, albeit with its own distinctive flaws. Long hailed as the home of democracy, America notoriously fell short in practice when it came to the denial of citizenship rights under slavery, that 'peculiar institution' in the South which became the root cause of the civil war. With the defeat of the South, slavery was abolished and the American constitution enshrined the principle of manhood suffrage in the Fifteenth Amendment (1870). But this great principle was subsequently mocked in its implementation by the persistently peculiar racial restrictions that continued to be imposed in the American South. And it is perhaps ironical that President Wilson, often remembered for his plea to make the world safe for democracy, was himself a Southerner who accepted such racial discrimination as a fact of life.

Plainly, none of this was perfect and none of it without anomalies. Yet we would be wrong to suppose that it was the lack of democratic power before the war that was the crucial impediment to a more equal distribution of wealth, since in all three countries the basic democratic mechanisms were in fact already established well before 1900. For much of the twentieth century, the move towards greater equality suggested that there was a natural link of cause and effect, from democracy to egalitarianism; indeed this process became part of the conventional wisdom about the workings of modern capitalism. It was mapped by famous economists who regarded it as axiomatic that the fruits of capitalist growth would continue to become more equally distributed, in a benign process. Other analysts more cynically suggested that the democratic system itself inevitably empowered the impoverished majority in self-interested strategies of redistribution, whether through high taxation, 'welfare' or budget deficits.

Either way, it was an egalitarian story – but only up to a point. That point, according to much of Piketty's data, is located in time somewhere around the 1970s, after which the previous trend went into fairly sharp reverse, especially in the English-speaking countries, leading to the sharp inequalities that have now reasserted themselves. This new political economy, contemptuous of the postwar consensus, found powerful voices in Margaret Thatcher and Ronald Reagan, whose ideological heritage is still with us today.

This points to the need to tell the story in a different way, no longer by lazily assuming that the potential of democratic power simply ensures that big money will be tamed – still less by supposing that revolution will otherwise ensue. What we once thought of as a general axiom of democracy has turned out to be the product of particular historical circumstances. In the English-speaking countries that had once led the way in introducing the highest rates of taxation on large incomes and hereditary estates alike, Piketty's conclusion is clear: 'It was war that gave rise to progressive taxation, not the natural consequences of universal suffrage.'[10] Hence we should now pay closer attention to contingency, not least to the impact of war and to the way that it reshaped the parameters of political and economic change.

In the First World War, as already noted, it was the ability of the democratic regimes to absorb shocks that was striking. Even though the French Third Republic tottered, it survived, despite a drastically shrinking economy. The veteran Radical Georges Clemenceau became the fifth wartime Prime Minister in 1917 and he survived as *Père la Victoire* in defeating Germany and in seeking the spoils of this victory. In the United States, the Democrat Woodrow Wilson won his uphill fight for re-election as a peace president in 1916; he nonetheless managed the entry of the United States into the war in 1917; he dramatically proclaimed his Fourteen Points for a peace settlement in 1918; and he made his triumphal progress to the Paris peace conference in 1919 at a dizzying peak of international esteem. Yet by 1920 his Democratic party was swept out of power, in both the Congress and the White House.

Not only did the American polity withstand all these stresses but its economy proved equally resilient. Widespread apprehensions that the wartime disruption of international trade and shipping would bring hard times in the United States proved unfounded. Instead, by 1918 a boom in manufacturing production that was directly linked to the needs of the belligerents helped push the US gross domestic product (GDP) to a level nearly 15 per cent higher than in 1913. This was what happened in the 'real economy', affecting virtually everyone, not just the financiers of Wall Street who had naturally seized their moment to topple the City of London from its primacy.

And the British experience? Here, by the end of the war, the economy was likewise about 13 per cent bigger than in 1913. Yet the numbers in the armed forces had meanwhile increased from 400,000 to 4.4 million – and, of course, over 700,000 combatants from the United Kingdom had meanwhile been killed. The capacity of the economy to grow in wartime Britain, despite simultaneously putting huge armies in the field, seemed counter-intuitive to many orthodox economists at the time, among whom the young Keynes has to be numbered.

In Britain, as in France, ministerial changes served as political shock absorbers. In fact, there were only two British prime ministers in the whole period 1908–22, both of them Liberals; but whereas Asquith left office a diminished figure at the end of 1916, his successor Lloyd George, rather like Clemenceau, was to be hailed as 'the man who won the war'. The fact that these two European leaders were able to play such a strong hand at the peace conference – and felt a political need to do so – was one reason for the ultimate demise of the ostensibly omnipotent American President. None of these outcomes was crudely determined by the locomotive of war. A lot depended on who was in the driving seat at the crucial moments. In short, the task of explaining what actually happened confronts us with a more than adequate agenda, and one that often demands a narrative giving attention to particular historical figures over a longer period, from Gladstone to Roosevelt.

4 THE POLITICS OF GUILT

Arguments about war guilt have played a disproportionately large part in fuelling disputes about the origins of the First World War. They have infused sober discussions about causation with passions that go beyond the immediate issues, largely because the attribution of guilt to Germany in the peace treaty of 1919 can itself be represented as one of the origins of the Second World War. Thus our understanding of some of the central events shaping the twentieth century is at stake here. Many views have been offered. A neglected factor, I suggest, is the influence of Anglo-American liberalism and its moralistic perspective.

Historically, the inescapable influence here is that of William Ewart Gladstone, the charismatic statesman who became the Grand Old Man of Victorian Liberalism. He inspired his legion of disciples with a highly moralised politics of conscience, taking the wrongs of the whole world as its tableau. Gladstone's extraordinary career needs to be understood; it was literally remade in the late 1870s when, in his late sixties and having already served a successful term as Prime Minister, he forsook a well-earned retirement and returned to the political stage.

The issue that moved him was not of his own making. The atrocities committed by the Ottomans upon their Christian subjects in Bulgaria had previously been publicised and politicised by others, of whom the young Liberal journalist W. T. Stead was perhaps the most significant. Here, then, was a great popular agitation in the making, one that lacked only a great populist leader. It was at this point that Gladstone was stirred to action himself, belatedly but magisterially. In the quiet of his study at Hawarden Castle, his country house, he had been pondering the theology of 'Future Retribution' or 'Eternal Punishment' – at once a subject of peculiar fascination in his own mind and also a key issue in religious debate at the time. Now he bundled his notes aside with an explanatory docket: 'From this I was called away to write on Bulgaria.'

Gladstone's authorised biographer, John Morley, himself an agnostic, published his highly sympathetic *Life* in 1903. By quoting this docket at the beginning of the relevant chapter Morley put its implied message into general circulation among a generation of latter-day Gladstonians. For the providential overtones are as inescapable as they are characteristic. The Bulgarian agitation is the emblematic episode in understanding the potency of the Gladstonian synthesis of conscience and what can be termed moral populism.

'Good ends can rarely be attained in politics without passion,' Gladstone reflected: 'and there is now, the first time for a good many years, a virtuous passion.' Here we see a politics of emotion, depending on high rhetoric to elevate the issues at stake and to persuade large popular audiences to subordinate their own immediate material grievances to great issues of right and wrong, starkly delineated. Max Weber, the pioneering German theorist of charismatic leadership, was surely right in identifying 'the fascination of Gladstone's "grand" demagogy, the firm belief of the masses in the ethical substance of his policy, and, above all, their belief in the ethical character of his personality'.

Admittedly, this style of politics was not wholly novel, in an era when the Americanisation of British politics was often remarked upon. Support for the North in the American civil war, because of the South's guilt over slavery, had itself been one of the causes that fed into the making of popular Liberalism in Britain in the 1860s. Here Gladstone had found himself on the wrong side, prematurely misidentifying the South with the sort of proto-nationalism that he lauded elsewhere; and he had to apologise for the lapse. The extension of the franchise in Britain was a crucial issue in the 1860s, when Gladstone characteristically claimed that new voters were 'morally entitled' to be included. This process of democratisation was intimately linked with the emergence of Gladstone as 'the People's William', which also paralleled the apotheosis of Abraham Lincoln, a more authentic man of the people and, in death even more than in his lifetime, a great iconic figure in Britain as well as in his own country.

From the 1860s, it is a new catchphrase, 'the English-speaking peoples', that characterises this strain of Anglo-American politics. In both countries a wide franchise made electoral politics democratic in a style that celebrated charismatic leaders like Lincoln and Gladstone, their popular image in each case fashioned into a sort of folk art. A range of common references fed into a style of politics better described as moral populism than in class terms.

The ease with which the Atlantic was crossed in this era is illustrated by the later career of W. T. Stead himself. He went on to flourish not only as a prominent Gladstonian journalist and eccentric crusader against sexual iniquity and prostitution in Britain – 'The Maiden Tribute of Modern Babylon' – but also as a muckraking journalist in the United States. Appropriately, he was to die in mid-Atlantic, when the *Titanic* sank in 1912. Sin and guilt infused Stead's worldview. Even as a young boy he had been moved to declare: 'I wish that God would give me a big whip that I could go round the world and whip the wicked out of it.'

So much for the punishment; but what about the crime? How to identify the criminals? This problem is easily resolved, at least in theory, by pointing to their evil intentions. Nobody can reasonably be expected to feel guilty about malign results that they did not intend or reasonably foresee. This is not only common sense and common usage but is congruent with the criminal law. Recent legal judgments in Britain, arising out of the use of 'joint enterprise' in bringing a prosecution, have reinforced the salient point that criminal guilt depends on proof of prior intention. Of course, in practice it is not always easy to establish what anyone intended, if only because there will often be disputes over the reasonably foreseeable results of actions and of their probable consequences.

The moralism of Gladstonian politics swept aside such quibbles. The politics of conscience confidently put a premium on intentions, since pure intentions were the hallmark of a clear conscience; and conversely any guilty parties could be identified by their self-evidently malign intentions. This was a populist projection of Gladstone's own sophisticated theological outlook: a projection that imperfectly reflected his own peculiar version of Anglicanism. We know from the volumes of the excellent modern edition of his meticulously kept diaries that Gladstone agonised over the meaning of his call to action over Bulgaria. The response to his pamphlet *The Bulgarian Horrors and the Question of the East*, written in August 1876, was overwhelming. The publisher had initially thought of a print-run of 2,000 copies; within a month 200,000 had been sold. A sequel, published as *Lessons in Massacre*, had originally been entitled *Who Are the Criminals?* The politics of guilt were proclaimed in a great series of public speeches which forsook the problems of eternal punishment for more immediate applications.

'My desire for the shade, a true and earnest desire has been since August rudely baffled: retirement & recollection seem more remote than ever,' Gladstone wrote in his diary on his sixty-seventh birthday, 29 December 1876. 'But [it] is in a noble cause, for the curtain rising in the East seems to open events that bear cardinally on our race.'[11] It was an issue of conscience for what Gladstone called 'our race', which should be interpreted as a reference to more than his compatriots in Britain. As so often, with his attachment to the 'concert of Europe', he was thinking of the civilised nations of Europe – and not just Europe. He sometimes wrote of 'kin beyond the sea' in a sense that embraced what we would now call the British diaspora or anglo-world, thus including all the English-speaking peoples within his proxy for a universal church.

For the scholarly Gladstone knew his Augustine; he revered the text *securus judicat orbis terrarum*, proclaiming that the settled judgement of the whole world must prevail. This is how he had expressed his view of the Franco-Prussian War in 1870, claiming that 'the general judgement of civilised mankind' had delivered its verdict: 'It has censured the aggression of France; it will censure, if need arise, the greed of Germany. *Securus judicat orbis terrarum.*' Germany's action in threatening Belgium and later in taking the provinces of Alsace and Lorraine was an affront to the concert of Europe, meaning the obligation of all the powers to enforce a conception of public right based on justice. It is little wonder that Gladstonians of a later generation, like the historian J. L. Hammond, stressed the universal aspect of 'the League of Nations mind' that Gladstone brought to politics and would quote his plea at the time of Britain's Second Afghan War (1878–80): 'Remember that the sanctity of life in the hill villages of Afghanistan amid the winter snows is as inviolable in the eyes of Almighty God as can be your own.'

Hence the wide significance – so it was revealed to Gladstone in 1876 – of the curtain now rising in the Ottoman Empire, exposing to the world the moral deficiencies of imperial rule under the Turks. Hence too the need for an old man to return, year by year, to the political platform. 'Sixty-nine years of age!' he wrote in his diary on 29 December 1878, reflecting on his stamina in a campaign that 'appears to me to carry the marks of the will of God', and one that was still going strong in its third year. 'For when have I seen so strongly the relation between my public duties and the primary purposes for which God made and Christ redeemed the world? Seen it to be not real only but so close and immediate that the lines of the holy and unholy were drawn as in fire before my eyes.' He marvelled at the way his health had held up. 'In the great physical and mental effort of speaking, often to large auditories, I have been as it were upheld in an unusual manner and the free effectiveness of voice has been given me to my own astonishment. Was not all of this for a purpose: & has it not all come in connection with a process to which I have given myself under clear but most reluctant associations.'[12] A year later, the story was similar, with the orator's confidence that 'the battle to be fought was a battle of justice humanity freedom law, all in their first elements from the very root, and all on a gigantic scale. The word spoken was a word for millions, and for millions who themselves cannot speak.'[13]

Now this was not an explicitly religious cause. It was resolutely secular in extrapolating, from Gladstone's own Christian faith, a system of political ideals that universalised conscience in terms of secular humanitarianism when calling for international action. It is largely because he kept a private diary that we can confidently point to a providential sense which Gladstone himself felt as his call to action. Not all later politicians in the Gladstonian mould have felt moved to such introspection, nor left such revealing records in their archives. Such providentialism is often documented less directly than in Gladstone's case.

With his spiritual candour balanced by deep subtlety and fathomless ambiguity, Gladstone made fine distinctions that were often swept aside in the flood of emotion that he tapped. Liberals who chose to take him as their leader had to take him on trust. In 1876 he reflected: 'We live, as men, in a labyrinth of problems, and of moral problems, from which there is no escape permitted us.' What he meant was that 'the prevalence of pain and sin' so limited the exercise of free will, in a social and economic system beset with all sorts of cross purposes, as to create problems that were intractable: 'Solution for them have we none.'

This does not suggest the temperament of a social reformer, despite Gladstone's own lifelong belief that the state had an ethical duty that sometimes made a case for intervention rather than for laissez-faire. In his later years as Liberal leader he was well aware of the intrusion of 'the social question' in politics, and made accommodations accordingly. Yet he was still ready to declare his own fundamental views in stark terms, in print if not on the platform. 'I believe in a degeneracy of man, in the Fall – in sin – in the intensity and virulence of sin,' he publicly proclaimed in 1888. 'No other religion but Christianity meets the sense of sin, and sin is the great fact in the world to me.' Those social reformers who felt otherwise, he maintained, 'have a very low estimate both of the quantity and the quality of sin: of its amount, spread like a deluge over the world, and of the subtlety, intensity and virulence of its nature'.

5 THE LONG SHADOW OF MR GLADSTONE

This book is not about Gladstone but it is inescapably concerned with the pervasive influence of the Gladstonian legacy. The lens through which many Anglo-American liberals looked at the world was accordingly one framed by guilt. This was natural, given their ideological inheritance: one that was later to be acknowledged not just in the era of Woodrow Wilson but in that of Tony Blair. The long shadow of Mr Gladstone has not been without influence in producing the world in which we live.

When liberals were confronted with violence, they regarded it as not just lamentable but criminal. They earnestly sought to identify the perpetrators of civil wars and international wars alike; they asked who could be blamed for causing such bloodshed, readily identifying guilty and innocent parties. Conscience then impelled them to action, or at least to take sides in a judgemental way – and perhaps to campaign for their own country to intervene, whether or not its 'selfish' national interest prompted such action. They invoked a higher conception of public right within a comity of nations. In this liberal vision, there was a fundamental optimism about intervention in foreign conflicts, in strategies of redemption that could put right the wrongs that had been done. There was a moral call to conscience that could not be ignored.

One Gladstone paradox is that of a great popular leader who simultaneously affirms the folly of state intervention in social and economic policy while proclaiming the virtue of government action in foreign politics. It was the same man, trapped in his moral labyrinth in 1876, who, within months, was to take up the cause of the Bulgarians, sharing with his plebeian followers a burning sense that these faraway problems, at least, were surely susceptible of solution. Likewise, when it came to applauding the assertion of Italian nationalism the British Liberals were united in offering British assistance for the Risorgimento, though their moral support for the Poles, like that for the Bulgarians, remained exactly that. When Gladstone himself took up the cause of Irish Home Rule in the 1880s, it is easy to understand why he was accused of 'Bulgarianising' it (and conversely why, as German Chancellor, the great realist Bismarck readily compared his own troublesome Polish subjects to the Irish).

It was again Hammond, that discerning guardian of Gladstone's reputation, who wrote in the late 1920s:

To a people without a theatre, without the arts that release the emotions, and bring them into play, the great Tsar, with his terrible hand closing over the liberties of the peoples at the other end of Europe, the despot at Vienna hunting the patriots of Hungary, the Pope at Rome making his dark religion more obnoxious by his wicked politics, were great stage villains, and men who prided themselves in ordinary life on sticking to business and keeping out feeling were swept away by this dramatic excitement.

A second paradox, of course, is that Gladstone himself, though later adopted as 'the People's William', was personally a figure from the elite of British society, with his education at Eton and Oxford, his inherited wealth, his grand London house and his country home at Hawarden Castle in north Wales. Yet this was the statesman who was to end his career declaring from the platform that 'upon one great class of subjects, the largest and most weighty of them all, where the leading and determining considerations that ought to lead to conclusion are truth, justice, and humanity, there, gentlemen, all the world over, I will back the masses against the classes.' He was speaking here, in 1886, with reference to Irish Home Rule, the mission that finally dominated Gladstone's career – though not quite his last call to action. Even after his retirement as Prime Minister in 1894, the reports of further oppression and bloodshed in the Ottoman Empire were a sufficient cause to enlist the final oratorical intervention of a man now in his late eighties. Known as 'the Armenian atrocities' at the time, they were to be repeated and exceeded in their scale and impact twenty years later, during the First World War.

Imperialism in all its forms emerged as the protean threat to this worldview, with no privileged exemption for the British Empire (though with some obfuscation as to what counted as 'imperialism'). A key issue was the Boer War, which broke out in South Africa only a year after Gladstone's death, waged against the Transvaal and the Orange Free State, the two small republics of Dutch origin which resisted British annexation. Imperialists in Britain obviously knew which side they were on; and it is hardly surprising that their opponents, the 'pro-Boers' in the Liberal party, freely appropriated their late leader's name.

In any posthumous cult, a crucial figure is the keeper of the bones of the saint. In 1899, while the Boer War was brewing, John Morley was already installed at Hawarden, working through the vast array of manuscripts that awaited him as Gladstone's biographer. Morley came from a modest professional background in the Lancashire cotton town of Blackburn and, sent to Oxford University, where he had happily immersed himself in the classics, he had then defied his father's expectation that he should become a clergyman and instead left the university without taking a degree. He became one of the foremost 'higher journalists' or 'public moralists' who made it their mission to lead liberal public opinion in Victorian England. Hence the gibe that he spelled god with a small 'g' but Gladstone with a capital letter. It is worth observing that Morley felt a special kind of bond whenever he found another Oxford man 'who knows his Aristotle', which helps explain not only his veneration for Gladstone but likewise his later loyal service in Asquith's cabinet for six years.

In September 1899 Morley was hauled away from the manuscripts at Hawarden and put on the train to Manchester to address a great anti-war protest meeting at the Free Trade Hall. The building was, of course, hallowed as the home of the Manchester School, where Richard Cobden and John Bright had made their names in linking free trade with universal peace, so long as Britain pursued a pacific foreign policy based on non-intervention. Morley had already served as Cobden's biographer and personally remained a cool Cobdenite non-interventionist for much of his career. We know from his research assistant at Hawarden that Morley had been privately brooding on 'cases of conscience for Gladstone and Gladstonians' (adding to the familiar litany of Italy, Bulgaria and Armenia the more surprising contemporary instance of Finland) and had pronounced: 'They presented no difficulties to men like Cobden and Bright.'

And now? The Boer War, it seemed to Morley, was a moment for virtuous passion. He knew that he was a small man who had to step into very large shoes but at the Free Trade Hall he rose to the occasion with a memorable speech, pitched in an emotional register that hit home with his audience. He roundly denounced the loss of life that the prospective war would bring: 'It will be wrong.' It might add to the Empire: 'It will still be wrong.' And though it might 'send the price of Mr Rhodes's Chartered up to a point beyond the dreams of avarice; yet even then it will be wrong'.

On these great, simple issues of right and wrong, Gladstonians were adamant. Now often identifying themselves as 'Radicals', it hardly mattered to them that Gladstone had been, at times, a sceptic about the agenda of modern liberalism, with its readiness to envisage state intervention in social issues. But he had, too, a dynamic view of politics, especially when humanitarian concerns were at stake. As the twentieth century opened, many liberals responded by instinctively applying their similarly moral perspective to a new reformist agenda on social issues. C. P. Scott, for example, who set his stamp upon the *Manchester Guardian* as its editor for half a century, was a champion of this New Liberalism of social reform, while remaining firmly Gladstonian in his outlook on the world. Scott certainly saw no contradiction here, confiding to a friend in 1899: 'More and more one feels that foreign policy is the touchstone of all policy.'

Scott's closest collaborator at this time was L. T. Hobhouse, later prominent as an academic sociologist at the London School of Economics but then working as a leader writer for the *Manchester Guardian*. An advocate of state intervention in social policy, unlike Morley, Hobhouse nonetheless remained a fervent admirer of both Morley and Gladstone in foreign policy. 'The Gladstonian theory', Hobhouse explained, 'is simply that men regarded as the members or as the rulers of a State do not cease to be, either as respects their rights or their duties, the subject of the moral law.' He had eagerly aided Scott in bringing Morley as their champion to the Free Trade Hall and it was the normally stolid Hobhouse who declared afterwards that 'Morley's one hour speech was worth months of ordinary life.' The emotion so gripped another prominent Liberal in the audience, who had bought a new top hat for the occasion, that, after leaping up to applaud Morley, he sat down on the hat. Gladstone himself could hardly have bettered such effects. And the New Liberalism that Hobhouse justified as a step towards social democracy in the twentieth century still self-consciously held true to the traditional Gladstonian maxims on international affairs and the primacy of a moral yardstick.

'The heart of Liberalism', as Hobhouse put it later, 'is the understanding that progress is not a matter of mechanical contrivance but of the liberation of living spiritual energy.' It is not surprising, then, that Hobhouse's *bête noire* in politics should have been the play-wright Bernard Shaw, who rivalled Sidney and Beatrice Webb as the public face (and voice) of the Fabian Society. With his self-conscious disdain for the old-fashioned liberal ethic of pure intentions, which he saw as now superseded by a Marxist analysis, Shaw well deserved Lenin's comment that he was 'a good man fallen among Fabians'. Shaw's contention was that Fabian socialists like himself were necessarily 'anti all the Liberal gods', and, working with Sidney Webb, he publicly expressed scorn in 1901 for what he saw as the disabling moralistic residue of Gladstonianism: 'a Liberal reform is never simply a social means to a social end, but a campaign of Good against Evil'. The mindset that Shaw criticised was quintessentially Gladstonian. It was still a potent force, twenty years after the great man's death in 1898, in shaping the way that not only Britain but also the United States responded to the First World War.

6 THOSE FOURTEEN POINTS

The Fourteen Points, as expounded by President Wilson in his famous speech to Congress in January 1918, are studded with appeals in the Gladstonian timbre. 'We entered this war because violations of right had occurred which touched us to the quick,' he claims, enunciating his commitment to 'the principle of justice to all peoples and nationalities, and their right to live on equal terms of liberty and safety with one another, whether they be strong or weak'.[14] Special mention is made (in Points 6, 7 and 8) of how justice should be applied to Russia, Belgium and France. These countries had a special status, if not formally as allies of the United States then as its co-belligerents, to whom the President showed himself naturally attentive, clothing their special interests in the raiment of 'unselfish sympathy', 'healing', 'international law' and 'the peace of the world'.

What follows reads like a roll-call of Gladstonian good causes. Speaking on behalf of the United States, but in terms that he well knew would strike a chord with British liberals too, Wilson laid out his Points 9–13. These apparently promise the Italians and the Poles satisfaction of their historic national claims; they acknowledge similar rights to the peoples of Austria-Hungary and Turkey, while going on to champion the cause of the oppressed nationalities within these two respective empires, implicitly promising 'an undoubted security of life and an absolutely unmolested opportunity of autonomous development' that the Bulgarians and the Armenians had lamentably lacked in the recent past. 'In regard to these essential rectifications of wrong and assertions of right,' Wilson concludes, 'we feel ourselves to be intimate partners of all the governments and peoples associated together against the Imperialists.' Here, concretely, is 'the principle of justice to all peoples and nationalities' for which Wilson pledges to fight. 'The moral climax of this, the culminating and final war for human liberty has come,' he declaims in a final, almost apocalyptic, paean.[15]

The politics of moralism and emotion plainly did not die with Gladstone. The role of noble rhetoric in uplifting the people to look beyond their own material interests was its staple. It is worth stressing that not all politicians have chosen to speak thus, for there was (and is) a choice here. For example, one alternative model of politics, highly rational in itself, is to think of parties as appealing to the self-interest of particular constituencies by offering a programmatic agenda of measures calculated to satisfy enough of the electorate to get elected.

By contrast, the British and American leaders in the two world wars of the twentieth century were adepts in a style of oratory that privileged pure intentions and uplifting emotional appeals, as some of their most famous phrases show. Lloyd George in 1914 committed himself to the war by invoking 'the great pinnacle of Sacrifice pointing like a rugged finger to Heaven'. Wilson in 1915 claimed for his country the virtue of being 'too proud to fight'. Roosevelt on his inauguration as President in 1933 asserted that 'the only thing we have to fear is fear itself'. Churchill, on assuming power in 1940, declared that he had 'nothing to offer but blood, toil, tears and sweat'. The language, in each specific case, was code for very different practical policies. But there is an obvious common element in the rhetoric of sacrifice, of pride, of fear and of tears – emotions of proven political potency.

The Fourteen Points can claim a canonical status in the history of liberal internationalism. Clemenceau liked to say, with an eloquent French shrug, that the Good Lord had been satisfied with only ten. But I will offer 'fourteen points of view' in the following chapters, forming a book that is more than an album of period snapshots. I seek to convey a series of personal and necessarily subjective insights, in different times and places, on some of the great issues of war and peace that have shaped the twentieth century. Wilson, Lloyd George, Churchill, Roosevelt and Keynes are all implicated in this story; each chapter in turn will seek to capture their own understanding of what was happening around them, with special scrutiny of some texts generated by these events – memoirs, diaries, letters and other published documents, along with some influential polemical tracts. Since this is only one way of telling a story that has many significant dimensions, my account certainly stakes no claim to be comprehensive or definitive. But there is a theme, which this prologue has sought to suggest.

The Locomotive of War is animated by the tension between two different ways of thinking about twentieth-century war and its impact. One is the essentially moralistic heritage of guilt, which was an inheritance from the nineteenth century that then became a legacy for the twentieth. Seeing the world in this perspective, when liberals looked at the origins of a war, any dispassionate causal analysis tended to become an issue of culpable moral responsibility. This is surely the premise of those endless debates about whether Germany was really responsible for the First World War, whether the Versailles Treaty was in turn responsible for the Second World War, and so on.

The other way of thinking about the two world wars is to look at their eventual outcome: at the reformed capitalist countries in the central decades of the twentieth century, with a marked egalitarian thrust in improving the life-chances of 'the 99 per cent', shaped by the locomotive of war. This was an outcome unforeseen by the Marxist prophets who originated this train of thought in the confident belief that they would be burying capitalism – a dream that finally died after the Berlin Wall came down. Nor did the Anglo-American post-war consensus prove to be the destination of history that many optimistic liberals once assumed, in the era before Thatcherism and Reaganomics put paid to reformist complacency. I hope that by casting the story in a more open-ended narrative, our understanding of what actually happened will be enhanced – sometimes in rather unexpected ways.

FOURTEEN POINTS OF VIEW

Part One

PEACE AND WAR

I

The Disciple as Prophet:
Thomas Woodrow Wilson

Ray Stannard Baker bears much the same relationship to Wilson as John Morley does to Gladstone. Each was a man of letters who had been a respected journalist before belatedly assuming a hands-on political role himself. Just as Morley was charged with the task of writing the *Life of Gladstone*, so Baker was selected as the authorised champion of Wilson: each given unique access to the great man's own archive and each informed by close personal understanding. Morley had produced three volumes: Baker outdid him by publishing eight, even if we do not count others on the Versailles Treaty. In a later generation, there was to be a definitive scholarly edition in no fewer than sixty-nine volumes of *The Papers of Woodrow Wilson*. But like Boswell on Johnson, in a sense Baker can never be bettered on Wilson, in faithfully capturing his hero's personal foibles and complexities.

As a boy, growing up in Georgia, Wilson had been simply 'Tommy'. He was the elder son, always privileged over his much younger brother, and was given his middle name in honour of his mother Jessie's family, the Woodrows, who hailed from the Scottish border country. The family of her husband, the Rev. Joseph Ruggles Wilson, had come to America from the Scots-Irish community in Northern Ireland. These links with Britain were relatively recent; Jessie Woodrow had herself been born in Carlisle, in the far north of England, though her father served as a Presbyterian minister in the Scottish mill town of Paisley.

The family was replete with Presbyterian ministers on both sides, looking back to the heroic days of the Scottish Covenanters of the seventeenth century, with their assertion of the idea of a solemn covenant to uphold the unflinching values of a godly people. When President Wilson, at the height of his international renown in December 1918, was fêted at the Mansion House in London, he told the well-fed guests who were assembled to salute him: 'The stern Covenanter tradition that is behind me sends many an echo down the years.'[1] Baker writes of the Bible as 'all his life, his daily companion and guide', so much so that Wilson successively wore out three copies. Baker comments, in some awe of this Calvinist heritage: 'These were chosen people, foreordained and predestined.'[2]

A belief in predestination, far from licensing moral complacency on the grounds that personal salvation was already assured, was a call to strenuous exertion by true believers. The consciousness of sin could thus be enhanced by the sense of having been saved through no personal merit but only by the grace of God. All were sinners, though some were redeemed through God's grace, as they should always be aware. Wilson evidently thought so; 'without quick religious life', as he put it, existence would be 'a furnace without fire'.[3] These were sentiments that he did not disguise from those who knew him well, like Baker and a few others in the tight circle of confidants on whom the President later relied in his White House years. But he made it clear, with some brusqueness if taxed on the subject, that he had no interest in pursuing, let alone debating, such arguments. Unlike Gladstone, Wilson did not wrestle with his own spiritual dilemmas, even in the confidential diary that he made intermittent efforts to keep.

Nor did he normally parade his personal religious beliefs in his political speeches. Like Gladstone, Wilson instead used his oratory to project universal moral and humanitarian values in a non-sectarian way, with an emotional uplift that was (in one sense of the word) catholic in its appeal. It was an unusual moment, nearing the end of his career on the platform, when he broke this rule.

'My fellow citizens, I believe in divine Providence,' he told a meeting in San Francisco in September 1919. 'If I did not, I would go crazy. If I thought the direction of the disordered affairs of this world depended upon our finite endeavor, I should not know how to reason my way to sanity.'⁴ This was hardly a sudden epiphany, even if its declaration came from a sick man now nearing the end of his tether. It was surely the same belief, rarely confided even to his closest friends, that he had held since his 'religious turning' in the early 1870s, which Baker identified as one of the important crises in his life.⁵

What we can document with confidence is that young Tommy became peculiarly fascinated by Gladstone from an early age – which initially seems puzzling. Here was a boy, born in Virginia and growing up in Augusta, Georgia, in a key area of the American South during and after the civil war. Surely there was plenty happening around him to absorb his attention? Surely there was plenty near at hand to stir his growing awareness of dramatic events and of great public figures in his own painfully divided country? And here was a boy who, for one reason or another, came very late to literacy, learning to read only when he was nine years of age, at a time when print was the indispensable information highway to the outside world.

Yet he clearly made up for lost ground with the intensity of his imaginative outreach, soon looking far beyond Georgia. We find him, in his early teens, sketching fantasy worlds, often detailed over several pages, projecting himself as a high-ranking admiral or general – not in refighting the battles of the civil war to snatch victory for the poor, defeated South, but instead imagining himself in the British service as Duke of Eagleton, Duke of Arlington or Marquess of Huntington. Many boys, of course, play such games of soldiers, only to outgrow them quickly in early adolescence, perhaps with some embarrassment. But Tommy Wilson, the favoured son of the manse, was different.

In 1873–4 he followed the family's vocational tradition by attending the Davidson Presbyterian College in Piedmont, North Carolina, where he developed an interest in the debating society (foreshadowing similar activities when he later went as a student to Princeton). He was a curious mixture of precociousness and immaturity, for at Davidson he continued to elaborate his fantasies about service in the Royal Navy – 'Commander-in-chief – Vice-Admiral Lord Thomas W. Wilson, Duke of Eagleton' et cetera – with full technical specifications supplied of the ships of his squadron, all built at Portsmouth 'according to plans drawn up by her celebrated commander Lord Wilson'.[6] He was seventeen at this time, still casting himself in this heroic posture, and in a world where Britannia ruled the waves.

During the previous year, however, he had already discovered another kind of role model. A cousin visiting the Wilsons noticed the portrait that now hung above Tommy's desk and asked who it was. 'That is Gladstone, the greatest statesman that ever lived,' came the reply. 'I intend to be a statesman too.'[7] This was no passing whim; when Wilson became president of Princeton University there was to be a portrait of Gladstone in his office. This was probably the painting executed by his wife, now surviving in the Woodrow Wilson Birthplace Foundation alongside two similar portraits, of her own father and of her father-in-law – privileged company to keep.

What had first attracted the boy to Gladstone? What affinity had he sensed? His recent religious crisis may have predisposed him towards the overt moralism that Gladstone preached. Moreover, Tommy was aware that, though his birthday was celebrated on 28 December, he had actually been born in the early hours of 29 December 1856. With his lifelong fascination with coincidences of personal numbers and dates, could it have escaped him that this was also the birthday of the Grand Old Man?

Whatever the portents, Gladstone henceforth came to occupy the psychic space that Lord Thomas W. Wilson had once commanded. Gladstone's speeches were well known in the United States, through the British as well as the American magazines to which the Rev. Joseph Ruggles Wilson subscribed, and through the syndicated newspapers that now used the transatlantic telegraph to reproduce political orations at a length that would not be countenanced today. We know that Tommy read an article in the *Gentleman's Magazine* for April 1874, written by the British parliamentary sketch-writer H. W. Lucy, who declared that there were only three true orators in the House of Commons, all of them on the Liberal front bench. One was William Edward Forster, largely forgotten today but at this time well known to Americans, not least for putting the term 'the English-speaking peoples' into general currency. He had been a notable partisan of the North in the civil war, as had John Bright, whom Lucy also singled out, less surprisingly, alongside his third and wholly unsurprising choice of Gladstone – whereas Disraeli was dismissed for lacking 'earnestness and simple conviction'.[8] Wilson was himself to write on Bright and Gladstone in two notable early essays, well worth close attention.

Wilson forged a lifelong link with Princeton College, where he was first a student (1875–9) and was subsequently, from 1890, to serve successively as a professor of political science and then (after the institution had assumed the title of university) as its president from 1902. Princeton, moreover, served as his platform for national fame, and thus as a stepping-stone to the Presidency of the United States. Why Princeton? Not only did it have a strong Presbyterian attachment but, although its location in New Jersey was not in the South, its recruitment of undergraduates had a much stronger Southern element than the Ivy League universities of New England.

In a sense, Wilson never really left the South, or at least never emotionally abandoned it. It was when he returned to North Carolina in 1909, to give an address on the great Southern hero Robert E. Lee that he declared that 'the only place in the country, the only place in the world, where nothing has to be explained to me is the South'. It was there, he explained, that he could 'discover a country full of reminiscences which connect me with my parents, and with all the old memories', which remained formative for him.[9]

'I have just received one of the finest letters I ever had from Tommy,' his father once declared. 'It is a regular love letter.'[10] The admiration was reciprocal and lasted until the old man's death. There was a natural shift over time in the dominant key of their relationship: from filial deference, as duly shown towards the Rev. Joseph Ruggles Wilson, to proud paternal acknowledgement of the eminence of his son, whom he (just) lived to see appointed as president of Princeton. At one time the father's hope had been simply of emulation by his son: 'Oh, my boy, how I wish you had entered the ministry, with all that genius of yours!'[11] But this genius had to find another channel of expression. The young man had already made it clear, before ever going to Princeton, that there would not be yet another member of the family to join the line of Presbyterian divines.

He was searching for another kind of public identity. And he concluded a letter to a friend in the summer of 1881: 'PS. You will see I am no longer "Tommy", *except to my old friends*,' and signed himself simply 'Woodrow Wilson'.[12] It was the name by which he was subsequently known to his doting family; to each of his successively adored wives; to the readers of his influential published writings on politics; to the American voters; and to the world that came to hang upon his words in the making of war and peace.

During his four years as a student at Princeton, Wilson had been instrumental in setting up a Liberal Debating Club. He devoted much time and attention to devising its constitution and to managing its affairs. Many of his friends, some of them with later careers in journalism, were likewise involved in debates that first sharpened their rhetorical skills. It was an era when there were particularly close links between the spoken and the printed word; great speeches were speeches that read well when printed verbatim.

The vocational utility of such activities was not lost upon Wilson, himself a contributor to student publications. 'What is the object of oratory?' he demanded in an editorial in the *Princetonian* in 1877.

'Its object is persuasion and conviction – the control of other minds by a strange personal influence and power. What are the fields of labor open to us in our future life and career as orators? The bar, the pulpit, the stump, the Senate chamber, the lecturer's platform.'[13] At the age of twenty he was evidently reviewing his future options with candid clear-sightedness. 'We went to college without an objective,' one classmate recalled. 'But Wilson always had a definite purpose.'[14]

The pulpit he had already rejected. The stump and the Senate chamber could wait; as it turned out, it was as the Governor of New Jersey rather than as a senator that Wilson finally ran for President. Meanwhile the bar clearly beckoned, hence Wilson's move to the University of Virginia's law school in 1879. But, having completed the first year there, with more oratorical than legal distinction, in the winter of 1880 his health broke down, in some psychosomatic way not clearly diagnosed at the time. He had had a similarly mysterious breakdown six years previously at the end of his first year at theological college. At any rate, these were not promising signals that either the ministry or the law was really his calling, though he persevered for the time being in his potential legal career.

Now with the name 'Woodrow Wilson' to hang on his plate, in 1881 he decided to set up a practice in Atlanta, in northern Georgia, chosen as a newly important industrial city enjoying sudden prosperity after the civil war: 'I think that to grow up with a new section is no small advantage to one who seeks to gain position and influence.'[15] Wilson went into partnership with a college acquaintance, Edward Renick, who proved agreeable enough and introduced him to political friends, notably Walter Hines Page, an anglophile and ideological sympathiser who was to serve as US ambassador to London during the First World War. All were keen Democrats and free traders.

But professionally it was another story. Wilson never had a case of his own; his principal client was his mother. He thus had plenty of time to keep up his copious reading, soaking himself in English literature, with his own copies of Milton, Shelley and Keats much treasured in his own little library, sitting on the shelf alongside works with a directly political bearing. Here was another imaginative world, at once isolating and comforting the highly strung young man who missed his coterie of Princeton friends; and he now longingly contrasted the established culture of southern Georgia, to say nothing of Virginia or Princeton, with the provincialism of Atlanta.

His library, however, gave him the opportunity for political and historical reflection. He was impressed by Edmund Burke's analysis of the organic growth of political institutions, by Walter Bagehot's pragmatic reflections on the workings of the British constitution, and by Henry Maine's emphasis on custom rather than contract in shaping social development. Wilson was no schematic or legalistic ideologue, never supposing that the world could be made anew by either fiat or revolution. Politics and history were deeply intertwined in the liberal story of progress. He was already deeply versed in English history and, just like many British Liberals, found J. R. Green's *Short History of the English People*, with its celebration of the Teutonic and Anglo-Saxon roots of English freedom, particularly stirring. 'To the American,' he had written of Green while still at Princeton, 'it was a vivid outline sketch of the progress of a people whose blood was coursing through his own veins, and whose traditions he was proud to claim as his own.'[16]

This was all very well, and highly educational no doubt; but where did it lead for an ambitious man of twenty-six, still financially dependent on his parents? He wrote to a friend whom he manifestly envied for beginning a PhD in Berlin, contrasting this happy fate with his own, 'buried in hum-drum life down here in slow, ignorant, uninteresting Georgia', and revealing that he was 'about to do what is the next best thing, for a fellow who is confined to the limits of this continent' – namely to throw up the law and instead study history, political science and German at Johns Hopkins University, leading to a PhD of his own as his passport to a new career. 'My plain necessity, then,' Wilson explained, 'is some profession which will afford me a moderate support, favourable conditions for study, and considerable leisure; what better can I be, therefore, than a professor, a lecturer upon subjects whose study most delights me?' This is how he triumphantly presented his supposedly sudden insight to his academic friend: 'Now here it is that the whole secret of my new departure lies.'[17]

Not, however, quite the whole secret. In April 1883 Wilson had, through the usual family network of social connections, met Ellen Axson, almost inevitably the daughter of a Presbyterian minister herself, and subsequently the love of his life. He was to keep 1,200 of their letters, exchanged over the next thirty years, in a sealed box that Baker, when beginning his work on the biography, was delighted to discover. The correspondence indeed reveals much, and not only about the closeness of their relationship but also about Woodrow's emotionally needy temperament. His letters to Ellen cover a wide range of subjects, not only personal and family, but comparing notes on literary and political topics. Moreover, they are often imbued with a fervour that ought to dispel any caricature of him as an austere and arid killjoy. Behind his public mask of intellectual severity, here was a man who brought passion and emotion to his politics – as he was quite ready to disclose.

'You know I am naturally extremely reserved,' he admitted to Ellen in beginning a 'stupendous epistle' of nineteen pages in October 1883; but he now felt able to unburden himself about future plans, clearly premised on wooing her as his wife, and finding sufficient means to support raising a family. He explained to Ellen that 'I left college on the wrong tack. I had then, as I still have, a very earnest political creed and very pronounced political ambitions.' So how had he gone wrong? He and his friends may have been right to make 'a solemn covenant that we would use all our powers and passions for the work of establishing the principles we held in common'; and right also to 'drill ourselves in all the arts of persuasion, but especially in oratory' as the means to this end. But then the false step. 'The profession I chose was politics; the profession I entered was the law,' he explained. 'I entered the one because I thought it would lead to the other.' He had been mistaken. As it was now practised in America, the law had become 'a jealous mistress', demanding that a man 'must be a lawyer *and nothing else*'.

Evidently, in opting for an academic career, Woodrow hoped to combine the attentions of a loving wife with those of a rather less jealous mistress. 'A professorship was the only feasible place for me,' as he put it to Ellen, 'the only place that would afford leisure for reading and for original work, the only strictly literary berth with an income attached.' It was thus clear from the outset that, for him, an academic career was no accidental stepping-stone to realising later political ambitions; it was a means calculated with this end always in view. 'But where does the oratory come in?' he demanded (rhetorically of course). Not in the lectures, perhaps, though he thought it should do so, when oratory was properly conceived in terms of its high rationale. 'Oratory is not declamation, not swelling tones and an excited delivery, but the art of persuasion, the art of putting things so as to appeal irresistibly to an audience.'[18]

Oratory was thus central to Wilson's conception of politics: a vocation in which he did not set out to be a great legislator, nor a great administrator, still less a great wirepuller. These were, if not simply tricks of his chosen trade, then necessary skills that the orator might do well to pick up later. In his first published book, *Congressional Government* (1885), he commented on how the great orators in British history, such as Hampden, Walpole, Chatham, Burke, Canning and Pitt, were in each case also famous for acquiring particular aptitudes – 'or, like Mr Gladstone, skilled in every branch of political knowledge and equal to any strain of emergency'.[19] Oratory was not a vulgar substitute for mastering the art of government: it was the means of mobilising consent by spreading a proper understanding of what was at stake. The subsequently famous historian of the American frontier, Frederick Jackson Turner, later a colleague of

Wilson, was paying the highest sort of compliment when he asked him, on one occasion, to tell Mrs Wilson that 'you, like Mr Gladstone, can make a budget interesting'.[20]

By 1883, then, Wilson had discovered that a legal career was not to be his pathway to his true vocation in politics, but that enlistment in the academic profession might well serve this underlying ambition. Moreover, it was a noble ambition, as seen in the careers of the statesmen he most admired, who were themselves, almost to a man, distinguished as great orators. And it was, significantly, within the constitutional framework of British politics, rather than within that of the United States, that Wilson saw the finest examples of the sort of political leadership that he most admired and most wished to emulate.

Virtually all the components of Wilson's conception of politics as a vocation are already apparent in his two essays on Bright and Gladstone, both published in the *University of Virginia Magazine* in successive months in 1880, but each having rather different origins. A couple of years previously, he had already identified the crucial difference between British and American politics: that a parliamentary career gave a long training in the requisite political skills whereas the changing composition of Congress failed this test. 'Why is it that Gladstone and Bright have so often been able to control and direct the current of public feeling and conviction in England?' he had asked. 'They give weight to any principle, power to any cause, from the mere fact that they represent an ability and integrity which the nation have seen tested by long public service.'[21]

This was one of the germinal ideas that Wilson was to later develop in *Congressional Government*, a critical work in more senses than one. He had put his point more stridently in an unpublished draft entitled 'Government by Debate', written in 1882, where he lectured his fellow Americans on what was needed. 'A ruling class must be created – not a ruling class of aristocrats or rich men, not a class boasting itself of hereditary privileges or prescriptive prerogatives, but a class of trained politicians, a profession of statesmen,' he proclaimed with a brashness that did not commend this work to any of the New York publishers who saw it. But, though put in different ways at different points in these years, Wilson's recipe for the making of statesmen was fairly consistent.

The idea of his composing a tribute to Bright in 1880 was thus no passing whim. Moreover this was first delivered as an oration to the Jefferson Society of the University of Virginia: a big public occasion that marked not only their early recognition of Wilson's aptitude as an orator but also his own temerity in tackling this particular subject. It may not surprise us that John Bright, the upright radical Quaker, is eulogised in the oration: 'His name has become synonymous with liberalism.'[22]

This was safe ground, as was Bright's record, along with that of his colleague Richard Cobden, in promoting the adoption of free-trade policies in Britain. The South, sharing a common interest in promoting the international cotton trade with industrial Lancashire, Bright's home, had always been pitted against the protectionist interests in the American North. '*Trade*, indeed, is the great nurse of liberal ideas,' Wilson declaimed. And so to Bright's reputation as an orator, with some epithets that Wilson had been honing for years. 'Grovelling minds are never winged with high and worthy thoughts,' he intoned, with all the moral gravitas that was to become his trademark. 'Eloquence consists not in sonorous sound or brilliant phrases. *Thought* is the fibre, thought is the *pith*, of eloquence.'[23]

If Bright lacked a classical education, this was clearly more than compensated by his grounding in the common texts of the English-speaking peoples. 'The Bible, Milton, and Shakespeare have been his most constant companions.' So far, so good. But the boldness of young Wilson's enterprise was now candidly acknowledged, before an audience in Virginia who all inevitably knew of Bright as 'a resolute opponent of the cause of the Southern Confederacy'. Was it therefore an invidious task to defend him? the orator mused – only to deny this in the starkest terms: 'But *because* I love the South, I rejoice in the failure of the Confederacy.'[24] This was indeed to be

Wilson's lifelong stance: readily acknowledging the legitimacy of a defence of states' rights rather than apologising for slavery, and accepting that the noble cause for which Robert E. Lee had fought was nonetheless doomed in modern America. The result, as he was to claim nearly thirty years later, was that 'the South has retained her best asset, namely, her self-respect'.[25] Perhaps the South had been too proud not to fight.

The oration on Bright was a triumph when delivered in March 1880, the published text a worthy memorial of the occasion. But Bright was only John the Baptist in the coming of the Liberal hour in Britain, now that the Bulgarian agitation had changed the landscape and Gladstone's famous campaign in his new Scottish constituency of Midlothian was in full spate. Compared with defending Bright, it was far more acceptable for Wilson, in his next essay, to apostrophise Gladstone in Virginia, and to do so at this high moment in the springtime of 1880.

The essay was only stating the obvious in saying that 'news of Mr Gladstone has long been peculiarly abundant', filling much space even in American small-town newspapers.[26] Breathlessly, Wilson's own chronicle was updated: 'The astonishing achievements and successes of Mr Gladstone's Midlothian campaign – news of whose triumphant issue has just reached us as I write – seem a fitting culmination to his career as a statesman.' The author's own partisanship was unabashed in delighting at Disraeli's electoral downfall – 'the brilliant reign of charlatanry is at an end' – and even higher sources of support for Gladstone were hinted at. 'Providence has been pleased to brighten his declining years with a new assurance of victory to the cause in whose name he has spent the magnificent energies of his nature,' Wilson declared.[27] This awed disciple could not have imagined that it would be another fourteen years before Gladstone's final departure as Prime Minister. But the crucial aspects of what was already a long and glorious political career were plain enough.

'Mr Gladstone has reasoned his way to the light; Mr Bright seems to have been born in the light,' Wilson asserted at one point, which may

THE COLOSSUS OF WORDS.

This Punch cartoon of 1879 conveys not only Gladstone's dominance during his famous Midlothian campaign but also his dependence on oratory. 'Passion is the pith of eloquence,' wrote the young Woodrow Wilson at this time in an admiring tribute to his hero.

read ambiguously as a judgement on his two heroes.[28] But in calling Gladstone 'the greatest English Liberal',[29] the author's ranking was now clear. The fact that, unlike Bright, Gladstone had notoriously given some credence to Southern pretensions to nationality during the civil war, though subsequently embarrassing for him in Britain, was not held against him in Virginia, of course. Moreover, as the author of a series of great budgets upholding free trade as having the sanction of ethics as well as of economics, Gladstone's name likewise appealed to an obvious Southern constituency. But the moral dimension in Wilson's encomium went far beyond any such calculations. 'His life has been one continuous advance, not towards power only – fools may be powerful; knaves sometimes rule by the knack of their knavery – but towards truth also the while.'[30] This morally strenuous progress towards the light was what mattered.

According to Wilson, Gladstone 'came gradually to allow full credit to the severe and inexorable processes of his keenly logical mind. And as soon as his mind was awakened his sympathetic affections enlisted his whole nature in the search after truth, fusing his reasonings and communicating their heat to the powers of his will.'[31] Thus passion was enlisted, not only within himself in support of the promptings of logic, but also in rallying support through communicating his moral appeal to the whole nation. It was integral to his statesmanship that Gladstone held 'a prominent place among the greatest orators'. Wilson had only recently, in commending Bright, suggested that thought was the pith of eloquence. He again reached for this epigram, but evidently with some significant second thoughts in now declaring: 'Passion is the pith of eloquence.' Virtuous passion released the energy to fight the good fight, as shown in Gladstone's great campaigns, those battles for righteousness under his generalship. 'For the principal qualities of his mind are warrior qualities – the qualities that display themselves in action.' In Wilson's admiring view, Gladstone's 'mind is habitually militant'.[32]

Whatever the other dimensions of his statesmanship, the central inspiration in Gladstone's example was clear. 'It is as an orator that

Mr Gladstone most forcibly appeals to our imaginations.' The force of his eloquence thus depended on more than a logical exposition of a case. It was a visceral process described in highly metaphorical language: 'The progress of Mr Gladstone's arguments is like the sweeping flight of an eagle from crag to crag and summit to summit.' And not, of course, mere flights of fancy or frivolous feats of resounding rhetoric, because 'under all and supporting all are the primitive, unchanging granite veins of conviction'.[33]

Here, then, was the 'keen poetical sensibility' that was discerned in Gladstone's oratory, despite Wilson's acknowledgement of the ponderous quality of his written prose. 'Great statesmen seem to direct and rule by a sort of power to put themselves in the place of the nation over whom they are set, and may thus be said to possess the souls of poets at the same time that they display the coarser sense and the more vulgar sagacity of practical men of business.'[34]

Wilson was twenty-three when he wrote in these terms of Gladstone; and he did so before his own abortive experiment with a legal career as his avenue to politics; before he married and had three daughters with Ellen; before he established himself as an academic authority on political science; before he rose to a position of increasing prominence as president of Princeton; before he was plucked away from academic politics to try his hand at the real thing as a reforming Governor of New Jersey; and well before, as President of the United States, he had to face an international crisis even more momentous than any that Gladstone had been called to confront. What made this remarkable trajectory possible, taking him into the White House in 1913, was partly the executive reputation that Wilson had meanwhile acquired in shaking up his university; it was partly his recognised academic expertise on the workings of the political system; but it was also crucial to his political credibility that he had made himself, through aptitude, study, training and practice, into an inspirational orator.

48

Essentially, then, Wilson's outlook on democratic statesmanship was already formed by 1880, and especially on the key role of oratory. 'Gladstone made good speeches,' Wilson would later maintain, 'but they are not good reading.'[35] The point was that writing made a different kind of appeal in communicating to instructed readers whereas other skills were demanded in turning ideas into deeds. 'Stripped for action, a thought must always shock those who cultivate the nice proportions of literary dress, as authors do,' he maintained in 1890, an author himself by then, but one evidently ready to strip for action if necessary as one of the 'leaders of men', as he called them, who were able to translate thought into action. 'The arguments which induce popular action must always be broad and obvious arguments,' he maintained, declaring it self-evident that 'the leader of men must have such sympathetic and penetrative insight as shall enable him to discern quite unerringly the motives which move other men *in the mass*'.[36]

This was not presented as a cynical view. Wilson was justified in anchoring such suggestions to the example of Gladstone, who liked to reflect on his own gift of timing in seizing on great issues. Virtually every reference Wilson ever made to Gladstone invites some suggestion of self-identification. 'Not only did he possess variety, but the force of his intellect was apparent to everyone,' this manifestly forceful professor had proclaimed in 1901. 'He stood for the type of what a man may make of himself when fired by high ambition and resolve.' But although such qualities were necessary and commendable, they did not go to the heart of the matter in understanding Gladstone's political potency. 'It was his moral force that enabled him to fill the benches of the House of Commons for hours at a time, it was his moral force which gave him his marvelous power over his fellow men, and finally it was the same force which made him the equal, if not the superior of any constitutional statesman of his time.'[37]

Gladstone was thus hailed not only for his ambition to raise the ethical tone of politics in an altruistic way but also for his ability – through what Wilson had termed his poetical sensibility – to translate his own sophisticated analysis into a simple visceral appeal to the masses rather than the classes, all the world over. This was indeed the proper function of passion and noble oratory in democratic politics: a belief that Wilson continued to affirm, exclaiming in 1909 (this was in his peroration to an address on Robert E. Lee): 'I wish there were some great orator who could go about and make men drunk with this great spirit of self-sacrifice.'[38] It is worth noting that this affirmation greatly impressed Baker, previously a Republican, when he read it at the time.

Wilson, through both precept and example, endorsed the legitimacy of the politics of emotion as the means of mobilising mass support for altruistic ends. Yet, to avoid misunderstanding here, there is need for some caution in terming him – as Gladstone has already been termed in my prologue – a moral populist. For Populism, in the context of American politics and especially with a capital letter, often refers to a grassroots political movement that came to a peak in the 1890s, with an emotional appeal that briefly captured the Democratic party. This was the basis of the presidential campaign waged in 1896 by the populist western Democrat William Jennings Bryan, 'the Great Commoner'. In taking up the cause of bimetallism, pitting his enthused followers against the iniquities of Wall Street and the gold standard, Bryan was a charismatic figure with his plea not to 'crucify mankind upon a cross of gold'. For this brand of populism, Wilson had little sympathy. His own version of liberal economics was based on the Gladstonian orthodoxies of free trade, balanced budgets and the gold standard; the Princeton professor seemed an aloof and, at that stage, a relatively conservative figure. Moreover, his later rival in progressive politics, Theodore Roosevelt, was a figure whom Wilson claimed to scorn for the moral emotionalism of his rhetoric (as did Baker), which may seem a selectively harsh judgement.

For all that, Wilson himself can be identified with an Anglo-American strain of moral populism that looked back not only to

Gladstone but to Lincoln. The fact that Lincoln had been elected as a Republican was, forty years on, no barrier to his veneration in this light. In 1909, in giving a commemorative address, Wilson entitled it 'Abraham Lincoln: a man of the people' – a label that he sought to reinterpret. Wilson duly hailed a self-made president 'whose glory it was to win the affection alike of those whom he led and of those whom he opposed, as indeed a man and a king among those who mean the right'.[39]

Resonant platitudes, of course, are apt to pad out any such address; but it is interesting how much space Wilson devoted to wrestling with the soubriquet 'man of the people' and in resisting the obvious sense that it depended on humble origins. Nor, apparently, did it mean 'a man who simply repeats the talk of the street-corners', but instead it meant one who heard 'the voices of the nation' and could harmonise them, 'so that he can speak what no man else knows, the common meaning of the common voice'. On the basis of this reinterpretation, a man of the people might evidently be born not in a log cabin but perhaps in a Presbyterian manse. To be called a man of the people was thus a function not of birth but (like Gladstone) of adoption by the people in a democratic age. 'We must always be led by "men of the people", and therefore it behooves us to know them when we see them.' And the task here was to find leaders who had not been 'too long submerged in a particular profession', since this was apt to deform their perspective. Wilson demanded: 'Are you not glad that Mr Lincoln did not succeed too deeply in any particular calling; that he was sufficiently detached to be lifted to a place of leadership and to be used by the whole country?' What should be admired was the coolness of someone who could 'smile at lawyers and turn away from ministers', proclaimed an orator who had like-wise turned away from both professions in his time.[40]

What was needed, he suggested, was not a man whose own heat and intensity sent a danger signal, but a leader with a more detached capacity: 'Anyone can stir up emotions, but who is master of men enough to take the saddle and guide those awakened emotions?'[41]

Wilson, an ostensibly cool man who was ready to enlist the politics of emotion, certainly fitted this job description. And in these terms he was clearly a moral populist: one who was to emerge on the international stage with a self-conscious Gladstonian pedigree. Wilson had even interjected into this same address on Lincoln a passing tribute to 'Gladstone, who knew how to rule men by those subtle forces of oratory which shape the history of the world and determine the relations of nations to each other'.[42]

Wilson manifestly made no secret of such opinions; virtually every reference to Gladstone quoted above was published at the time. But in the context of the First World War, in which the President proclaimed American neutrality in 1914, to call him an anglophile was a highly charged way of characterising him and his policy; so it is now necessary to ponder what kind of an anglophile Wilson really was.

———————

Wilson first crossed the Atlantic to Britain in 1896: a long voyage in those days, both literally and figuratively, and undertaken by comparatively few Americans. Nearly forty, he travelled in recuperation from a medical problem – possibly a small stroke – that had incapacitated his right hand. This was to be a cycling holiday with his brother-in-law, Stockton Axson, and the trip apparently did the trick. Woodrow wrote back to Ellen with enthusiasm about what he saw, especially the ancient universities. The town of Cambridge 'seemed to me rather mean', he admitted, 'but the colleges most of them beyond measure attractive, – some of them exceedingly beautiful'.[43] Partly this was a professional mission; he was charged with luring the eminent legal historian F. W. Maitland to visit Princeton. Maitland declined: not so Wilson's enthusiasm. Writing home to Ellen from 'the heart of the Shakespere country' he told her: 'My heart burns with a keen remorse that I should be here without you, – in this inexpressibly beautiful region, where England is to be seen looking as I had dreamed it would look, and where memories crowd and haunt so as to fill the mind and heart to overflowing.'[44]

Whatever could be better than this? The answer was to be revealed after cycling for four more days: 'a mere glance at Oxford is enough to take one's heart by storm'. As he walked around the ancient quadrangles, each college seemed more beautiful than the last. 'I have seen as much that made me feel alien as that made me feel at home since I came to England,' he admitted to Ellen, 'and have been made on the whole to love Am. more rather than less, – for all Eng. is so bonny and so full of treasure for the mind and fancy, – but Oxford! Well, I am afraid that if there were a place for me here Am. would see me again only to sell the house and fetch you and the children . . .'[45] It was only a holiday romance, of course, and the Princeton professor was to return refreshed to his duties and to the bosom of his family without putting his house on the market. Still, it was just as well that such letters were not published in 1915 or 1916 when Wilson was running for re-election on his record of keeping the country clear of any anglophile embraces.

In 1899 Wilson went cycling again in Britain with Stockton Axson. This pair of stern Presbyterians now spent some time in Dumfries, in 'Burns country', enthusing over the 'quaint little tavern which Burns most frequented here', marvelling at 'the table about which the poet and his cronies used to gather, and the chair in which he used to sit and hold forth for their delectation'. Stockton even dared to sit on this notorious toper's chair, so his sister was told.[46] A month later they had worked their way south, partly by rail but also by cycling up to eighteen miles a day. 'And Cambridge at the end of the ride!' Woodrow exclaimed to Ellen, still back at home in Princeton. Though Oxford was still judged 'more beautiful and impressive', there was something to be said for the River Cam and the Backs. 'The river is full of boats for hire, and Stock. and I took one and paddled slowly from end to end of the beautiful place, with unspeakable quiet pleasure.'[47] The next day, *Baedeker* in hand, Woodrow noted that 'there is much more architectural consistency here than at Oxford, – with the result that there are no monstrosities here such as there are at Oxford, but a sameness of satisfying style, – except where Sir Christopher Wren has touched the original design to spoil it.'[48]

This is where business and pleasure happily intersected. For when Wilson shortly afterwards became president of Princeton, ambitious to raise both its profile and its pedagogical record, he not only looked to the example of England's ancient universities but aimed to set this aspiration in stone. 'By the very simple device of constructing our new buildings in the Tudor Gothic style we seem to have added to Princeton the age of Oxford and Cambridge,' he purposefully assured the alumni in 1902; 'we have added a thousand years to the history of Princeton by merely putting those lines in our architecture which point every man's imagination to the historic traditions of learning in the English-speaking race. We have declared our derivation and lineage.'[49] This was at once a significant cultural declaration and an efficient fund-raising ploy in his plan to transform the university, constructing quadrangles to enshrine a teaching regime based on tutorials, all on the Oxbridge model.

In 1906, perhaps as the result of over-exertion in his efforts to rebuild Princeton, Wilson woke up with blindness in one eye, probably a symptom of another small stroke. The prescription was for a further long visit to England, this time for several months with his family, based at Rydal in the Lake District. This was, of course, 'Wordsworth country'; Woodrow and Ellen loved it; and the cure again seemed successful. But the stubborn president returned to his duties at Princeton more determined than ever to drive through his plans for reshaping the university in accordance with his own blueprint, which included a graduate school on the campus. If he had been ready to settle for such a school on a nearby adjacent site, he might have been able to achieve his essential academic objectives; but he insisted on the integrity of his original proposal, all or nothing, at the expense of alienating crucial support within the university. He took the fight to the public platform, infusing and inflating his rhetoric with lofty aspirations that Baker later attributed to a religious crisis. In this episode, Wilson revealed characteristic responses that were to cloud his final years in the White House.

His duties at Princeton notwithstanding, Wilson again returned to the Lake District in 1908 – hardly a convenient itinerary to squeeze into the summer vacation – and this time by himself. 'My wish is fulfilled: I am back in sweet Grasmere,' he reported to Ellen, 'though I have not yet seen the friends.'[50] The social connections they had formed clearly reinforced their attachment to the Lakes, which they may even have contemplated at some point as an ultimate retirement home. All of this speaks mainly to the cultural hold of England and Scotland upon Wilson's imagination. He cultivated few political links and commented little on current British political issues.

Although in Britain during the summer of 1899, when the South African crisis had been brewing, and when Gladstonians like Morley were voicing their fervent condemnation of British aggression, Wilson seems to have taken scant notice. He was certainly not drawn into controversy about imperialism in principle and instead envisaged a parallel American role in emulating Britain's example. Kipling's well-known plea for Americans to 'take up the white man's burden' was in this idiom. Wilson confessed at this time that he had not wished the United States to occupy the Philippines but accepted the outcome: 'We have the islands, and the question now is what are we to do with them.'[51] There was a clear racial element, perhaps not surprising in a Southern white man who upheld a colour bar, in Wilson's view here. 'The "consent" of the Filipinos and the "consent" of the American colonists to government', so he argued, were 'two radically different things, – not in theory, perhaps, but in practice, – and practice is "the whole duty of man" in politics, i.e. what is practicable, workable'.[52] This is the voice of expediency rather than of moral principle, with a pragmatic view of 'colonial politics', as he put it to his colleague Frederick Turner, 'concerning which we must, whether we will or not, take our lesson from England in any case'.[53]

On his 1908 visit to Britain, Wilson was to meet Morley himself. Their encounter took place in the slightly bizarre setting of Andrew Carnegie's enormous Scottish castle, which the famous Gladstonian philanthropist had financed from the profits of the American steel industry. Viscount Morley of Blackburn, recently ennobled to spare his attendance in the Commons, was by now nearly seventy, serving in Asquith's Liberal cabinet as Secretary of State for India. It was less as a politician, however, than as a literary model that Wilson appraised and appreciated him. 'What he said had that flavour of sincerity and simplicity which I so love in the best English men,' he wrote to Ellen, 'and was expressed as you would imagine he would express it, – with an elegance natural to a real man of letters and a deliberation (such as I greatly admire but have not) characteristic of a man who thinks both before and while he speaks.'[54]

Here was a sense of style, and a consciously detached mien, that Wilson himself liked to emulate. He too became the intellectual in politics. Ray Stannard Baker conveys a vivid sense of the prevailing atmosphere while the votes were being counted at the Democratic party convention in Baltimore, to decide the nomination for presidential candidate in 1912. Wilson was at the official Governor's cottage – in fact a substantial and imposing residence – on the New Jersey coast. He remained intermittently in touch by telephone with the protracted horse-trading at the convention, in which he initially seemed to stand little chance. Calm and aloof, he went off to play a round of golf during the early ballots and then, Baker tells us, 'for a time he read Morley's *Gladstone* – "a great book"'.[55] They shared, of course, a highly favourable view not only of this biography but of its subject – and surely did so as Gladstonians rather than simply as anglophiles. Baker does not say that Wilson was called away at this point to run for President; but the call from Baltimore duly came through.

A Man of the People:
David Lloyd George

'Most of the leading actors in the Great War, both Statesmen and Warriors, have committed to writing the story of the part they played in it,' wrote Lloyd George in the preface to his own *War Memoirs*, first published in 1933. He included 'President Wilson (through Mr Baker)' among the works he listed. 'My shelves groan under the burden of war autobiographies,' was Lloyd George's ritualistic complaint; but then he promptly explained how he had been persuaded to follow 'the example set me by those who figured so prominently on the stage where I also occupied a not inconspicuous position'.[1] It was not only the false modesty that was disingenuous here. The whole story of how he came to compose his book was told in a way that concealed one motive – money, of course – while only hinting at his other obvious agenda, defence of his own record.

Lloyd George had stood on a high peak of fame at the end of the war. In 1922, the year that he lost office as Prime Minister, it was announced in the London *Evening Standard* – one of the newspapers owned by his crony Lord Beaverbrook – that Lloyd George had signed 'the biggest deal in the history of publishing' for his memoirs. The sum concerned amounted to £90,000, which today would be worth at least £4 million (say $6 million). 'After seventeen years in office,' Lloyd George explained, 'I have retired a poor man, and it is absolutely imperative that I should turn to writing as a means of livelihood.' But the huge book advance looked rather like literary war profiteering, or so Lloyd George's political enemies claimed. The adverse publicity induced him to issue a statement, promising that the proceeds of his memoirs would be donated to charity.

This hasty pledge in 1922 naturally lessened his own incentive to publish. What he would have written at this time will never be known. It was to be ten years later – amid a cynical public mood that no longer celebrated the outcome of the war – that Lloyd George, nearing seventy, actually began the book, evidently with mixed feelings. Yet he warmed to his task. He found that he enjoyed writing and said that he wished he had started at fifty. He now had an advance worth slightly less than before, but one that he felt free to pocket himself; and he delighted in the fact that the sum involved was much bigger than that for a similar contract recently signed by his old friend and rival Winston Churchill to add a final volume to his work *The World Crisis*. So much did Lloyd George relish his experience as an author, refighting old battles and settling old scores, that after the sixth and final volume of his *War Memoirs* had been published at the end of 1936, he turned to writing the 2,000 pages of *The Truth about the Peace Treaties* (1938). His breathtaking claim there is that it was 'written without any consideration of the effect which a plain statement of the truth may have upon present controversies'.[2] Still, the story that he had to tell as an author was indeed remarkable – even if there were private revelations that it was still prudent to omit and public issues on which it was now tempting to change his tune.

Though born in Manchester in 1863, David Lloyd George was quintessentially Welsh. Not only was he fluent in the language but he grew up with a keen sense of alienation from the English establishment, especially the landlord class whom he saw as parasitic upon his own compatriots. 'I was brought up in a workman's home,' he later claimed, admittedly when addressing an audience of trade unionists. He made the most of his upbringing in the cottage of his uncle, Richard Lloyd, the village shoemaker, who had adopted his infant nephews, David and William George, on their father's death. The boys' mother, born Elizabeth Lloyd, had successfully appealed to her brother when facing this extremity, and she was glad to leave Manchester and return to the village of Llanystumdwy, on the edge of Snowdonia, where the beautiful Lleyn peninsula juts out into the Irish Sea.

Uncle Lloyd thus took the place of the father whom the orphans had barely known. It was David, the elder of the boys, who was pampered as the favourite and alone allowed to assume the name of his mother's family, the Lloyds, thus becoming known as Lloyd George (unlike his brother William George). In his later career, David had to face intermittent campaigns to call him 'Mr George', usually inspired less by the fact that this was the legally correct form than by a combination of political spite and social snobbery. Undiminished, he remains Lloyd George to posterity. And from the first, he grew up with a sense of entitlement that allowed him, quite without compunction, to exploit his indulgent family and to eclipse his younger brother. There are some obvious parallels with Woodrow Wilson here.

Uncle Lloyd had ensured both boys a good schooling, leading not to university but directly to a professional career as solicitors. Even in his days as a cabinet minister, Lloyd George liked to refer to himself as just a Welsh country attorney, by which he must have meant that William was left minding the law firm (Lloyd George and George) that financed his brother's spectacular rise in politics. 'Here was a Welsh boy,' William wrote of his brother in his own autobiography, 'and an orphan at that, with no state education other than that provided by a village school, who, by dint of his almost unaided efforts rose to the highest post in the land.' This was true enough, and also very magnanimous.

The fact is that the brilliant political career of Lloyd George could never have got off the ground without Uncle Lloyd to steer the boys down the path to a suitable profession, nor subsequently without an endlessly supportive brother. William was left to slave at his desk alone, with a nominal law partner who could do his fair share of the work only when Parliament was not sitting, yet a partner who thought that having his own illustrious name on the letterhead fully justified him in drawing upon the proceeds of this family firm to foot the bills that beset a young backbencher. Members of Parliament were still unpaid in those days and it was fully fifteen years after his election to the Commons that Lloyd George was first appointed to government office in 1905, as President of the Board of Trade, with a salary of £2,000 a year. Only then did he secure a settled income of his own; and when he became Chancellor of the Exchequer a couple of years later, this brought his annual salary up to £5,000, which would be worth at least £400,000 today. It was indeed a remarkable ascent: financially, politically, professionally and socially alike. For few solicitors – lawyers working at the more humble end of their trade – succeeded in even getting elected to the House of Commons in those days.

The lawyers who made a political mark were more often barristers, with all the prestige of the metropolitan bar to inflate their reputations, as Lloyd George could well see when he looked around him at Westminster. A top barrister could earn enough at his day job in the London courts to finance a career in the House of Commons, which met mainly in the evening. The pre-eminent example was Herbert Henry Asquith, who was, by the time he became Home Secretary in Gladstone's last government in 1892, already spoken of as a future leader of the Liberal party.

Asquith's rise was far from effortless, though a classical scholarship to Balliol College, Oxford, helped to create the impression that his successive triumphs were always assured. In fact, Asquith too had lost his father as a boy; he too had become dependent on his mother's family to provide him with an education. In his case this had meant moving to London, away from the austere Nonconformist milieu of his birthplace in industrial Yorkshire. The skills that Asquith had acquired as a barrister, notably when deployed in the politically charged exposure of the iniquities of the reporting by *The Times* on Parnell's leadership of the movement for Irish Home Rule, were crucial in transforming him from a struggling Liberal backbencher into a potential future prime minister.

Political fame marched with upward social mobility in Asquith's career. He always professed deep affection for his first wife, who died suddenly in 1891, clearly intending his description of her as 'not the least anxious for me to "get on"' as a tribute to her sweet nature. But his second marriage – to Margot Tennant, the daughter of a wealthy Scottish industrialist who had become a Liberal grandee – was itself a statement about the circles in which the new Home Secretary now moved. The register at their fashionable wedding in Mayfair was signed by Gladstone, a family friend of the Tennants, and he had obligingly postponed a cabinet meeting that clashed with the event.

Margot was a woman who made her own idiosyncratic impact felt. She reshaped her husband's social life in a way that reflected both her own wayward aesthetic aspirations and her keenly focused ambitions for him. One symbol was her disdain for his first name, Herbert, which was discarded on Margot's whim after their marriage in 1894. It had seemed a good enough name to Gladstone, who had had his own son christened Herbert, but Margot was now even grander than the Grand Old Man. She insisted that her husband be called Henry, or just referred to as HHA, as henceforth became customary, though Margot would surely have been mortified by the practice of a number of recent historians in reinventing a Prime Minister called Herbert Asquith (rather like talking of President Thomas Wilson).

The careers of Asquith and Lloyd George were to become interlocked and intertwined. They were to serve, successively, as Britain's last two Liberal prime ministers. The Liberal party was to find itself fatally divided between their followers. Their names became codewords for sharply different styles of Liberalism: Lloyd George as the plebeian man of business with coalitionist instincts and dirty hands, in contrast to an aloof Asquithian aura compounded of liberal purity and elitist disdain. Their two families were to perpetuate a great posthumous feud into the next generation, leaving a dense undergrowth of deeply rooted myth and luxuriant misconception.

Yet there was a curiously durable mutual respect between these two essentially self-made men, reflecting some strong affinities.

They shared a mutual recognition of the outstanding gifts that had made their rise possible; and they knew that, in each case, this had been achieved against the odds and without the independent financial resources that sustained most of their colleagues. In his *War Memoirs*, when describing the response to his appointment as Prime Minister, Lloyd George still made a point of writing that 'it was necessary to bear in mind that there had never been a "ranker" raised to the Premiership – certainly not one except Disraeli who had not passed through the Staff College of the old Universities'.[3] There was some truth in this, but it was a comment not only on the cards that the young Mr George had been dealt but on how he had subsequently played his hand, in a game that he was always determined to win. For if Asquith had a carefully cultivated patrician air that belied his family roots, it was with equal care that Lloyd George always burnished his own image as 'the cottage-bred man'.

Lloyd George was truly a man who lived in more than one world. One was that of his native Wales, where Welsh was a living language which he used in electioneering in his constituency, and which also served him as a useful code into which he could discreetly lapse in family letters from faraway Westminster. And it was London, of course, that was the centre of another, wider world that he set out to conquer. As a cabinet minister in two posts with direct economic responsibilities, first at the Board of Trade and then at the Treasury, Lloyd George became fully briefed on the role played by the City of London in acting as the global financial regulator, operating through the gold standard so as to balance the flows of international transactions under the free-trade regime that was the bedrock of Liberal economic policy. This was the heart of the Empire, with a global diaspora of white settlement looking to London for finance and offering opportunities for British investors. Lloyd George went along with all this happily enough and made investments himself, not always wisely.

Two very different worlds, but which came first? In chronology at least, it was obviously the milieu of the Welsh language, of Welsh chapels, of Welsh history and culture – the world that first gave its talented young champion his chance. His gifts were apparent from an early age: a handsome and vibrant young man whose charismatic appeal inspired devotion from men and women alike. He was not embarrassed that he stood only five foot five. Though Etonians, like those who literally looked down on him in Parliament, were as tall then as today, Lloyd George was actually about average height for men of his generation in Wales – the shortest in the United Kingdom – so even his diminutive stature was typically Welsh. He was a natural orator in either Welsh or English: rarely sticking to any cryptic notes he had made but instead improvising his speeches through his own sharp wits and his uncanny sense of empathy with his audiences.

It was rather remarkable that, aged only twenty-five, Lloyd George had won the Liberal nomination for the Caernarvon District of Boroughs. But this was a rather remarkable sort of parliamentary constituency. It represented, as its name suggests, the borough of Caernarvon, with its ancient castle where Lloyd George, by then as Constable of the Castle, was to stage the investiture of a new Prince of Wales in 1911 – in Wales itself for the first time since the title had been appropriated by the English crown in the Middle Ages as a handy title for the heir to the throne. The King and Queen attended the ceremony; their son (later Edward VIII) was coached to speak in Welsh for the occasion. The Constable himself, who had masterminded the whole pageant with his genius for public relations, made himself conspicuous only by the elaborately self-effacing way that he conducted himself, since everyone knew full well that he was the real power behind the throne. Little wonder that Churchill later called him 'the greatest Welshman which that unconquerable race has produced since the age of the Tudors'.

The Caernarvon Boroughs constituency also included the nearby boroughs of Bangor, Conway and Pwllheli. Also within the district, bounded by mountains and sea, there lay not only the modern seaside resort of Llandudno but also smaller towns with evocative Welsh names like Llanfairfechan, Penmaenmawr and Criccieth. It was to Criccieth that Uncle Lloyd had moved the family after Dafydd (as the family called him) began working there as a solicitor; it was in Criccieth that the firm of Lloyd George and George was then established. Here in the heart of this north-west corner of Welsh-speaking, chapel-going north Wales, the young man was already regarded as the local prodigy. In an opportune by-election in 1890, he was elected a Member of Parliament at twenty-seven – as young as those lofty aristocrats who had always been able to enter the House with youth on their side (and thus build the sort of long parliamentary career of which Professor Wilson had written enviously in his *Congressional Government*).

Lloyd George exploited this special opportunity from first to last. In the 1890 by-election he had squeaked home with 50.2 per cent of the vote, increasing his share somewhat in the following General Election. Even in 1900, a bad year for the Liberals when the South African War made Lloyd George's exposed position as a 'pro-Boer' vulnerable, he polled 53 per cent; and in the good years of the Liberal revival, when he was a cabinet minister, he polled over 60 per cent in each of the three General Elections of 1906, January 1910 and December 1910. Thus by the outbreak of the world war his local position was already impregnable; and he was to hold the seat for nearly fifty-five years in all (until he accepted an earldom shortly before his death). Not Gladstone, nor Asquith, nor Churchill, to name but three, enjoyed such electoral security, near to home. And Lloyd George took full advantage of it, swiftly making an impact at Westminster through his ready eloquence and quickness in debate. His young wife Margaret had already been told what to expect. 'My supreme idea is to get on,' he had written while courting her, and he declared himself 'prepared to thrust even love itself under the wheels of my Juggernaut' in the process.

They were to remain married for over fifty years, through thick and thin. Margaret came from a locally prominent Methodist family and remained rooted in the culture of their home in Criccieth while David increasingly led his other life, centred on Westminster. He had been brought up by Uncle Lloyd as a Baptist but this sectarian affiliation was more evident in his radical politics than in his own spiritual commitment. His religious faith does not seem to have survived the death of his favourite young daughter, Mair, at the end of 1907, at a moment when he was already in the Liberal cabinet and within reach of further promotion. 'Some hand from the dark', as he privately mused, now struck at him at the very moment 'when I have been put on a sort of pinnacle, just so that I should become the target for this cruel blow'. His abiding sense of destiny and providence was bound up with his secular ambitions, which always came first. 'Dearest Maggie' remained his loyal wife because, often in Criccieth herself in later years, she learned

David Lloyd George was a rising MP on the Opposition backbenches when this family photograph was taken in 1904. His wife Margaret holds baby Megan; their elder daughter Mair was to die three years later, just as her father stood on the threshold of high office. 'Some hand from the dark' had struck; the event finally destroyed his own religious faith.

to tolerate his infidelities in distant London – a situation far from unique at Westminster, though one that was to be taken to extraordinary lengths by Lloyd George, with characteristic insouciance.

The *War Memoirs* remain discreetly reticent on such matters. In writing of his appointment to head the new Ministry of Munitions in 1915, Lloyd George makes the point that he had 'no office staff except my two able Private Secretaries', one a fellow Welshman who served as a reliable henchman throughout ten years of his master's ministerial career, and the other identified as 'Miss F. L. Stevenson', who was 'the first woman secretary appointed by a Minister'.[4] This is the sole reference to her; but she certainly had more than a walk-on part in the drama.

Remarkably, from 1913 until her own death in 1941, Margaret Lloyd George had to accept that her husband had embarked upon a virtually bigamous relationship. In Wales, he lived with Margaret; and when she made one of her visits to London, discreet arrangements were put in place (sometimes hurriedly) to maintain all the outward forms of family life. But during the increasingly long stretches of time when his wife was away, Lloyd George lived with another woman, and one whose own diary provides us with an extraordinarily vivid account of a man to whom she had unique access, and whom she was ultimately to marry after Margaret's death.

Frances Stevenson was a politically astute young woman of progressive views and considerable ability, a graduate of London University in classics. She was twenty-three and Lloyd George forty-eight when they first met in 1911, and he engaged her as tutor for his young daughter Megan. The relationship developed; he offered her a position as his official secretary in the Treasury, as she later put it, 'on his own terms, which were in direct conflict with my essentially Victorian upbringing'. She recalled that he gave her a book on the Irish leader Parnell, whose career had been retrieved from political calumny in 1889 (partly through Asquith's agency) only to be spectacularly destroyed in 1890 through a divorce case, at just the time that the young Lloyd George had entered Parliament. Gladstone, seeing his final attempt to implement Irish Home Rule now in jeopardy, had sought to limit the damage by repudiating Parnell, simply on politically expedient reasoning.

Here was a lesson in conventional morality that Lloyd George took to heart with pragmatic forthrightness. In a sense he had always lived by a double standard, with one way of doing things in Wales and another in London. Frances hesitated until the end of 1912, considered more prudent alternatives for herself, but then accepted Lloyd George's renewed pleas; and the bargain with convention was duly struck. The price was eternal watchfulness, with Frances seldom riding in the government car 'in case people fix on it for a scandal', as her diary admits. 'Never mind! We are "doing" the world in spite of its spitefulness,' so Lloyd George reassured her, adding: 'If you pay homage to it in certain things, you can defy it in others as much as you like.'[5]

In the decade before the First World War, it was the Liberal party that made the running in British politics. It was traditionally the party of Peace, Retrenchment and Reform – a fine slogan in its day but one that was now subverted in all three respects. First, it was a Liberal government that took Britain into the war that broke the European peace in 1914. Second, retrenchment was an odd way to describe the striking increase in public spending for which the government was responsible: up by 30 per cent in eight years. Third, though some of this rise was a result of reform initiatives, notably in social legislation, there was also a big increase in the defence budget, notably for the new super-battleships, the dreadnoughts, commissioned in a barely disguised naval race with Germany.

Though the dynamics of the Liberal government were now geared to social reform and domestic policy in a way that marked a sharp break with the Gladstonian agenda, the Liberal party's factional politics remained highly charged with nostalgic Gladstonian rhetoric over foreign policy. Here too Lloyd George presented himself as outwardly conventional. 'My interests were definitely centred on more domestic matters; on the special concerns of Wales, and on the education controversy, free trade, Home Rule, the land question and social reform,' he recalled in 1933. 'In foreign policy I had always been, as I am today, an ardent advocate of the rights of small nationalities, and I had been trained to believe in a peaceable settlement of the differences which arose between the nations of the world.'[6]

The young Lloyd George may once have nurtured his private reservations about the aged Gladstone, but he was to wax fulsome in appealing to the memory of the posthumous Gladstone. In 1892 the Grand Old Man had paid a ceremonial visit to Caernarvonshire, which the district's novice MP had naturally exploited at the time and continued to exploit in the opening pages of the *War Memoirs*, which include a vivid tableau. 'Mr Gladstone was passionately pro-French in his general attitude,' Lloyd George claimed. 'The Bismarckism of blood and iron never appealed to him. He was essentially a Liberal in foreign affairs.'[7] We need to remember that this was written well after the Great War, as was the graphic account of Gladstone's table talk on this occasion – 'a wonderful panegyric on the people of France', which, so Lloyd George assures the reader, 'more or less represented the Radical attitude towards the French Republic and its citizens at the time when I came into active politics'.[8] It is true that, when the Dreyfus case polarised French politics and society – with the Radical politician Georges Clemenceau prominent in defending the wrongly accused Captain Dreyfus against an array of anti-semitic, Roman Catholic, upper-class and militaristic prejudices – Lloyd George knew which side he was on as a Welsh Dreyfusard.

The impression that the *War Memoirs* conveys can be called a post-war perspective in more senses than one. Lloyd George was writing in the light not only of the war of 1914–18 but also of the Boer War of 1899–1902. It was over this conflict, closely identified with Joseph Chamberlain as Colonial Secretary in the Conservative government, that the opposition Liberal party had found itself awkwardly divided. Asquith and his closest colleagues Edward

Grey and Richard Haldane were termed 'Liberal Imperialists', though their acceptance of annexation here (much like Wilson over the Philippines) was more politically pragmatic than ideologically fervent. Some of the passion excited by their label as 'Liberal Imperialists' was retrospective, but the term proved as indelible as Lloyd George's own label as a 'pro-Boer'.

In origin at least, 'pro-Boer' was a pejorative term, suggesting that those who opposed Britain's resort to force were simply unpatriotic. But of course they themselves claimed the higher sanction of morality for the stand they took. In September 1899, at the outbreak of the South African War, Lloyd George was visiting western Canada, to investigate prospects for Welsh immigrants on this remote Pacific shore of the British Empire. He was thus largely reliant for news on the copies of the *Manchester Guardian* that his brother sent him – 'The London papers are sickening reading & I don't get them,' William explained. Lloyd George had already formed a friendship with the *Guardian*'s editor, C. P. Scott, whom he knew as a fellow Liberal backbencher in these years. It was Scott who had recently organised the notable protest meeting in Manchester at which Morley repeatedly called any such war 'wrong' – whatever its outcome, 'wrong'.

Lloyd George was himself to make many passionate denunciations of 'Joe's war', by which he meant that the resort to arms had not been necessary but had been provoked by Chamberlain for ulterior ends, notably to serve the interests of the bondholders in South African goldmines. At the war's outbreak, while still in Canada, Lloyd George had sent home his private expostulations which ('so long as my hopes that the English will get a black eye are omitted') he relied upon Margaret and William to publicise. 'I am still at boiling point over it,' he told them. 'It is wicked.' And as the war actually progressed, it got worse. It was waged, Lloyd George later proclaimed in one speech, against 'a little country, the total of whose population was less than Carmarthenshire', thus appealing to his Welsh followers in a style that was thoroughly in character, and to be repeated in 1914 with a belligerent rather than a pacifist twist. Lloyd George rekindled the flame of Gladstonian rhetoric, in which no foreign or imperialist war could assert an overriding patriotic obligation to support 'my country, right or wrong'; in which the right to self-determination of any nation, however small, was always an overriding moral issue; and in which war therefore posed a high issue of conscience, in choosing between right and wrong.

These were high stakes, generating a commensurately high level of emotional commitment. Little wonder that the pro-Boer agitation forged lasting bonds between many of those who took part in it. They had had to wind themselves up to brave the hostility of the street. This was true psychologically for Scott, whose big demonstration in 1899, starring John Morley, was at least on his home ground in Manchester. It was true physically for Lloyd George, whose attempt two years later to speak in Birmingham, which was Chamberlainite territory, led to a riot from which the police rescued 'this most virulent anti-Briton', as the Tory press had billed him. Lloyd George was smuggled out of the hall, hurriedly dressed in police uniform himself, and snatched from real personal danger. Here was a battle in itself; the confrontation ended with the deaths of two people, one of them a policeman. It was a night to remember.

Though the hostilities were concluded in 1902, the Boer War left a potent residual legacy. Indirectly, it contributed to the eventual collapse of the Conservative government, since Chamberlain soon opened his next big campaign to save the Empire, this time through proposals for imperial preference on the new tariffs he wanted to impose on food imports. This initiative in 1903 backfired, since its immediate effect was to reunite the Liberals around free trade, and also to precipitate some Conservative defections (of which the most prominent was that of the young Churchill). Asquith was brought back into a central role as the free-trade champion best fitted to follow Chamberlain round the country, exposing the fallacies of protection. The Liberals, now in an informal alliance with the nascent Labour party, duly achieved their landslide free-trade victory at the General Election of 1906, essentially on this negative ticket.

The new Liberal government ostensibly put the divisive issues of the Boer War behind it. At the top, Sir Henry Campbell-Bannerman was a stopgap prime minister, a rich man who had accepted the party leadership in 1899 only after Asquith withdrew his own obvious claims, noting that for him to lead the party while in opposition would 'cut me off from my profession and leave me poor and pecuniarily dependent'. The two men had then formed a good working relationship, Asquith ready with the oratorical sledgehammer that the easy-going leader knew he could not wield himself. His canny and unassuming leadership style eventually made 'C-B' into a minor cult figure, a process assisted by his death after only a couple of (rather barren) years in office, and he was to be extravagantly mourned in retrospect for his ability to transcend Liberal factionalism. He had indeed quelled his own instinct to campaign more actively against the Boer War in favour of keeping the party together, simply trusting that its luck would change (as it did).

Likewise, in forming his government in December 1905, C-B was magnanimous. Of course he gladly gave high office to his own factional supporters: John Morley at the India Office and the lawyer Robert Reid, elevated to the Lord Chancellorship as Lord Loreburn. But C-B also forgave everyone their past sins, as long as they had stuck to the Liberal party. He even found a junior ministerial post at the Colonial Office for the Tory renegade Churchill.

Indeed Churchill's first task in government was to assist in granting self-government to the new Union of South Africa. This was C-B's own most significant policy initiative, and he characteristically opted for magnanimity in victory, in the hope that it would lead to goodwill in peace – sentiments that Churchill was to echo in later life. This strategy essentially traded leniency towards the Boers for their acquiescence in imperial annexation (and it gave them licence to impose highly illiberal restrictions upon the native peoples). Liberals later liked to point to the way that the former Boer generals Botha and Smuts duly led South Africa into the Great War as a loyal dominion of the British Empire. Both Lloyd George, who had once fought against the Boer War, and Churchill, who had once fought in it, were to seize on this same point. It was a vision tinctured with some idealisation of the nobility of the pastoral, Protestant, straight-shooting farmers who were now the master race of the Veldt.

It was only after Asquith had succeeded the dying Campbell-Bannerman as Prime Minister in 1908 that social reform became central to the Liberal agenda. One early measure was the introduction of non-contributory old age pensions, which obviously required a new budget strategy; and the later development of a contributory but state-subsidised scheme of national insurance, for both health-care and unemployment, extended the range of state intervention. Here was obvious potential for division between the adherents of Gladstonian doctrines of individualism and a minimal state, on the more traditional wing of the party, and, on the other wing, the advocates of this New Liberalism, which had obvious affinities with social democracy. Yet, surprisingly perhaps, the party did not splin-ter along such lines, that is, between left and right on how to reform capitalism in the twentieth century.

Instead, issues of foreign policy proved much more explosive and divisive. As narrated in Lloyd George's *War Memoirs*, it was the persistent factional division of Boer War days that continued to haunt the Liberal cabinet. In his account, we find that Asquith, Grey and Haldane remain identified as Liberal Imperialists, while the author pointedly reasserts his own pro-Boer credentials. 'There was a percep-tible difference of attitude between the two sections on questions of foreign policy,' he explains. 'The old pro-Boers inherited the pacifist doctrines of Mr Gladstone.' As for the old Liberal Imperialists, he suggests, their previous suspicion of France had 'altogether vanished, even from the stubborn mind of Sir Edward Grey, but for it was substi-tuted a worrying distrust of the designs of Germany'.[9] This certainly makes for a good story, pregnant with forebodings for the future; but whether it is quite the whole story is another question.

Asquith did not form a Liberal Imperialist government in 1908. Although his close ally Haldane would have liked to become Lord Chancellor, Lord Loreburn was instead kept in place until 1912. And, with a warm intellectual respect that was fully reciprocated, the new Prime Minister made Morley a viscount and kept him in the cabinet as Lord President of the Council even after the India Office proved too taxing for this septuagenarian. Moreover, Asquith made three other key appointments. To replace himself as Chancellor of the Exchequer, he chose Lloyd George, previously at the Board of Trade. Next, he moved Winston Churchill from the Colonial Office and made him, at only thirty-three, the new President of the Board of Trade. These two men not only cooperated closely on inter-departmental economic and social issues: their close working relationship was animated by a growing friendship, in which Lloyd George was always acknowledged as the senior partner. Their dramatic promotions naturally stole the headlines. The Prime Minister's other big decision was altogether less striking but equally significant: he kept his old comrade Edward Grey as his Foreign Secretary.

Looking back, Churchill pointed to the way in which Asquith adroitly ensured that his own authority as Prime Minister went unchallenged, and did so precisely by his unforced recognition of Lloyd George's talents. For Asquith knew that his own reputation as a Liberal Imperialist still provoked, among the Radical wing of the party, a degree of distrust that he needed to dispel. 'He resolved to ally to himself the democratic gifts and rising reputation of Mr Lloyd George,' was how Churchill put it, depicting the cabinet, like C-B's before it, as 'a veiled coalition', but one in which Lloyd George had now been made 'the second man in the Government'.[10]

Conversely, though duly established as Asquith's lieutenant, Lloyd George found that his own reputation as a Radical and a pro-Boer pursued him, sometimes in paradoxical ways. It was now that he came to exercise a kind of influence on foreign policy that was unusual in a Chancellor of the Exchequer. Sir Edward Grey himself came from an old Whig family; he had succeeded to his grandfather's baronetcy at the age of twenty and another ancestor was the Lord Grey who was credited with the Reform Act of 1832. Grey represented just the sort of cool-tempered, privileged aristocrat whom Lloyd George typecast as, at best, an anachronism in the modern Liberal party. Yet Grey's own politics showed an acute awareness of the rising power of Labour, and not in any hostile sense: he mused on the possibilities of bringing a better social order even though it might not seem such to those of his own kind who had more than £500 a year (at a time when this was ten times the unskilled wage). Grey strongly supported the National Insurance Act, Lloyd George's brainchild. And, hindsight apart, the differences at the time between Grey's cautious calculations in foreign policy and Lloyd George's own impulsive responses were more in style than in substance, as the Germans were belatedly to discover.

In 1908 the German ambassador, Count Metternich, who professionally knew a lot about the British Foreign Secretary, took up an invitation from Grey to find out more about the new Chancellor of the Exchequer, of whom Metternich was relatively ignorant. 'He knew that I belonged to the more pacifist group in the Cabinet,' was how Lloyd George later put it.[11] For a pacifist of any stripe, he proved more robust and less tractable than might have been expected, warning Metternich not to suppose that the cabinet was divided about the principle of maintaining British naval supremacy. True, Radicals had often coupled their pleas for retrenchment in military spending with this kind of support for the Royal Navy as Britain's true guardian, thus hoping to make a large standing army unnecessary. 'It was absolutely necessary for the security of these Islands that we should retain our Naval superiority,' one member of Asquith's cabinet wrote later – not Winston Churchill but Lord Loreburn in his book *How the War Came* (1919).[12]

And already in 1908, Lloyd George was saying even more than this. He stated that, if challenged in the naval race, Britain would be pushed into raising a large army, just like Germany, where the Prussian army was virtually a state within a state; and Britain would have to do this by adopting conscription, viewed in Britain as the hallmark of Bismarckianism. When Lloyd George's comment on conscription was reported to the Kaiser, the latter's laconic comment was simply: 'It would do them good.'[13]

In the Liberal canon, of course, conscription was anathema. It did not matter that Lloyd George might be speaking hypothetically, or bluffing, or seeking to bargain with the Germans. Whatever was a good Liberal doing in even thinking such a thing? Perhaps an answer can be found in the fact that in 1910 Lloyd George was prepared to contemplate a grand coalition with the Conservatives, as a means of breaking the political deadlock that was currently destabilising the British political system. The issues at stake were cumulatively inter-connected. Lloyd George's 'People's Budget' of 1909 had imposed new taxes, not least on land; the House of Lords had, in response, displayed a new level of constitutional intransigence in rejecting a budget; the Liberal government's riposte, in stripping the second chamber of its veto power, in turn opened the door to the passage of Home Rule for Ireland. To Lloyd George, as to his cabinet colleague Churchill, a national bargain covering all such issues promised a constructive solution. Lloyd George himself offered a proposal of national training for defence, as part of a bipartisan package.

Admittedly, this was not universal conscription, more like the (democratic) model of the Swiss militia; and at the time the tentative coalition proposal fell to the ground anyway. But here is a clear enough signal of the way that Lloyd George's mind was working. In November 1914, while the battle of Ypres was raging, he recalled these 1910 negotiations in the course of a breakfast conversation with Frances Stevenson. He told her that he had 'suggested a system of Ballot Conscription in this country' and maintained that, had this been accepted, 'we should have had a million men ready in this country on the outbreak of war'.[14]

Lloyd George subsequently repeated and inflated this claim, arguing that 'there would by 1914 have been a body of trained young men aggregating between a million and one-and-a-half-million, fit for incorporation in our armies, shortly after the declaration of war'. By then they would presumably have been equipped with the weapons that in fact took eighteen months of warfare to produce. If, instead of the nineteen battalions of Territorial soldiers who were thrown into the battle of Ypres, there had been 300 or 400 battalions, already fully trained in a militia, the outcome 'would not have been a stalemate, but a victory which might have liberated Flanders and ended the War'.[15] Again, as Metternich and the Kaiser had discovered, this was at odds with Lloyd George's reputation as any kind of 'pacifist'.

The public display of this other face of Lloyd George came in the international crisis of 1911. The Germans had sent a gunboat to the Moroccan port of Agadir, which the French regarded as within their own sphere of influence. The Anglo-French entente of 1904, though not a military alliance, had from its beginnings made a priority of settling clashes of colonial ambition between the two countries. It was only to be expected, then, that Grey and the Foreign Office would be sympathetic to the French position, in resisting this German initiative. What was not expected was the intervention of Lloyd George, who used his speech as Chancellor of the Exchequer, given annually at the Mansion House in the City of London, to issue a warning to Germany on 21 July 1911.

It was not so much what he said as the fact that it was Lloyd George who said it. Churchill later put the point plainly: that foreign policy had been in the hands of ministers 'drawn entirely from the Liberal Imperialist section of the Government', though 'kept in equipoise by the Radical element, which included the venerable figures of Lord Morley and Lord Loreburn, on whose side the Chancellor of the Exchequer and I had usually leaned'. It was this perception that gave 'peculiar importance' to the Mansion House declaration.[16] Lloyd George's *War Memoirs* simply endorsed Churchill's account of this episode, including the claim that nobody had foreknowledge of what Lloyd George would do in this situation. 'Working with him in close association, I did not know,' Churchill claimed. 'No one knew. Until his mind was definitely made up, he did not know himself.'[17]

Once his mind was made up to support the Foreign Office's firm line, Lloyd George, however chary of ever calling himself a Liberal Imperialist, became the most formidable recruit that Grey could have hoped for. No wonder the Foreign Secretary was delighted to let the Germans hear directly from this newly galvanised Iron Chancellor. But, in the light of this incident, Lloyd George's complaints (in 1933) that the cabinet was kept in the dark about Grey's foreign policy and possible military commitments have a rather hollow ring. Admittedly, Loreburn had already alleged as much (in 1919): 'This concealment from the Cabinet was protracted, and must have been deliberate.'[18] Yet in July 1911, as C. P. Scott's diary records of a breakfast to which he had been summoned at 11 Downing Street on the morning after the big speech, 'Lloyd George spoke warmly of Grey and said he was very good in showing him (Lloyd George) everything' – an impression far from that conveyed by Loreburn, whom Lloyd George at this time called 'petulant, unreasonable', repeatedly 'rubbing Grey the wrong way', and now isolated in a cabinet that he was to leave within twelve months.

What is true, of course, is that some of the top permanent officials at the Foreign Office were already intensely suspicious of Germany. The obvious names are those of the dyspeptic Sir Arthur Nicolson, the permanent under-secretary, and his deputy Sir Eyre Crowe, author of an influential analysis of Germany's rising ambition, conscious or unconscious, to play the role of a great power. Yet Grey was not their puppet. He had first been appointed as a junior minister at the Foreign Office in 1892 by Gladstone, who thought highly of his abilities and whose moral earnestness about the concert of Europe Grey shared. And some glaring inconsistencies arise if we suppose that, as Foreign Secretary, he shut out the old Gladstonian Radicals from his inner counsels, when we also consider that, on taking one of his fishing holidays, Grey would hand over his brief at the Foreign Office either to Haldane *or to Morley*. Moreover, Lloyd George's own account specifically identifies Morley and Loreburn among the handful of senior cabinet ministers whom Asquith and

Grey took into their confidence, and who were thus 'expected to make any contribution on the infrequent occasions when the Continental situation was brought to our awed attention'.[19]

The fact is that, as the Agadir crisis revealed, the wholly unawed Lloyd George was ready enough to inform himself, when he chose; ready enough to assert the imperial dimension in British foreign policy, when he chose. Above all, Lloyd George was both ready and able to make his own stance decisive, as the Mansion House speech had shown in its inception, its delivery and its delayed impact. Count Metternich was shortly afterwards relieved of his post as German ambassador, apparently incapable of advising the Kaiser on what to expect of the second man in the British government.

Lloyd George's claim to have been the standard-bearer for 'the pacifist doctrines of Mr Gladstone' is thus far too simple. In his day, Gladstone could surprise his own cabinet with his readiness to contemplate war in a good cause, to defend public right, as he did over the threat to Belgium from Prussia in 1870. Having guaranteed Belgian integrity, Gladstone told the House of Commons, the British could hardly stand aside if it were threatened with extinction. Suppose that a similar dilemma were again posed, would self-professed 'Gladstonians' feel bound by their reputation as 'pacifists'? The young Woodrow Wilson surely had a point in claiming that Gladstone's mind was 'habitually militant'. At any rate, the issue was not simple, even for a man like Lloyd George who relied not on scholarly exegesis but on his own intuitions. Not only in his instinctive readiness to use the powers of the state for new ends but also in his combative response to the German threat, Lloyd George was already a nascent war leader, perhaps fearful of war itself but not of his own capacity to lead. It took the crisis of 1914 to dispel persistent misconceptions to the contrary.

Aristocrat and Soldier:
Winston Spencer Churchill

There are so many good stories told about Winston Churchill: so many of them so often repeated that they become canonical. One favourite came from the pen of Violet Bonham Carter who, as Asquith's daughter, had an early opportunity to meet the remarkable young man who was virtually her father's protégé in the cabinet that he formed in 1908. Shortly beforehand, in the last days of C-B, it had seemed to young Violet that 'rather commonplace people' did best in politics – 'Winston the only in-the-least *unusual* one'. More than half a century later she was to publish her graphic account of their first meeting; it was in the early summer of 1906, she says, and she recalls how she was summarily pressed by him to reveal that she was nineteen. '"And I," he said almost despairingly, "am thirty-two already. Younger than anyone else who counts, though," he added as if to comfort himself . . . and ended up with words I shall always remember: "We are all worms. But I do believe I am a glow-worm."'

This is just the sort of story that ought to be true. Alas, at the relevant point in 1906, Churchill was only thirty-one, and the encounter went curiously unmentioned at the time in her diary. Moreover, it was not until April 1908, after his promotion to the cabinet, that Violet wrote to a friend about a weekend house party: 'I was quite amused & liked Winston (whom I'd never properly spoken to before) very much.'

It is true that a friendship indeed later developed. But it was one distinctly more passionate on Violet's side, since their first proper discussions evidently took place in the same month that Winston declared his love for his future wife, Clementine Hozier. 'Whether he will ultimately mind her being as stupid as an *owl* I don't know,' Violet wrote when the news of the engagement was announced, adding: 'Father thinks it spells disaster for them both.' In 1908 this was the hot gossip that Violet confided to her close friend Venetia Stanley – whose subsequent intimacy with Violet's revered father was to spell its own potential danger for Asquith's premiership. For any gossip travelled quickly in this small world, inhabited by a tight-knit, socially active and highly privileged coterie, of which some leading Liberals were both critics and members.

None more so than Churchill. 'In those days English Society still existed in its old form,' he reflected in 1930. 'It was a brilliant and powerful body, with standards of conduct and methods of enforcing them now altogether forgotten. In a very large degree every one knew everyone else and knew who they were.' He wrote this in his memoir *My Early Life*, deploying a well-judged sense of distance and irony with his practised literary skill; and he wrote, above all, as an insider. For he was himself an aristocrat, born in 1874 in Blenheim Palace, the home of his grandfather, the 7th Duke of Marlborough. After the death of both the 8th Duke (his father's elder brother) in 1892 and of his own father in 1895, Winston was himself for a couple of years next in line to the dukedom; and this tantalising prospect was dashed only when his cousin 'Sunny', the 9th Duke, produced a male heir in 1897. 'Everywhere one met friends and kinsfolk,' Churchill recalled. 'The leading figures of Society were in many cases the leading statesmen in Parliament, and also the lead-ing sportsmen on the Turf.'[1] Little wonder that his own champagne lifestyle is well known; it is likewise well known that he kept race-horses himself in later life; also that he became a leading statesman in Parliament.

What we now know about the distribution of wealth in that era helps substantiate such impressions. In Britain the top 1 per cent of incomes accounted for over 20 per cent of all income in 1910; and the top section that constituted 'Society' was an even smaller elite, enjoying an even more precipitous level of privilege. It was the top 0.1 per cent that took an 11 per cent share of all British incomes at this time.[2] Now these were incomes that supported whole families, rich or poor, in an era when the convention in all classes was that the male head of the household was responsible for supporting his family, whether as the breadwinner working for wages or as the heir to a great estate with its rentier income. But how many families are we talking about?

In 1910 the number of inhabited houses in Great Britain was 7 million. The parliamentary electorate, which supposedly included the head of every household, was likewise 7 million. So this figure seems about right; and out of these 7 million families, there were 7,000 lucky families who enjoyed incomes a hundred times greater than the average. Moreover, though industrial and financial sources of wealth made a significant contribution in 1910, this was often as a supplementary part of the investment portfolio of owners of landed estates. The number of landowners in Great Britain with more than 1,000 acres each has been author- itatively calculated as 7,000; and if we include Ireland, this figure also corresponds with a pioneering statistical estimate made back in 1880, showing that 7,000 families then owned 80 per cent of all the land in the United Kingdom. Despite agricultural depression, causing some sales, great estates still remained the norm thirty years later.

This is what we know now from modern research; it is what Winston Churchill knew from the cradle. In 1880 there had been ten dukes who each had an annual income of at least £100,000 (say £8 million today). Alas for young Winston, he knew all too well that the Duke of Marlborough was not one of them. To sustain their high status, the Marlboroughs had too little rental income and too many spendthrifts; the costs of maintaining a vast palace were met by sell- ing many of the Old Masters on its walls. Worse still, though his cousin 'Sunny' enjoyed his ducal income at Blenheim, supplemented by the proceeds of an American marriage, Winston came from the cadet branch of the family since his father Lord Randolph Churchill (who died when Winston was twenty) was only a younger son of the 7th Duke. And Lord Randolph's brilliant marriage to the New York heiress Jennie Jerome had actually brought yet another spectacular spendthrift into the family. Hence Winston's lifelong dependence on his own literary earnings. His hard-working professional career was as a writer; but no member of Asquith's cabinet knew better than Churchill that his ancestral class was now in the firing line when fiscal policy and hereditary privilege became interlocked issues in Liberal politics.

The crucial turn had come with Asquith's last budget as Chancellor in 1907. There was henceforth a distinction between 'earned' and 'unearned' income (taxing the latter more heavily) and a move towards progressive rates plus increased estate duties. The stakes were dramatically increased by Lloyd George's budget of 1909, provocatively introducing new taxes on land and further increasing the levels of estate duties – red rags to aristocratic bulls, of course. It was this budget that the huge Tory majority in the House of Lords, still dominated by the landed interest, chose to reject. The conflict could not have been dramatised in more picturesque terms by W. S. Gilbert himself.

> The quarrel between a tremendous democratic electorate and a one-sided hereditary chamber of wealthy men has often been threatened, has often been averted, has been long debated, has been long delayed, but it has always been inevitable, and it has come at last. It is now open, it is now flagrant, and it must now be carried to a conclusion . . . Why should five hundred or six hundred titled persons govern us, and why should their children govern our children for ever?

The author of this fine democratic rhetoric was not the Chancellor responsible for 'the People's Budget', Lloyd George, who had himself memorably described the House of Lords as 'five hundred men, ordinary men chosen accidentally from among the unemployed'. These were actually the words of the President of the Board of Trade, Winston Churchill, whose insights on the respective governing capacity of 'their children' as against 'our children' had particular piquancy. Though the overall impact of the new Liberal fiscal policy may have been modest by post-war standards, to pre-war opponents it already seemed like the beginning of the end. In 1909 the top rate of income tax, charged on unearned incomes above £2,000 a year, was increased to 5.8 per cent and a new 'super-tax' was levied at a 2.5 per cent supplementary rate on incomes of over £5,000 (the same salary as a cabinet minister). Thus the top tax rate was now 8.3 per cent. One effect was that those on incomes of over £10,000 a year (say, over £800,000 today) found themselves paying 8 or 10 per cent of their income in all forms of taxation. This could be seen as either a modest tribute to the fairness of progressive taxation or a gross affront to everything that society stood for.

The Liberal journalist A. G. Gardiner, who was a keen supporter of the budget and on easy terms with Lloyd George personally, published a sympathetic portrait of him in 1913. 'It is doubtful whether any statesman has ever aroused such bitter hostility in "Society",' Gardiner reported, and reflected on the fact that this animus against the Chancellor seemed to increase the higher one moved in the social scale. 'I can only dimly imagine what happens when duke meets duke,' commented this self-made editor of the rather plebeian *Daily News*, quick to admit that he did not move in such circles. But Churchill did so – whenever he met his own relatives.

Churchill's ear was likewise innately attuned to the prejudices of the '1 per cent' in the City of London. He keenly appreciated that they had never before had to listen to a Chancellor like this one; and he realised that this was one reason why Lloyd George's speech at the Mansion House in 1911 had so baffled them. 'His City audience,' Churchill recalled, 'whose minds were obsessed with the iniquities of the Lloyd George Budget and the fearful hardships it had inflicted upon property and wealth – little did they dream of the future – did not comprehend in any way the significance or the importance of what they heard.'³ Churchill knew better, if only because he comprehended within his own person such sharply conflicting perspectives on the society into which he had been born. In his own way he was as enigmatic as Lloyd George, as difficult for contemporaries to read – and fully as much distrusted.

Violet Asquith, a child of her intensely political upbringing and already her father's political confidante, knew the case against Churchill. 'He appeared to have found fighting a rather too congenial occupation in the past,' was her summary of it. 'Had he got Liberalism in his bones? Would he stay put?' Churchill had been trained as an officer cadet at Sandhurst; he had gone into the army; he had fought in imperial wars on the North West Frontier of India, in the Sudan and in South Africa; he had made his name as a war correspondent; and he had entered Parliament as a Tory MP.

All this made a striking contrast with the demeanour of Violet's beloved father, schooled in Latin and Greek through prize-strewn years at Balliol College, Oxford, with his ethic of stoicism and restraint often expressed allusively in a dead tongue with which young Winston had been barely on speaking terms. For once, he was an outsider. John Morley, at the height of the Boer War division in the Liberal party, could still admiringly call Asquith's mind 'twenty times as good as Russell' (meaning the former Liberal Prime Minister, the 1st Earl Russell, not his grandson Bertrand). Conversely, in August 1914, Asquith saluted Morley as 'the greatest source of the moral authority of the Government' and went to extraordinary lengths in imploring him to stay in his cabinet. None of this was lost on young Violet. 'My father and his friends were mostly scholars, steeped in the classical tradition, deeply imbued with academic knowledge, erudition and experience,' she reflected later. 'Their intellectual granaries held the harvests of the past.'

The young officer of the 4th Hussars had no granary except what he constructed for himself. Hence the poignancy of his recollection that, posted to India in his early twenties, he had belatedly 'resolved to read history, philosophy, economics, and things like that; and I wrote to my mother asking for such books as I had heard of on those topics'.[4] Churchill's army career was indeed heroic, not least intellectually in testing his courage as an autodidact. After he eventually became Prime Minister, Margot Asquith patronisingly claimed that she had known Winston when he had never heard of Robert Louis Stevenson and had thought Blake was an admiral. This is a calumny. Her husband had appreciated much better that Churchill's failings could not be put down to any lack of assiduity in doing his homework. It was in early 1915, after several months of war, that Asquith wrote an unusually acerbic comment, regretting that 'Winston hasn't a better sense of proportion', in one of his confidential missives to Venetia Stanley, concluding: 'He will never get to the top in English politics, with all his wonderful gifts; to speak with the tongues of men & angels, and to spend laborious days & nights in administration, is no good, if a man does not inspire trust.'[5]

It was not only in the Asquith household that Churchill's well-wishers harboured persistent doubts of this kind. Liberal uneasiness about his martial spirit was real and widespread. Gardiner's political portraits were widely respected, and he wrote two about Churchill. In the first, in 1908, he readily acknowledged how hard Churchill worked in reading up on his ministerial briefs, not least in social policy, and in mastering the democratic case. 'But don't forget that the aristocrat is still there – latent and submerged, but there nonetheless,' a colleague was quoted as saying. And while Gardiner conceded that he was 'the most interesting figure in politics', he stuck by his suggestion that 'the whole spirit of his politics is military'. Five years later, by which time Churchill had become First Lord of the Admiralty, Gardiner declared: 'You may cast the horoscope of anyone else; his you cannot cast.' But he also reiterated, in monitory mood: 'Remember, he is a soldier first, last and always. He will write his name big on our future. Let us take care he does not write it in blood.'

These are not retrospective comments but those of a shrewd political supporter at the time. It was already the case, before Gallipoli or the carnage of the western front, that Churchill's reputation was that of a brilliant young politician who could not be trusted with such a serious business as that of making war. True, as a proud descendant of the great Duke of Marlborough, he was hardly likely to believe that the only justification for waging a war was a scrupulous moral judgement about its particular merits. Instead, as Gardiner had put it: 'His school was the barrack-room; his university the battle-field.' For Lieutenant Churchill, it was the natural, honourable, patriotic course to take up arms for his country, whatever private doubts he might harbour about the wisdom and justice of any particular campaign.

Conversely, he respected his opponents for doing the same, as he went out of his way to state when he became a Tory MP. He made sure that his carefully crafted maiden speech from the backbenches was given as soon as possible, in February 1901. The South African War was then at a critical stage, apparently offering a window for negotiations (a window soon to be closed). Lloyd George, speaking from the Opposition backbenches, had accordingly put down an amendment urging a ceasefire but, persuaded by his own party leaders that this was not the right moment, he sat down without putting it to the vote.

Churchill, all geared up to contest the amendment, thus had the rug snatched from under him. With his memorised speech in his head, this boyish twenty-six-year-old found himself with no amendment to oppose and had to improvise his opening. But he still subjected Lloyd George's pieties to scathing sarcasm. 'No people in the world received so much verbal sympathy and so little practical support as the Boers,' Churchill claimed, before adding a personal thrust: 'If I were a Boer fighting in the field – and if I were a Boer I hope I should be fighting in the field – I would not allow myself to be taken in by any message of sympathy, not even if it were signed by a hundred hon. Members.'[6]

It was this sentence that reverberated through the House. The Irish Nationalist members cheered the first half of it, the Conservative backbenchers the second part; and Churchill's claim became a talking point. He expanded on what he meant by suggesting that the patriotic duty to support one's country could rarely be out-trumped, since the rival arguments were usually so complex. 'Neither side has a monopoly of right or reason.'[7] Hence the implied value judgement in his original comment, that the Boer who fought bravely 'was the best kind of Boer'. This was indeed the ethic of a soldier; but it was one that also easily translated into a political context, and, having first fought him, Churchill subsequently treated Lloyd George as the best kind of pro-Boer. For it was this early confrontation across the floor of the House of Commons that had led to their personal introduction afterwards. Lloyd George had said: 'Judging from your sentiments, you are standing against the light.' Churchill had replied: 'You take a singularly detached view of the British Empire.' Or so he benignly recalled this exchange, nearly thirty years later, in that evocative volume *My Early Life*.[8]

Some of what Churchill wrote in *My Early Life* should be read as a teasing exercise in ambiguity. 'So a lot of people were killed,' runs his account of the first military action he saw, on the Afghanistan frontier in 1897, 'and on our side their widows have had to be pensioned by the Imperial Government, and others were badly wounded and hopped around for the rest of their lives, and it was all very exciting and, for those who did not get killed or hurt, very jolly.'[9] There are evidently subtly different senses of a favourite word like 'jolly', not all of them to be resolved simply by consulting the dictionary. This author often pleases his friends and his critics alike, since both can find ample confirmation of their own preconceptions.

We see how the author's air of nostalgia can serve as a foil. It allows him to hint at a more sinister significance in a soldierly career that had begun with little more than the consuming pleasures of horsemanship. 'Every day long hours were passed in the Riding School, at Stables or on the Barrack Square,' he writes. This was a severe discipline, requiring new officers to undergo the same rigours as the troopers they were to lead by example. There were furtive smirks from the men when an officer fell before their eyes in training, as he was more or less bound to do at times. 'Mounting and dismounting from a bare-backed horse at the trot or canter; jumping a high bar without stirrups or even saddle, sometimes with hands clasped behind one's back; jogging at a fast trot with nothing but the horse's hide between your knees, brought their inevitable share of mishaps.' Churchill discreetly mentions straining 'my tailor's muscle on which one's grip on a horse depends'. But such painful injuries simply had to be endured – 'I suffered tortures.'[10]

It is needless to ask whether he gave in or doggedly persisted through adversity to glory. For glory, of a kind, there surely was. He takes his ignorant readers through some of the technicalities in order to convey a full sense of these imperishable memories. 'There is a thrill and charm of its own in the glittering jingle of a cavalry squadron manoeuvring at the trot; and this deepens into joyous excitement when the same evolutions are performed at a gallop,' he recalls. 'The stir of the horses, the clank of their equipment, the thrill of motion, the tossing plumes, the sense of incorporation in a living machine, the suave dignity of the uniform – all combine to make cavalry drill a fine thing in itself.'[11]

Such passages are vividly drawn and surely truthful to experience. The author cannot resist offering his lament for the spectacle of the cavalry charge: 'It is a shame that War should have flung all this aside in its greedy base, opportunist march, and should turn instead to chemists in spectacles, and chauffeurs pulling the levers of aeroplanes or machine guns.' And he goes on in this vein, now assuming the mien of a crusty old colonel himself, in delivering his aphorisms. 'War, which used to be cruel and magnificent, has become cruel and squalid,' he declares. 'In fact it has been completely spoilt. It is all the fault of Democracy and Science.'[12]

None of these one-liners, however, ought to be taken literally, apart from their context. Of course the memoirist wants us to empathise with his young self, the neophyte who is being inducted through his thrilling exercises in horsemanship into the military mystique. But once Churchill has indulged in his inflated panegyric on the charge, he reserves for himself the further pleasure of deflating the whole exercise. 'Afterwards when we were home in barracks, these enthusiasms in my case were corrected' – and not only by recalling how many more cavalry divisions the Germans had, but by posing a sharper reminder of the imperatives of modern military technology. He records 'wondering what would happen if half a dozen spoil-sports got themselves into a hole with a Maxim gun and kept their heads'.[13]

It is true that Churchill saw the real face of battle, not just the display of the parade ground. Present in the Sudan at the battle of Omdurman in September 1898, in his ambiguous role as embedded war correspondent and serving officer, Churchill observed for himself how Sir Herbert Kitchener's British and Egyptian troops confronted their Islamic enemy ('Dervishes'). Churchill was a full participant in the fighting, not least when confronting one of the Dervish warriors who unexpectedly appeared in the midst of the British cavalry, whereupon Churchill shot him with his pistol at very short range. 'He fell on the sand, and lay there dead. How easy to kill a man!' he writes, thirty years later, adding: 'But I did not worry about it.' And perhaps his comment is extenuated by the impression of shared dangers and risks – 'the fight was with equal weapons, for the British too fought with sword and lance as in the days of old'.[14]

Yet this can hardly be the whole story. For Churchill has just told us how he watched, 'spellbound', as the Dervish charge headed into the artillery barrage that Kitchener had carefully planned, deploying the advantage of his new supply line on the railway that had now been constructed. 'I saw the full blast of Death strike this human wall,' Churchill writes, observing how it took down men 'by hundreds', reducing them to 'shapeless heaps' upon the ground. 'One saw them jumping and tumbling under the shrapnel bursts; but none turned back.'[15] Admittedly, some loose ends are apparent in a story that maintains: 'Nobody expected to be killed.'[16] Nobody, that is to say, on the *British* side of this desperately unequal struggle – in which, nonetheless, Lieutenant Churchill's career might well have been abruptly terminated.

These are complex reactions to battle: at once celebrating victory and grieving its cost, and written by a man who had undeniable first-hand experience. It is too easy to read Churchill's abiding nostalgia for his soldierly career as a sinister indication of an immature enthusiasm for military glory – as though he was simply ambushed by the reality of the western front, with no premonition of the impact of the locomotive of war.

For even as a young Tory politician, he had offered the House of Commons a notable caution against glib talk of a European war under modern conditions. 'In former days, when wars arose from individual causes, from the policy of a Minister or the passion of a King, when they were fought by small regular armies of professional soldiers, and when their course was retarded by the difficulties of communication and supply, and often suspended by the winter season, it was possible to limit the liabilities of the combatants,' he conceded. But in the twentieth century, 'when the resources of science and civilisation sweep away everything that might mitigate their fury, a European war can only end in the ruin of the vanquished and the scarcely less fatal commercial dislocation and exhaustion of the conquerors.' This was no soldier's panegyric upon war, nor upon its likely aftermath. 'Democracy is more vindictive than Cabinets,' the young Churchill warned in 1901. 'The wars of peoples will be more terrible than those of kings.'[17]

In politics, Churchill followed his own star. Party loyalties and factional allegiances, which meant little to him personally, were motives that he observed in others, almost as an outsider. His political evolution was nothing if not eclectic. In the course of twenty-five years he ran through more political variations and permutations than conventional party loyalists would have imagined possible, still less desirable.

He started loyally enough, as the filial son of Lord Randolph Churchill, whose famous slogan – it was hardly a policy – had been Tory Democracy. In 1897, a couple of years after Lord Randolph's death, Winston was writing to his mother of going into politics himself, with a manifesto that balanced 'Reform at home' with 'Imperialism abroad'. He toyed with the fancy that, but for Irish Home Rule, this stance might make him a Liberal. But the emphasis was definitely on imperialism by 1900, when he was elected as Conservative MP for the Lancashire borough of Oldham. This was the so-called 'khaki election', with none more khaki than Lieutenant Churchill.

Yet he was soon restive. *My Early Life* ends with Churchill as a young MP, pondering an after-dinner tip-off from the great Joe Chamberlain: 'Tariffs! There are the politics of the future, and of the near future.'[18] In a cotton-spinning town like Oldham, however, dependent alike on imported American cotton and on an export trade to the whole world, tariffs did not seem a good idea. In 1904 Churchill crossed the floor of the House of Commons; two years later, in the General Election, he was elected as Liberal MP for the central financial district of Manchester, where Unionist free traders in the business community flocked to his standard. So he had somehow managed to be on the winning side in both the Tory triumph of 1900 and the Liberal landslide of 1906.

This was already an unusual political path, inevitably provoking adverse comment, not just imputing political opportunism but alleging ideological inconsistency. Churchill, though claiming to be an imperialist, had spurned Chamberlain's novel tariff proposals, aimed at binding together the British Empire. True, he was by no means alone in rejecting Chamberlainite tariff reform; so did many conventional, centrist politicians whose instincts were to stick with what they knew. But Churchill was of a different temperament and, having adopted the Liberal cause, he did it in spades. It was now that his early alliance with Lloyd George flourished; like him, Churchill developed a close relationship with C. P. Scott and the 'progressive' politics of the *Manchester Guardian*, working for cooperation between Liberals and Labour. Churchill's book *Liberalism and the Social Problem* (1909) collected his speeches arguing for an interdependent policy of state-sponsored social reform to which the Lloyd George budget was the key. The editor of the *Nation*, the leading left-wing Liberal weekly paper, H. W. Massingham, contributed a notably enthusiastic introduction. 'Mr Churchill came to Liberalism from the same fold as Mr Gladstone,' he claimed.[19]

Yes and no. True, both statesmen had renounced the conventional Conservatism of their era in favour of more radical political strategies and alliances. But Winston Churchill had certainly not been brought up on any pieties about Mr Gladstone – 'an old man in a hurry' was what Lord Randolph had memorably called him. Moreover, the way that young Churchill talked about social reform certainly did not sound Gladstonian. One of the government's key legislative achievements, the path-breaking scheme of unemployment insurance enacted in 1911, was of Churchill's own making while he was President of the Board of Trade. Now state insurance was an idea that fastidious Liberals thought tainted through its association with Bismarck's Germany; but Churchill's mindset was different, as he had long made clear, not least to his cabinet colleagues. He had presumptuously offered advice to Asquith on a social reform strategy for his new cabinet in 1908, despite his own lack of previous expertise. 'Dimly across gulfs of ignorance I see the outline of a policy wh I call the Minimum Standard,' Churchill wrote, and he had no compunction in declaring that the country needed 'a sort of Germanised network of State intervention & regulation'.[20]

This was no passing whim. After barely nine months as a cabinet minister, he once more took up his pen to instruct Asquith. Churchill pointed again to the example of Germany, and in a spirit more admiring than hostile. 'She is organised not only for war, but for peace,' he claimed. 'We are organised for nothing except party politics.'[21] Churchill was so proud of his turn of phrase that he gave it a public airing in *Liberalism and the Social Problem*. 'Look at our neighbour and friendly rival Germany,' he reiterated. 'I see that great State organised for peace and organised for war to a degree to which we cannot pretend.' He even repeated the gibe about only being organised for party politics – 'and even for purposes of party politics we are not organised so well as they are in the United States'.[22]

So why not draw upon the experience of Germany in social policy? The agenda seemed clear enough to Churchill. To Asquith he specified labour exchanges, which were within his own ministerial responsibilities, and linked this with national insurance not only for sickness but (unlike the German model) for unemployment too. He advocated state intervention in forestry, in roads and in the railways; and also a modernisation of the existing poor law and the provision of compulsory education to the age of seventeen. Such were his proposals to 'thrust a big slice of Bismarkianism [sic] over the whole underside of our industrial system'.[23]

Did the iconoclastic Churchill really propose to replace the portraits of the Grand Old Man hanging in reverent Liberal homes with images of the Iron Chancellor? The fact is that, though strikingly expressed, such views were not uncommon at the time. The humbling early setbacks in Britain's recent campaign in South Africa had demonstrated the locomotive effect of even a small war. Rudyard Kipling's 'The Lesson (1899–1902)' was terse and telling: 'We made an Army in our own image, on an island nine by seven.' For Churchill the ex-soldier, Britain's military capacity was one obvious issue when he contemplated future 'wars of peoples'. But he was also aware of the current talk of 'national efficiency' in a wider sense, when the poor physical stock of many of the recruits who came forward had turned military questions into social issues. Tariff reformers pointed to the way that free trade neglected the social consequences of a doctrine of cheapness. The Liberal social reformer Charles Masterman, later close to both Churchill and Lloyd George, had asked whether all was well at 'the heart of the Empire', at home in Britain's slums. It was the Fabian socialists Sidney and Beatrice Webb who had first talked of instituting a 'national minimum' as a benchmark in collectivist social legislation. Churchill now self-consciously discovered the poor and saw a mission for himself in taking up their cause. He did so as an intellectual magpie with no conscience about stealing ideas and with little scruple about any ideological inconsistencies in developing a social policy fit for the twentieth century.

And yet, throughout his career, there was indeed an inner core of consistency to Churchill's political beliefs. From first to last, he was undeniably an imperialist: one who, as a young soldier, had unapologetically fought the wars of the British Empire and who, as a veteran Prime Minister, still preferred to talk of the Empire rather than the Commonwealth. But he had little time for schemes of imperial federation, which some urged as a political necessity in a twentieth-century world that would be dominated by superpowers. Nor, crucially, did Churchill accept the Chamberlainite claim that only the adoption of imperial preference and tariffs could ensure the survival of the British Empire.

Instead, Churchill relied essentially upon sentiment to sustain an empire that had been founded upon a free-trade basis since the repeal of the Corn Laws in the 1840s. Here, if anywhere, he was the legatee of the Gladstonian tradition, as established by the great free-trade budgets of the mid-nineteenth century. Here too was the firm principle to which Churchill sought to cling in all his political peregrinations. When the Conservatives abandoned free trade, he left them in 1904; when, in effect, they abandoned preferential tariffs in 1924, he was to return – as a free trader still.

The imperialism of free trade was thus fundamental to Churchill's political outlook. He had had no formal academic schooling in economics – or in anything else for that matter – but had, as usual, made himself a master of the arguments through his own efforts. In public speeches he held up the beauty of the self-regulating flows of worldwide trade; he marvelled at the way that imbalances were automatically corrected through international transfers of gold; and he hailed the role of the Bank of England in adjusting its rate of interest so as to correct any disparity. Here was the basis not just of British prosperity but of a benign pattern of interdependence based on a division of labour, from which Britain's colonies benefited through their buoyant exports of food to the mother country, while the low prices of colonial imports simultaneously benefited the British consumer.

What folly, then, to threaten imperial unity by protectionist meddling! How noble a contrast, so Churchill proclaimed in 1907, was the vision of the free traders, 'who look forward to larger brotherhoods and more exact standards of social justice, value and cherish the British Empire because it represents more than any other similar organisation has ever represented, the peaceful cooperation of all sorts of men in all sorts of countries, and because we think it is, in that respect at least, a model of what we hope the whole world will some day become'.[24] It was virtually the League of Nations in scaffolding.

There was one possible threat to this beatific world order. Uniquely among the great powers of Europe, Britain had sacrificed its own agricultural production on the altar of free trade. The effect of the repeal of the Corn Laws in 1846 had been delayed by a generation. But then, from the 1870s, a combination of factors, notably lower freight rates in steamships and the extension of North American railways, opened up competition, halving wheat prices in Britain and doubling the quantity of wheat imports. As to the Dominions, Canada became Britain's granary; Australia and New Zealand its abattoir. When Napoleon talked of a nation of shopkeepers, the population of Great Britain was little more than 10 million, fed mainly on British food; by 1911 the population was over 40 million, fed on imports.

The maintenance of the imperialism of free trade now depended, more than ever, on keeping the sea routes open. This, of course, was the unique task of the Royal Navy. In 1894, when Gladstone retired, the naval estimates were £15 million; in 1902, following the Boer War, the estimates for the first time reached over £30 million. The Liberal Imperialist R. B. Haldane commented in the House of Commons that 'the Commerce of this country was something approaching £1,000,000,000 and the estimates only amounted to some 3 per cent of that. That was not an extravagant premium of insurance.' Maybe not. But ten years later, when Haldane was Asquith's Secretary of State for War and Churchill was First Lord of the Admiralty, the naval estimates were now heading towards £50 million – an increase from a premium of 1.5 per cent to one of 5 per cent in twenty years. Why?

Churchill had two productive years at the Board of Trade, his first cabinet post. Then, in February 1910, Asquith moved him to the Home Office, where his record was more mixed, though somewhat controversial, as always. He was remembered for the so-called 'Siege of Sidney Street' – involving anarchists, gunfire and Churchill's personal appearance at the scene – and for his brushes with the 'suffragette' agitation, militant on both sides, of course. It was in October 1911 that the Home Secretary, after only twenty months in this post, received an invitation from the Prime Minister to join him at his Scottish home. Asquith clearly had more in mind than the ritual of golfing together. It was on the way back from the links that he abruptly disclosed his thinking about an obvious lack of coordinated defence planning. He now asked Churchill to move yet again, this time to become First Lord of the Admiralty.

We have Churchill's own inimitable account of the episode in his *World Crisis*, a work originally published in the early 1920s. He mentions that the proposal that he should go to the Admiralty had first been broached back in 1908. At that point, he had rejected this 'glittering post' only because it would then have meant directly displacing one of his own aristocratic uncles, the previous incumbent. 'This time I had no doubt what to answer,' Churchill explains. 'All my mind was full of the dangers of war. I accepted with alacrity.'[25]

Gazing out over the Firth of Forth, his sense of the moment was crystallised by the sight of two Royal Navy battleships, silhouetted in the distance. And, on going to bed in his room that night, he found on the table a large Bible. No believer in orthodox Christianity, Churchill had faith mainly in himself, with a strong sense of personal destiny. When the Bible opened randomly at the ninth chapter of Deuteronomy, he eagerly seized upon its menacing hints about divine policy towards the threat posed by the alien Anakims: 'Understand therefore this day that the Lord thy God is he which goeth over before thee; as a consuming fire he shall destroy them, and he shall bring them down before thy face: so shalt thou drive them out, and destroy them quickly, as the Lord has said unto thee.'[26] Under such portents Churchill began his fateful spell of three and a half years at the Admiralty. Contemporaries like Gardiner, of course, did not at the time have the benefit of these particular providential insights to enlighten them about his mindset.

Churchill's record in the cabinet had actually been provokingly mixed on naval issues. As he later acknowledged, his cooperation with Lloyd George was not just in the field of domestic reform: they also sought to 'restrain the froward both in foreign policy and in armaments'.[27] This use of the archaic term 'froward', with its original connotations of perverse or even naughty, is plainly a piece of obfuscation, to conceal Churchill's subsequent embarrassment. What he meant was that the two of them wanted to restrain spending on armaments. True, young Winston had sometimes claimed that 'the tattered flag of retrenchment and economy' was the great cause for which his father, Lord Randolph, had nobly sacrificed his political career. At any rate, these were the terms in which he and

Lloyd George opposed just the sort of increased defence spending that Churchill later acknowledged to be justified by events.

The problem was the German naval programme, itself an indirect reflection of Germany's growing economic power. In 1880 Britain had accounted for 23 per cent of the world's manufacturing output, nearly three times as much as Germany; in 1913 Britain had 14 per cent, Germany 15 per cent. The Franco-Prussian War of 1870–1 had demonstrated Bismarck's readiness to assert the power of the Prussian army to control the destinies of continental Europe; and Gladstone was not alone in his consternation. But Bismarck's veto on building a large German fleet signalled his unwillingness to breach the global Pax Britannica, which had been underwritten by the pre-eminence of the Royal Navy since the time of Nelson. The young Churchill fully recognised this priority, soldier or not. 'With such a Navy we may hold any antagonist at arm's length and feed ourselves in the mean time, until, if we find it necessary, we can turn every city in the country into an arsenal, and the whole male population into an army,' he told the House of Commons in 1901. 'Sir, the superiority of the Navy is vital to our national existence.'[28]

It was only after Bismarck's fall that this superiority was challenged by the young Kaiser Wilhelm II. A grandson of Queen Victoria, an honorary admiral in the Royal Navy, Wilhelm was deeply ambivalent in his feelings towards Britain; he loved wearing his admiral's uniform but lacked a fleet of his own, and now had the power to command one. In 1897 he dramatically promoted Admiral Alfred von Tirpitz, who shared his ambition to challenge Britain on the seas, which was the obvious rationale for expanding the High Seas Fleet.

The traditional British policy was to maintain a 'two-power standard'. This meant that the Royal Navy should match the strength of the next two strongest powers, usually France and Russia. Britain's treaty with Japan in 1902 allowed concentration of the British fleet in European waters; then, after the Entente Cordiale of 1904, France was no longer considered a threat and so was eliminated from this calculation; and the fleet of France's ally Russia was hardly a factor after its devastating defeat by Japan in 1904–5. All this temporarily eased matters for the Royal Navy, still with its huge historic endowment of capital ships, and confident of its immense superiority over Tirpitz's naval building programme. Temporarily too, the advent of a new class of battleship reinforced Britain's advantage, since the Royal Navy alone possessed the formidable HMS *Dreadnought*, launched in 1906, and its sister ships in this class.

These dreadnoughts, however, spelt the obsolescence of all other battleships – not least the existing capital ships of the Royal Navy. The new technology, once adopted by Germany too, thus hypercharged the naval race, at a wholly new level of expense. Henceforth, to maintain its supremacy in the North Sea, and protect the shipping channels, the Royal Navy had to keep on building new dreadnoughts at a greater rate than the German High Seas Fleet. Any proposed acceleration in the German programme thus triggered a potential crisis for Britain in responding. This was not because, even at the peak of Tirpitz's ambitions, he was capable of outbuilding the British fleet but because the Royal Navy needed an assured margin of superiority in capital ships. Hence the provocative nature of the Germans' naval law in 1908, increasing their new construction to four dreadnoughts per year, since their clear motive was to challenge the Royal Navy.

The Liberal government was consequently racked by this issue. Churchill and Lloyd George cooperated in cabinet, as 'economists', to resist an immediate acceleration of the British programme. Churchill was the most junior member of the cabinet and as President of the Board of Trade had no departmental responsibility in this matter; but he nonetheless prepared for the cabinet a detailed critique of the projections that had been presented by Reginald McKenna, First Lord of the Admiralty. Instead, Churchill's paper not only counted old capital ships alongside new but also alleged that any German superiority in dreadnoughts would be marginal or temporary. 'Instead of jerky construction in response to the gossip of naval attachés & the whisper of Krupp's backyard,' he told Asquith, '& after recurring friction between the Admiralty & the Cabinet, we shd make our plans with something of the precision & foresight of our German rivals.'[29] The *World Crisis*, though printing lengthy extracts from any documents that vindicate Churchill's prescience, omits his lengthy attempt to disparage McKenna's froward proposal.

In the end, new dreadnoughts were indeed sanctioned by the cabinet. This was accomplished, largely without rancour, after an adroit move by Asquith to rephase the schedule of their construction, with four begun immediately and another four later. 'The Admiralty had demanded six ships: the economists offered four; and we finally compromised on eight,' was how Churchill subsequently put it, graciously adding: 'But although the Chancellor of the Exchequer and I were right in the narrow sense, we were absolutely wrong in relation to the deep tides of destiny.'[30] By the time he went to the Admiralty himself in 1911 (in effect, switching jobs with McKenna), Churchill had ceased to be an 'economist' and had instead become a big spender, at least on the Royal Navy.

He was, of course, not immune to the romantic appeal of his new post. This is readily apparent in reading his description of the fleet manoeuvres that he attended in the spring of 1912, aboard the official yacht, HMS *Enchantress*, which was 'to become largely my office, almost my home'. From it the new First Lord marvelled, like the assembled guests from around Europe, at the precision of the great fleet's manoeuvres. 'Every anchor falls together; their cables roar through the hawser holes; every propeller whirls astern.' Looking along the lines, stretching for miles, 'they might have been drawn with a ruler', and this great demonstration of British naval prowess was not lost on anyone: 'The foreign observers gasped.'[31] They were clearly joined in their awed admiration by one former cavalryman who had once lavished years of his life in perfecting equine display with the same impressive effect.

This too was all very jolly. But Churchill's experience at the Admiralty served to sharpen his retrospective sense of a

UNDER HIS MASTER'S EYE.

SCENE—*Mediterranean, on board the Admiralty yacht "Enchantress."*

MR. WINSTON CHURCHILL. "ANY HOME NEWS?"

MR. ASQUITH. "HOW CAN THERE BE WITH YOU HERE?"

As First Lord of the Admiralty, Churchill wrote later, the official yacht HMS Enchantress was 'to become largely my office, almost my home'. It is quite true that he entertained the Prime Minister aboard on more than one Mediterranean cruise, and the conversation imagined between them was at least a poetic truth.

fundamental transformation in the nature of warfare, within his own professional lifetime, into 'a mere disgusting matter of Men, Money and Machinery'.[32] In 1911 the naval problem was not only quantitative but also qualitative. The objective was still to sustain a supremacy that went back to Nelson's victory at Trafalgar, fought between creaking old wooden ships dependent on winds and tides for their ability to manoeuvre. But, in the twentieth century, it was the revolution in naval technology, symbolised by the coming of the dreadnought, that gave Germany its crucial opportunity to challenge the Pax Britannica and the imperialism of free trade that depended upon it. The locomotive of war was being retooled. In the process, the heavy investment by government was creating what can be termed a warfare state.

It was partly a numbers game, with each German initiative triggering a proportionately larger British counter-move. There was a frantic search for a new formula to replace the traditional two-power standard. Various options were canvassed – perhaps a 60 per cent margin over Germany in dreadnoughts; but perhaps only in the North Sea; or perhaps matching the Austrian and Italian fleets in the Mediterranean too; or perhaps including older capital ships in the Mediterranean; or perhaps reinforced by potential Canadian dreadnoughts. By 1912 it was agreed that the Royal Navy should withdraw dreadnoughts from the Mediterranean, to which France would conversely relocate its fleet. This would, of course, leave the French coasts on the Atlantic and the English Channel vulnerable to potential attack from the German High Seas Fleet – unless the Royal Navy intervened. Did this constitute a moral obligation for Britain? It was a worrying question, not foreseen when the making of the Entente Cordiale had been so warmly welcomed by francophile British Liberals.

The Admiralty plans concentrated on a supremacy in dread-noughts in the North Sea, geared to German plans. 'I had been

thinking that if the old German programme had been adhered to,'
Churchill reflected in January 1912, 'we should have built 4, 3, 4, 3,
4, 3 against their six years' programme of 2, 2, 2, 2, 2, 2. If their new
programme stands, as I fear it must, and they build 3, 2, 3, 2, 3, 2, we
cannot build less than 5, 4, 5, 4, 5, 4.'[33] His own recurrent suggestion
was that Britain and Germany should agree to take a 'naval holiday',
and this proposal became part of the mission to Berlin undertaken
at this time by Haldane, who was trusted alike by Asquith, Grey
and Churchill. No agreement proved possible, less because of the
naval numbers than because of the German insistence, in return,
on a guarantee of British neutrality in a war between Germany
and another continental power. But why would the Germans have
wanted such a guarantee except to facilitate an invasion of France?
This was Grey's reaction: another worrying question for him, not
least in wondering about the status of the more emollient German
Chancellor, Bethmann Hollweg, in such negotiations. 'It is clear that
Grey has no idea who is master here, namely myself,' was what the
Kaiser commented.

It was not just the number of dreadnoughts that was at stake in
the naval race. Since Britain's numerical supremacy, measured in
dreadnoughts, was itself the result of the technological advance that
had put the dreadnoughts into a league of their own, it followed that
any further qualitative improvements could also affect the balance
of power at sea. The race would be won by the fleet with the newest
super-ships, driven by the fastest engines, protected by the thick-
est armour-plating and equipped with the biggest guns that a vessel
could carry. Chapter VI of the *World Crisis* is called 'The Romance
of Design'.

Here, even before his appointment, the new First Lord had
already become persuaded of the central role of Lord Fisher, who
had served as First Sea Lord, the professional head of the navy,
from 1904 to 1910. Fisher had become a legend in his own lifetime, not least through his own idiosyncratic gift for self-publicity.
'For at least ten years all the most important steps taken to enlarge,

improve or modernize the Navy had been due to Fisher,' Churchill claimed, listing notable achievements like the water-tube boiler, the 'all big gun ship', the introduction of the submarine, 'the great naval programmes of 1908 and 1909' (almost thwarted by the opposition of Churchill and his friend Lloyd George, of course) and, not least, the introduction of the 13.5-inch gun.[34]

It was the charismatic, self-dramatising Fisher who brought such issues alive for Churchill. Fisher had been an undeniably central figure for decades at the Admiralty; also an undeniably divisive one, as suggested by his famous maxim, 'Favouritism is the secret of efficiency.' On his appointment in October 1911, Churchill consulted Fisher at once and almost decided to take the gamble of bringing him back as First Sea Lord at the age of seventy-one, before opting for a safer choice in Admiral Sir Francis Bridgeman. But the spirit of Fisher pervaded Churchill's thinking. 'Until I got to the Admiralty,' as he subsequently put it, 'I had never properly appreciated the service which Mr McKenna and Lord Fisher had rendered to the Fleet in 1909 by their big leap forward from the 12-inch to the 13.5 inch gun.'[35] Here was the intersection of a seemingly mundane technical issue with the imperatives of twentieth-century grand strategy: what sort of fleet could provide the Nelson touch in maintaining British naval supremacy?

What was needed was a means of delivering the big punch. This was the case that Fisher made, serving as Churchill's far-from-grey eminence in schooling him with the arguments he needed to override the risk-averse fainthearts at the Admiralty. For the irrepressible Fisher now insisted that the big punch needed a 15-inch gun – a further increase of 1.5 inches, which was unprecedented. The lure was that this promised to increase the weight of shot from 1,250 to nearly 2,000 pounds. The scientists who were consulted were ready to go ahead but could offer no certainty. Churchill's own gut instinct carried him through the moment of anxiety. He told his First Sea Lord, Bridgeman: 'Risks have to be run in peace as well as in war, and courage in design now may win a battle later on.'[36]

The immediate moral of Churchill's story was that it worked. But the gun, as always, dictated the design of the ship. A new gun generated new imperatives in optimising ship design. Current battleships were planned to carry ten 13.5-inch guns; a ship carrying ten 15-inch guns would have to be over 600 feet long, with engines capable of delivering 21 knots, given the need for armour that would now reach a thickness of 13 inches. 'For less armour you could have more speed: for less speed you could have more armour, and so on within very considerable limits,' Churchill suggests.[37] To create a Fast Division that could steam at 25 knots would require engines with an additional 50,000 horsepower. Solution – the boilers to provide this could be accommodated in the space vacated by replacing ten guns with eight!

'But even this would not suffice,' Churchill admits. 'We could not get the power required to drive these ships at 25 knots except by the use of oil fuel.' The case for oil likewise depended on an interlocking series of options. Oil took up less of the ship's capacity so the cumulative efficiency-gains were now decisive. 'The use of oil made it possible in every type of vessel to have more gun-power and more speed for less size or less cost.'[38] The decision was, in that sense, obvious, but still far-reaching in its implications. Each link forged the next, as Churchill put it – and thus led, link by link, to an Anglo-Persian oil agreement that became, in due course, the origin of the multinational oil giant British Petroleum (BP). One result of Britain's longstanding involvement in modern Iran has been the periodic deployment of the Royal Navy in the Gulf; it seems ironic that, in a circular way, the origin of the Anglo-Iranian connection should lie with the perceived needs of that same fleet. 'A decision like this involved our national safety as much as a battle at sea,' Churchill suggests. 'It was as anxious and as harassing as any hazard in war. It *was* war in a certain sense raging under a surface of unbroken peace.'[39]

Yet it would be wrong to infer that, in planning for war, Churchill was himself planning to break the peace. He had done his best in

February 1912 to help Haldane's mission to Berlin by publicly airing his thoughts on the naval issue. 'The purposes of British naval power are essentially defensive,' he explained in a speech in Glasgow, and he purported to make the same benign assumption about other great powers. 'There is, however, this difference between the British naval power and the naval power of the great and friendly Empire – and I trust it may long remain the great and friendly Empire – of Germany,' he continued. 'The British Navy is to us a necessity and, from some points of view, the German Navy is to them more in the nature of a luxury.' This was no more than he had been saying for a dozen years. In the current context, however, it was not surprising that his notion of the *Luxus Flotte* was ill received by German readers, who could hardly be expected to sympathise with his plea that 'the whole fortunes of our race and Empire, the whole treasure accumulated during so many centuries of sacrifice and achievement, would perish and be swept utterly away if our naval supremacy were to be impaired'.[40]

This fervent imperialist now found that he had stirred up more trouble than he had naively anticipated. Yet his guiding assumptions about the maintenance of the British Empire on the basis of peace and free trade were longstanding Liberal platitudes. And Churchill himself belatedly acknowledged, with some self-irony, how these highly moral intentions might sound in foreign ears. 'We have got all we want in territory,' he explained in March 1914, 'but our claim to be left in undisputed enjoyment of vast and splendid possessions largely acquired by war and maintained by force, is one which often seems less reasonable to others than to us.'

Whether all this seemed reasonable or not to Tirpitz, by 1913 he had concluded that there was little point in pressing beyond what he had already achieved. Thereafter, the German naval building programme was implicitly settled at the relative balance that the British Admiralty could accept – 60 per cent superiority of dreadnoughts. If Britain had thus won the numbers game against Germany, it was with little gain thereby. Simply in order to maintain its supremacy over the German High Seas Fleet in the North Sea, a tacit British obligation to protect the northern French coasts had thereby been incurred. None of this strengthened British security, as Lloyd George still liked to complain, all too conscious that the claim of social reform upon his budgets remained at the mercy of burgeoning naval estimates. From 1908–9, before 'the People's Budget', to 1913–14, the last peacetime fiscal year, central government expenditure increased by 33 per cent; but naval spending rose by 52 per cent.

Yet when Lloyd George had warned in his Mansion House speech in 1911 that he would not accept a situation 'in which peace could only be preserved by the surrender of the great and beneficent position Britain has won by centuries of heroism and achievement', he was speaking for the Liberal cabinet as a whole. It was a warning rather than a threat; and as such it worked – on that occasion. In the *World Crisis* Churchill made the most of the story of Agadir: the crisis that had failed to ignite a European war. 'Soft, quiet voices purring, courteous, grave, exactly-measured phrases in large peaceful rooms,' he wrote of the preparations he observed being made around him in Whitehall, at the hub of the machinery of government.

So now the Admiralty wireless whispers through the ether to the tall masts of ships, and captains pace their decks absorbed in thought. It is nothing. It is less than nothing. It is too foolish, too fantastic to be thought of in the twentieth century . . . No one would do such things. Civilization has climbed above such perils . . . Are you quite sure? It would be a pity to be wrong. Such a mistake could only be made once – once for all.[41]

4

How the Liberals Started
a World War

Germany was not Asquith's only problem in the summer of 1914 – hardly his most acute worry at all. Even Churchill, relying on the Prime Minister's discreet support in safeguarding naval supremacy, did not seem anxious. 'The spring and summer of 1914 were marked in Europe by an exceptional tranquillity,' he wrote later. 'Ever since Agadir the policy of Germany towards Great Britain had been not only correct, but considerate. All through the tangle of the Balkan Conferences British and German diplomacy laboured in harmony.'[1]

This was indeed the case, as the interlocked and internecine Balkan conflicts of 1912–13 had shown. The weakening of Ottoman influence had seen Russia flexing its muscles as the protector of the Slavs; but Grey had apparently established a good working relationship with the German Chancellor, Bethmann Hollweg, who showed himself ready to restrain his Habsburg ally in its Balkan ambitions, while France was encouraged by Britain to restrain its Russian ally. An ambassadors' conference held in London (rather than in partisan Paris) in 1913 saw Grey, as chairman, using his freedom from the entanglements of formal alliances to good effect, in ostensibly defusing the Balkan powder keg. He worked well with the French ambassador, Paul Cambon, finding him more conciliatory than his government in Paris. Perhaps, then, the Entente Cordiale was the best British compromise in such a wicked world, allowing the British Foreign Secretary this sort of latitude. He did not like to call

Britain's further informal link to Russia a Triple Entente, if only because good Liberals were wary of supporting the Tsar, but Grey's little joke was that he could not himself prevent such references any more than he could prevent split infinitives.

Asquith was focused on problems nearer home. He had now been Prime Minister for six years, with legislative achievements unmatched since the first Gladstone government, forty years previously. Old age pensions, health insurance, labour exchanges and unemployment insurance were striking novelties, though soon accepted as the foundation of a twentieth-century welfare state. Free trade had been defended, not inertly, but through innovative budgets; and when the House of Lords had blocked this strategy, it was Asquith himself who took command of the constitutional crisis, facing down the Lords, securing the agreement of the new King George V to create hundreds of Liberal peers if necessary, and thus passing the Parliament Act in 1911, limiting the veto of the second chamber. This was as real an extension of democracy in Britain as any of the famous Reform Acts. Likewise, Grey's acute awareness of the importance of public opinion was Gladstonianism brought up to date. 'The idea that one individual, sitting in a room in the Foreign Office,' as he put it later, 'could pledge a great democracy definitely by his word, in advance, either to take part in a great war or to abstain from taking part in it, is absurd.'

Asquith, then, had good reason for pride. He had kept his cabinet together, often by opting for boldness. When Lloyd George's characteristically lax handling of his personal investments had blown up into the Marconi Scandal in 1912, he had survived with the robust support of the Prime Minister, as he did not soon forget. This was the formidable partnership at the heart of the Liberal government. And Asquith was no less effective in holding together its parliamentary and electoral support.

The General Election of 1906 had been a freak landslide for the Liberals; the real test came in the two elections made necessary by the constitutional crisis in January and December 1910. In both elections the voter turnout was well over 80 per cent, among the highest of the twentieth century. In December 1910 the formal party strengths in the House of Commons were 272 each for the Liberals and the Unionists, 42 Labour and 84 Irish Nationalist. Today this may look like a 'hung Parliament', yet the fact is that the government could rely upon a solid majority of over a hundred. In the first place, Labour, representing trade-union interests, was not really an independent party in that era; there was an informal but effective electoral pact with the Liberals. So in virtually all the seats won by Labour there was no Liberal opposition; accordingly, in the House of Commons the government enjoyed solid Labour support.

A further reason for the Liberal government's parliamentary strength was the position of the Irish Nationalists. In December 1910 they won eighty-four seats, again without Liberal opposition, and they continued to support a government pledged to passing an Irish Home Rule Bill. After the Parliament Act, the vast Unionist majority in the House of Lords could only delay the implementation of such an Act for two years. The fact that Asquith steered a Home Rule Bill through the Commons in 1912, and thus stood ready to implement it in 1914, was a bitter charge against him in Unionist eyes, seeking to justify the extreme and unconstitutional lengths of their resistance. Their argument was that the Liberals had bought Irish support for dismembering the United Kingdom. Liberals argued that they had been committed to Home Rule since Gladstone's day, while 'New Liberals' like L. T. Hobhouse and his friend the classicist Gilbert Murray were as passionate as any of the old guard in their determination to uphold the rights of small nations.

Beyond these well-rehearsed, setpiece partisan contentions, however, there is a highly significant piece of electoral arithmetic that often goes unremarked. The fact was that, quite apart from Ireland, in December 1910 the Asquith government had achieved a progressive majority of fifty-nine from England, Wales and Scotland – 314 seats to 255. (The Conservatives relied on the support of seventeen

Ulster Unionists.) By-elections eroded this majority by 1914. But only if the Irish Nationalists used their parliamentary strength to bring down the Liberal government was it in any hypothetical danger; and since such an action would simply install a Unionist government, pledged to thwart Home Rule at all costs, the unreality of this scenario is surely apparent. However much the Conservative and Unionist opposition resented the situation, they had little chance of overthrowing the Liberals, short of the next (peacetime) General Election.

It was thus a Liberal government that would call the shots in 1914, on foreign affairs as on domestic or Irish issues. If there were decisions to be made on war or peace, it would be on the basis of arguments that swayed Liberals and progressives, just as the arguments about naval policy had been resolved in these terms in earlier years. This was a situation in which Asquith's own skills should not be overlooked. A cryptic warning to his opponents during the ongoing Home Rule struggle – 'wait and see' – was later used to caricature his leadership style; but under ordinary peacetime conditions he remained the indispensable man. His oratorical mastery in the House of Commons, deploying a barrister's deft command of his brief, was paralleled by his adroit and patient handling of his cabinet, timing his own interventions to build consensus in the direction that he favoured. The Liberal party owed him a lot; his leadership was unchallenged.

In July 1914 the immediate problem was, of course, Ireland. The Unionist opposition to Home Rule now concentrated on the position of Protestant Ulster, raising the spectre of armed resistance with moral support from the Conservative leadership, and even loose talk of mutiny by some right-wing army officers. Indeed the mishandling of such a threat led to Asquith taking over the War Office himself in late March 1914. Gun-running, on both sides, was already a reality by the summer. The possibility of amending the Home Rule Act so as to defer its implementation in Ulster – a course favoured by Lloyd George and Churchill – was actively canvassed.

Little wonder that Asquith's cabinet found its time so largely pre-empted by these complex and intractable issues.

Asquith turned for solace to his young confidante Venetia Stanley. His emotional dependence upon her now reached new levels of intensity – but mainly, it seems, in his letters. 'There is nothing (as you know) that I would not show you: so great and deep is my trust,' he had told her in February.[2] She found herself better briefed than many cabinet ministers, as the Prime Minister let her into the secret of the policy-making methods that had served him well. 'And those Navy estimates, with all the memories which cluster around their cradle, promise to go through on oiled castors, with hardly a murmur of protest,' he wrote with satisfaction in March 1914. 'Am I not right in my fixed belief that the Expected rarely happens?'[3] On 30 June he reported from Westminster on his busy day: first, War Office business all morning, next, a dreary formal lunch, 'thence here for an "obituary" on the Austrian royalties; and after a ridiculous debate, nominally on my salary, but in reality an attempt to rake up the ashes of Marconi', he at last found himself free to send off yet another letter to Venetia.[4] She knew, of course, if only from the newspapers, that the 'Austrian royalties' were the Archduke Franz Ferdinand and his wife, assassinated two days previously in the Bosnian city of Sarajevo. Having made this oblique reference to the event, Asquith during the next three weeks sent Venetia seventeen further letters, replete with all manner of political gossip, before he again alluded to the developing European crisis.

Only on 24 July did the Prime Minister feel any need to bring Venetia up to date. He reported that the cabinet had heard 'Grey's statement of the European situation, which is about as bad as it can possibly be'. It was the speed with which it then eclipsed all other issues in Britain that took virtually everyone by surprise. Asquith's report shows him plainly relying upon Grey's reading of events:

Austria has sent a bullying and humiliating Ultimatum to Servia [sic], who cannot possibly comply with it, and demanded an answer within 48 hours – failing which she will march. This means, almost inevitably, that Russia will come on the scene in defence of Servia & in defiance of Austria; and if so, it is difficult both for Germany & France to refrain from lending a hand to one side or the other. So that we are within measurable, or imaginable, distance of a real Armageddon, which would dwarf the Ulster & Nationalist Volunteers to their true proportion.

The chain of events was thus sketched cogently enough. Asquith knew much less than we do today about the convoluted political context in Bosnia-Herzegovina itself, a Balkan province formally annexed by Austria as recently as 1908 and regarded by ethnic Serb nationalists as their own. But he knew well enough that the Habsburg Empire was bound to make some demand for redress once the heir to the imperial throne had been assassinated; he knew that the Russian Empire was likely to champion its Serbian clients; he knew that the German and Austrian empires, as allies, would undoubtedly respond to Russian intervention; he knew that France, as Russia's ally, could then be drawn in; and this chain indeed led, link by link, to the prospect of a major European war. But, on Friday 24 July, Asquith still concluded: 'Happily there seems to be no reason why we should be anything more than spectators.'[5]

Within ten days, he knew better; and that flexible word 'happily' became stretched in new dimensions. By that point the alliances had done their work in mobilising the rival armies across Europe. 'Happily I am quite clear in my own mind as to what is right & wrong,' he told Venetia after a crucial cabinet meeting on 2 August, almost unprecedented for taking place on a Sunday morning. The Prime Minister summed it all up in six points. The first two denied any British obligation to give military assistance to France, still less to Russia. The next three points, however, acknowledged that there were 'ties created by our long-standing and intimate friendship with France'. Moreover, since it was 'against British interests that France shd. be wiped out as a Great Power', it followed that Germany should not be allowed 'to use the Channel as a hostile base'. These three points implicitly added up to some kind of support for France in a war launched by Germany. Finally, Asquith mentioned British 'obligations to Belgium to prevent her being utilised & absorbed by Germany'.[6]

Belgium was a good deal nearer to the British coast than Bosnia-Herzegovina. Moreover, its independence had been formally guaranteed by the Treaty of London (1839) under the concert of Europe, an obligation famously recognised by Gladstone in 1870. And if, in 1914, the distant Balkan crisis, in which Britain had no direct interest, had become a preoccupation of the cabinet with a remarkable suddenness, this was now to be exceeded in every way by the exploding Belgian crisis. When Bonar Law, the Conservative leader, had told Asquith that morning (Sunday 2 August) that his party was ready for war in support of France and Russia, there was no mention of Britain's treaty obligations towards Belgium. At this stage only Asquith and Grey, along with Haldane and Churchill and perhaps a couple of other cabinet ministers, evinced any commitment to intervention by the British government.

And what kind of government, *if not a Liberal government*, could that possibly have been? Lord Beaverbrook was later responsible for the notion that Churchill was already after a coalition; and others too have freely assumed that 'a coalition government' would in any case have taken Britain into the war. But the Conservatives and their Ulster Unionist allies were still fifty seats short of even a bare majority in the House of Commons – hardly a good basis on which to commit the country to war. As Lloyd George later put it: 'In the 1914 Parliament the Conservatives, in fact, constituted the largest party in the House, but they could not attract the support of any other section.'[7] Any idea that Labour would have supported the Unionists is a fantasy. Any idea that the Irish Nationalists would have done so is even more bizarre. And hardly more conceivable is the notion that Asquith, with his barely concealed contempt for Bonar Law, was remotely contemplating such a coalition, still less splitting the party that he had spent his best years in nurturing, healing and conciliating. The Prime Minister's efforts were directed instead to keeping any decision for war in Liberal hands. It followed that the decisive arguments would be those that spoke to distinctive Liberal concerns, in Asquith's day as in Gladstone's.

Churchill's mind, of course, was not programmed in quite that way. His grasp of the language of Liberalism was somewhat self-conscious – yet another tribute to his capacity for self-tuition. In one sense he was a notional coalitionist, who had little difficulty in persuading himself that a great national issue like war would readily justify him in putting country before party. But in the political world at this time there was no Liberal cabinet minister more distrusted by the Conservatives than Churchill himself, so his exclusion from any actual coalition was always likely – as he was to discover in due course. Churchill had his own reasons, then, for doing his utmost to keep the Liberal cabinet together. This meant not embarrassing Asquith with any show of bellicosity that would simply alienate support from more squeamish Liberals. It likewise meant using the personal relationship that Churchill had established with Lloyd George to ensure that the second man in the government was kept on board.

If we read Churchill's *World Crisis* and Lloyd George's *War Memoirs*, we get rather different perspectives on the coming of war. One obvious reason for this is that these post-war versions were themselves written in very different contexts. In the early 1920s, when the early volumes of the *World Crisis* were published, Germany's responsibility for the war was generally taken for granted in Britain, in a way that Churchill's account reflects.

By 1933, however, when Lloyd George's first two volumes were published, this was no longer the case. One notable publication had been the posthumous *Memorandum on Resignation* (1928), carefully composed by John Morley, justifying his own departure from the cabinet yet respectful towards all his former colleagues, except for one – 'The motives of Lloyd George were a riddle.'[8] The latter's *War Memoirs*, while affecting to ignore Morley, display an evident anxiety to suggest that he too thought war might have been avoided. By then, of course, the Liberal party was in fragments and there was bad blood between the old Asquithians and Lloyd George, who was equally vindictive in reliving these quarrels. Edward Grey, whose later career had seen him venerated as the great apostle of *bien-pensant* internationalism, became the posthumous target for Lloyd George's pent-up barbs, which stud the pages of the *War Memoirs* with a persistent contempt that is inconsistent with their actual dealings before 1916. The general effect is to reconstitute the British Foreign Secretary as one of the sleepwalkers who missed every opportunity to avert Armageddon: 'The nations slithered over the brink into the boiling cauldron of war without any trace of apprehension or dismay.'[9]

It was admittedly a ritual complaint among the Radicals that foreign policy was in Liberal Imperialist hands. Likewise the Foreign Office was reproached for not disclosing any secret commitments that compromised Britain's freedom of action. Yet, as the Agadir crisis had shown in 1911, Lloyd George was fully capable of involving himself in such matters when he chose to do so; and from this date, at the latest, no member of the cabinet could have been unaware of the military contingency planning for possible joint action with the French (as Morley's account admits). Moreover, the concentration of the British fleet in the North Sea, and that of the French fleet in the Mediterranean, were matters of public debate at the time. The rest was emotion and goodwill, refreshed in 1914 by the public celebration of the tenth anniversary of the Entente Cordiale. Such were the ties with France of which, on Sunday 2 August, Asquith wrote in two letters – not only in one gossiping to Venetia Stanley but in another replying to the Conservative leader, Bonar Law. The sinister significance of 'secret diplomacy' was a familiar Radical trope;

but at the time most members of Asquith's cabinet listened atten-tively to Grey whenever he chose to call their attention to an issue of foreign policy.

This is what he had done on Friday 24 July 1914. The classic account is in Churchill's *World Crisis*, which records how even his own soldierly mind had been focused not on the threatening devel-opments in the Balkans but upon the cabinet's more immediate and compelling Irish difficulties. The reaction of Austria to the Sarajevo assassinations, however, had now produced 'an ultimatum such as had never been penned in modern times. As the reading proceeded it seemed absolutely impossible that any State in the world could accept it, or that any acceptance, however abject, would satisfy the aggressor.' Whether it seemed quite so conclusive at that moment is doubtful. Conscious that Austria indeed had a real grievance, Grey was to press the Serbians to make amends, only to find their concil-iatory response curtly brushed aside by Austria without further negotiation. In sombre hindsight at least, and with fitting phrases to match, Churchill described the impact of Grey's announcement as it sank in around the cabinet table: 'The parishes of Fermanagh and Tyrone faded back into the mists and squalls of Ireland, and a strange light began immediately, but by perceptible gradations, to fall and grow upon the map of Europe.'[10]

Hence further strangely lit cabinet meetings over the next week or so. Churchill pursued his twin objectives. The way he explains them in the *World Crisis* is true up to a point. He stresses the pacific temperament of the cabinet: 'At least three-quarters of its members were determined not to be drawn into a European quarrel, unless Great Britain were herself attacked, which was not likely.'[11] And, later citing Morley's *Memorandum* in support, Churchill reaffirmed that any prior public commitment by Grey to support France 'would have resulted only in his complete disavowal by four-fifths of the Cabinet and three-quarters of the House of Commons'.[12]

So Churchill was right to think that more time was necessary before any decision for war could be taken; and he was also to be proved right in personally ensuring that the Royal Navy was prepared for the worst. The practical point was that the fleet should not be dispersed after its annual manoeuvres; Churchill himself gave the orders here, confident of Asquith's support. Second, though the *World Crisis* claims that Churchill from the start appreciated the full salience of the Belgian issue in persuading the cabinet's doubters, this seems a highly unlikely piece of foresight. But it is true that he kept up his personal pressure on Lloyd George, playing for time as the cabinet met day by day in a fast-changing situation.

In those pre-war days, there were no official cabinet minutes, just the letters that the Prime Minister (or a deputy) had to send to the King after each meeting. Thus on Thursday 30 July Asquith reported that, having reviewed the Treaty of 1839 guaranteeing Belgium's neutrality and 'action which was taken by Mr Gladstone's Government in August 1870', it seemed doubtful how far any single signatory was obliged to act alone. The cabinet formally considered that 'the matter if it arises will be rather one of policy than of legal obligation'.

It was a Liberal fetish in that era to invoke the formula: 'Remember what Mr Gladstone said in . . .' And now the cabinet itself was doing it. Obviously, the great authority on such matters was Morley's *Life of Gladstone*, which stated that in 1870 the cabinet had taken 'a decision to which Mr Gladstone then and always after attached a high importance'. He had successfully sought to prevent either France or Prussia, or both, from carving up Belgium against its will. This would have been, in Gladstone's view, 'a crime' that 'would come near to an extinction of public right in Europe, and I do not think we could look on while the sacrifice of freedom and independence was in course of consummation'. Or so Morley's biography quoted Gladstone as telling John Bright on 4 August 1870.

And forty-four years later, the keeper of the shrine, Viscount Morley of Blackburn, Lord President of the Council, was himself at the cabinet table to advise. Morley was the biographer not only of Gladstone but also of Cobden; and the two loyalties were

BRAVO, BELGIUM.

In August 1914 the violation of Belgian neutrality belatedly but inexorably became the focus of Liberal concerns. This Punch *cartoon depicts the issue in terms that had a lasting effect upon not only the war but also the subsequent peace.*

uneasily entwined within him. Could Gladstonian moralism out-trump Cobdenite pacifism? At the end of July 1914 Lord Morley sided with the large majority of his cabinet colleagues in thinking that there was now no such crime as that of 1870 in prospect, and no such extinction of public right as Gladstone had envisaged: just a ruse to manipulate the Belgian situation. Indeed, by the time the cabinet met on the morning of Sunday 2 August it had received a diplomatic warning that the Belgian government, purporting to be confident that no German violation of Belgium was intended, did not wish for foreign intervention; and the mantra of the cabinet Radicals, including Morley, was thus that they could not be 'more Belgian than the Belgians'.

It had never been a secret from anyone that what made France uniquely vulnerable to invasion was its frontier with Belgium. Hence its historic status and international treaty guarantee. Moreover, the great cities of Belgium and the strategic railways all lay in the north, around Brussels; this was what mattered, whether to the German high command in planning an invasion or to Britain as a guarantor of Belgian neutrality. By contrast, the possibility of a minor, techni-cal infringement of Belgian sovereignty – a traverse, as it was often termed – should an invading German army cross the sparsely inhab-ited south of the country, had long been a familiar scenario.

As such, a transit or traverse of this kind was discounted as a *casus belli* both by the Belgian government and by a large majority of the British cabinet. Lloyd George had himself discounted it at this time, apparently with the aid of a map, all on the assumption of a minor infringement at worst, with no Belgian resistance. Only in his *War Memoirs* do we encounter the claim that Grey ought to have issued a warning to Germany about Belgium and 'could at any stage of the negotiations have secured substantial unanimity among his colleagues on that point'.[13] But which point? A wholesale violation of Belgian sovereignty was simply not a point that had been contem-plated by any member of the cabinet until the events of the night of 2–3 August.

What the two cabinet meetings held that Sunday actually authorised was a naval commitment to the French, to whom it came as
some small relief. The French ambassador, Cambon, set on also
receiving military support, remained noisily sceptical about British
'honour'. Conversely, the naval decision had threatened cabinet
unity that morning. The former labour leader John Burns, President
of the Board of Trade, tearfully announced that he must resign and
worked on a reluctant Morley to join him. Morley was recorded as
saying: 'You all know my views, those of a lifetime, I cannot renounce
and if you persevere in intervention, I cannot return to this room.'
Both ministers were nonetheless persuaded by Asquith to return, at
least for one further cabinet meeting that evening. In Morley's case,
he attended after spending the afternoon in rumination at his club,
as his later *Memorandum* explained: 'Felt acutely what Mr Gladstone
had often told me, that a public man can have no graver responsibility than quitting a Cabinet on public grounds.'[14]

Churchill, always ready to jump the gun, had already ordered
the mobilisation of the fleet. 'The Prime Minister, who felt himself
bound to the Cabinet, said not a single word, but I was clear from
his look that he was quite content.'[15] Churchill, grateful for tacit
approval from this quarter, but still worried as the day unfolded
that a majority of cabinet ministers might join in resigning, set
about ensuring that Lloyd George was not among them. This too
chimed with Asquith's view. He had previously assured Venetia that
'Ll. George – all for peace – is more sensible & statesmanlike, for
keeping the position still open.'[16]

The account of the coming of war in Lloyd George's *War Memoirs*
was not only composed a decade after that in the *World Crisis* but
explicitly deferred to Churchill's fuller account of all these matters.
What Lloyd George himself added was a cameo on the role of public
opinion that weekend. 'I shall never forget the warlike crowds that
thronged Whitehall and poured into Downing Street, whilst the
Cabinet was deliberating on the alternative of peace or war.' Monday
was the August bank holiday, and apparently just as jingoist. Lloyd

George, walking from Downing Street to the House of Commons with Asquith, allegedly said to the Prime Minister: 'These people are very anxious to send our poor soldiers to face death; how many of them will ever go into battle themselves?'[17] It is true that Asquith shared his impression of the 'cheering crowds of loafers & holiday makers'.[18] But it was natural that there should be crowds in public places – it was a sunny holiday for ordinary Londoners enjoying a rare day off work – though modern estimates of numbers suggest only 10,000 more than normal, in a city of 7 million. Above all, what now seems highly questionable is whether the popular mood was bellicose – the crowd of over 10,000 in Trafalgar Square was there for an anti-war demonstration. But though Lloyd George, by 1933, may have been seeking to protect himself from charges of being a warmonger himself, he was right to point to the crucial role of public opinion in Britain, as every member of the Liberal cabinet appreciated.

Luckily we have at least one source that is untainted by hind-sight. During cabinet meetings Churchill often used to exchange hastily scribbled notes with Lloyd George; he did so at the meetings on 2 August; and though Lloyd George tore up most of them after reading, the scraps were subsequently collected by Frances Stevenson and pieced together. So the evidence has a compelling sense of immediacy (though dating these fragments is not always easy).

It was evidently on Sunday 2 August that Lloyd George asked: 'Would you commit yourself in public *now* to war if Belgium is invaded whether Belgium asks for our protection or not.' To which Churchill simply replied, 'No.' This was consistent with what the cabinet had so far agreed, having received no appeal from Belgium – instead, a 'keep out' notice that very morning. So it was probably at the second meeting of the cabinet, on the Sunday evening, that Lloyd George offered some cautious advice to his impetuous young colleague: 'If patience prevails & you do not press us too hard tonight we might come together.'

This was exactly what Churchill had wished to hear. 'Please God – It is our whole future – comrades – or opponents,' he responded. 'The march of events will be dominating.' Lloyd George came back at him: 'What is your policy?' In an answer that exactly reflects the limited facts known on that Sunday evening, Churchill replied: 'At the present moment I would act in such a way as to impress Germany with our intention to preserve the neutrality of Belgium. So much is still unknown as to the definite purpose of Germany that I would not go beyond this.' This was all in line with what Asquith and Grey were proposing at that moment. Churchill added: 'Moreover public opinion might veer round at any moment if Belgium is invaded & we must be ready to meet this option.'

Churchill then piled on the personal appeals to Lloyd George. He invoked their long cooperation. He reminded Lloyd George of his part over Agadir, and implored him to remain involved in settling the issue. Otherwise, they would be tragically opposed for the rest of their lives – 'I am deeply attached to you & have followed your instinct & guidance for nearly 10 years.' Together, so Churchill suggested, 'we can carry a wide social policy'; and he added a final plea for Lloyd George not to withdraw his support from the decision the cabinet had now taken to protect the French coasts. 'The naval war will be cheap – not more than 25 millions a year.'[19]

It was the Marquess of Crewe, Lord Privy Seal, unencumbered with departmental duties, whom Asquith entrusted with writing the letter to the King that Sunday evening. He confirmed that the French – but not yet the Germans – had been told of the naval commitment to protect France. Conversely, Cambon had the less welcome news that there was no decision for British troops to be sent overseas. Crewe then added a short paragraph, evidently carefully drafted.

As regards Belgium, it was agreed, without any attempt to state a formula, that it should be made evident that substantial violation of the neutrality of that country would place us in the situation

contemplated as possible by Mr Gladstone in 1870, when inter-
ference with Belgian independence was held to compel us to take
action.

———

By the end of Sunday 2 August 1914, a great European war had
indeed started. The German declaration of war on Russia had been
in response to Russian mobilisation, which was in turn a response
to mobilisation by Germany's ally Austria, which had ordered
mobilisation as its means of getting satisfaction from Serbia – the
ultimate suspect in this chain, held responsible for the assassination
at Sarajevo. True, Serbia's complicity in the irredentist campaign
for incorporation of ethnic Serbs within its borders was, as we
now know, much more extensive than was acknowledged, still less
proved, at the time.

Even then, however, it was notorious that the whole Balkan imbro-
glio had many rights and wrongs (especially the latter). The British
Foreign Secretary's own recent experience had instilled this lesson.
'Our idea', he had explained to Cambon on 29 July, 'had always
been to avoid being drawn into war over a Balkan question.' Hence
his apparently successful efforts throughout 1913; hence his attempt
in late July 1914 to convene another ambassadors' conference in
London, only to find himself disconcertingly snubbed this time by
Bethmann Hollweg. So who was now in charge in Germany? Was
it really Bethmann? Or was it his master, the Kaiser, with his fitful
interventions – alternately provocative and conciliatory – in the
interstices of his cruising holiday in the Baltic? Or was it the military
high command, with steadfastly fixed war plans that were evidently
unknown to well-meaning German diplomats, like the ambassador
in London, who still worked until the last moment to avert British
intervention?

It was indeed an extraordinary thing that a great European war
should have broken out as a result of this Balkan crisis. But in Britain

it was evident that the Liberal cabinet was not going to go to war over this. It would have meant supporting the Russian Tsarist regime in its pro-Slav campaign on behalf of its Serbian clients. Morley spoke for many in repeatedly making clear his abhorrence of the Russian connection. In the *Daily News* of 1 August its editor, A. G. Gardiner, had affirmed that 'we will not shed a drop of English blood for Tsar or Servia' in arguing for non-intervention. Whatever hesitations had been expressed about the ties generated by the Entente Cordiale, most Liberals were, like Lloyd George, instinctively francophile – 'You know I am much more pro-French than you are,' he had warned C. P. Scott. But virtually no Liberals, least of all the trouble-makers on the left, were russophile.

'Russian autocracy was almost as unpopular with the people of these islands as Bolshevism is today,' Lloyd George wrote in 1933.[20] Little wonder that Grey had tried to suppress the term 'Triple Entente'; little wonder that he toyed with notions of limiting the European war to one on the eastern front, with the western front between Germany and France perhaps frozen in some kind of armistice. But then, as he kept telling the French, he did not actually know the terms of their alliance with Russia. Above all, Grey did not appreciate that Germany had only one war plan – one that made a European war on two fronts inescapable.

Grey was not alone in his innocence of such vital matters. The Kaiser, for one, did not know that the programmed assault on France through Luxembourg and Belgium foreclosed all other options. So much for the decision-making capacity of autocracy. It was only when the crunch came, in the early days of August, that none of the schemes for limiting the war proved feasible, if only because of the plans of the German high command. The sole plan in existence – a refinement of the notorious Schlieffen Plan – was for the German army to fight a war on two fronts: first in the west, quickly knocking out fragile France, and only then in the east against the lumbering Russian giant. Moreover, a quick war against France depended on smashing through Belgium, with the locomotives of war literally speeding the German advance. Any sort of discreet traverse or transit through the south of Belgium was beside the point; this needed to be a full-scale invasion, capturing control of the country's railways and strategic northern cities.

Tacit Belgian consent for this sort of assault could hardly be presumed. Bethmann and the other civilian leaders had won the concession (as early as 26 July) that an ultimatum would be drafted, seeking the Belgians' agreement to a German passage through their country. This was perhaps in the hope of appeasing the British by the reasonableness of such a procedure. The much redrafted German ultimatum was actually sent on the evening of Sunday 2 August, requiring compliance by 7.00 on Monday morning. Unexpectedly (at least to many Germans), the Belgian King and his ministers were now united in rejecting the demands.

'The Germans, with almost Austrian crassness, have delivered an ultimatum to Belgium & forced themselves on to their territory, and the Belgian King has made an appeal to ours,' Asquith reported to Venetia Stanley on Monday, sensing a dramatic change in the political weather.[21] Churchill later called King Albert's appeal 'decisive' for the cabinet that reconvened yet again in Downing Street. 'Discussion was resumed on Monday morning in a different atmosphere, though it seemed certain that there would be numerous resignations.'[22] Burns's resignation was definite, if only because of the naval commitment. Morley likewise wrote to Asquith, resigning not on this ground but fearing that, if he stayed, 'vital points might arise that would make my presence a tiresome nuisance'. Lloyd George 'seemed astonished', so Morley later claimed, when told of this letter – '*But if you go, it will put us who don't go, in a great hole.*'[23]

There were two more ministers (Sir John Simon and Lord Beauchamp) who now joined Burns and Morley, making four dissidents in all. Significantly, Lloyd George was not among them, and he successfully appealed for them to appear in their places in the House of Commons that day while the Foreign Secretary made his keenly awaited speech. Lloyd George himself was well aware of the swing in opinion. His *War Memoirs* state that 'Belgium was responsible for the change. Before then the cabinet was hopelessly divided – fully one third, if not one half, being opposed to our entry into the War. After the German Ultimatum to Belgium the Cabinet was almost unanimous.'[24]

This is a bit too simple, in telescoping the speed of the conversion, not only in his own case but also in Liberal opinion in the country. Lloyd George had just received a minatory telegram, warning against British intervention, from Scott, the editor of the anti-war *Manchester Guardian*: 'No man who is responsible can lead us again.' Events were changing every hour, news lagged, rumour filled the gap. 'I am moving through a nightmare world these days,' Lloyd George wrote hastily that day to his wife. 'I have fought hard for peace & succeeded so far in keeping the Cabinet out of it but I am driven to the conclusion that if the small nationality of Belgium is attacked by Germany all my traditions & even prejudices will be engaged on the side of war.'

The cabinet that met on the morning of Monday 3 August had, as its main business, to consider the terms in which Grey should explain events to the House of Commons that afternoon. Throughout the crisis Grey had stressed the importance of carrying public opinion with him. Thus he had told the Russians: 'I do not consider public opinion here would or ought to sanction our going to war in the Servian quarrel.' Cambon had become bored, then infuriated, with Grey's constant pleas about what public opinion would sanction him to do. Conversely, the Germans had been warned that 'our attitude would be determined largely by public opinion here, and that the neutrality of Belgium would appeal very strongly to public opinion'. In this context, in a democracy it makes little sense to pose a sharp distinction between the reasons for decisions and the arguments advanced to justify them (unless, of course, some 'dodgy dossier' compromises such arguments).

Grey, acting in good faith, knew all along that he had to have reasons that he could justify. And now he had his chance, not only to test the prevailing wind in the Commons but to make the political weather himself. It was a great parliamentary moment. The House was packed, with a double row of chairs, most unusually, placed up the central aisle. That Grey would be listened to with close attention was not in doubt. What was much more doubtful was that this aloof figure, with his lack of charismatic appeal and oratorical skills, could change anyone's mind.

Hansard tells us that Grey stood up to speak soon after 3 p.m. He acknowledged that the present crisis 'originated in a dispute between Austria and Servia'. But he insisted that, whereas France had become involved through honouring its alliance with Russia, Britain's position was different. 'We are not parties to the Franco-Russian Alliance,' he stated. 'We do not even know the terms of that Alliance.' He reiterated that the Russians had always been told not to expect support from Britain in any Balkan crisis. The relationship with France, however, was rather different, as indicated by the disposition of their respective fleets. Grey asked the House 'how far that friendship entails obligation – it has been a friendship between the nations and ratified by the nations – how far that entails an obligation let every man look into his own heart, and his own feelings, and construe the extent of the obligation for himself'.

His own sense of the obligation was obvious. 'The French coasts are absolutely undefended,' he declared, meaning that the French fleet was concentrated in the Mediterranean; and here he allowed himself an uncharacteristic rhetorical appeal. 'My own feeling is that if a foreign fleet engaged in a war which France had not sought, and in which she had not been the aggressor, came down the English Channel and bombarded and battered the undefended coasts of France, we could not stand aside and see this going on practically within sight of our eyes, with our arms folded, looking on dispassionately, doing nothing!' This was, of course, the rationale of the cabinet's decision for naval intervention.

Grey had now been speaking for about half an hour. 'And, Sir,' he continued, 'there is the more serious consideration – becoming more serious every hour – there is the question of the neutrality of Belgium.' He rehearsed arguments that had consumed the cabinet's attention for a couple of days but which must have been unfamiliar to many MPs. Grey took them back to what Mr Gladstone had said in the House of Commons in August 1870, quoting him at tortuous length on the complex nature of the British obligation under the Treaty. 'The Treaty is an old Treaty – 1839 – and that was the view taken of it in 1870,' Grey acknowledged, making the point that it had manifestly been in Britain's interest to become a signatory to it. 'The honour and interests are, at least, as strong to-day as in 1870,' he concluded, 'and we cannot take a more narrow view or a less serious view of our obligations, and of the importance of those obligations than was taken by Mr. Gladstone's Government in 1870.'

With the news still coming in as he spoke, this was his declared benchmark. It was now that he captured the mood of the House. Grey left little doubt that he was himself committed to full British participation in an appalling war that he had hoped to avert. 'We are going to suffer, I am afraid, terribly in this war whether we are in it or whether we stand aside,' he admitted. The speed with which the Belgian situation had emerged and was now eclipsing other factors in British eyes was his final message. 'I believe the country, so quickly has the situation been forced upon it, has not had time to realise the issue,' he suggested. 'It perhaps is still thinking of the quarrel between Austria and Servia, and not the complications of this matter which have grown out of the quarrel between Austria and Servia.' Grey, knowing his audience, transposed the issue into a higher realm of moral judgement, framed in his penultimate quotation from Gladstone: 'whether under the circumstances of the case, this country, endowed as it is with influence and power, would quietly stand by and witness the perpetration of the direst crime that ever stained the pages of history, and thus become participators in the sin'.

'Grey made a most remarkable speech,' Asquith reported to Venetia Stanley, '– about an hour long – for the most part almost conversational in tone & with some of his usual ragged ends; but extraordinarily well reasoned & tactful & really cogent – so much so that our extreme peacelovers were for the moment reduced to silence; though they will soon find their tongues again.'[25] In the cabinet, he now found the resignations of Simon and Beauchamp hurriedly withdrawn, leaving only Burns and Morley as the ministers whom he had to replace. Churchill later gave a benign account of how he tried to persuade Morley, for whom he felt a surprising sense of affinity as a literary figure, to 'wait for two or three days more, everything would be clear, and we should be in full agreement. The Germans would make everyone easy in his conscience.'[26] But Morley, who had again gone to ruminate in his club rather than listen to Grey's speech, remained set on quietly taking his leave at the age of seventy-five, still reluctant to acknowledge the sudden primacy of the Belgian issue. 'To bind ourselves to France is at the same time to bind ourselves to Russia,' he warned Asquith in rebuffing the Prime Minister's third and final personal plea.[27]

On the evening of Monday 3 August, the cabinet insisted that Germany should withdraw its ultimatum to Belgium. Instead, the news came overnight that the German army was advancing. After the next cabinet on Tuesday the 4th, Scott, who had been summoned from Manchester by Lloyd George, was briefed by him on how things now stood: 'Up to last Sunday only two members of the Cabinet had been in favour of our intervention in the War, but the *violation of Belgian territory* had completely altered the situation.' Actually there had been more than two members for intervention – maybe as many as six – but the salient point was the Belgian issue, on which the clock was now ticking. The Foreign Office, having received no satisfactory assurances from Berlin, sent the Germans an ultimatum expiring at 11 p.m. GMT. Ministers gathered as the hour approached. It was now that Sir Edward Grey, nearing the close of his only two days of eloquence in an allotted span of three score years and ten, is said to have uttered the words: 'The lamps are going out all over Europe; we shall not see them lit again in our life-time.'

With no German response, the United Kingdom was thus at war. That it was still united was one blessing. The Irish crisis had been pushed aside – for the moment. The Irish Nationalists, under their leader John Redmond, supported the declaration of war. Bonar Law had already assured Asquith of Conservative support. The Labour leader in the House of Commons, Ramsay MacDonald, resigned over the declaration of war and was replaced as leader by Arthur Henderson, who supported it. Asquith and Henderson each lost a son in the war; Law was to lose two; Redmond lost a brother.

It was with conflicting emotions that the Liberals had entered the war. On 4 August Scott had been told that 'at a Cabinet meeting Grey had burst into tears – an extraordinary and moving thing in a man so reserved', as even the unenthused old editor had to admit, adding: 'Very different was Churchill's light-hearted irresponsibility.' True, Churchill's demeanour throughout the crisis had contrasted with that of most of his Liberal colleagues. While the ministers waited for the ultimatum to expire, so Lloyd George later told the story, not only to Frances Stevenson but to Margot Asquith, of all people, Churchill dashed into the room, his face 'radiant', and full of all his naval plans.[28] As Winston himself had admitted to Clementine, his apprehensive Liberal wife, a few days earlier: 'Everything tends towards catastrophe & collapse. I am interested, geared-up and happy. Is it not horrible to be built like that?'

Lachrymose or exuberant, the Liberal cabinet, with only two resignations in the process, had resolved upon intervention in the European conflict. Not only that: the whole of the British Empire was now carried into war by the British decision. This was obviously true of the colonies directly under British rule; and it was true also of the Indian Raj, which possessed the only large standing army immediately at Britain's disposal. Equally significant, the self-governing Dominions were also committed to the war, without their formal consent but with their effective support, even in the case of South

Africa. In anglophone Canada, in Australia and in New Zealand, the war was a popular cause from the outset, as the amazing flow of volunteers into their armed forces subsequently confirmed.

During the war, the Dominions were to enlist 1.3 million soldiers, of whom a million served overseas, mainly on the western front. Of these, 144,000 were killed, with a slightly higher casualty rate than was suffered by British troops. This was not a token commitment. Canada, with a population of 8 million, sent 458,000 troops abroad, some of them recruited from Newfoundland, which additionally sent over 9,000. Australia and New Zealand, with a combined population of just over 6 million, sent 444,000. South Africa, with a white population of 1.4 million, had 136,000 troops serving, 50,000 of them in German South West Africa; and 44,000 black South Africans also served in labour brigades in France. The Indian Army recruited 827,000 combatants and 446,000 non-combatants. In 1913, the total strength of all the British armed forces had been only 400,000.

It was because of the participation of the British Empire that a European war became a war that was worldwide in its scope. Canadians found themselves fighting in France, Australians and New Zealanders in Turkey; South African troops directly contested Germany's colonies in Africa. Japan was drawn in too as Britain's ally, taking the war to the Far East. And just as the fuse of the European war had been lit in the Balkans, the trigger for this world war was the Belgian issue, with its unique pull upon Liberal sensibilities.

The Royal Navy guaranteed the integrity of imperial communications, its priority to keep the sea lanes open. This is why it had been built up to its current strength in matching the German challenge. Moreover, it was because of that challenge, notionally requiring the Royal Navy to sustain its 60 per cent superiority in the North Sea, that the British fleet had been concentrated there, with the concurrent redeployment of the French fleet to the Mediterranean. So the consequent exposure of the French coasts, generating the moral obligation for the Royal Navy to protect them, was itself the clear result of the new German naval policy. In this sense, the need for every man (as Grey had put it) to 'look into his own heart, and his own feelings, and construe the extent of the obligation for himself' can be called one of the moral consequences of Admiral Tirpitz.

Asquith did not lose as many cabinet ministers as he had expected; nor did he find 'our extreme peacelovers' either as numerous or as intractable as he had predicted to Venetia Stanley. In fact, many prominent Liberals underwent dramatic conversion, if not through hearing Grey's actual words then through the abrupt shift in the terms of the argument during Monday and Tuesday 3–4 August.

This was true not only of Liberal MPs but of the intellectuals and publicists, notably those who had come together to found the British Neutrality Committee on Sunday. They included Leonard Hobhouse and the historian J. L. Hammond, both of them closely connected with Scott and the *Manchester Guardian*; also their mutual friend the Oxford classical scholar Gilbert Murray and the historian G. M. Trevelyan; and since A. G. Gardiner, the editor of the *Daily News*, was also numbered among the dozen present, it is not surprising that his paper printed their letter urging non-intervention. This appeared on the morning of Grey's speech. Several of the signatories were present in the lobby of the House of Commons while Grey spoke. Murray had actually got into the visitors' gallery of the Commons, and so fundamental was his conversion that he was (with Hammond's assistance) to compose a widely read pamphlet, *The Foreign Policy of Sir Edward Grey*, in exoneration of a man whom they declared to have been misjudged, not least by themselves.

For after Grey's words about Belgium had sunk in, many upright Liberals had second thoughts. The change of tack by Liberal journalists was set up in type for their readers to see: in the *Daily Chronicle* of 3 August there was a leader arguing against intervention and on 4 August one arguing for it, both written by R. C. K. Ensor (who himself later published a discerning history of these events). Gardiner's *Daily News* was much the same, and Lloyd George's *War Memoirs* tellingly juxtaposes its reports of those same dates.[29] The British Neutrality Committee was formally constituted at a meeting at noon on 4 August, at a meeting that now also included Trevelyan's Cambridge friend

Bertrand Russell. But their friendship was to prove as short lived as the committee itself; the two men quarrelled as they walked down the Strand, Trevelyan now persuaded of Grey's case and Russell scornful, and they did not speak again for thirty years. The next day the hastily formed committee was equally hastily dissolved.

The *Manchester Guardian* was the toughest nut to crack. Scott was faced with the choice of breaking with Lloyd George or breakfasting with Lloyd George, and chose the latter, as previously. This gave his host the opportunity to convey his side of the story over the coming weeks, with long explanations of why it was a 'substantial violation', rather than a technical infringement, of Belgian neutrality that had seemed crucial. Likewise Russell challenged Hammond as to whether he had been aware of the (allegedly obvious) fact that Germany would make such a violation. 'Personally I was not,' Hammond admitted. The Kaiser could have pleaded the same. But as Hammond later put it in his biography of Scott, the invasion of Belgium 'gave to the war from its first day an implacable temper', and the fact that 'the Allies held that Germany should be punished for going into Belgium' made an insuperable obstacle to a negotiated peace.

The news coming out of Belgium, day by day, had sharpened this point. Within a month the German army's action in razing the medieval heart of the university city of Louvain (Leuven) became a highly publicised event. It was this sort of verifiable vandalism, rather than disputable human atrocity stories, that first led to the use of the term 'Huns' at this time, understandably enough in the original context. In the 1920s, of course, such stories of German 'frightfulness' were to be sweepingly dismissed as Allied propaganda, with an indiscriminate scepticism that has itself been revised by modern historians. The shock impact in 1914 is perhaps difficult to recapture in the light of twentieth-century experience. Lloyd George's reaction to the burning of Reims cathedral in September – 'It has moved him more than anything else since the outbreak of the war,' noted Frances Stevenson – may thus seem rather exaggerated (and in this case it turned out to be so).[30] But his own fervour in the prosecution of the war was by this time ready to be shared with the public.

Before Lloyd George's speech of 19 September in the Queen's Hall, London, he had been unusually apprehensive and agitated. But his nerves fed into a great oratorical performance, striking the chords of the politics of emotion. He made Belgium the heart of his case, with Britain's need to defend its integrity, as in 1870, a key issue. 'I am not going into details of outrages,' he said. 'Many of them are untrue, and always are in war.' But he now also alluded to the Serbian case, by analogy; and in a wholly idiosyncratic thrust, he contrasted Belgium and Serbia with the '6-foot-2 nations' on the German model. 'The world owes much to the little 5-foot-5 nations,' Lloyd George declaimed, presumably drawing himself up to his full height. Nor was this the only allusion to Wales, for its landscape was invoked in his closing passage: 'the stern hand of Fate has scourged us to an elevation where we can see the great everlasting things that matter for a nation – the great peaks we had forgotten, of Honour, Duty, Patriotism, and, clad in glittering white, the great pinnacle of Sacrifice pointing like a rugged finger to Heaven'.

This oration was not couched in an idiom that has worn well. But to contemporaries it was the real thing. 'The Prime Minister said with tears in his eyes that it was "a wonderful speech",' so Frances Stevenson reported. 'Sir Edward Grey said he wept when he read the peroration.'[31] We have to reconcile such sentiments with the fact that, three weeks earlier, Lloyd George had written in rather different terms to his wife, with reference to their nineteen-year-old son Gwilym, indicating what was necessary. 'Beat the German Junker but no war on the German people &c,' he assured her. 'I am not going to sacrifice my nice boy for that purpose. You must write Wil telling him on no account to be bullied into volunteering abroad.'

Lloyd George was not the only Liberal to be caught on the hop, adjusting his moral compass with some awkwardness. As editor of the *Manchester Guardian*, Scott stopped writing leaders himself for a while, but then resumed; and he remained in close touch with his ally Leonard Hobhouse, well remembering the sound pro-Boer pedigree that he shared not only with Leonard but with his formidable sister Emily, notable for her brave exposure of the humanitarian record of the

British army in South Africa. On 2 August Leonard had told her: 'The Jingoism of the *Times* clique baffles the imagination & we are evidently in the greatest danger.' On 4 August, in despair, Hobhouse had pleaded to a well-connected uncle: 'Could not Morley be persuaded to resign for his name's sake?' On the day, his wish had come true.

In several ways, it was all too like the Boer War. And just as Hobhouse had viewed that as a moral issue, so his perennial antagonist on the left, Bernard Shaw, took the polar-opposite view. 'You don't understand this war a bit: you are not interested in Weltpolitik and Realpolitik,' Shaw sternly told Beatrice Webb. 'Belgium is not the outstanding fact: it is the outstanding excuse.' Shaw thus scorned this war, on the same sort of reasoning with which he had earlier extenuated the war in South Africa. Conversely, by the end of 1914, Hobhouse had come to his own clear view about what was at stake, and now presented to his anti-war sister the mirror-image of the Shavian lecture: 'Nearly all those who sympathised with the Boers as a small nation struggling for freedom now sympathise with the Belgians struggling for freedom.'

These were indeed the terms on which, with whatever reluctance, Liberals supported this war. And with British intervention, the European war that had begun over Serbia was transformed into a global conflict – the designation First World War was soon invented, though the Great War remained the most common description at the time. Uniquely, what the British brought into this struggle was the support of a vast diaspora of European settlement in three continents, as well as the might of their Indian Raj. It was a world war that the Liberals would not have started over the Serbian issue. It was only when the Belgian dimension emerged that they were persuaded of the case for intervention, on Gladstonian arguments that had a unique resonance for them. Having inexorably moralised the issues that started the war, British liberals were to find that they had ineluctably moralised the terms of the peace that was to end it. And in this, in a way that reinforced the worldwide dimension of the war, they were to be aided and abetted in their moral fervour by American liberals.

Goodbye to the Garden of Eden: John Maynard Keynes

Like Churchill, Bertrand Russell was immensely well connected in British society, but whereas the Churchills were Tories the Russells had been Whigs since the time of the Glorious Revolution of 1689. Lord John Russell had served as Liberal Prime Minister before Gladstone and (though later rated 95 per cent intellectually inferior to Asquith by Morley) was treated with due respect in retirement as the 1st Earl Russell. Young Bertrand (the future 3rd Earl) had been orphaned at the age of four and brought up by his formidable grandmother. It was she who, when hosting Mr Gladstone for dinner in 1889, without any other male in the household, left her young grandson to entertain the Grand Old Man when the ladies withdrew, in the custom of the day. Gladstone made only one remark, but it was one which his teenage host was to remember all his life: 'This is a very good port they have given me, but why have they given it me in a claret glass?' One way or another, throughout a long and eminent career, Russell knew everybody.

In his autobiography he recorded that he had first met John Maynard Keynes in Cambridge through the undergraduate's father, who taught formal logic, and was 'an earnest Nonconformist who put morality first and logic second'. The Keyneses and the Russells plainly came from very different social worlds. Born in 1883 in the heart of the Cambridge academic establishment, the boy was always known by his middle name, Maynard, if only to distinguish him from his father, John Neville Keynes, who was known as Neville. In Russell's view this was not all that distinguished the younger Keynes, whom he came to know well as a colleague in pre-war Cambridge: Keynes as a Fellow of King's College, Russell as a Fellow of Trinity College, often discussing common philosophical interests. 'Keynes's intellect was the sharpest and clearest that I have ever known,' Russell declared in old age. 'When I argued with him, I felt that I took my life in my hands, and I seldom emerged without feeling something of a fool.'

Maynard's parents would not have been surprised by any of this. They doted on their offspring, from his birth in 1883 to the memorial service for Lord Keynes of Tilton in Westminster Abbey in 1946, which they both lived to attend. The Royal Economic Society's admirably authoritative thirty-volume edition of Keynes's *Collected Writings* would have seemed to them nothing less than fitting as a monument. Neville and Florence spent sixty-seven years of married life at 6 Harvey Road, Cambridge, a house built in the 1880s near the station, with the William Morris wallpaper still on the walls when Maynard would later return, from negotiations in Whitehall or Washington, for one of their regular Sunday lunches. Little wonder that his authorised biographer, Roy Harrod, wrote of 'the presuppositions of Harvey Road' as an unspoken but unquestioned ethic of enlightened reform to be sponsored by an intellectual elite using the tools of persuasion.

The elder Keynes had a career that made him a discreetly influential figure in the administration of a university still struggling to emerge from its monastic origins. He was the trustworthy, pedantic, unassuming man in the back room who helped more famous men to get things done. Alfred Marshall, the leading British economist of that era, served as professor of political economy from 1885 to 1908; he became instrumental in establishing economics as a separate undergraduate course (called Tripos in Cambridge) in 1903 – previously the subject had been taught mainly within the moral sciences Tripos – and in all this Marshall was loyally aided by

Neville Keynes. But neither by temperament nor by upbringing was Neville's elder son (who had two siblings) fitted to remain in any back room. Maynard's own career duly blossomed, living out his parents' ambitions for their always precocious child.

It is apparent, then, that Neville and Florence, who herself subsequently became the first woman mayor of the City of Cambridge, were actually rather well connected – not in the tradition of the established orders in Church and state but within an intellectual aristocracy that strenuously prized talent. Neville had been a Baptist, Florence a Congregationalist, the daughter of the Rev. John Brown, latterly a renowned pastor in Bedford, and with an array of Dissenting forebears to rival the pedigree of Woodrow Wilson. For Neville and Florence, chapel-going was of less importance than the moral ethic that fed into an axiomatic Liberal affiliation in politics. When Chamberlain's tariff-reform campaign had been launched in 1903, a manifesto supporting free trade was published in *The Times*, signed by fourteen leading economists including Marshall. Neville Keynes privately considered this overt, partisan intervention by academics tactically unwise (though it was just the sort of thing that Maynard would get up to in future). Neville and Florence agreed with the fourteen about free trade itself, of course, and their own commitment to the Liberal cause was unwavering. Everything was to be settled by debate, with competitive, unprotected free trade not only in commerce but in religion and in ideas too.

Maynard simultaneously accepted many such presuppositions and also rebelled against other moral strictures as Victorian relics. In Cambridge he was a member of a highly select discussion society, generally known as the Apostles, who affected to idolise the teachings of the moral philosopher G. E. Moore (though Russell, another Apostle of an earlier vintage, thought his younger friends had misunderstood their mentor). The way Keynes later put it was simple, claiming that the only part of Moore they did not accept was his injunction that general rules should always be followed. 'We entirely repudiated a personal liability on us to obey general rules,'

Keynes explained. 'We claimed the right to judge every individual case on its merits, and the wisdom, experience and self-control to do so successfully.'[1]

Keynes said this in 1938, talking to his own close friends. They were a coterie, known by then simply as 'Bloomsbury', and could be expected to understand him, even when he immediately added a further comment – couched in characteristically mischievous terms – claiming that this stance made them 'in the strict sense of the term, immoralists'.[2] Of course, to anyone not familiar with their in-group allusions, this could suggest that Apostles and members of Bloomsbury had been concerned only with intense personal relations and that Maynard himself was thus insulated from political problems. There were, however, those who knew him rather better, like the economist Sir Austin Robinson, who later commented that 'beneath a Georgian skin there peeped out from time to time an almost Victorian sense of moral purpose and obligation; neither Eton, nor Cambridge, nor Bloomsbury had obliterated wholly his heritage from generations of Keyneses and Browns'.

The fact was that Keynes delighted in supposing that he had the best of both worlds, enlightened but with advantages that he took for granted. When, as a young student of mathematics, he decided he needed formal instruction in economics, family connections ensured that he got it from Marshall himself. Though he was later to challenge the Marshallian orthodoxy in economic theory, Maynard was also the keeper of the flame. He continued to uphold his great teacher's contention that 'the bare bones of economic theory are not worth much in themselves' unless they could yield practical conclusions: 'The whole point lies in applying them to the interpretation of current economic life.'[3]

In his personal life, Maynard was likewise an ambiguous figure, coming of age in Edwardian Britain. If this was an era when the outward sexual proprieties were strictly policed in Britain, this was literally so in the case of homosexual conduct. Until the 1960s sexual acts between men were punishable by law – if the men were caught, of course, which was another matter. In practice, social station offered a degree of protection for illicit sexual relations, discreetly maintained but not publicly acknowledged. This was certainly the state of affairs in King's College, Cambridge, where Keynes was admitted as an undergraduate in 1902 after his schooling at Eton College. These two institutions, both products of the *ancien régime* and founded by King Henry VI, had always been closely linked – indeed until 1873 only Etonians had been eligible as scholars or fellows of King's. This was surely a primrose path to tread.

Maynard's homosexuality as a young man was something that had to be hushed up in his own lifetime. His surviving brother, Sir Geoffrey Keynes, connived at this and Sir Roy Harrod's biography, published in 1951, is full of personal insight on virtually every aspect of his hero's life except this one. Yet within Maynard's own milieu his sexuality was accepted, whether with a worldly shrug or a frisson of exaggeration. He told his friends of his days at Eton in terms that suggest a frenzy of adolescent amours. Certainly as an undergraduate, protected as he was within the walls of all-male colleges, he indulged more freely in what he and his friends teasingly called 'the higher sodomy'. In his private papers, defiantly preserved for posterity, is a list that he once compiled of his sexual partners, year by year, from 1901 to 1915. This includes many of his friends, like the writer Lytton Strachey, but also – following his couple of years in London working as a civil servant at the India Office – a number of casual pick-ups: 'Stable boy of Park Lane', 'Auburn haired of Marble Arch', 'Lift boy of Vauxhall'.

Here Keynes was clearly transgressing not just the line of conventional morality but also the class line. Such liaisons on the streets of London, under the noses of the constabulary, exposed him to risks that could have destroyed even the most promising career. Churchill's retrospective comment that in those days society had 'standards of conduct and methods of enforcing them now altogether forgotten'[4] sounds the warning note, but it was a warning of which young Maynard showed himself recklessly oblivious. And he got away with it.

He had taken a lot for granted, as he came to realise. 'What an extraordinary episode in the economic progress of man that age was which came to an end in August 1914!' he writes in *The Economic Consequences of the Peace* (1919). There he describes the way of life of 'the upper and middle classes, for whom life offered, at a low cost and with the least trouble, conveniences, comforts, and amenities beyond the compass of the richest and most powerful monarchs of other ages'. It was a system perfectly attuned to ministering to the tastes of a man very much like himself. Thus he 'could order by telephone, sipping his morning tea in bed, the various products of the whole earth', in a world where trade and travel alike were unrestricted. If planning to travel abroad, he 'could despatch his servant to the neighbouring office of a bank for such supply of the precious metals as might seem convenient' and, 'bearing coined wealth upon his person', experience the tangible benefits of an international gold standard.[5] Under this regime, the gold sovereign, for the last forty years, had been freely exchangeable for $4.86 or 25.5 French francs (and vice versa). Here is the picture of a privileged man, and one who had hardly realised how lucky he was.

In retrospect, Keynes is implicitly admitting that he was among those who had 'regarded this state of affairs as normal, certain, and permanent, except in the direction of further improvement, and any deviation from it as aberrant, scandalous, and avoidable'. And he identifies 'the serpent to this paradise' in the shape of militarism and imperialism, racial and cultural rivalries, monopolies and restrictions, all of which had seemed to him insubstantial before 1914.[6] His vignette constitutes a beguilingly plausible snapshot, though retrospect is not always a reliable lens. We need rather more evidence than his *Economic Consequences* supplies about how the serpent entered the garden.

On Sunday 2 August 1914, so Russell recalled, he met Keynes hurrying across the Great Court of Trinity College, intent on getting to London. He was seeking the assistance of his brother-in-law, A. V. Hill, recently married to Margaret Keynes. Hill was to become a distinguished physiologist, awarded the Nobel Prize in 1923. But in 1914 he was a junior research Fellow of Trinity and – his immediate relevance to Keynes – the proud owner of a motorcycle with a sidecar. 'Why don't you go by train?' Russell asked, only to receive the cryptic answer: 'Because there isn't time.'

It was the August bank holiday weekend, with the railways crowded. And Keynes had just received an urgent letter from a friend in the Treasury, Basil Blackett: 'I wanted to pick your brains for your country's benefit and thought you might enjoy the process.' Keynes reached Whitehall in time for tea that afternoon, having alighted from the sidecar at the end of the street to keep up appearances, and was immediately plunged into the midst of a major crisis that foreshadowed many others in his career, tendering crucial advice at the highest levels of government.

As we have seen, the cabinet was by now meeting a couple of times most days, faced with the fast-developing war situation. As with the politics, so with the economics: it was the Austrian ultimatum to Serbia on 23 July that had suddenly brought a new awareness of the seriousness of the position. It came 'like a bombshell', said the *Bankers' Magazine*; the word on the Stock Exchange was 'the worst day since 1870'; and the impact on London of the panic in other European financial centres intensified daily. The effects were already apparent across the Empire; the shares of the Canadian Pacific Railway fell by 15 per cent in ten days. On 30 July the Paris Bourse postponed settlement of accounts for a month. Customers who depended on immediate liquidity were left high and dry. There were immediate knock-on effects for the London Stock Exchange, which was in those days bigger than the Bourse and Wall Street combined. Established, respected trading firms were 'hammered'. Bank rate was successively raised from 3 per cent to 4 per cent, to

8 per cent, to 10 per cent, and the Stock Exchange was closed on Friday 31 July.

On that day too, the high-street banks tried to avoid paying customers in gold. Their story was that they feared hoarding by customers and preferred to hoard it themselves. But those high-street customers who had been fobbed off with Bank of England notes (five pounds denomination and upwards) then had the right to demand gold in exchange at the Bank's headquarters in Threadneedle Street. Keynes was to chastise the high-street banks for their behaviour in the September issue of the *Economic Journal*, of which he was the youthful editor: 'On Friday, July 31st, and Saturday, August 1st, the shameful sight was seen of a queue of persons outside the Bank of England waiting to cash notes which had been forced on them by their bankers.'[7] In rebuking them for imperilling the fabric of confidence, Keynes made his economic point in the language of moral repugnance. Since the bank-holiday weekend had now begun, the real crunch would not come until the next full business day, Tuesday 4 August. Hence the urgency of Blackett's request and of Keynes's motorcycle journey.

Blackett had served as secretary of a recent Royal Commission on Indian finance and currency. Keynes, who had had a brief spell as a civil servant in the India Office before his election as a Fellow of King's in 1908, served on this Commission – his first book, published in 1913, was on the same topic. Hence his friendship with Blackett. And Keynes had another useful friend in high places: Edwin Montagu, four years older than himself. His father, Samuel Montagu, created Lord Swaythling in 1907, was famously wealthy as a foreign exchange dealer and notable as a Jewish philanthropist. The son, now Liberal MP for one of the Cambridgeshire seats, served successively as private secretary to Asquith, 1906–10; as a junior minister at the India Office, 1910–14; and, since February 1914, in effect as Lloyd George's deputy at the Treasury as the Financial Secretary. Montagu knew about money; he knew the two most powerful figures in the Liberal government; he knew many secrets; and he knew Venetia Stanley, to whom he had proposed in 1912, only to be turned down – for the moment at least.

'I owed – rather surprisingly – nearly all my steps in life to him,' Keynes privately admitted later. It was Montagu who had encouraged him to participate in student debates in the Cambridge Union Society; again Montagu who had enlisted Keynes in electioneering in the strongly Nonconformist villages near Cambridge in the General Elections of 1906 and 1910. (The workers at the jam factory at Histon depended on the consumption of their products worldwide, jar by jar, and were duly buttered up by Montagu, spoon-fed on the benefits of free trade by Montagu's persuasive friend.) 'In 1913 when he was at the India Office,' Keynes acknowledged, 'it was he who got me put on the Royal Commission on Indian Currency, which was my first step into publicity (my name was known to no-one outside Cambridge before then).' Another Commissioner, Sir Robert Chalmers, had been impressed by Keynes's keen questioning, which was another useful link, since Chalmers was currently permanent secretary at the Treasury and was, after serving as Governor of Ceylon, to return to that post in wartime, jointly with Sir John Bradbury. Keynes acquired an awed respect for both these formidable mandarins.

In August 1914 Keynes had just turned thirty-one. He was the same age as Churchill had been in December 1905 when he was made a junior minister. Now Keynes too exploited his connections and was given his chance to shine. He stepped into a situation where the outcome was highly fluid. On Saturday 1 August Asquith and Lloyd George had signed an important assurance, demanded of them by the Governor of the Bank of England, Sir Walter Cunliffe. This letter indicated their willingness, if it proved necessary, to suspend the Bank Act of 1844, meaning its statutory obligation to restrict its internal advances to a fixed level proportionate to its holdings of gold. (And the level of these gold reserves, of course, was affected by external flows, either to or from the rest of the world.) Montagu had served as messenger to Downing Street in securing the ministers' signatures, business that had to be transacted in the interstices of the two fraught cabinet meetings that day.

This proposal to suspend the Bank Act was not unprecedented. It had happened in earlier financial crises (in 1847, 1857, 1866 and 1890), enabling the Bank of England to act as 'lender of last resort' in preventing the markets from freezing up. The new development in 1914 was that the banks would start issuing a printed sterling paper currency to replace gold sovereigns. Now under the Bank Act, the Bank of England was legally bound to exchange its own notes for gold if customers demanded it. But the smallest Bank note in circulation was the 'fiver', which in today's money would be worth about £400. Hence the emergency plans to print notes of a smaller denomination, for one pound and for ten shillings, to be available as soon as the banks reopened.

As Governor of the Bank, Sir Walter Cunliffe cut a bluff figure in a world where bluffing was often important. He had a no-nonsense disposition that impressed Lloyd George, who once asked how he knew which foreign-exchange bills were safe and received the reply: 'I smell them.'[8] Since this was much like the way in which the Chancellor of the Exchequer himself operated, there was a natural affinity here. 'His manner was not propitiatory to strangers, but when you got to know him he was a genial, kindly man, and I liked him,' was how Lloyd George's *War Memoirs* put it. 'I relied on his shrewdness, his common sense and instinct.'[9] This was written well after the post-war peace conference and the setting of a figure for reparations, in which Cunliffe's sense of smell played a notable part.

In 1914 Lloyd George's only quarrel with Cunliffe was a joking relationship over the printing of the new paper currency notes. Should they be the hallowed Bank of England notes or the allegedly inferior notes, now hastily being printed by the Treasury? In the end there was only time to print the Treasury notes, signed by Bradbury as permanent secretary, and hence soon dubbed 'Bradburies'. This actually got the Bank off the hook in the end since, unlike its own notes, Bradburies were not to be literally 'as good as gold'; they did not carry the guarantee for free exchange with gold sovereigns; and they thus fell outside the terms of the Bank Act – which, in the end, did not need to be suspended after all. But Bradburies were explicitly legal tender, so the question was whether the public would accept them. With three extraordinary bank holidays declared for 4, 5 and 6 August, everyone was now working to the deadline of Friday 7 August as the first working day of this new system.

In this way, with much improvisation on a hand-to-mouth basis, Britain scrambled into the adoption of 'fiat money'. The country was forced by the war emergency to adopt a paper currency for internal use: a contingency so little considered or foreseen that no such notes had been printed in advance of the actual crisis. But Britain, unlike every other country on the international gold standard, had not immediately decided to lock up its own gold reserves, instead maintaining the 'specie payment' that backed international transactions. Hence Keynes's later compliment to the authorities: 'The Bank of England alone met the international catastrophes of August, 1914, without suspending specie payments and without availing herself of emergency privileges.'[10] Britain had thus refused to abandon the international gold standard, one of the verities of the Garden of Eden.

That the currency crisis of August 1914 was resolved in this way owed much to Keynes's influence. His role was to advise on whether the government should, in effect, quit the gold standard altogether. He was briefed by Blackett on the evening of 2 August and he spent the next few days in the Treasury. His first task, working until late on 3 August, was to compose a memorandum, of which only two copies survive: Bradbury's as permanent secretary and Lloyd George's as Chancellor. First it dealt with the magnitude of any possible drain on the country's gold reserves, which Keynes currently estimated, in round terms, as £28 million in the Bank of England plus £15 million held by high-street banks. This was all qualified by the likelihood that other countries might send gold to London, or take it for their own use. Who knew what might happen? Perhaps the United States might send gold, attracted by that 10 per cent interest rate, or perhaps not since it would have to be shipped across a suddenly far

Lord Kitchener, Britain's best-known soldier, became quite literally the face of the recruitment campaign. The war challenged many entrenched liberal assumptions, of which voluntary enlistment was one and the gold standard another – as the young Keynes was progressively to discover.

from tranquil Atlantic Ocean; or perhaps France might take gold, perhaps as much as £10 million. But even that last 'perhaps' could be borne, Keynes thought. So his advice to stick with 'the rules of the game' under the gold standard was fairly confident: 'It is useless to accumulate gold reserves in times of peace unless it is intended to utilise them in time of danger.'[11]

What may now strike us as surprising is the smallness of the sums at stake. This total of £43 million of gold, even at today's values, would only be worth about £3.5 billion, and there were voices at the time arguing that the reserves needed to be bigger. These small reserves, however, were only the lubrication in the great hydraulic machinery of international transactions. In 1913, the last full year of peace, Britain's exports totalled £637 million and imports £719 million, leaving a visible trade gap of about £80 million. So here was the trade that was being financed through the gold standard, with flows that had to balance in the long run, because imports had to be paid for, not by gold transfers, but by exports. And the visible trade deficit was more than covered by Britain's net surplus of £120 million on services and, above all, by a further net surplus on investment income from the rest of the world of £200 million. Hence the ease with which Britain, as a creditor country, financed its own imports under free trade; and, moreover, painlessly accumulated the proceeds of an overall current account surplus of £235 million, which could be left to increase British investments throughout the Empire and the wider world. It would have been absurd to imagine this surplus as accumulating in London as vast gold reserves, for which there was simply no need. A creditor country had special advantages, especially when London was the world's financial centre.

This was certainly Keynes's view. For here was the Garden of Eden in economic statistics: the reason why 'the products of the whole earth' had been so readily available to the privileged classes. After the August crisis was over, Keynes made the complacently anglocentric comment: 'The principle that the Bank of England can afford a small reserve, because it always lies within its power to influence the exchanges of the world within a very brief period, has again been justified.'[12] And this was not mere hindsight on his part; it also vindicated his foresight. Writing against the clock on 3 August, Keynes had not needed to cite the trade figures to make his point about the folly of capitulating to panic at this moment, but his confidence in the system's powers of adjustment – from the perspective of a creditor country – had nonetheless underpinned his advice.

'If the foreign drain is not likely to be very large,' so he assured the Treasury, 'and the internal drain can be obviated by other means, it is difficult to see how such an extreme and dangerous measure as the suspension of cash payments can be justified.'[13] The foreign drain, then, was a well-justified risk that should be taken. Otherwise this default would needlessly besmirch London's reputation and impair confidence, which was actually a great national asset. For Keynes, 'London's position as a monetary centre' was pre-eminent because of 'complete confidence in London's unwavering readiness to meet the demands upon her'. Hence he stressed that 'the vital point is that we should not repudiate our external obligations to pay gold, until it is physically impossible for us to fulfil them'.[14]

The internal drain, on the other hand, could be obviated by practical, pragmatic measures, since the internal currency in everyday use was another question. 'Suspension of the Bank Act' (which he assumed to be inevitable at that point) was a well-rehearsed form of words that implied too much, since it muddled internal and external commitments to honour payments in gold. 'Indeed *one* important object of the suspension of the Bank Act is to enable the internal circulation to be filled with emergency paper, in order that all or nearly all our gold may be available for a foreign drain,' Keynes argued. 'This object falls to the ground if no gold is to be used for the latter purpose.' The point was to continue meeting foreign demands in gold, through the Bank of England, 'while making it extremely difficult and inconvenient for the ordinary man to get gold'. All the evidence was that 'people take very readily to notes', and that 'most people will have no option but to use notes for a time'. So Keynes made light of the theoretical objections to a paper currency by appealing to the common sense of ordinary people: 'They may soon discover that they are quite well adapted to their purpose.'[15] A century later, this looks like an open-and-shut case.

At the time, these arguments had to persuade one key figure, the Chancellor himself. He was given Keynes's memorandum on 4 August, a momentous day, with war now inevitable. Blackett recorded that Lloyd George 'asked who Keynes was, and on being told that he was a friend of mine, expert in currency, said it was monstrous that Treasury officials should call in outsiders on their own responsibility. But he read the memorandum . . .' On the following day, it became apparent to his officials that Lloyd George was learning fast. 'He has clearly imbibed much of Keynes' memorandum and is strong against suspension of specie payments,' Blackett observed.

On 6 August, Keynes wrote to his father, saying that he had just heard that 'it was my memorandum [that] converted Lloyd George'.[16] And by 8 August Blackett, in his private diary, was wryly celebrating his boss's conversion by his young friend: 'It took some time to teach him, but he promises now to reach the front rank of financial experts, if his present knowledge makes him retain a taste for the pure finance side of the Treasury work which he has hitherto entirely neglected.' It was an impressive learning curve of which both pupil and teacher had some reason to be proud. But Lloyd George, living through 'some of the busiest and most anxious days I ever spent' did not pause to acknowledge any such debt, which is eminently understandable.[17] Nor did he do so in publishing his *War Memoirs* in 1933, which is also understandable for different reasons (as will emerge below in chapter 13).

Keynes, after relishing his own busy few days in the Treasury, was not offered further employment at this point and instead returned to Cambridge – on the train this time. That was the end of the war crisis for him, except for writing about it with new authority. He did so not only for the *Economic Journal*, with its largely British circulation, but also for the *Quarterly Journal of Economics*, where he assured his mainly American readers: 'Great Britain is a creditor nation, not only in the sense that she has large permanent foreign investments and an annual balance available for increasing them, but also in the sense that she habitually loans to foreign centres large sums of money which are repayable *at short notice*.'[18] This was true enough at the time of publication (November 1914), during the four rather frustrating months that were to pass before the Treasury required the author's further services.

For Lloyd George, of course, it was business as usual, but more so. In retrospect he claimed that the decision to keep to the 'rules of the game' on international gold payments, 'which marked the main difference between our treatment of the situation and that adopted by other countries, was one which in fact did greatly help us to recover financial normality, because it tended towards a restoration of confidence which was so vitally necessary at the moment'.[19] His next big decision that week was to empower the Bank of England to guarantee all the bills drawn on London before the outbreak of war on 4 August – a total that amounted to about £350 million (at a time when the annual budget was under £200 million).

Lloyd George made a bold proposal for 'cold storage' of these bills, while a moratorium kept the Stock Exchange closed for the time being. He was not deterred by the official advice that this might cost £50 million, nor by the estimate in the *Economist* that the figure could be as high as £200 million. Lloyd George's priority was to get trade moving, to get the Stock Exchange open again, and thus to get on with winning this war; and in this he was largely justified by events. After 157 days, the London Stock Exchange reopened in January 1915; Wall Street had reopened in the previous month. The immediate costs to the Treasury of its guarantee to the Bank of England involved a payment of £39.5 million in 1915; but this was subsequently offset by successive repayments, so that in the end the Treasury got back £46 million, giving a net profit of £6.5 million to the taxpayer on Lloyd George's wild speculation. The Treasury made this calculation in 1926 but, with customary prudence, never published it.

On 8 August 1914, the House of Commons voted the government a war credit of £100 million, and in November a further £225 million. Government spending in the fiscal year ending March 1914 had been about £190 million; in 1915 it turned out at £560 million; in 1916 it hit £1,560 million; in 1917 almost £2,200 million and in 1918 almost £2,700 million. Even though up to half of this sum is accounted for by inflation, this is at least a sixfold increase. If we look at public expenditure as a percentage of national income (GDP), it was around 7 per cent in 1890, in the heyday of Gladstonian finance; it was around 10 per cent by 1914 under Asquith's and Lloyd George's peacetime regime; and then, within four years, it reached a wartime peak of around 50 per cent. After the First World War, by the same measure, this proportion was rarely less than 20 per cent.

Lloyd George had introduced a supplementary budget in November 1914, so he later explained, aimed at 'paying our way as far as possible by current taxation'.[20] This was a fine Gladstonian principle, sternly visiting the costs of war upon taxpayers to instruct and chastise them. It proved a vain hope well before 1918; great loans were to be raised both at home and – increasingly – in the United States, generating the protean problem of war debts.

But it is certainly true that Lloyd George imposed heavier taxation. He doubled the rates of income tax and super-tax, each previously levied at maximum rates of 1s 4d in the pound, so that standard-rate income-taxpayers now paid 2s 8d in the pound (13.3 per cent) and those super-taxpayers on incomes over £8,000 a year paid a combined top rate of 5s 4d (26.6 per cent). By 1918 the standard rate of income tax had reached 5s 0d (25 per cent) and super-tax on incomes over £10,000 was charged at an additional 4s 6d (22.5 per cent). This represented a top marginal tax rate of 47.5 per cent for the lucky '1 per cent' who now paid it, and their new misery was compounded by the fact that £10,000 was now worth only half of what it had been in the prelapsarian paradise before 1914.

In retrospect, Lloyd George regretted that later war budgets relied too much on loans, and paid such high interest rates on them. Had British investors proved unwilling to subscribe at lower rates, he suggested, 'there would have been a clear and popular ground for the conscription of capital for war purposes – a step which would have been an appropriate corollary to the conscription of man-power which we were soon to introduce'.[21] These were steps about which Keynes, now a Treasury official himself, had acutely mixed feelings.

Knight-Errant of Progressivism: Franklin Delano Roosevelt

According to the wits, we see two countries divided by a common language. And according to their constitutions, one was a monarchy with an entrenched aristocracy that controlled one chamber of Parliament, while the other was a republic founded on the will of 'we the people'. Until the end of the nineteenth century there was still loose talk of possible war, pitting the United States, which had long hankered after Canada, against Great Britain, still jealous of its own interests on the American continent. But Britannia could no longer rule these waves; the diplomatic détente at the turn of the century (formalised in the Hay–Pauncefote Treaty) reflected a balance of power that had long been shifting, tipped by demography.

In the mid-nineteenth century the population of the United States had been roughly the same as that of the United Kingdom (including Ireland). In the early twentieth century the American population climbed to over 90 million, twice that of the British isles. Some of this was natural growth through the respective birth rates; but immigration into the United States from continental Europe fuelled the process, with a surge of 'New Americans' who lacked any Anglo-Saxon pedigree. Moreover, American democracy, socially as much as politically, was a standing reproach to the reign of privilege in the Old World. Wilsonian rhetoric, of course, often played to this perception, not least in legitimating American warmaking and peacemaking.

Yet these stylised contrasts cloak some points of congruence. Tracts were written to explain why there was no socialism in the United States; but actually there was almost as little revolutionary socialism apparent in Britain. It was certainly not evident in the foundation of the Labour party, which established its bridgehead in the House of Commons through an informal 'progressive alliance' with the Liberals. It was in this way that social reform was brought into mainstream politics, which suggested some parallels with the rise of the 'progressive movement' in contemporary American politics, as many intellectuals and publicists on both sides of the Atlantic well appreciated.

True, the American party system was much different. In particular, the ideological progressives were notably divided, as the 1912 presidential election was to show, between the supporters of Wilson as the Democratic candidate and the insurgent Theodore Roosevelt (known as TR), who split the Republican vote, thus facilitating Wilson's election. A couple of years previously, when Leonard Hobhouse had made an academic visit to the United States, he had been surprised, as a British progressive, by some things he found. The big surprise to him was to find that Americans were no longer complacently individualist in outlook: 'They are in full revolt against the domination of capital.' And this, he suggested, was the American twist on progressivism, 'that England is faced by the problem of poverty and America by the problem of wealth'. Another surprise to him was linked: it was the name of Roosevelt, 'in stirring the conscience of America on the subject of wealth and its power', that was most often mentioned. As to the political impact, though the 'old, unreal party division between Democrats and Republican subsists', so Hobhouse reported: 'The real distinction is between the Radicals and the Conservatives, two terms which one hears in conversation with a frequency which rather surprises an Englishman.' At least this was what intellectuals evidently told each other, and some of them – faced with the Roosevelt–Wilson contest in the 1912 election – voiced their hope that the Democrats too would subsequently split, thus creating a clear ideological division between progressives and conservatives.

What actually happened was that Wilson, once in office, had by 1916 virtually cornered the market among self-conscious progressive supporters. Ray Stannard Baker's own odyssey is interesting. Coming from a Republican family, his early approval of Roosevelt had ended when TR attacked muckraking journalists. Several years later, Baker heard Wilson give a speech in New York to an audience of bankers, including the prominent figure of J. P. Morgan, who took offence at its tone (and whose friction with the Wilson administration in wartime, when the Morgan firm acted as the British government's agent, became a recurrent problem). It was Baker's high opinion of Wilson as an orator – he carried around a clipping of the address on Lee in which Wilson spoke of making men drunk under the influence of oratory – that sealed his commitment to the improbable ambition of electing this high-minded professor as President. 'But the miracle happened: it really happened!' It was in the 1912 campaign, then, that this former Republican began working for Wilson; many other progressives from that tradition supported Wilson by 1916.

Wilson, partly by being in the right place at the right time, thus established his progressive or liberal constituency. And this was integral to his image in international politics. Wilson was now seen by sympathetic British observers as acting in a 'collectivist' way, or what was described as a 'Hamiltonian' style by American supporters of his domestic policy; and meanwhile, in foreign affairs, the President maintained a 'Gladstonian' stance that had international (or internationalist) resonance.

This travelled well to Britain, if not to Germany. For in Britain liberals put a similar emphasis on concepts of international law, even though in Germany such talk tended to be dismissed as unrealistic given the imperatives of 'military necessity'. This measure of congruence in the Anglo-American liberal vocabulary can be glimpsed by juxtaposing a couple of contemporary comments (italics supplied in both examples). One is from an American journal of progressive views. 'What *liberals* need to obtain from Mr Wilson', the *New Republic* wrote in 1916, 'is some assurance that his later preference for a governing government will not prove to be as fugitive as his earlier preference for doctrinaire freedom.' Conversely it was the British journalist A. G. Gardiner who stated, in a book published in late 1915: 'It is because no man in a conspicuous position in the democratic world to-day is so entirely governed *by principle and by moral sanctions* that President Wilson is not merely the first citizen of the United States, but the first citizen of the world.'

In significant respects, then, the British and American political systems exhibited affinities in their political culture. But just as the British were somewhat more 'democratic' than the artefacts of an ancient constitution might initially suggest, so the Americans could not entirely escape the taint of privilege in the formation of their political elite. It was not just that money provided the 'sinews of war' in American politics at least as much as in Britain: what can hardly be ignored is the social influence of the 'old money' in recruiting the men who disproportionately dominated the system. Perhaps aristocracy does not need resonant titles or ivy-clad castles to become an entrenched political reality; in practice the dynastic principle was alive and well on the free soil of North America, nurtured by family connection and upbringing alike.

The Education of Henry Adams, as written by the man himself in 1905, remains an instructive chronicle. Henry Adams had been born in Boston in 1838, the son of Charles Francis Adams, who became American minister in London during the civil war. The boy grew up acutely conscious that he was the grandson of John Quincy Adams, sixth President, and the great-grandson of John Adams, second President. 'The true Bostonian always knelt in self-abasement before the majesty of English standards,' the book observes, with characteristic irony, in the same register as one might say that rules are made to be broken.[1] Young Henry's education, in the formal sense of the term, had a certain inevitability for a 'Boston Brahmin' of his generation. 'The next regular step was Harvard College,' is how he puts it, fastidiously employing the third person throughout his account.[2] And the sense of 'education', in an intangibly pervasive sense, is what the whole book conveys. 'If Harvard College gave nothing else, it gave calm,' Adams explains. 'For four years each student had been obliged to figure daily before dozens of young men who knew each other to the last fibre.'[3] Moreover, they were to go on knowing each other as members of a predestined elite, stamped with the 'self-possession' of Harvard men, especially of those insiders who were members of the Hasty Pudding Club, a venerable undergraduate society of which five American presidents seem to have been members – John Adams and John Quincy Adams, naturally; and later, Theodore Roosevelt, Franklin Roosevelt and John Fitzgerald Kennedy.

Henry Adams, declaring that 'social advantages were his only capital in life', found that he could live off this capital very agreeably.[4] He knew everybody, in the way that members of any aristocracy do in any country, even perhaps in the Great Republic. 'Mr Harrison was an excellent President,' Adams comments later[5] – referring to Benjamin Harrison, who served as twenty-third President, 1889–93. It was his friend Benjamin's grandfather, William Henry Harrison, who had been elected ninth President in 1841 (though he served for only one month before his death from pneumonia).

A commendation of notable warmth is bestowed on John Hay, who was to become Secretary of State from 1898. The young Adams had met the young Hay (then Lincoln's private secretary) in Washington back in 1861, as he indulgently recalled. 'Friends are born, not made, and Henry never mistook a friend except when in power.'[6] Back in Washington in the 1890s, Adams found that his welcome in the Hay household inexorably ushered him into the Republican inner circle. 'In a small society, such ties between houses become political and social force,' he comments. 'Without intention or consciousness, they fix one's status in the world.' He thus moved easily between these nearby houses, 'with Theodore Roosevelt equally at home in them all', almost daily.[7] Little wonder that he later salutes the

Hay–Pauncefote diplomacy for its statesmanship in bringing détente with the British Empire: 'After two hundred years of stupid and greedy blundering, which no argument and no violence affected, the people of England learned their lesson just at the moment when Hay would otherwise have faced a flood of the old anxieties.'[8] Hay was to conclude his tenure at the State Department (he died in office in 1905) under the Presidency of Theodore Roosevelt – the bearer of a family name, just like the names Adams and Harrison, that was to be borne by more than one occupant of the White House.

The imposing house at Hyde Park where Franklin Delano Roosevelt was born and where he had grown up as part of the Hudson River squirearchy. It is not as big as Blenheim Palace, where Winston Churchill was born, more comparable with Chartwell, later Churchill's country home.

Franklin Delano Roosevelt grew up as one of the Roosevelts of Hyde Park, some eighty miles north of Manhattan. He was born there in 1882 in the amply appointed family house overlooking the Hudson River, just north of the town of Poughkeepsie. The Delanos, his mother's family, had prospered in the China trade (though FDR later balked at any mention of opium). He came from what has aptly been called 'unsnubbable stock'. Cousin Theodore was one of the Roosevelts of Oyster Bay on Long Island, and, though only distantly related genealogically, was to show himself persistently helpful in furthering young Franklin's political ambitions. Blood was thicker than party affiliation here, even when TR, the former Republican President from 1901 to 1909, became the presidential opponent of Wilson, of whom FDR was, already by 1911, a prominent supporter through their common progressive commitment. FDR had been elected as a reform Democrat to the New York state assembly, representing his family fiefdom in the district of Poughkeepsie, in the previous year. Already a brilliant campaigner, he had quickly made his mark in fighting the corrupt Tammany Hall machine, notorious for its organisation of the immigrant voters in New York City.

The Roosevelts too had once been immigrants, of course. They were Dutch in origin, with an obvious ancestral partisanship when the South African War broke out in 1899. 'Hurrah for the Boers!' the teenage Franklin wrote home from his boarding school to his parents, who carefully preserved all the early letters.[9] These were to be published by the family after his death in three volumes, which also include diaries with some uncharacteristically revealing entries by a man later famous for keeping his cards close to his chest.

Culturally, the fact is that the Roosevelts were hardly less anglophile than the Adamses in many of their social assumptions. Franklin visited Europe frequently in his youth, always sailing via England, which gave him more familiarity with 'the old country' than he later chose to recall. These trips were undertaken so that his elderly father could enjoy the curative waters at Bad Nauheim. This was medicinal; the family did not really like Germans, though again, when being too anglophile seemed suspicious to American isolationists in the 1930s, it sometimes suited FDR to maintain otherwise.

At the time, Franklin openly welcomed the Anglo-American rapprochement of the Hay–Pauncefote era. 'What a change has come over English opinion in the last few years!' he wrote home to his mother, Sara, from England in 1905.[10] The nature of his entrée to English society can be judged from his first solo visit at the age of twenty-one. He had been invited to stay with the Cholmeleys, friends of his parents, at their country house, Easton, near Grantham, where the baronet owned about 11,000 acres. Franklin was favourably impressed but far from overawed. 'This house is a Dream of Nirvana,' he reported to his mother, '& as the situation much resembles ours I am taking notes & measurements of everything.'[11]

Sara had been widowed in 1900, when Franklin was eighteen. The death of his father at seventy-two brought him even closer to his mother, who was now aged forty-six and was to live for another forty years. She henceforth extended her own formidable influence over the household, not least over her own son, the sole offspring of her husband's second marriage. Though Franklin had a half-brother nearly twenty-eight years older than himself, he was virtually an only child and had been pampered as such. As a small child he was kept in skirts, eccentric even in that era; he had long curls, not cut off until he was well into boyhood; he was not allowed to bathe without Sara until he was eight. Franklin from the first led a life in which useful introductions always eased his path. When he was five Sara had taken him to Washington, where President Cleveland naturally received them at the White House. 'Everyone is so charming to us,' Sara commented. 'Even Franklin knows everybody.'

The wider Roosevelt clan proved equally supportive in that era. In old age, TR's daughter Alice maintained, with implausible but implacable conviction, that the very name Roosevelt was pronounced differently by the rival branches of the family; but her father had not shared any such antipathy. While still in the White House himself, TR blessed Franklin's marriage in 1905. The bride was Eleanor

Roosevelt, the high-minded niece of the President. Virtually everyone at the wedding was called Roosevelt: the difference was only between the Roosevelts of Oyster Bay and the Roosevelts of Hyde Park; and Franklin's much older half-brother had actually been given Roosevelt as a forename as well as his surname, and was thus always known as 'Rosy'. Since her alcoholic father's death in her childhood, Eleanor had been protected by TR in an almost paternal role, and he now took to signing off as 'your affectionate uncle' to FDR too.

The marriage seemed blessed, emotionally and also materially. Franklin had a private income of $5,000 a year; Eleanor had the same; so their joint income would be worth about $300,000 in today's terms. The Roosevelts' four-month honeymoon was financed by Sara. 'We have ordered thousands of dollars worth of clothes,' Franklin reported to her from Brown's Hotel in Mayfair, 'and I am going to send you several cases of champagne, as I know it is needed at Hyde Park.'[12] The expenses of the Hyde Park estate were largely defrayed by Sara, who had inherited a million dollars from her father (say $30 million today). The most obvious difference between FDR and the English aristocrat Churchill, each impeccably well connected in furthering his keen political ambitions, was that the American could lay his hands on more family money.

Many people were surprised by the Roosevelt marriage. They saw Franklin as the flamboyant, outgoing playboy of his college years – at Harvard, where else? – a member of the Hasty Pudding, of course (though faced with a long-resented blackball after nomination for the prestigious Porcellian Club). Franklin was a vibrantly handsome man, usually attracted to young women with more blatant physical charms than the awkward and self-consciously earnest Eleanor. Certainly the match had not been encouraged by Sara Roosevelt, though she now settled for an ongoing role for herself in supervising, on strict lines, the rearing of the six babies whom Eleanor dutifully produced during the years 1906–16. One of them – significantly endowed with the name Franklin Delano Roosevelt, and born in 1909 – lived for only a few months; in 1914 exactly the same name was passed on, like a precious heirloom, to another son. Like his elder brothers James and Elliott, Franklin Delano Roosevelt Junior was literally to support his polio-stricken father in his later political career. There was a strong sense of family here, with an almost dynastic connotation.

Virtually every summer since Franklin's childhood, the Roosevelts had gone in style to the house on the sea that his father had built at Campobello island, New Brunswick, off the Canadian coast. Sara continued this practice; Eleanor too in due course, accompanied by the steadily increasing number of children. But from the time of his appointment as Assistant Secretary of the Navy in 1913, FDR was to be left alone for weeks on end, attending to his duties in the heat of Washington, until he could join Eleanor and the children.

Assistant Secretary in a major department was a fine appointment for a man in his early thirties. The US Navy had become more of a force in recent years, not least through the enthusiasm of TR as President, with his flamboyant notion of a 'great white fleet'. But it was naturally the Secretary of the Navy, Josephus Daniels, who enjoyed frequent contact with the President as a member of his cabinet. Daniels was a former journalist, with pacific if not pacifist views and none of the navalist enthusiasm of a Churchill or a Roosevelt; but Wilson felt a debt towards a loyal supporter who had handled his electoral publicity well. As Assistant Secretary, FDR was in a relatively junior position, remote from Wilson's entourage, and concerned more with implementing policy than with making it. In the summer of 1914, his own views on the European situation differed from those of Daniels, towards whom FDR evinced an air of kindly condescension in his dutiful letters to Eleanor, far away in Campobello.

It was during this summer that Franklin began a relationship that – in a vulnerably clandestine manner – had a duration almost exactly as long as the world war itself, and an aftermath that lasted into the Second World War. Lucy Mercer was a personable young woman of whom everyone spoke well. She came from a formerly eminent Roman Catholic family that had seen better days, and was as seemingly perfect a choice for Eleanor's social secretary as Frances Stevenson had initially seemed for the Lloyd George household. In time Eleanor was to become suspicious of her husband's attentions to this particular member of her own domestic staff; Lucy's transfer to the Navy Department in the summer of 1917 did not help matters; and at the end of the following year there seems to have been a confrontation between husband and wife, which was retailed with malicious glee in the later gossip of the Oyster Bay Roosevelts, notably by TR's daughter Alice ('Princess Alice').

Yet in the end there was to be no open scandal. The affair remained discreet, and Washington insiders as well connected as Jonathan Daniels, son of Josephus, later claimed never to have met Lucy Mercer nor to have heard her name (though it was his straitlaced father who abruptly removed her from official employment in October 1917). A Roosevelt divorce or annulment was indeed avoided, seemingly at the price of allowing Eleanor to lead an almost wholly separate private life from FDR, though with common political commitments still uniting them in the public eye. And Lucy went on to marry a respectable widower after the war; rumours were not publicly aired until after FDR's sudden death in 1945 at Warm Springs (with Lucy present); and stories of an affair were still being dismissed as preposterous by FDR's authorised biographer in the 1950s.

Yet we now know enough to see that Roosevelt was himself sitting on a potential time-bomb during the First World War. He must surely have realised, if only after Lucy Mercer's sudden discharge from her official duties, that his own future prospects were potentially imperilled, and at just the time that his career was taking him into new circles of power. 'I had a very good time with Lloyd George,' he wrote home during an official visit to London in the summer of 1918, adding that 'what impressed me more than anything else was his tremendous vitality'.[13] These two charismatic and ambitious men had a lot in common, perhaps more than they realised; indeed their political careers might be read as a tribute to the creative energies released through marital infidelity.

For in neither case does their own intense commitment to politics, or their focus on waging world war, appear to have suffered any disabling distraction. Roosevelt was one of the first in the Wilson administration to sense the potential significance of the European war for the United States itself. 'To my astonishment on reaching the Dept.,' Franklin had written to Eleanor on Sunday 2 August 1914, 'nobody seemed the least bit excited about the European crisis – Mr Daniels feeling chiefly very sad that his faith in human nature and civilization and similar idealistic nonsense was receiving such a rude shock.' It was obviously not a crisis that immediately threatened the United States itself, but the Assistant Secretary was already fired up and clearly knew where his sympathies lay: 'Rather than long drawn-out struggle I hope England will join in and with France and Russia force peace *at Berlin*!'[14] Within days, the first part of his scenario, at any rate, was realised. 'Thank God England has gone in in earnest,' he wrote on 10 August.[15] And it soon became apparent to his intimates that, much like his bellicose uncle Theodore, he was burning for the United States to get into the war itself. The fact that this was by no means the official line of the Wilson administration obviously inhibited any public affirmation of such views; but it clearly did not suppress these visceral instincts. 'Roosevelts are born and never can be taught,' was how Henry Adams had put it.[16]

The British War Effort:
Churchill, Lloyd George, Keynes

When Britain went to war, Asquith had been acting temporarily as his own Secretary of State for War since March 1914. On 5 August he replaced himself at the War Office in a dramatic new appointment, bringing in Field Marshal Lord Kitchener, once Lieutenant Churchill's commander in the Sudan and now his closest cabinet colleague in waging war by land and sea. It was indeed a great symbolic move. It was Kitchener who punctured any navalist complacency in the cabinet and instead warned it of a war that would put millions in the field, and for years rather than months. It was Kitchener's image, all brass hat and mustachio, that stared out from the posters urging enlistment; and the stream of volunteers staunched cries for conscription from the Conservatives, for the moment at least. This was, at the time, the largest volunteer army raised in any country in recorded history. The numbers in the British armed forces doubled to 800,000 during 1914 and reached nearly 2½ million by the end of 1915. The volunteers from the Empire were a further bonus. What need, then, for any talk of conscription?

Though they kept it to themselves for the moment, Lloyd George and Churchill both privately thought otherwise. Lloyd George's view, as we have seen, was that some obligation for military service would have served Britain well, and Churchill likewise later wrote that 'the counsel of perfection at the outbreak of a life-and-death struggle would have been for Parliament to decree Universal service'.[1] This was not because either of them held the naive view that the problem was simply that of putting enough men into uniform: not if this induced skilled workers to quit vital jobs and become untrained, ill-equipped soldiers with insufficient munitions at their disposal.

In fact, each of them was unusually ready to think the unthinkable about the locomotive of modern war, which each characterised in similar terms. Indeed when Lloyd George came to compose his *War Memoirs*, he echoed some similar phrases in Churchill's published writings: 'Modern warfare, we discovered, was to a far greater extent than ever before a conflict of chemists and manufacturers.'[2] Admittedly, it was in a wartime speech to the Trades Union Congress that Lloyd George had already described the war as 'a conflict between the mechanics of Germany and Austria and the mechanics of Great Britain'.[3]

Lloyd George soon educated himself about the supply chain when it came to producing the tools of modern warfare. He found the Kitchener regime at the War Office over-trustful of the traditional arm's-length methods of procurement, with its attendant delays: 'there was a genuine, though mistaken, under-estimate of the capacity, skill and adaptable engineering ability of the nation at large'.[4] Instead, the momentum of recruitment meant that, within months, all too many skilled workers 'had already fallen in futile battles, owing largely to lack of guns and ammunition they could have helped to provide'.[5] The result was that 'during the first seven or eight months of the War, when enthusiasm for enlistment had been at its height, the most vital industries suffered losses which no subsequent efforts could altogether repair'.[6]

These comments, of course, were written in hindsight. But in his memoirs Lloyd George was also able to quote at length from his advocacy at the time. Thus in February 1915 he had told the cabinet: 'I do not believe Great Britain has ever yet done anything like what she could do in the matter of increasing her war equipment.' He claimed it would be possible to 'double our effective energies if we organised our factories thoroughly'. And the costs of doing so could well be borne by a nation committed to the task: 'The population ought to be prepared to suffer all sorts of deprivation and even hardships whilst this process is going on.'[7] Here is the background to the specific charges that Lloyd George laid against the Kitchener regime in the spring of 1915, alleging a literally fatal lack of sufficient high-explosive shells on the western front, thus exposing British troops to intolerable casualties. This alleged 'shells scandal', once it became public via the newspapers owned by Lord Northcliffe, was one of two reasons for Asquith's decision to reconstruct the government on a coalition basis at the end of May.

The other reason centred on Churchill. As First Lord of the Admiralty, his reiterated claim was that the fleet had been ready when war came – even Kitchener conceded that much. But the reality of war showed that, rather like the nuclear deterrent in a later era, the super-dreadnoughts constituted an armoury too dangerous and too precious to use except in a last resort that never eventuated. The only major setpiece naval engagement was to be that off Jutland in 1916, leaving the British with more casualties on the day but equally leaving the German High Seas Fleet with an aversion to putting to sea again. Thus it sat out the war in harbour, while the Royal Navy, nervous only of being caught napping at its great base at Scapa Flow, patrolled the seas with no direct engagement with the enemy that it had been constructed to confront. The naval deadlock at sea was paralleled by a military stalemate on the continent. The outcome of the battle of the Marne, when the Germans failed to reach Paris in September 1914, meant that the Schlieffen Plan had failed; and, as Churchill later put it, this 'decided almost at its beginning the fate of the war on land, and little else was left but four years of senseless slaughter'.[8]

Could nothing have been done to avert such a fate? Here is the rationale for the Dardanelles expedition and the invasion of Gallipoli. The merits of Churchill's case in handling the operation are best explored later, in the context of the early 1920s, but his central strategic argument needs to be addressed now. At the Admiralty, the First Sea Lord, Lord Louis Battenberg, with a name almost as Teutonic as that of the royal house, had resigned in October 1914; and Churchill's decision to bring back Lord Fisher, now aged seventy-three, introduced a personality quite as strong as his own as his professional counsellor. The fact that Fisher rose early in the morning, when Churchill liked to sleep, and that the old man faded in the evening, when Churchill liked to work on, meant that their shifts became, in Fisher's enthusiastic words, 'very nearly a perpetual clock'.[9] But it obviously did not make for a full meeting of minds, as became apparent when their two clocks did not chime together.

The Dardanelles was widely considered to be Churchill's baby. He boasted of this in early days, so Lloyd George told Frances Stevenson, saying that it was 'entirely his own idea'.[10] And it was indeed a brilliant conception, aimed at exploiting British naval superiority in a new theatre of operations. The Ottoman Empire decided at the end of October 1914 to join the German Empire and the Habsburg Empire in a war that obviously threatened Russia and made control of the waterway from the Mediterranean to the Black Sea into a key concern. On their western shore, the narrow straits at the Dardanelles were guarded by the Gallipoli peninsula; and to the north-east, through the Sea of Marmora, lay Constantinople and the Bosphorus. It was not the only way of developing an eastern strategy – Lloyd George was already toying with ideas for mobilising the Balkans – but it was the one with most appeal to the Admiralty. Fisher's suggestion that old battleships might be deployed, without compromising the British supremacy of dreadnoughts in the North Sea, was seized on by Churchill as an element of his own plan.

On this basis, the War Council that Asquith had set up accepted Churchill's plan in January 1915. Older, and therefore expendable, battleships would form part of a naval flotilla aiming to force the straits, with Constantinople as the objective. Churchill stressed the importance of this psychological impact. If no headway were made, he argued in January 1915, 'we can pretend that it is only a demon-stration', which was 'important from an Oriental point of view'.[11] So far, so bold; or perhaps so ambiguous. Then at some point Fisher got cold feet, and wanted the army involved too, and had to be jollied along by his young master; and, once a decision had been taken in February for boots on the ground, Kitchener's support wavered too. Crucially, a naval exercise to force the Dardanelles with otherwise superfluous naval forces had morphed into a scenario that included landing troops on the Gallipoli peninsula.

By the beginning of March 1915, as the *World Crisis* acknowledges, the Anglo-French naval operations flagged and faltered. Ships were sunk. 'To statesmen or soldiers, ships in time of war possess no sentimental value,' Churchill observes.[12] But the admirals, as he discovered, evidently had a stubborn streak of sentimentality, caus-ing the naval action to be called off, which meant that it was now up to the army, with British and French troops reinforced by those in transit from Australia and New Zealand (ANZAC), who had reached Egypt and were now diverted from their intended destina-tion in France or Flanders. This was also the time when the shell shortage was becoming a key issue. 'But though the available ammu-nition was hopelessly insufficient for a great offensive on the Western Front,' Churchill argues, 'it was enough to sustain adequately the much more limited operation which was impending in Gallipoli.'[13]

On 25 April the troops were landed on the bare unsheltered beaches, with their steep cliffs held by the enemy. All to no avail. By the middle of May, as Churchill acknowledges, the interlock-ing nature of the two crises, over munitions and Gallipoli, meant that 'events were now to supervene in the political sphere which were destined fatally to destroy the hopes of a successful issue at the Dardanelles and preclude all possibility of a speedy termi-nation of the war'.[14] Instead, the speedy termination of his own tenure at the Admiralty was to follow. First, Fisher jumped ship; then Churchill set about replacing him; next, Lloyd George told him that the Conservatives were about to make the shell shortage into a confidence issue and that the dual nature of the crisis made a national government necessary. Asquith had already decided as much, and, when he saw Churchill, posed the question, with its barely concealed subtext: 'What are we to do for you?'[15] It was obvious that Churchill was finished at the Admiralty. He had come to suppose that either Kitchener or himself would be made the scapegoat, but Kitchener's public image still made him indispensable (just as Fisher's protected his reputation, even in retirement).

Gallipoli was a disaster – not in simply stalling one man's meteoric rise but more importantly for the men now stranded on the peninsula. All told, over 400,000 British Empire troops served, 60,000 of them 'Anzacs'; and 80,000 French troops. By the time of the evacuation in January 1916, a total of 46,000 Allied troops had died, including 8,700 Australians and 2,700 New Zealanders, which was not to be forgotten in the Antipodes.

In the formation of a coalition government, Churchill had become the most conspicuous casualty, with the Dardanelles now hung around his neck. He was demoted to a sinecure as Chancellor of the Duchy of Lancaster, sweetened only by his continuing membership of the Dardanelles Committee, which now replaced the War Council. Asquith knew that he could not save Churchill and did not try; he could not even save his friend Haldane, now a declared conscriptionist but still a victim, in the right-wing press, of his longstanding intellectual sympathies for German culture. 'Not all done by rosewater!' Churchill later reflected on Asquith's ruthless coup. 'These were the convulsive struggles of a man of action and of ambition at death-grips with events.'[16] Nor could Lloyd George have saved Churchill, even if he had tried, which he did not, as he made clear to Frances Stevenson, who reflected: 'It seems strange that Churchill should have been in politics all these years, & yet not have won the confidence of a single party in the country, or a single colleague in the Cabinet.'[17]

Churchill was to resign his ministerial post in November 1915. At that point, resuming his previous military career, he went to serve in the trenches himself. He faced life-threatening dangers, as he had known he would. It was not his courage but his judgement that was in question. In linking his criticism of the strategy of the western front with an eastern adventure now branded with failure, Churchill had compromised the whole case put forward by the 'easterners'.

By default, the strategic commitment to the western front was now stronger than ever. Moreover, the advent of a Conservative element in the coalition government strengthened support for conscription as the only means of putting the necessary vast armies into the field. Asquith's partnership with Lloyd George held firm for the moment. Lloyd George was justified in reproducing in his *War Memoirs* a facsimile letter from the Prime Minister, thanking him for his 'incalculable help and support' – it had, claimed Asquith, displayed 'the lightning streak of nobility' that elevated their long partnership.[18] But the centre of gravity in the new government was now shifting, in ways that increasingly divided Asquith's supporters from Lloyd George's, and put the Asquithians on the defensive.

May 1915 was a stressful month for Edwin Montagu. Since February he had been a member of the cabinet. On 25 May the key offices in the coalition government were finally decided: Asquith and Grey to continue as before, likewise Kitchener, but Lloyd George to leave the Treasury (with a reversionary right) in order to start, from scratch, an entirely new Ministry of Munitions. The Conservative leader, Bonar Law (whom Asquith unwisely disparaged), had to be satisfied with the Colonial Office while his predecessor, Arthur Balfour (whom Asquith genuinely esteemed) was readily given the Admiralty. Some other Liberal ministers would clearly have to make way for Conservatives. On 26 May Montagu found that he was luckier than other personal friends of Asquith, like Haldane or Churchill, and had not lost his job as Financial Secretary to the Treasury, though he temporarily relinquished his cabinet rank. He thus continued at the Treasury under the new Chancellor of the Exchequer, Reginald McKenna, a highly partisan supporter of Asquith. It was on 29 May that Montagu travelled to The Wharf, Asquith's country home near Oxford, steeling himself to discuss a matter of keen mutual interest.

Just over two weeks previously Asquith had been told by Venetia Stanley of her engagement to Montagu, a man whose family wealth made him the conventional good match, despite the equally conventional drawback of his Judaism. 'As you know well, *this* breaks my heart,' Asquith responded.[19] He met Venetia for a farewell half-hour on 23 May, amid the Prime Minister's tense negotiations in reconstructing his government. He had a lot on his mind; but, again, no time for rosewater. By the time he agreed to talk to Montagu in the following week, Asquith appeared urbanely resigned to the situation; he had other young confidantes, including Venetia's sister; and civil social relations were to be maintained with Montagu, a man who still had peculiarly easy access to the Liberal elite, Asquithians and Lloyd Georgians alike.

'It was he who got me called to the Treasury in 1915 during the War,' Keynes explained later, referring to his appointment as a junior civil servant in January 1915. 'It was he who got me taken to Paris in February of that year for the first inter-Ally Financial Conference and so established me in my war work. It was he who introduced me to the great ones (I first met Lloyd George in a famous dinner party of 4 at his house; I first met McKenna through him; I first met Margot sitting next to her at dinner in his house).'

All this is borne out by contemporary evidence. Asquith had already told Venetia, back in February, about 'a clever young Cambridge don called Keynes' who was now briefing him on food prices.[20] And soon Margot Asquith was to become the bridge partner of this same 'Treasury man Keynes' – together they won £9 off Montagu and his partner – when Maynard made his own first visit to The Wharf later that year. This sum would be worth at least £500 today, so playing bridge brought financial rewards as well as those social advantages of which Margot briskly advised her new protégé, telling him that he would otherwise have remained unknown. As it was, when he was part of a country house-party along with the Prime Minister, so the story goes, they were announced as 'Mr Keynes and another gentleman'. There was little such interaction between Keynes and Lloyd George, no man for long hours at the bridge table.

Keynes's rise to a position of influence within the Treasury was to come under McKenna, like himself a Liberal who naturally gravitated towards Asquith. In 1915–16 the Treasury was inevitably at the heart of an intense conflict over what sort of war to fight, how to fight it and how to pay for it. In a total war, as Keynes was later to argue from a position of great influence during the Second World War, the whole resources of the nation could and should be mobilised towards a single end. After 1940, he thus helped redefine the problem of how to pay for the war within a command economy that temporarily departed from the norms of peacetime finance. Currency controls became an integral part of this system. But in the First World War, as he saw in retrospect, exchange control 'was so much against the spirit of the age that I doubt if it ever occurred to any of us that it was possible'.[21]

The young man's captivation by the outlook of the Treasury was as much cultural as it was purely financial. He reacted with the sensibility of a connoisseur to his surroundings. He regarded the traditional Treasury ethos with some awe and quickly developed an appreciation of its austere charms. 'Things could only be done in a certain way, and that made a great many things impossible, which was the object aimed at,' he wrote after the war. 'And supported by these various elements, it became an institution which came to possess attributes of institutions like a college or City company, or the Church of England.' Passages like this remind us that, although Keynes's family background was rooted in Nonconformity, he was himself a natural member of the establishment, imbued with ingrained common-room loyalties. Little wonder that Lloyd George, with his totally different Welsh background, felt so little affinity – social, academic, traditional or whatever – for this milieu, and, as Keynes put it, 'had no aesthetic sense for the formalisms, and no feelings for its institutional aspects'.[22] Lloyd George was simply not a man to be put down by what he saw as the condescension of an alien elite. He was quite unabashed when he farted in public.

McKenna upheld the traditional Treasury orthodoxies as established in Gladstone's day. And at the time he had no more ardent supporter than Keynes, who liked to say that he had been 'brought up' on such assumptions in Cambridge. Orthodox economic teaching – what Keynes later termed 'classical economics' – taught that the role of government was to get the financial framework right and then expect the 'real economy' to follow, in making the necessary adjustments. With the right financial disciplines in place, market forces ought to do the trick – if not, so much the worse for those who resisted them.

Thus the role of government was ideally confined to upholding a holy trinity. First it should balance its own budget, whatever the current state of the trade cycle. It should also uphold free trade in all exports and imports, with no protective tariffs or preferential trade deals. Finally, it should maintain the international gold standard, pegging the external value of the currency to gold (which in peacetime meant pegging the pound sterling to the US dollar at $4.86). Free trade and the gold standard were mutually supportive in balancing the books in international trade and transfers. Here was what Bradbury immortally dubbed the 'knave-proof' fiscal constitution, to be maintained through thick and thin. Even in wartime? Yes, so far as Bradbury, and also his colleague. Chalmers, were concerned. One or both of these men served as permanent secretary at the Treasury, either separately or jointly, from 1911 to 1919, thus throughout Keynes's own time there and throughout the war.

What often escaped direct comment in wartime was the role of bank rate. In peacetime, it was the great equilibrator of this system, correcting any drain in the Bank's international gold reserves by raising the rate, thus attracting hot money to London. So long as

Britain had been a creditor country, this mechanism had been almost invisible in its adjustment effects in Britain, since the whole world generally adjusted to British prices. Even in the crisis of August 1914, bank rate had stayed at 10 per cent for only a few days, and then fell back to 5 per cent, at which it remained for the next couple of years (and never exceeded 6 per cent during the war). This may suggest 'business as usual' but in fact Britain's pre-war balance of payments surplus quickly moved into deficit. Yet bank rate remained immobilised in its historic task; and raising it would, of course, have thereby raised the cost of financing war loans.

The Treasury held fast to its established doctrine, and Keynes continued to admire it for doing so. Britain did not formally go off gold until 1919, consistent with his own advice in 1914. The day-to-day rate against the dollar fluctuated, but the Treasury aimed to peg it at $4.76 and thus clung to a sort of shadow gold standard. Behind the shadow was the reality that Britain, the great creditor nation of 1914, was now running up debts, overwhelmingly to the United States. In peacetime Britain had easily financed a current deficit on visible trade with the United States, of around £70 million pre-war; but by 1915 this deficit was £180 million and by 1917 over £300 million. American supplies were vital to sustain the expenditure of blood and treasure on the western front, and Britain was increasingly paying for the war by borrowing in the United States, initially through its agent in New York, J. P. Morgan and Co.

The Treasury priority was understandably to satisfy Wall Street that all the consequent bills could be met on the due dates. McKenna sternly defended this view, which Lloyd George derided at the time and mocks in his *War Memoirs*. His account of the arguments in the autumn of 1915 identifies Keynes along with Bradbury as the authors of 'two dismal papers', circulated to the cabinet. Of the two documents, Lloyd George calls Keynes's 'more alarming and much more jargonish'.[23] Their case, that it was only just possible to struggle on until the end of the financial year, 31 March 1916, had not impressed him as Minister of Munitions; nor was it to do so subsequently as Prime Minister. His *War Memoirs* invoke Churchill's satirical rendering of the Treasury position: 'Put the British Empire at one end of the scale and the 31st of March at the other, and the latter would win every time. That was Mr McKenna's view.' Lloyd George also claims to have known that 'it was part of the campaign that the Treasury were waging against my great gun programme', meaning an unexampled British military commitment on continental Europe. Above all, he claims vindication since 'the hour of indicated doom struck' in 1916 and the British economy survived.[24]

Here was a fundamental crisis, in both British military strategy and financial strategy. Britain's indebtedness in dollars was successively increased by the position of its allies. External finance became Keynes's brief at the Treasury by early 1916, and, in an informal talk that he gave at the Admiralty in March, he could be frank: 'We have one ally, France. The rest, mercenaries.'[25] This was, of course, the traditional 'British way in warfare', as it was later dubbed by the military historian Basil Liddell Hart, with British power exerted through a double-sided strategy: 'by sea-power on the enemy, by financial support to all possible allies'.

All this made for a stark difference with Germany, military and economic alike, in an interdependent way. As Keynes had put it in September 1915: 'If this country could do without substantial imports and if we ceased subsidising allies, our position would be comparable to Germany's.'[26] Such subsidies to various effective allies in continental Europe had thus helped deliver many historic triumphs so long as mercenaries, paid from London, served as an alternative to raising mass armies in Britain.

But this war was to be different. In May, the one real ally, France, found its honourable intentions beyond its means; within a year, Britain was financing all French purchases too, in addition to those of Russia, Belgium, Serbia and (following its belated entry into the war on the Allied side) Italy. Loans were raised on Wall Street: the Anglo-French loan of October 1915 for £250 million; another £250 million in September 1916; then £300 million in two tranches in the next month; and £250 million, also in two tranches, in January 1917. All of these were at either 5 or 5.5 per cent.

Such were the immense new strains put upon 'the rules of the game'. The gold standard set a fixed exchange rate, which the British balance of payments could no longer justify; yet the Bank of England could not support sterling through interest rates for policy reasons, but was nonetheless obliged to honour specie payment by paying out its diminishing gold reserves. In peacetime the gold standard may have given Britain the best of all possible worlds. But clinging to it in wartime intensified the strain of servicing the dollar loans, though facilitating the process of raising them in the first place – so long as Britain's bluff was not called. The real moral was perhaps that the British way in warfare was no longer viable (though an American version of it might well be an option for the United States).

Keynes represented the Treasury at an inter-departmental committee in October 1916. 'Of the £5 million which the Treasury have to find daily for the prosecution of the war, about £2 million has to be found in North America,' he announced. Liquidation of the substantial British assets in the United States was necessary but insufficient, though this also provided collateral for further loans. Keynes's conclusion was stark: 'It is hardly an exaggeration to say that in a few months time the American executive and the American public will be in a position to dictate to this country on matters that affect us more nearly than them.'[27]

These were weeks of crisis for Britain – military, political and financial. Despite the great Somme offensive starting in July 1916 (in which Raymond Asquith, the Prime Minister's eldest son, was killed) there was stalemate on the western front, which made Asquith's regime appear complacent. The wartime public, as Churchill later put it, 'demanded a frenzied energy at the summit; and effort to compel events rather than to adjudicate wisely and deliberately upon them'.[28] Here, from someone who knew both men well, was the contrast between Asquith and Lloyd George, who was now ready to cooperate with the Conservatives in forcing the issue.

THE NEW CONDUCTOR.

OPENING OF THE 1917 OVERTURE.

Churchill later wrote that the war 'demanded a frenzied energy at the summit' – hardly Asquith's style. In December 1916 he was replaced as Prime Minister by Lloyd George, who was to be subsequently vindicated by victory – partly because his hunch about the economic potential of the locomotive of war proved well founded.

As a result, a second coalition was formed under Lloyd George on 6 December.

Later that month there was a run on the currency reserves. In this desperate situation, the Treasury chiefs unblinkingly supported the Bank of England's commitment to specie payment. 'They had been brought up', Keynes later explained, as though admiring officers who dutifully went over the top in the trenches, 'in the doctrine that in a run one must pay out one's gold reserve to the last bean.' Even in 1939, when he wrote this, Keynes added: 'I thought then, and I still think, that in the circumstances they were right.' He recalled Lloyd George's question as the new Prime Minister: 'Well, Chalmers, what is the news?' 'Splendid,' was Chalmers's reply, adroitly putting his own gloss on figures that he airily reported to uncomprehending ministers, while Keynes 'waited nervously in his room, until the old fox came back triumphant'.[29] The bluff worked, not only on the ministers but also on the markets. The next test loomed on 31 March 1917.

Lloyd George wrote later that, whereas the Conservatives had entered the war with 'a note of exhilaration', the Liberals had 'promptly if unhappily followed a course prescribed by the greatest of their leaders in 1870', and only, as he maintained, when the invasion of Belgium was at stake.[30] For most Liberals, just as the great external issue in causing the Great War was Belgium, so the great internal issue in fighting it was conscription. It was not only the Liberal leadership that was divided over this issue but also a much wider constituency of their supporters and ideological bedfellows.

Today we are accustomed to the idea that conscription proved uncontentious in Britain during the Second World War. We know that there was a recognised category of conscientious objectors who were permitted to serve their country in non-military occupations. We are not surprised that in peacetime the principle of conscription was reintroduced into post-war Britain under the name National Service, on which many people still look back with a degree of nostalgia, albeit underpinned by misconceptions about the alleged social utility of the experience for the generation of young men who went through it. But the past is another country; in the moral universe of most British Liberals in 1914, they did things differently, working from different kinds of assumptions.

Keynes was one among many for whom conscription posed a fundamental issue, irreducibly defined in moral terms. The political pressure to introduce it had been mounting throughout 1915, fuelled by the frustrations of the deadlock on the western front, with demands for more soldiers for the next big push. Voluntary attestation of willingness to serve ('the Derby scheme') had been the last chance for persuasion to produce the right numbers; and, in any event, the Treasury still insisted that the economy could not stand the strain of recruiting and supporting a bigger army. As so often before, Asquith had played a waiting game; he hoped that he had yet again chosen the right moment to act when it became clear that the Derby scheme had failed to meet its targets at the end of 1915.

Asquith now proposed a carefully crafted conscription measure, as desired by most of his Conservative ministers and also by the increasingly impatient Lloyd George. Four cabinet ministers offered their resignations, all of them firm Asquithians. They included not only Sir John Simon, who had almost quit on 3 August 1914, but also Grey and McKenna too, whom Asquith was fiercely determined not to lose. This time it was Simon alone who stuck to his resolve and resigned. The legislation passed the House of Commons in January 1916, opposed by most of the Irish Nationalist party along with a few dozen Liberal and Labour MPs, thus fragmenting the majority that had long sustained the Asquith government in both peace and war. For the moment, however, it seemed that Asquith himself had yet again ridden out the storm, though with open disaffection among many Liberals in the country.

Bloomsbury was not only the district of London where Keynes now lived: it was also the designation for his neighbours in the coterie of writers and artists who were his closest friends. Many of the males had previous Cambridge affiliation as Apostles. Lytton Strachey was quintessentially Bloomsbury; Bertrand Russell, though an Apostle, was not; but both now urged Keynes to resign from the Treasury; and both were strongly opposed to the war itself as well as to compulsory military service. Russell was to lose his lectureship at Trinity College, Cambridge, as a result. Strachey maintained his refusal to aid the war effort by flamboyantly asserting his position as a conscientious objector, which was an option that Liberals had managed to insert into the legislation. This covered secular as well as traditional religious objections, such as Quakers (like John Bright) had long maintained.

Keynes's position was distinctive in several ways. Plainly he was not a pacifist, unable to accept any war at any price; at school during the Boer War, he had been attracted to the cadet corps (though he did not join in the end) and neither he nor his parents were pro-Boers. Nor did he think it wrong for Britain to have got into this particular war. In an anonymous article published in early 1916, he revealed his own attitude towards advocates of an early peace. Their argument depended, he maintained, on showing that a deadlock was recognised on both sides; and also on showing 'that an early peace is likely to be durable', by which he meant that Germany would not simply exploit any such armistice to prepare for future retaliation. 'Pacifists must show that a different result is probable now, and unless they can do that, the most convincing demonstrations of a "deadlock" are in vain.'[31] So an assessment of relative probabilities was invoked, perhaps not surprisingly by a scholar whose own *Treatise on Probability* (1921) was still a work in progress, held over for the duration of hostilities.

'Had the will for peace in Germany been wholehearted and strong and really widespread, it would not have been so easy to bamboozle the people in August 1914,' Keynes argued, adding: 'It was necessary to bamboozle them as it was.'[32] So much for the history that had already happened; but, looking ahead, in the spirit of Lincoln, it seemed improbable to him that, even in Germany, all the people could be fooled all the time. Keynes was, of course, still at the Treasury when he wrote this; he had not resigned over the Military Service Act; he had his own qualms about the methods by which the war was now being waged; but this was not a sufficient reason for him to refuse to do his job in financing these operations. And since his vital work at the Treasury gave him exemption from conscription under the new Act, it did not require him to do anything about his own status.

Yet at the end of February 1916, three days before the deadline, he had registered his official objection to serving. 'I claim complete exemption because I have a conscientious objection to surrendering my liberty of judgement on so vital a question as undertaking military service,' he wrote, adding the significant clarification: 'I do not say that there are not conceivable circumstances in which I should voluntarily offer myself for military service.' Simon, on resigning from the cabinet because he thought conscription wrong, had voluntarily joined the Royal Flying Corps, as a good liberal following his own conscience. Likewise for Keynes, it was back to the principle of his longstanding argument against Moore: 'I am not prepared on such an issue as this to surrender my right of decision, as to what is or is not my duty, to any other person, and I should think it morally wrong to do so.'[33]

The only puzzle is why Keynes should have felt it necessary to make out this case at this moment. After all, the Military Service Tribunal, to which it was addressed, could see perfectly well that this tiresome Mr Keynes already had exemption because of his vital work at the Treasury. The tribunals were busy enough already, overloaded with appeals that were overwhelmingly on domestic grounds from married men or from workers in essential industries, with probably less than 2 per cent on conscientious grounds. Maybe Keynes had still been thinking of resignation when he applied.

Certainly he showed little interest in the formal outcome of his application. Pleading that he was too busy at the Treasury, in March 1916 he did not even turn up to hear his own case, which was naturally dismissed on the grounds that he had exemption already. The symbolic nature of his affirmation was surely his main motivation, reaffirming his own early beliefs by still claiming 'the right to judge every individual case on its merits'. And there is equally little difficulty in understanding his reasoning here, once one has got past the paradox of an 'immoralist' argument for a moral decision, on an overriding moral issue.

The upshot was that the Treasury renewed Keynes's exemption in August 1916, for the duration of the war. And though McKenna was to face political exile in December 1916 along with Asquith, Keynes stayed at the Treasury, as gloomy as ever in his forecasts. On 31 March 1917, the hour of doom duly struck again, and Britain again survived.

To this extent, Lloyd George was vindicated by events, as he did not let anyone forget. Moreover, there is an historical irony here. For he had been proved right in supposing that Britain could survive all the strains imposed on it in 1915–17, because (as a later generation of Keynesians would have explained) the full capacity of the economy had been crucially underestimated by the Treasury mandarins – and none more guilty in this respect than the young Keynes himself. It was Keynes who had provided an exhaustive analysis, supposedly proving that no men could be 'spared' for conscription because there was no 'margin', in the process minimising the potential of any resources currently unemployed.[34]

This 'Treasury view' had supposed too readily and dogmatically that the limits on domestic production had been reached, without realising that the cumulative force of expansion itself created further resources by taking up the slack in the economy. The best estimates we now have of GDP, with 1913 as the baseline, show a small increase of about 2 per cent in 1914; and then from 1915 to 1917, sustained levels around 10 per cent higher than pre-war, and higher still in 1918. Clearly the raising of great conscript armies, diverting men out of productive employment, still allowed the economy to expand, despite all the forecasts.

The fact that the 'real economy' had grown under a wartime expansion of effective demand, albeit with some leakage into inflation, would today seem unsurprising to any economist who applies a Keynesian perspective. But to Maynard Keynes himself financial survival seemed like sheer, uncovenanted good luck, a view inevitably coloured by the Treasury spectacles through which he had looked at such issues. It is true that raising bank rate was no easy option; true that American imports could not all have been substituted by increased British production; true that currency controls might have been necessary. So Keynes continued to think that his own caution had been justified at the time, in assessing future probabilities on the basis of the available knowledge, in line with his own preferred methodology. He could point out that the second hour of doom was averted only with the aid of a German U-boat campaign that brought the United States into the war – 'we dragged along with a week or two's cash in hand until March 1917 when the U.S.A. came in and that problem was over'.[35]

Over? Not quite, not yet, not as it seemed at the time. On 2 April 1917, while the United States Congress was still debating whether to enter the war, Bonar Law (who was now Chancellor of the Exchequer) reported to the cabinet that the gold reserves would last about three weeks; after which the British assumption was that the Americans would thenceforth finance the war. Any such assumption was anathema to the US Treasury, to whom Law had to explain himself in July; and he did so in a Note drafted by Keynes. This cited statistics to show that Britain's support of the Allies was still running at a level '*more than double* the assistance afforded them by the United States, and that the assistance the United Kingdom has afforded these other allies much exceeds the assistance she has herself received from the United States'.[36] Moreover, the portfolio of British investments in the United States – now much exaggerated in American eyes – was hardly an adequate source of the money needed.

As with many British Liberals, Keynes's hopes came to be pinned upon the intervention of the Americans under their inspiring leader, President Wilson. Yet, in line with Keynes's own warnings, the flexing of American power brought a new phase of problems, not least because dollar loans were soon to be made from government to government. In the *Economic Consequences of the Peace* he was to summarise the final position over war debts, with statistics that may not be exact but remain indicative of orders of magnitude. Thus Britain owed £842 million to the United States (the only British debt) but was owed £508 million by France, £467 million by Italy, £568 million by Russia, £98 million by Belgium and £20 million by Serbia and what became Yugoslavia (plus £79 million elsewhere).[37] The total owing to Britain on account of its wartime sustenance of these 'mercenaries' was thus £1,740 million, a sum that comfortably exceeded its debt to the Americans – on paper at least.

Maynard himself had reflected to Florence Keynes at the end of 1917 that the war 'probably means the disappearance of the social order we have known hitherto' and professed himself not altogether sorry. 'The abolition of the rich will be rather a comfort and serve them right anyway,' he mused. 'What frightens me more is the prospect of *general* impoverishment. In another year we shall have forfeited the claim we had staked out in the New World and in exchange this country will be mortgaged to America.' This was indeed salient among the economic consequences of the war; it was a perverse consequence of Keynes's own aptitude in running up these debts in the United States; and it was thus an unwitting consequence of the Treasury orthodoxy that he still espoused.

The American Way in Warfare: Wilson and House

Everyone agreed that Colonel House's appearance was remarkable only for its apparent insignificance. Of course the man was not really a colonel – this was just a courtesy title bestowed on Edward Mandell House in his native Texas, though he was to find that, when he later hobnobbed with the German high command, they took his rank at face value and talked shop to him in military language. One way or another, it was as Colonel House that he became an historical figure. Equally inescapably, this public identity from first to last depended on his uniquely close relationship with President Wilson.

Though it was to end forlornly, their friendship had a fairytale beginning in November 1911, when Wilson was no more than Governor of New Jersey and a presidential aspirant. House had immediately sensed a man of destiny whose ambitions he could serve. Wilson warmed magically to this unassuming Texas wire-puller, soon telling him: 'My dear friend, we have known one another always.' Or so House recorded the remark a few years later in compiling his reminiscences, but it is perfectly consistent with the tone of other exchanges between them. House fully realised at the time that he was helping to make history; he wanted history to judge him fairly; he knew that historians are prisoners of the documents available to them; he made sure that his own documentary trail was replete not only with his correspondence but with his own memoranda, his own memoirs and, above all, his own meticulously kept diary, as dictated to a faithful secretary.

It was House, then, who became Wilson's uniquely trusted 'silent partner' and his authorised emissary. A well-heeled amateur in high politics – his millionaire father had left an estate including 250,000 acres in Texas – Edward House had thrown up his own university education at Cornell and settled for a role in the backroom of several political campaigns in his native state, at that time largely Democrat. But he could not stand the heat (literally); he preferred Massachusetts; and he turned down Wilson's offer of a cabinet post in sultry Washington, DC, instead paying flying visits to the White House from either New York or New England – not forgetting his annual visits to old England which had also become a regular routine. So he already knew British politics unusually well, and he thoroughly approved of the social legislation of the Liberal government. Just after his first meeting with Wilson, one of House's friends commented: 'I think the first thing he would do would be to import Lloyd-George and make him Wilson's Prime Minister.' Failing this, House lent strong support, as a White House insider, to the new President as he pursued his progressive agenda. But it was House's expertise in European affairs that Wilson valued most highly.

In the summer of 1914 the Colonel again took the transatlantic liner, but this time not seeking personal recreation so much as international reconciliation. Perhaps naively, he thought that a friendly visit to Britain and to Germany by a known confidant of the American President might do the trick. House was determined to operate independently of the State Department, where William Jennings Bryan was now installed as Secretary of State; though the anglophile ambassador to London, Walter Hines Page, Wilson's old friend from his days in Georgia, was at this point on highly amicable terms with the Colonel. 'I gave it as my opinion', House reported to Wilson after a lunch with Sir Edward Grey, 'that international matters could be worked out to advantage in much the same way as individuals would and I thought that most of the misunderstandings were brought about by false reports and mischief-makers and if the principals knew of the facts, what appeared to be a difficult situation became easy of solution.'[1] This was written on 26 June, with the Archduke Franz Ferdinand already en route to Sarajevo.

Like Page, House was favourably impressed by Grey, who in turn expressed his warm admiration for what Wilson 'had done for international morals'. Wilson's decision, implemented earlier that month, to honour the terms of the Hay–Pauncefote Treaty over international equality of tolls on the newly opened Panama Canal – despite inconveniently abolishing the preferential terms initially allowed for American ships – was undoubtedly better received in London than in Washington. Its significance was far more than a commercial concession to British interests: it was simultaneously an affirmation of the principles of international law and of free trade. As Wilson now put it in his Fourth of July address: 'And so I say that it is patriotic sometimes to prefer the honor of the country to its material interest.' He adopted a true Gladstonian tenor here on the universality of moral commitments: 'When I have made a promise as a man, I try to keep it, and I know of no other rule permissible to a nation.'[2] Little wonder that the British Liberals who met House, notably Asquith and Grey, liked what they heard. 'Of course I needn't tell you that they are all charmed with House,' Page assured the President.[3]

House sailed for home on 21 July, arriving in Boston eight days later, by which time Austria and Serbia were already exchanging fire. 'For the moment, I do not see what can be done,' he wrote to the President, 'but if war comes, it will be swift and terrible and there may be a time soon when your services will be gladly accepted.'[4] Both of these assumptions were to be proved wrong, of course. Wilson, now increasingly distracted by a mysteriously nagging illness that afflicted his wife Ellen, replied from the White House on 3 August. He commiserated with the way that unfolding events in Europe had dashed his friend's hopes, then added: 'but we must face the situation in the confidence that Providence has deeper plans than we could possibly have laid ourselves'.[5]

When we look at the first year of hostilities from the viewpoint of the United States, there are two key moments when some clear response from the White House might have been expected. The first is obviously the inception of a world war with Britain's intervention on 4 August 1914 over the German violation of Belgian neutrality; and the second – at least as dramatic for Americans – is the sinking of the British passenger liner *Lusitania* by a German U-boat on 7 May 1915, with 128 Americans among the 1,198 lives lost. Here, one might suppose, a man of Wilson's background, historical knowledge, moral compass and inspirational eloquence might have been expected to sound the tocsin for his fellow Americans. On each occasion, however, his immediate reaction seemed muddled and uncertain. It may be a significant pointer that he tended to make overt references to providence (like that in his letter to House) only at moments of personal stress, virtually throwing up his hands in the face of problems that he currently had no wish to confront.

Woodrow and Ellen Wilson had been married for nearly thirty years. All the evidence is that the marriage was close and supportive and, though Woodrow had apparently written some indiscreet letters to at least one female admirer, he was deeply committed to Ellen, whose advice he valued in general, and whose good opinion of Edward House had eased the Colonel's entrée to the Wilson inner circle. The only political figure as close to the family was William McAdoo, the forceful Treasury Secretary, recently married to Eleanor, the youngest of the three Wilson daughters; and McAdoo's ambivalent position as son-in-law, loyal cabinet minister and possible presidential successor was less easy to manage than House's role as court favourite. As such, House had the President's full confidence, whereas Bryan as Secretary of State did not and was to be increasingly cut out of the top-level contacts that were established with the British government.

It was to House that Wilson confided all his hopes and fears – especially the latter in August 1914. Ellen had finally been diagnosed with a kidney disease which, by the time of House's return to the

United States, had become life-threatening. 'Mrs Wilson's condition is giving me a great deal of anxiety, but we are still hoping and the doctors are doing noble work,' Wilson wrote to House on 6 August; but by that evening she was dead.[6] For ten days the President remained incommunicado before he felt able to 'get my head above the flood that came upon me' and was 'at last able to speak with some degree of composure about the unspeakable loss I have suffered', as he confided to House in thanking him for his support – 'May God show me the way!'[7]

It is in this context that we can better understand not only what Wilson now said about the European situation but what he did not say. Of course, nobody expected the United States to participate in the war itself, which represented exactly the sort of foreign entanglement that the Great Republic had traditionally forsworn. Under Bryan, the most that could be expected of the State Department was pious hand-wringing (of the kind scorned by FDR). Still, the Belgian minister to the United States thought it worth asking at the end of August for some reaction to what was happening to his country: 'Such a crime as this concerns the whole world.'[8] When House and Wilson finally met again a few days later, in a vacation setting that permitted relaxed discussion, there was no dissent from this perspective on the Belgian situation, with the destruction of Louvain now the focus of concern. House recorded that 'I found him as unsympathetic with the German attitude as is the balance of America. He goes even further than I in his condemnation of Germany's part in this war, and almost allows his feeling to include the German people as a whole rather than the leaders alone.'[9]

No such opinions leaked into presidential pronouncements. Naturally, when Wilson received an official Belgian delegation, he opened by assuring them: 'You are not mistaken in believing that the people of this country love justice, seek the true paths of progress, and have a passionate regard for the rights of humanity.' Then he told them: 'You will, I am sure, not expect me to say more.'[10] Maybe this was only proper in view of the need to establish the facts in a scrupulous fashion, without precipitate haste; after all, in December 1914 the British government thought it right to appoint an official inquiry into alleged atrocities, under the chairmanship of Lord Bryce, formerly British ambassador to the United States and a respected academic colleague of Professor Woodrow Wilson – and still his friend. Meanwhile the White House resisted any attempts to involve it in the Belgian issue, even in relief appeals; and the view in the State Department was even stricter in displaying ostentatious neutrality.

The President had laid down the official policy in August. It was his first public statement since his wife's death and was phrased in formidably exacting terms: 'We must be impartial in thought as well as in action, must put a curb upon our sentiments as well as upon every transaction that might be construed as a preference of one party to the struggle before another.'[11] There was clearly some tension between this standard and how he and Colonel House might talk in private.

They thus differed from the Secretary of State. To Bryan, with his overt populist distaste for these atavistic Europeans, the obvious course was to keep clear of their quarrels in every way – not to offer any provocations and not to engage with disputes that were simply no business of the United States. 'My dear Mr President,' he wrote in January 1915, after one of his rare visits to the White House: 'Another matter I had intended to speak to you about this morning was the statement explaining why we have taken no action on the invasion of Belgium by Germany.' The legal counsellor at the State Department, Robert Lansing, was keen on this idea at the time, but his draft left Wilson perplexed. 'This note is entirely sound and conclusive from the lawyer's point of view,' he explained to Bryan, 'but I fear it will make the impression of a technical defense against the charge that we have not performed a duty suggested by moral considerations and the general sense of thoughtful men throughout the world.'[12]

Like Gladstone, Wilson knew that there was more than diplomacy at stake; like Gladstone, he knew that there was a time for action but also a time for silence; and, like Gladstone, he prided himself on his own sense of timing. This was the same man who had written, in his bereavement in August 1914, to Sir Edward Grey: 'I feel that we are bound together by common principle and common purpose.'[13] As President, he now insisted that nothing be said to explain why the United States saw no such common principle at stake in making any response to the Belgian predicament.

Yet the treatment of this small nation was by no means forgotten and was to trigger highly significant repercussions later. What Wilson and House keenly appreciated in private was that Belgium was the crux of the issue for their friend Grey and the British Liberals, and hence would inevitably bulk large in any talk of possible peace terms. They certainly did not need the lecture that the more outspoken Page, as ambassador in London, addressed to Bryan. 'The war has already revealed two great facts,' Page wrote in September, 'first that all Europe has been living on the brink of a precipice and second that Germany has done a grievous and irreparable wrong to Belgium.' And this reading of the war made for an equally irresistible reading of the only sort of peace proposals that would justly satisfy the British government: 'Any terms that England will agree to must provide for an end of militarism forever and for reparation to ruined Belgium.'[14]

Where did such ideas come from? Page candidly acknowledged his source as 'Grey's wholly private talk to me not to be quoted to anybody nor made public'. And here, only one month into the war, we find an expression that is pregnant with implications for the future. If we look up the term 'reparations' in the *Oxford English Dictionary*, we are quickly led to its usage in the Treaty of Versailles, in a sense that has become standard. Yet the ancient sense of 'reparation' simply as a synonym for 'repair' – 'reparation nail' was one specific variant – could be extended to 'making amends'. Dr Johnson's *Dictionary* (1755) quotes Dryden: 'I am sensible of the scandal I have given by my loose writings, and make what reparation I am able.' He did not mean financially. The word is obviously Latin in origin, so it is not surprising to find that *Le Grand Robert de la Langue Française* gives much the same usage in French, and with the plural *réparations* specifically tied to the 1919 sense.

Whatever its exact provenance, the usage influentially revived by Grey quickly became a term of art. It had the inestimable virtue of avoiding the invidious overtones of 'indemnity', which may have been functionally equivalent, but (as the dictionary again tells us) was a usage associated with what the Germans had imposed on France in 1871. Indemnity had become an historically tainted term; reparations were freshly minted, almost as soon as the lamps had gone out all over Europe.

Notwithstanding, when House shortly chimed in with much the same line of thinking, it was in his own slightly modified language. He told Wilson that 'an agreement for general disarmament and an indemnity for Belgium' would content the British.[15] A couple of days later, the British ambassador, Sir Cecil Spring-Rice, was amplifying the Foreign Secretary's message, that 'a cruel wrong has been done to Belgium' and that the question was: 'Is Germany prepared to make reparation for these acts?'[16] House again translated the signals for the President: 'The surmise that all England wants is a permanent guaranty of peace, by disarmament and other effective measures, and a proper indemnity for Belgium, is quite right.'[17]

Indeed these became the terms for the peace mission that Wilson was to propose. He broached the idea to House in early December, as a finesse upon Bryan's plea for the US President to offer his good offices as mediator. The twist was that House would actually go to Europe, in full knowledge of what the British would accept, and seek the approval of the Kaiser for these essentially similar conditions: 'One being the indemnity of Belgium, and the other such a reduction of armaments as would insure lasting peace in Europe.'

The Germans would understand what 'indemnity' meant, so they did not need education about the difference between that and the concept of 'reparation'. House thus had his brief – and also recorded the word of caution that he had been given about his own role: 'Going back to Mr Bryan, the President said that he, Mr Bryan, did not know that he, The President, was working for peace wholly through me, and he was afraid to mention this fact to him for fear it would offend him.' Should Bryan be told? 'I advised not telling him for the moment,' House noted, with his normal penchant for using the back stairs. Another bit of cautionary advice was to be given to Page, who was upsetting the State Department with his overt pro-British despatches.[18]

By the beginning of 1915, the Wilson administration had thus found an indirect means of atoning for what the British saw as its strange blindness about Belgium in August 1914. What was now continually repeated in covert messages between Grey in London and Spring-Rice in Washington, and between Colonel House and the White House, was that the core of any peace terms would comprise disarmament plus a form of German financial atonement for the crime committed against Belgium. When Page's legal adviser at the US Embassy in London visited Washington in January 1915, he was made the bearer of an important message from Grey, to be conveyed discreetly to the President. The gist was 'that the time had not yet come for peace overtures or even the discussion of possible terms of peace', but that Wilson should know that, when the time came, the Allies would insist upon certain essential points. 'At the head of the list was reparation for Belgium so far as reparation was possible, and how that could be accomplished was a question which had not yet been worked out.'[19] This was an oral message, and never was a truer word spoken.

Unlike Belgium, a subject which it was often not politic to mention in Washington, there was always a lot to be said about the sinking of the

Lusitania. The shock of this news in May 1915 made it a memorable moment, like the deaths of FDR or JFK later, for a whole generation of Americans. It was left to their President to translate emotion into policy. In the *World Crisis*, Churchill offered his measured judgement that during the world war Wilson 'played a part in the fate of nations incomparably more direct and personal than any other man'.[20] This ranking, made by the deferential colleague of Lloyd George and the warm admirer of Georges Clemenceau, remains impressive – more so than the author's criticism that Wilson simply missed a golden opportunity to bring the United States into the war. 'What he did in April, 1917, could have been done in May, 1915.'[21]

Could it? Aficionados of the myth of the English-speaking peoples have always thought so. Theodore Roosevelt privately maintained at the time that this would have been a good thing. Conversely, among Americans suspicious of the political influence of too many patrician WASPs like Roosevelt and his accomplice Henry Cabot Lodge, it has often been tempting to depict the United States' ultimate rally to the British side as regrettable but culturally foreordained.

It is undeniable that some influential Britons hoped that this would be the case. In 1913 Sir Cecil Spring-Rice, though now physically ailing, achieved his ambition to serve as British ambassador in Washington, a city that he already knew well as an erstwhile friend of John Hay and Henry Adams, of TR and Cabot Lodge, the cream of (mainly Republican) society. 'The feeling of nearly everyone with whom I speak is very friendly,' Spring-Rice reported to Grey in September 1914, 'but then the friends I have here are those who would naturally be friendly.' As to the (Democratic) President, the good news was that when the ambassador started reciting Wordsworth – 'We must be free or die, who speak the tongue / That Shakespeare spake' – it was Wilson himself who had all the words by heart and spoke feelingly of their import. 'You and Grey are fed on the same food and I think you understand,' responded the ambassador (and duly reported it all to the Foreign Office).[22]

In such a perspective, it is all too easy to suppose that Wilson's course was plotted by the compass of anglophilia, tempered only by the need to negotiate awkward electoral squalls. Yet there is a sense in which his own Gladstonian ambitions made Wilson increasingly critical of the British government, whenever it seemed to him to fall short on sensitive issues. He felt himself a much misunderstood man, all the more keenly relishing the sympathy of those who intuitively appreciated his real outlook. In that event, he could quickly reciprocate, as he had with House, in giving the Colonel the authority to speak for him as a uniquely favoured roving ambassador – and one who Wilson hoped would discover like-minded sympathisers overseas.

By January 1915 it had been agreed that House would travel to Europe with his subtle scheme for mediation. Before sailing on the *Lusitania*, the pride of the Cunard fleet, he made the journey from New York to Washington for a final confidential briefing (behind the backs of the State Department) on all the complex issues that arose. 'After dinner the President read from A. G. Gardiner's sketches of prominent men,' noted House, who already knew from a previous visit of Wilson's interest in the Liberal editor's biographical essays. 'I was surprised that he preferred to do this rather than discuss the matters of importance we had between us,' House commented in his diary.[23]

This may well have seemed surprising; but it was neither slighting towards House nor a sudden whim. We know that Wilson had recently begun such readings from Gardiner, as a highly literate British Liberal who had an unusually keen appreciation of American politics. Gardiner's sympathetic essay on Bryan in *Prophets, Priests and Kings* (1908) seized on the moral dimension that the Great Commoner projected, making an invidious contrast with current British politicians: 'Oratory fell to earth when Gladstone and Bright ceased to wing it with spiritual passion.' We know that Wilson read this; also the essay on Morley in the same volume.

Moreover, Gardiner had now published a successor volume, *Pillars of Society* (1913). This included a profile of the new President of the United States, in whom it found an eager reader. On the subject of TR, his rival, Wilson would hardly have been displeased by Gardiner's comment: 'Mr Roosevelt clothes the poverty of his thought and the vagueness of his purposes in a tumultuous whirl of words.' Wilson himself, by contrast, was hailed as more than an orator: 'He is that rare combination, a thinker who loves action, a scholar and a man of affairs, one who reads Greek and writes short-hand, who combines a luminous idealism with the practicality of a plumber and a sunny smile with ruthless purpose.' Such were the texts, fashioned from old articles in the London *Daily News*, that Wilson, now bereaved and lonely, liked to read out loud to his close circle of companions after an early dinner.

Having been given at least three doses of this particular tonic at the White House, House set off on the *Lusitania*, accompanied only by his wife and secretary. On his safe arrival in London in early February 1915, it is no surprise to find that he soon dined with 'our friend A. G. Gardiner', and was afterwards able to assure Wilson: 'I think now he will be able to write of you in a way that will be help-ful.'[24] The point is surely rather more than the purposeful cultivation of a receptive foreign journalist: it is that Wilson and House and Gardiner all shared a similar liberal and internationalist perspective and thus 'spoke the same language' in a rather deeper sense than shallow rhetoric about 'the English-speaking peoples'.

Under the stresses of wartime, relations between these peoples certainly needed constant attention. It was not because of personal friction at the top. 'Sir Edward Grey', House now assured the President, 'looks upon the situation as fairly and dispassionately as we, but he cannot act alone.'[25] It was not just that France and Russia were unprepared to back down. There was also pressure for one kind of territorial claim against Germany – contrary to Grey's general principle – over which he was now 'in conflict with Colonial opinion', so House explained to Wilson, because South Africa and Australia had no intention of relinquishing their own annexation of German colonies.[26] Such were the complexities of a world war in which the Dominions had their own views, their own voices – and some of their own troops currently headed for the Dardanelles. In any case, Germany was not remotely ready to entertain the idea of Belgian reparations, which was Grey's bottom line; and in the end House had to concede that no peace terms were at present viable. Page was more strident in making the same point in language that showed the incompatibility of the views of the US ambassador with those of the State Department, of which he was nominally a servant.

What Grey persistently impressed upon House was that, whereas Germany had a natural advantage in waging war on land, Britain's comparative advantage was at sea. So it was necessary and natural for Britain to exploit this through a policy of blockade, which – since modern technology rendered obsolete the traditional kind of close blockade of particular ports – had to be made effective by declaring an exclusion zone over the sea routes to Germany, enforced through the supremacy of the Royal Navy. But it surely followed that the Germans' preferred counter-measure was not to deploy their precious High Seas Fleet to challenge this supremacy; it was to use the U-boat, in which their own technology was superior.

So each side was naturally playing to its own strengths, in a game where the law of the sea had not caught up with the technologies of twentieth-century warfare. New guidelines had to be improvised, incident by incident. A further twist was that, in the American civil war, Britain had been all in favour of neutral rights, whereas the Union government in the North had been all for blockading the South; so many of the precedents asserted on each side sounded paradoxical (or hypocritical). In any case, the Declaration of London (1911), which was supposed to govern these matters, had not been ratified by the respective governments, which invalidated its authority in British but not in American eyes. The practical issue in March 1915 was that the United States reluctantly accepted a restriction of safe passage under Royal Navy protection on the vital sea routes that gave access to the Atlantic. This obviously abridged 'the freedom of the seas', which became a high-sounding slogan that the Germans now deployed, exciting British suspicion whenever it was mentioned. But the freedom for civilians – notably American civilians – to sail in safety was also subject to the German threat of a U-boat blockade of Britain, to be enforced in ways that remained disputable.

It was against this background that the sinking of the *Lusitania* took place on 7 May – a matter of keen personal concern to House, of course. On 9 May, he cabled in a private code to the White House: 'Think we can no longer remain neutral spectators. Our action in this crisis will determine the part we will play when peace is made, and how far we may influence the settlement for the lasting good of humanity.'[27] On the following day, the President spoke in Philadelphia, extemporising from his own notes as usual, to an audience of 15,000, including 4,000 newly naturalised citizens. 'You have taken an oath of allegiance to a great ideal, to a great body of principles, to a great hope of the human race,' he told them. He adopted an elevated view, earnestly advising them 'not only always to think first of America, but always, also, to think first of humanity'. But this was no call to arms. 'The example of America must be a special example,' he enjoined; but it was an example displayed through a commitment to peace rather than war. Hence the great rhetorical flourish, appealing to the crowd's emotions: 'There is such a thing as a man being too proud to fight. There is such a thing as a nation being so right that it does not need to convince others by force that it is right.'[28] When the speech was later edited for publication in a proposed (but aborted) book, Wilson deleted the first of these two sentences.

Perhaps his own emotions at this point had been running unduly high, clouding his judgement on the proper response from a president. The fact was that Wilson had fallen in love: suddenly swept off his feet by Edith Bolling Galt, a vivacious and wealthy widow in her forties, whom a cousin had introduced into the White House circle during House's absence. Day after day in early May, Wilson was now writing her frequent, lengthy, extravagant, passionate letters. On the day that the *Lusitania* was sunk, he implored her: 'all that you have a right to decide, if you are going to be fair to me is, *can you love me for my own sake and do you want me for your life's joy?*'[29] The next day, as the news broke: 'Prudence is an impertinent intruder *this week*, and Wisdom intolerable!'[30] On the day of his great public speech – 'I know I am going to see you and am all aquiver with the thought' – he seemed unsure whether he was in Philadelphia or New York, and it was in this disorientated condition that his words tumbled out that evening.[31]

They were not well chosen, as he soon had cause to realise. His disclaimer, that he had not had the *Lusitania* in mind and was not declaring American policy, simply reinforced an impression of vacillation. In reaction, on 11 May he drafted a strong Note, warning Germany of consequences and demanding some 'reparation'; next he sought to appease Bryan by an off-the-record press briefing that a peaceful resolution of the matter was nonetheless in view; but the tone was subsequently stiffened again in a second draft Note to Germany – which Bryan refused to sign, and instead resigned at the beginning of June 1915.

House had not yet docked on his return from Europe and he craved a spell of quiet recuperation on Long Island. Instead he received a flying visit on 24 June from the President, who came to deliver a personal briefing on these important developments. 'Colonel House has been Secretary of State, not I, and I have never had your full confidence,' Bryan had apparently told the President, which was more or less true. Accordingly, the choice of a successor who would not prove 'troublesome' was now discussed between Wilson and House, and here the more compliant figure of Robert Lansing seemed to fit the bill. But there was clearly more on the President's mind, as House's diary records with some coyness. 'He then said, I have an intimate personal matter to discuss with you. You are the only person in the world with whom I can discuss everything.' Of course, the well-briefed House already knew what it was; and he knew too that he had better approve of the plan for the happy couple to get married. This was prudent on the Colonel's part, not least so as to court Edith's goodwill, but it also reflected his own concern for the President's personal well-being, as he noted in his diary: 'When I spoke of how much depended on him and how anxious I was that he might maintain his health and strength he said his belief was that Providence did not remove a man until his work was finished.'[32]

———

This man's work was far from finished. On the U-boat crisis, he had fumbled his way to a stand-off that made him look like a strong President: one who had got Germany to modify the conditions under which it would now use its U-boats, at once minimising their effectiveness against Britain and their lethal consequences for American citizens. So long as the German high command believed that they could deliver victory on land without resorting to this ultimate weapon at sea, the U-boat issue was unlikely to provoke an American declaration of war. Instead, Wilson was free to lay the basis for a carefully modulated re-election campaign, focusing attention on the kind of European peace that the United States could use its influence to achieve. It was Grey who had spoken of such a settlement, with international cooperation to underpin it, as one of the key British demands, alongside Belgian reparation. But the ideas that Wilson developed were no subservient projection of anglophilia.

For Wilson had all the traditional American suspicions of the imperialist and navalist side of British policy. He had faith in the American mission to uphold the tenets of liberalism with a democratic purity that was untainted by the narrow prejudices of the Old World. The concert of Europe was dead; but long live democratic world governance. So Wilson felt himself increasingly able to propose a vision of international politics that the United States had unique authority to further in the twentieth century, because American principles were now the true principles of mankind. This was the impulse behind a series of notable speeches that developed a distinctive Wilsonian view of a League of Nations as essential to a lasting peace settlement. The vision was publicly disclosed in his address to the League to Enforce Peace in May 1916; it was developed in his 'peace without victory' address to the Senate in January 1917; it was implicit throughout his War Address of April 1917; and it became canonical in the Fourteen Points, as proclaimed in January 1918.

It was not an ethereal vision; it was rooted in immediate political concerns, both at home and abroad. As it became obvious that this war would not be over by Christmas 1914, or 1915, or 1916, it was fundamental that Wilson should be re-elected President in order to exert the wholesome influence he craved. In the end, he managed to squeak home, despite losses on the eastern seaboard, because the South held firm and unexpectedly strong progressive support materialised in the west – always Bryan's home territory (and a base that, even out of office, he helped to mobilise for the Democrats). When Woodrow Wilson woke up on 8 November 1916, he found himself still in the White House, still with Colonel House creaking up and down the back stairs – but now with the second Mrs Wilson in the presidential bed, determined that her influence too would be felt in affairs of state, on which the besotted Woodrow kept Edith as fully briefed as Henry Asquith had once kept his beloved Venetia.

By this point, the President actually appeared far less sympathetic to the Allies than he had in the first year of the war, in private as in public. Thus we can find him telling House (in May 1916) of 'the altogether indefensible course Great Britain is pursuing with regard to trade to and from neutral ports and her quite intolerable interception of mails on the high seas carried by neutral ships'.[33] Ireland was another sore point, after British suppression of the Easter Rising. Grey was still there (until December 1916 at least) to iron out some of these particular difficulties but was also increasingly weary in tone in the comments that he sent privately to House. 'I understand that the President is disappointed at the want of response to his speech about a League of Nations,' Grey wrote in August 1916. But it was

© Punch Limited

BRINGING IT HOME.

PRESIDENT WILSON. "WHAT'S THAT? U-BOAT BLOCKADING NEW YORK? TUT! TUT!
VERY INOPPORTUNE!"

*British views of American policy were often simplistic – why on earth did the United States
not respond to German naval aggression by declaring war? One reality was indeed that
President Wilson had to get re-elected in 1916. And Wilson himself was by no means a
biddable anglophile.*

Wilson's 'statement of indifference to the causes and objects of the war' that particularly jarred and provoked doubts: 'If feeling in the United States is one of congratulation that they did not intervene to prevent the violation of Belgium or to avenge the loss of life in the "Lusitania", can they ever be expected to intervene?'[34]

Any such imputations now simply infuriated Wilson rather than shaming him in any way. He instructed House to write to Grey 'in the strongest terms' to inform him of the true resolve of the people of the United States, who 'were growing more and more impatient with the intolerable conditions of neutrality, their feeling as hot against Great Britain as it was at first against Germany and likely to grow hotter still' – not only that, but to tell Grey, in effect, that Ambassador Page had evidently gone native in faraway London and 'no longer represents the feeling or the point of view of the United States'.[35] Indeed plans to replace Page were currently afoot, though later shelved.

Wilson's equal scorn for 'German militarism' and 'British navalism' was evident in the drafts of the peace note that he was now preparing. When it was published, somewhat delayed by Asquith's sudden political demise, in late December 1916, it had a poor reception in Britain. Gardiner's *Daily News* was by this time not so much partisan towards Asquith as prominently critical of Lloyd George, who nonetheless did not exclude its editor from those summoned to Downing Street for briefing on Wilson's note. 'It is very bad,' Lloyd George assured a sceptical Gardiner. 'It is a pro-German declaration.' After nearly two and a half years, the President seemed finally to have achieved his ambition to be 'impartial in thought as well as in action'.

The culmination of this line of thought (or feeling) was the 'peace without victory' speech in January 1917. 'No covenant of cooperative peace that does not include the peoples of the New World can suffice to keep the future safe against war,' Wilson argued in claiming the right of a neutral country to participate in fashioning its terms. And the reason that 'it must be a peace without victory' was simple: 'Only a peace between equals can last.' There was certainly no deference to British sensibilities in claiming: 'The freedom of the seas is the *sine qua non* of peace, equality, and cooperation.'

Wilson now claimed for himself a unique status among world leaders in his freedom to broach such issues. He explained that he was proposing an updated Monroe Doctrine, extending freedom from outside interference to all nations, not just in the Americas; yet this cosmopolitanism was simultaneously distinctive to his own country. 'These are American principles, American policies,' he declaimed to his compatriots. 'We could stand for no others.' There was, of course, an echo here of Luther's famous affirmation – 'here I stand: I can do no other' – which was an aptly elevating appeal to sentiment, honed for deployment in future oratory. And the point was that these were the principles 'of every modern nation, of every enlightened community', because they were 'the principles of mankind and must prevail'. This is why he had posed the rhetorical question: 'May I not add that I hope and believe that I am in effect speaking for liberals and friends of humanity in every nation and of every programme of liberty?'[36]

By 1917 Wilson could be confident of a positive response from liberals across Europe, especially in Britain. It is worth pondering on why this was so. In a third book of biographical essays, *The War Lords*, published in late 1915, Gardiner had supplied an updated cameo of Wilson. (His earlier essay had meanwhile been put on Edith Galt's reading list by the President as part of her pre-nuptial preparations.) Gardiner parried the obvious objections that British Liberals had made, especially about American silence over Belgium, conceding that the President might well have asked for an independent court of inquiry into alleged atrocities. Actually, since Lord Bryce's report for the British government had received such widely favourable publicity in the United States when published only days after the *Lusitania* sank, it served this function. Today it is easier to determine dispassionately whether the German army used notably brutal methods, since the fact that it did so is broadly corroborated by historical research. What obfuscated the issue in 1915 was the prurient fascination that both the British and American public had with suggestive overtones of sexual violence, as in the post-Bryce comment of the *New York Tribune*: 'While our own women were only slain those of Belgium were outraged.'

Gardiner's main reason for endorsing Wilson's stance, as early as 1915, was simple: 'This war is, ultimately, a war for the Government of the world.' Hence the continuing sense of affinity between this prominent Liberal journalist in London and the increasingly confident champion of liberalism in the White House – not forgetting, of course, the peripatetic Colonel House. It was an article that Gardiner had published in the *Daily News* just as House left London for home at the end of February 1916 that particularly caught this mood. Of course House had appreciated its immediate usefulness in election year, telling the President that 'I also want to suggest it as a campaign document later.'[37] What is more striking in retrospect is the prescient way that Gardiner sketched Wilson's hints of an expanded Monroe Doctrine, calling on the New World to redress the balance of the Old (as Canning's famous declaration had once put it). 'It is President Wilson's part to give that vision a worldwide scope,' declared Gardiner. When House dined at the White House at the end of March 1916, he was glad to find this article duly brought out, and read aloud to general compliments and approval. 'The President smiled and said: "I seem to see something of the Colonel's fine Italian hand in this article."'[38]

This compliment was gracious as well as shrewd. But it would be naive to attribute any later initiatives in Wilsonian statecraft either to Machiavellian manoeuvres on House's part or unique inspiration on Gardiner's. All three of them were already well versed in the canons of nineteenth-century liberalism, which it was only natural for them to draw upon in the changed situation of a world war that the United States was finally to enter in April 1917.

Wilson's uneasy equipoise over the freedom of the seas depended, in the end, on the German army overruling the German navy in restricting U-boat operations. This veto was lifted in early 1917, dashing any hope of the 'peace without victory' that Wilson's speech to the Senate had recently proposed and leading him instead on an inexorable path of confrontation. His loyal but restive Assistant Secretary of the Navy, of course, had long been privately contemptuous of 'a lot of the soft mush about everlasting peace which so many statesmen are handing out to a gullible public'.[39] For Franklin Roosevelt, as for his famous Republican cousin, the American decision for war came as a welcome relief.

It was in this radically different context that the President addressed a joint session of Congress on 2 April 1917. In terms of analysis, there was nothing new in what he said: only the facts had changed. So after a brief recapitulation on the effects of unrestricted submarine warfare on all vessels, 'whatever their flag', he offered a simple response: 'It is a war against all nations.' It was indiscriminate in its effects: 'The challenge is to all mankind.' And it came, not from the German people, with whom he pursued no quarrel, but from their autocratic government – a government all too similar in kind to that now recently overthrown with the deposition of the Russian Tsar. Here was the great simplification of the meaning of the war: 'The world must be made safe for democracy.' This was why the Americans would 'fight without rancour and without selfish object, seeking nothing for ourselves but what we shall wish to share with all free peoples'; it was why they were committed to 'a universal dominion of right by such a concert of free peoples as shall bring peace and safety to all nations and make the world itself at last free'. The peroration, as in January, echoed Luther in its call to the United States: 'God helping her, she can do no other.'[40]

Spending all that day with the President, House allowed himself to wonder how much of the address he had himself contributed. He noted that Wilson seemed quite unconscious of this – 'I think it is quite possible that he forgets from what source he receives ideas and suggestions.' On returning to the White House that evening after the speech had been delivered, House put the matter of originality and provenance differently, assuring Wilson that he had now gone further than any previous statesman. 'He seemed surprised to hear me say this and thought perhaps Webster, Lincoln and Gladstone had announced the same principles.'[41] It was no doubt Daniel Webster's eloquent equation of American nationalism with liberty that secured his place in Wilson's pantheon of nineteenth-century predecessors.

There is a sense in which both perspectives are valid. Wilson was indeed drawing upon the liberal canon of the nineteenth century, but he did so self-consciously as an American and in the context of a new century in which war, revolution and democracy had a more immediate salience. Even as he spoke, Lenin and Trotsky were already fomenting a further kind of revolution, confident in their belief that war was the locomotive of history in aiding and abetting their project. They too made an appeal that went beyond any national frontiers yet enlisted national sentiment behind it. Mischievously perhaps, they too were to espouse the slogan of self-determination for all subject peoples (not least for the Irish, as the Easter Rising in 1916 had served to remind everyone). Their calculation was that self-determination could unlock and unleash suppressed social tensions; it would thus produce the kind of revolutionary turmoil that the Bolsheviks needed. Their claim, in updating Marx in this way, was to install the proletariat in power, as a proxy for a 'universal class' that would represent the true interests of all.

This was far different from the liberal vision of Woodrow Wilson. When he invoked 'a universal dominion of right' as the means to 'make the world itself at last free', he did so as the First Citizen of the United States. It was for his own country that he claimed this universal character, with no interests to advance except the common interest. It was unthinkable, then, to suppose that this high role might be vitiated by any selfish concerns of the United States, as he had explained in October 1916: 'It is inconceivable that America should wish to take anything away from any other nation in the world.'[42] Would he have thought this 'inconceivable' for any other country? Of course not – only by appealing to 'American exceptionalism' could the claim be made.

Looking back a century later, it is hard to escape a sense that this was one of the great climacterics of modern history. Lenin and Trotsky offered the prospectus for a worldwide revolution that would supersede capitalism, both in its original home (Britain) and ultimately in the country where the modern capitalist system had now achieved its most advanced levels of development (the United States). Their proxy for the universal class might be found in backward Russia; but the ultimate unwinding of the skein of history, as Trotsky put it, would vindicate his vision. Even in the 1960s it was possible for historians to appropriate this kind of analysis in contrast with the supposedly capitalist and imperialist worldview of Wilson. Yet today few would accept the idea that Trotsky had successfully identified the universal class he needed to accomplish the overthrow of capitalism: still less that the Soviet Union embodied it. By contrast, though the notion of 'American exceptionalism' may seem risible to many non-Americans, it would clearly be premature to proclaim its demise in the United States itself.

How could a man as intelligent as Wilson have explained the unique status he claimed for his own country? 'The power of the United States is a menace to no nation or people,' he was to affirm in February 1918. 'It will never be used in aggression or for the aggrandizement of any selfish interest of our own. It springs out of freedom and is for the service of mankind.'[43] This was a rhetorical claim, announced as self-evident, and with long historical roots; but he had already offered one particular suggestion that is worth unpacking. 'We are the clearinghouse for the sympathies and principles of mankind,' he explained in his war address in April 1917.[44] Here was an implicit subtext that was to come to gestation, nine months later, in the Fourteen Points. Indeed, as long ago as May 1915, he had offered the providential claim: 'It is as if humanity had determined to see to it that this great nation, founded for the benefit of humanity, should not lack for the allegiance of the people of the world.'[45] Here was the taproot of exceptionalism, planted by the founding fathers of the Great Republic and still flourishing.

It is also relevant that, as a politician, Wilson needed to recruit political support. He did so, like Gladstone before him, not by making sectional appeals to the electorate but nonetheless in ways that had particular resonance for the feelings of downtrodden and excluded citizens. When the Grand Old Man had once rhetorically proclaimed to mass audiences that shepherds and fishermen, rather than scribes and pharisees, had been Christ's first disciples, it did not mean that he simply tailored his political agenda to winning the shepherd vote or the fisherman vote. But, as Wilson had always recognised, populist arguments were necessary for the orator to mobilise wide support. The Fourteen Points, to be proclaimed in January 1918, simultaneously proclaimed Wilson's internationalist ideals but also had traction in particular constituencies.

Their highly specific nature is often forgotten. This affected the co-belligerents of the United States. It was not just that Point 7 accommodated the interests of Belgium and France, but Point 6 (Russia) was still notably supportive of the faltering war effort on the eastern front, despite the Bolsheviks' seizure of power and their current efforts to negotiate a separate peace at Brest-Litovsk, which provided 'the acid test' for the Germans' (specious) commitment to self-determination. Then there was Point 9 (Italy), which a large number of Italian-Americans read in a sense more expansive than its careful drafting perhaps warranted. Point 10 was solicitous for 'the peoples of Austria-Hungary', who likewise swelled the ranks of American immigrants. Similarly, Point 11 remembered Romania, Serbia and Montenegro, just as Point 13 nourished the dream of a Polish state that had lived on in the minds of so many Polish-Americans. And Point 12? The subject nationalities of the Ottoman Empire found acknowledgement in its terms; and the particular resonance was that occasioned by the Armenian massacres of 1915, which became a burning issue for the Armenian community in the United States (though for the State Department a nagging embarrassment almost as much as Belgium had once been). Here, then, was another level at which the great American clearing-house took on a tangible significance, reinforcing this President in promising to bring updated liberal principles to the rescue and redemption of the whole world.

FOURTEEN POINTS OF VIEW

Part Two

WAR AND PEACE

Agenda for the Hall of Mirrors:
Clemenceau, Lloyd George, Wilson

There was to be no 'peace without victory' in 1917. And there was to be no victory either, even though the French and British were now reinforced by American support. Not until November 1918 was an Armistice negotiated. Though it was a moment that had been long in coming, it came quickly in the end and was invested with conflicting expectations.

The peace treaty with Germany was eventually signed on 28 June 1919 in the magnificent palace that Louis XIV had built at Versailles. The building contained both a *salon de la guerre* and a *salon de la paix*, though whether war led to peace or peace to war was a matter of opinion. The palace's dazzling central feature was the *galerie des glaces*, the Hall of Mirrors, with its seventeen mirror-clad arches, each with twenty-one mirrors serving to reflect the views of the outside world – with some distortion – through seventeen long windows. In 1871, to France's humiliation, this was where the victorious Bismarck had declared Wilhelm I German Emperor; and in 1919 the Hall of Mirrors was again pointedly chosen, this time by Clemenceau, *Père la Victoire*. In a well-known painting by Sir William Orpen, Clemenceau, in the chair, turns with some animation towards Lloyd George, on his left, thus momentarily ignoring, on his right hand, President Wilson, whose steely gaze seems fixed on some more distant object. These were indeed the three men who were finally to be responsible for the Treaty: made responsible for it by their compatriots, held responsible for it by posterity.

Everyone who was anyone seemed to be in Paris in January 1919 when proceedings began. Franklin and Eleanor Roosevelt, determined to save their marriage, were already established at the Ritz when the President arrived from London, and they were to sail back to the United States in his company the next month. FDR had been in Europe the previous summer and had been distinctly more impressed by Lloyd George than by the latter's abrasive cabinet colleague, Winston Churchill, now restored to cabinet office as Minister of Munitions. Churchill was thus again seeing plenty of Lloyd George, his boss. And Churchill had already met Woodrow Wilson in London, both at 10 Downing Street and at a glittering reception held at Buckingham Palace (where the President had taken some satisfaction in slyly rebuking him over British naval pretensions). One session of the peace conference was to bring the two men into further conflict, when Wilson openly scorned Churchill's proposals for Allied intervention against the Bolsheviks.

The official agenda for the peace conference was settled amicably enough. Behind it lay the real agenda, which was different when looked at through French eyes, or British eyes or, still more, through American eyes: in each case for the obvious reason that it reflected a different experience of war in the preceding years. To understand this we need to take a retrospective view on what shaped the real agenda for Clemenceau, Lloyd George and Wilson.

At the official opening of the conference, Georges Clemenceau was elected to preside. He was proposed by Wilson, who claimed to 'know how much he is united with us, and with what ardour he is working for that which we ourselves desire'. Lloyd George had been equally gracious. 'When I was at school,' he said, 'M. Clemenceau was already one of the moving forces in French politics.' This was all well said in the golden morning of amity, at the beginning of a year that ended with a wintry welter of mutual reproaches on all sides, foreign and domestic. 'La morale de cette histoire?' Clemenceau was to declaim to his faithful secretary in his retirement. 'C'est que j'ai eu grand tort d'avoir quatre-vingts ans en 1920.' He had not actually been quite eighty years old, even if it later seemed a great fault (*grand tort*) to have been so old: fifteen years older than Wilson, twenty-one years older than Lloyd George – and, for that matter, more than thirty years older than Churchill, or forty than Roosevelt.

In the eyes of FDR himself, however, who had met Clemenceau in July 1918, declining vitality was hardly the problem. 'He almost ran forward to meet me and shook hands as if he meant it; grabbed me by the arm and walked me over to his desk and sat me down about two inches away. He is only 77 years old and people say he is getting younger every day.'[1] Likewise Churchill recalled his first impressions of Clemenceau as the new French premier in late 1917, when the visiting British Minister of Munitions watched him facing down the opposition in the Chamber. 'He looked like a wild animal pacing to and fro behind bars, growling and glaring; and all around him was an assembly which would have done anything to avoid having him there, but having put him there, felt they must obey.'[2] Churchill registered the impact of the stark way that Clemenceau declared his policy: 'I will fight in front of Paris; I will fight in Paris; I will fight behind Paris.'[3] This admiring tribute was published in *Great Contemporaries*, which Churchill had sent to his publishers just three years before the summer of 1940: his own homage to the oratorical inspiration of a man who was already known before 1914 as 'the Tiger' on account of his long and combative career in French politics.

It is true that the French often looked through different spectacles on the great issues of war and peace that tortured Anglo-American consciences during the twentieth century. This 'First World War' that broke out in 1914, was it really the first of its kind? Such was never the French view. For them it had meant, yet again, a patriotic war against German armies, in a pattern that struck them as all too familiar, all too predictable, all too intractable, in its causes and its probable consequences alike. It was, in particular, barely forty years since the last German soldiers had left France after marching into Paris in 1871. The costs of that war to France were palpable, measured in both blood and treasure. Not only had French patriots died during it but the costs of the war were subsequently levied on French taxpayers. In exacting the traditional spoils of war, Bismarck, as Chancellor of the new Reich, got his own way on most – but not all – aspects of the peace terms that France had been forced to sign.

The victorious Germans had imposed an indemnity, to be paid off before their occupation ended. It seemed enormous at the time: 5,000 million francs. But a full settlement was made by the end of 1873 – a one-off, fixed-sum levy of about a quarter of the annual French national income. It was an external transfer payment financed in short order as a capital sum, which it took French taxpayers decades to pay off internally, but this harsh measure was accepted as the necessary cost of getting rid of the German occupation, even though the victors also annexed the two provinces of Alsace and Lorraine to the new German Empire.

All this rankled. For decades the French toyed with the notion of revenge; and though *revanchiste* politics cannot be directly blamed for causing the war in 1914, once this had started, the French agenda was clear. Revenge would indeed be exacted upon the old German enemy; the restoration of the two lost provinces was naturally a prime war aim; and it was taken for granted that victory would be sealed by the exaction of an indemnity on Germany. In all of this there was a great deal of sentimental investment by the French, but it did not require any agony of moralising on their part to identify the issues and interests at stake.

Georges Clemenceau was in this sense not exceptional – though he was clearly a man of exceptional abilities, not least in his gift for plausibly personifying France. But what has often been overlooked is the extraordinary nature of the old man's anglophone connections. He had qualified in medicine in 1865, under Napoleon III, but his Radical opinions made him a marked man and he emigrated to the United States and dabbled equally in medicine, teaching and journalism for four years before marrying an American wife (later to be divorced by him for her outrageous adultery, though his own peccadilloes were not denied).

Clemenceau's English was excellent, whenever he chose to use it. He was particularly fond of American slang. But when he once ran into Gladstone at Cannes, the British Prime Minister spoke French, and the overawed French political journalist followed suit. Gladstone's diary for 9 February 1883 confirms the authenticity of this meeting, arranged after they had met at dinner: 'Saw Comte de Paris – Duke of Argyll – M. Clemenceau.'[4] Through the indiscretion of another guest, who was the Paris correspondent of the *Daily News*, her account of their exchanges, perhaps none too accurate, found its way into newspapers worldwide. 'Much life, it is said, was on both sides infused into the conversation which ran upon the gay science – love, as it appeared to the Greek dramatists,' was how she described some of the exchanges. Either through modesty or inadvertence, Clemenceau did not allude to this privileged encounter with the Grand Old Man in his gossip with the British ministers in Paris in 1919. 'What about your Gladstone,' he demanded of Lloyd George on one occasion, 'what sort of man was he?' Lloyd George's response – 'He was a very great man' – was immediately capped by Bonar Law adding, 'He was a very great humbug.'[5]

What did Clemenceau make of these Anglo-Saxon liberals, with their panoply of earnestly expressed convictions? He has rarely been given credit for the extent to which he understood them, sympathised with many of their aspirations and, in turn, hoped that they would extend their understanding and sympathy to himself and his countrymen. He had good friends in England, across a wide political spectrum, from the Maxse family, with their links to high Conservative circles, to the far left, represented by H. M. Hyndman, the founder of the Marxist Social Democratic Federation. It was the eccentric francophile Hyndman who, in the desperate summer of 1918, determined to publish a biography of Clemenceau, and

received a handwritten letter from the embattled Premier supporting the project.

Hyndman understood his subject well, much better than most
of the British or American public did. Thus it was not surprising
in France that Clemenceau had famously championed Dreyfus; he
had published over 600 articles in support of 'the man on Devil's
Island' (a destination to which the young Clemenceau might himself
have been condemned by the Bonapartists). Yet it was Zola and
Picquart who were better known at the time in Anglo-American
eyes. Hyndman knew that this was the same Clemenceau who, as
a Radical politician, had scorned Napoleon III's provocation of
Prussia in 1870 and had viewed the course of that war with despair –
'as I have heard Clemenceau say himself, it was almost impossible
for a patriotic Republican to desire victory for the French armies'.
Yet the declaration of a republic had changed the situation: 'This
was the moment when England should have interfered decisively
on the side of her old rival.' A democratic war against a militarist
autocracy thus became exemplary – perhaps in 1918 too? In later
years, when Clemenceau was asked for his own preference among
the many biographies that had by then appeared, he answered at
once: Hyndman's.

Could none of the Americans who thronged Paris at the end of the
First World War grasp the significance of what was now happening
or see the situation through Clemenceau's eyes? Even at the beginning of August 1918 the Allied armies had found themselves hard
pressed in defending French soil; it was then only a fortnight since
the Germans had been at Château-Thierry, a mere forty miles east of
Paris and the scene of the first major engagement by the US Army.

This was the context for FDR's own meeting with Clemenceau.
'He jumped up, took me over to a big map with all the latest troop
movements and showed me the latest report from General Degoute,
covering progress north of Château-Thierry up to one hour before – a
fine advance by the French and American troops north of Fère-en-
Tardenois and to within a very short distance of the Vesle.' This

was the river on which Reims itself stood. The doughty Premier followed up with 'a hair-raising description of the horrors left by the Boche in his retreat', on which FDR readily accepted Clemenceau's testimony. 'These things I have seen myself,' FDR was told by 'the wonderful old man', who spent his weekends visiting the front. One vignette in particular stood out: 'A Poilu and a Boche still standing partly buried in a shell hole, clinched in each other's arms, their rifles abandoned, and the Poilu and the Boche were in the act of trying to bite each other to death when a shell had killed them both – and as he told me this he grabbed me by both shoulders and shook me with a grip of steel to illustrate his words, thrusting his teeth forward towards my neck.'[6]

So graphic were some of these images that in later years FDR was to appropriate the memories as his own. 'I have seen war,' he was to declaim as President in 1936, as though he had personally witnessed such events. Certainly his feelings were stirred in 1918, and even his vocabulary shifted. It is notable that before meeting 'the Tiger', FDR's diary always writes of 'the Germans'. Thus when he had met the pugnacious King George V, 'the subject switched to the Germans and he told me a lot about the atrocities in Belgium and northern France', even specifically mentioning Château-Thierry, recently retaken by US troops. In response FDR mentioned his own experience in having gone to school in Germany (during his father's convalescent visits) and the King not only spoke of his own schooling in Germany for a year but, 'with a twinkle in his eye', added: 'You know I have a number of relations in Germany, but I can tell you frankly that in all my life I have never seen a German gentleman.'[7]

With the King, then, it was the banter between two cosmopolitan members of an international elite. But FDR's report of his later visit to inspect the Château-Thierry battlefield, now secured by the Allies, discloses families 'remembering always their good fortune in having got away before the arrival of the Boche, ready to start in again even from the ground up, but constantly impressing upon their children what the Boche has done to Northern France in these four years'. True, 'the Boche line' remained worryingly close (at least until the reverses suffered by the German army on 8 August), thus highlighting the good fortune of those villages where 'the Boche had never entered them'; though there was one unlucky village, shelled 'first by the advancing Boche', then by the French and by the Americans, 'and finally by the retreating Boche'.[8]

Worse was to come. There was one little church which 'remained just as the Boche had left it', its use as a hospital evident from the 'various articles of Hun clothing', and all 'done deliberately and maliciously by the Huns', with further danger lurking behind the observation of 'a Hun plane, probably doing photographic work'.[9] Even on his further visit to France in January 1919, FDR was writing home to his mother of what 'the Boche' and 'the Huns' had left behind.[10] It was not uniquely the French, still less uniquely Clemenceau himself, who approached the peace conference still infused with the passions of a war that only five months previously had hung in the balance.

The speed and scale of the final German collapse took almost everyone by surprise. At the time, the British could hardly believe it; later, the Germans refused to believe it when a victors' peace was imposed on them. Virtually everyone had become inured, over the years, to the futility and deadlock on the western front. Lloyd George's *War Memoirs* remain full of scorn for the 'Westerners' who persisted in believing that it was in the trenches that Germany had to be confronted with superior Allied power. 'At first they deluded themselves with the assurance of speedy victory,' he comments. 'Later on, the Western Front became the shrine of Moloch, demanding and justifying such sacrifice as even its most infatuated priest would not have dreamt of offering had he known in 1915 what this worship meant.'[11] Hence no sufficient exploration of the alternatives

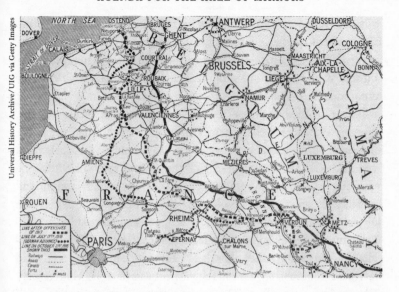

The end of the war came very suddenly, after a long stalemate on the western front and German advances as late as July 1918. At the time of the Armistice, the Allies did not realise how close they were to victory – nor did the Germans acknowledge how close they were to defeat.

in the east, if not in the Dardanelles then in the Balkans. But, after Gallipoli, it had seemed to the Asquith government that the western front was the only real option. 'The infatuation of a break-through which still haunted the western generals like a disease of the mind still prompted them to organise another and, as they thought, over-whelming attack on the German entrenchments.'[12] In 1916 came the bitter, blood-soaked defence of Verdun by the French, to be followed by the great offensive by the British on the Somme under their new commander-in-chief, Sir Douglas Haig.

It was the well-connected Haig who quickly became Lloyd George's *bête noire*. The action had already begun in the Somme valley when Lloyd George accepted appointment as War Secretary on 6 July 1916 in succession to Kitchener, who had been drowned at sea while on a mission to Russia. Towards Haig, Lloyd George reserved a personal antipathy that went beyond his robust disagreements with Sir William Robertson, a man who had risen from the rank of private to become the Chief of the Imperial General Staff, and who still enjoyed a plenitude of power inherited from the Kitchener regime. With Robertson's support, Haig was virtually irreplaceable as commander-in-chief.

This remained the case despite the expensive failure on the Somme, with more casualties on a single day (1 July) than any army in British history had ever suffered. On that day 20,000 British soldiers had died (as compared with the total of 53,000 US soldiers who died in combat by November 1918). All this put a premium on final victory. Grimly, resolutely, Haig confided his objective in his diary at the end of July 1916: 'The war must be continued until Germany is vanquished to such an extent as to be obliged to accept whatever terms the Allies may dictate to her.'

In November 1916 Haig still felt that this was obvious. Conversely, Frances Stevenson found 'D.', as she now called him, 'feeling very sick with everything' – and everyone too, evidently. 'He says they have made a muddle of the whole war, & he fears it is too late to do anything. He says the soldiers are quite right in resenting his inter-ference – that he has no right to dabble in strategy – all the same, he feels certain that they are running the country on the rocks.' To her at least he made no secret of his despair: 'The Germans are cleverer than us, he says, and they deserve to win. (Very broadminded, of course, but not very helpful.)'[13]

Hence Lloyd George's recurrent temptation to suppose that the deadlock on the western front might be broken by an imaginative redeployment of resources so as to catch the enemy off guard in some other theatre. A favourite plan was to concentrate on the Italian front instead: perhaps to surprise the enemy or simply to get Italian troops to do more of the fighting. But the idea that Italy was in some way the enemy's soft underbelly was a theory that few experts found plausible in the First World War (even before the Italian debacle at Caporetto in late 1917). Lloyd George's counsels of restraint on the western front were thus often weakened in their effect because his alternative seemed to be an implausible attempt to defeat or detach Germany's Austrian ally, perhaps in the Balkans. Hence Haig's incredulous and dismissive note in his diary of a conference in Paris (16 November 1916): 'Lloyd George asked several questions with a view to having more troops sent to Salonika!' Yet again, 'unanimously' in the end, they all endorsed the western priority.

The Somme had been a prelude to Lloyd George's bid for power and he frankly dreaded a repetition under his leadership, once he became Prime Minister in December 1916. But since the soldiers insisted that victory against Germany had to be won by mastering its armies in the field, this necessarily meant that the western front had to have priority. This may have been Asquith's grand strategy, *faute de mieux*; it likewise became Lloyd George's, *faute de mieux*. For Britain, the internal politics of the war therefore turned to a large extent on whether the generals or the politicians would finally prevail.

Part of Lloyd George's difficulty here was temperamental, since his own brand of courage was not at all physical and he was better at supplying large amounts of high explosives than personally withstanding their proximity. He was no Clemenceau or Churchill, striding into danger in the course of asserting his presence on the spot as the man in command. Instead, Lloyd George visited the front as little as possible: one reason why he saw so little of Haig. This meant not only that they established notoriously poor mutual comprehension but also that Lloyd George's search for an alternative commander-in-chief was handicapped by the simple fact that he did not meet many generals, who, whatever their other deficiencies, were often to be found in places disagreeably close to guns and shells and mines and mortars.

From all this, then, Lloyd George flinched. And a good thing, too, it might be thought, given the results of Haig's unflinching courage, Haig's unflinching steadfastness and Haig's unflinching fortitude, as he ordered wave upon wave of his soldiers into action. But Haig had powerful friends, including the King, who at one point 'suggested that non interference should occur in Haig's position: that after all he was a great British soldier, & his position & prestige was the first thing to be considered'. The Stevenson diary is our (partisan) source here and it has Lloyd George responding heatedly to His Majesty: 'The most important thing seems to me that the lives of our gallant soldiers should not be squandered as they were last summer, but that they should be used to the very best advantage.'[14]

Presumptuous but wily as always, Lloyd George tried to thwart Haig by indirect ploys. This was one reason why the new British Prime Minister often favoured the claims of French generals who seemed less keen on refighting another Somme. Hence the short-lived supremacy in the early part of 1917 of Robert Nivelle, a man who was fluent and articulate in English, his second language (rather like Lloyd George himself, and Clemenceau too). Recently a colonel, now suddenly a general, Nivelle came up with plausible ideas that made him, in Lloyd George's eyes, a fit person to exercise supreme command over all Allied troops, and especially over Haig.

Early in 1917 there was 'a trial of strength between him and Haig', as the Stevenson diary reports at some length. Frances records Lloyd George remarking to her: 'Haig does not care how many men he loses. He just squanders the lives of these boys.'[15] Her account, of course, is biased but also uniquely well informed, given her official access to the Prime Minister as his principal private secretary in addition to their personal intimacy. He told her at this time, hearing the news of his revered Uncle Lloyd's death, that she was 'his only devoted friend now – that I shall have to fill the old man's place'.[16]

In Stevenson's eyes, then, Nivelle's dizzy rise soon looked like over-promotion. His tactical successes with the creeping barrage turned out not to be easily translated into a strategy for a large-scale breakthrough, to be attempted mainly by French troops on the Aisne. By the time this 'surprise attack' was launched in April 1917, it was no surprise at all to the Germans. By May it was clear that no breakthrough had been achieved; but 270,000 French soldiers had been killed. And the political impact? 'Nivelle has fallen into disgrace, & let D. down badly after the way D. had backed him up at the beginning of the year,' wrote Stevenson, now well aware that Haig had 'come out on top in this fight between the two Chiefs, & I fear D. will have to be very careful in future as to his backings of the French against the English'.[17]

All of this licensed Haig in his own optimistic plan for winning the war in 1917. This was the Flanders offensive. It was not, of course, to be the first battle for Ypres, nor even the second – these had both taken place in the early months of the war; and perhaps that fact indicates that the strategic position of Ypres was inherently worth a third battle, sooner or later. If so, Lloyd George preferred later. He countered Haig's blithe prospectus with a bitter appeal to experience. Yet Lloyd George was reluctantly persuaded to assent; and perhaps Haig's commitment to back off quickly if the position became untenable was the best that could be secured (though Nivelle had promised much the same).

In the event Third Ypres, launched in June 1917, conformed to Lloyd George's forebodings. It proved impossible to stop Haig when, in subsequent months of increasingly sodden weather, he insisted that his troops must push on through the mud towards the bombed-out quagmire that had once been the village of Passchendaele. Hence the bitterness, if not the accuracy, of Lloyd George's later charges against Haig: 'He never even saw the ground on which his greatest battles were fought, either before or during the fight.'[18] If Lloyd George can be credited with putting the initial case against Third Ypres as strongly as he was able, nonetheless, having given the generals carte blanche through his own political weakness, he was never subsequently in a position to rein back Haig until the total British casualties at Ypres had reached 275,000, of whom 70,000 were killed.

In the spring of 1918, then, it was still the Germans who could pull off a surprise on the western front. They had been liberated from fighting on their eastern front once the Bolsheviks capitulated to German peace terms at Brest-Litovsk; and the American intervention, though increasingly decisive in tipping the balance, was frustratingly delayed in its impact on the battlefield. General John Pershing ('Black Jack'), whom Wilson had recently chosen to lead a punitive expedition into Mexico, retained the President's confidence as commander-in-chief; and what we can call the Pershing doctrine was that American troops should be sent to the western front only as part of a separate US army. 'Pershing wanted to fight his own battle and win his own victories with his own Army,' Lloyd George observed. 'Haig wanted his own offensive on his own front, ending in his own breakthrough.'[19]

The Pershing doctrine was a fine patriotic conception but it necessarily took time. At the end of 1917, after nine months, there were only 175,000 American troops in France; by the beginning of June 1918, which saw the initial engagement at Château-Thierry, there were 650,000 troops; and the plan for 1919 envisaged no less than 3½ million. *Formidable!* But, meanwhile, the western front might be breached, the Allied armies might be separated, the Channel ports might be taken, Paris might fall – or so the worst-case scenarios still suggested. On 12 April, Haig had issued his order of the day: 'With our backs to the wall and believing in the justice of our cause each one of us must fight on to the end.' It sounded all too like the noble but doomed note struck in Captain Scott's diary amid the invincible wastes of the Antarctic.

On 14 April, in a desperate hour, Marshal Ferdinand Foch had, at least nominally, been made commander-in-chief of all the Allied armies. In May the Pershing doctrine was relaxed a little after a desperate appeal to Washington by Lloyd George, working closely with Clemenceau and Foch in Paris. 'If House had been present,' Lloyd George commented later, 'we should have got a better agreement.'[20] As it was, Wilson relied on Pershing's advice and the Allied leaders had to be satisfied with some increase in the rate at which US troops were shipped to Europe. Their long-anticipated impact on the battle for Château-Thierry in July was notable, but mainly in spelling out to the Germans what was in store.

In fact, the hubris of the German high command, with their over-extended supply lines and overweening ambitions, masked a chronic internal crisis within Germany. Churchill was unusual in discerning this, in a cogent analysis drafted on 3 August: 'The *Appearance* of power is with the enemy & the *Reality* of power is with us.'[21] Indeed, soon enough the tide of war turned; and in the process Haig found himself vindicated by the impressive British victories that finally pushed the Germans back in the summer of 1918.

On 8 August the breakthrough came at Amiens. Hardened Australian and Canadian troops, rather than raw British conscripts, were prominent in the assault. The use of artillery was now much more sophisticated, and so, as Churchill let nobody forget, was the use of a new weapon of war that he had sponsored: 'The Germans were unable to resist the tanks.'[22] About 400 were deployed, with an impressive initial impact; and when, having quickly gained miles rather than yards of territory up the Somme valley, they became ensnared in old fortifications, Haig defied Foch's call to press on regardless. He had finally learned a bitter lesson and insisted on time to regroup. Lloyd George, by then conditioned to disbelief in Haig's promises, was slower to appreciate the significance of all this than his *War Memoirs* later admitted: 'The reports of the battle received by the Cabinet from the front showed how little even the victors understood the immense effect of the triumph they had won.'[23] What this does not spell out is that 'the victors' included himself; but he quickly sensed that, having suffered the long agonies of trench warfare, he suddenly had a triumph on a Roman scale to exploit.

Five months is a long time in politics. In August 1918 the outcome of the war had still seemed uncertain; by January 1919 the victors were meeting in Paris to dictate their terms. Clemenceau, in purposefully hosting the conference, already had a mental scenario in which the final act would be German submission in the *galerie des glaces*. Lloyd George arrived in Paris with a stunning electoral endorsement. He had called a General Election three days after the Armistice; it was held a month later; the way in which he had won it simultaneously saluted 'the man who won the war' and constrained his negotiating position. Wilson's position was no less ambiguous, with his international reputation now at its zenith but, after congressional elections in November 1918, with the Republicans ascendant in domestic politics. All this shaped the agenda in Paris.

It is understandable that, in August, Lloyd George had initially discounted well-founded claims that the Germans' morale was now flagging, with few reserves and inadequate rations to sustain their further resistance. But he certainly made political capital out of his victories in the next three months, as did Clemenceau of his. For it was the British and French advances that now caught the headlines, at least in Europe, with Pershing as slow to learn new lessons as Haig had once been. In its battles around the old fortress of Verdun, the US Army suffered casualties worse than at Gettysburg or Antietam, though these were efficiently hushed up at the time by American war correspondents in the war's final days.

Wilson remained reliant on Pershing's own account of these matters. On shipboard to Europe, the President continued to talk privately about 'how we saved the world' and claimed that the Allies realised that they would otherwise have been beaten: 'They all acknowledged that our men at Chateau Thierry saved them.'[24] Such misconceptions about the strength of his negotiating position obviously inflated his own sense of how far he could determine the shape of the peace. Conversely, the more that public opinion, in Britain as in France, saw this as their own victory, the more difficult it was for Lloyd George or Clemenceau to satisfy high expectations in quite different directions.

The final, painful, long-promised and long-delayed German defeat in the land war had actually been foretold by the outcome of the war at sea. In 1917 the U-boat campaign had threatened to cut off Britain's maritime supply line and thus to render support from the United States ineffectual. The implementation of the convoy system in the summer of 1917 addressed this problem. The myth is that it was Lloyd George's personal intervention that overturned the professional scepticism of the Admiralty, in which case his reputation as the man who won the war would be as well founded as his *War Memoirs* persistently suggest. True, he came round to the idea of convoys, as did the Admiralty itself, and the system indeed proved an effective answer to the German menace below the waves. This was crucial, for otherwise it might well have been the British rather than the Germans who were starved out in the end. As it was, on land as at sea, Germany had lost its bet in its race against time.

At the beginning of October 1918 a new civilian German government sued for an armistice. The military leaders now adroitly disowned a war that had ended in defeat, fostering a subsequent legend of a 'stab in the back' by their political opponents on the left. Thus the Germans, under the liberal Prince Max of Baden, negotiated with the Americans, accepting Wilson's undertaking that peace terms would be on the basis of his Fourteen Points. They saw this as an essentially American offer, to make a peace that proclaimed these disinterested principles, qualified by specified conditions that spoke to the realities of the war situation. For though Wilson had, back in January 1917, in the days of American neutrality, spoken of his hopes for a peace without victory, the Allies had, twenty months later, suddenly become conscious of how near they were to achieving victory. Moreover, the Americans were fully aware of this in appending conditions to what they agreed with the Germans.

Foch may not personally have delivered this victory as supreme commander but he knew how to exploit it under the Armistice. For the military terms that he imposed in negotiating it are a clear indication that the Allies were now in a position to call the shots (or, on the German side, lack of shots). The Kaiser was now deposed, which was as Wilson required, and the successor regime accepted conditions more consistent with defeat than with an open-ended negotiation. The net effect was explicitly stipulated by Wilson as providing Germany with no opportunity of resuming hostilities should the treaty talks break down.

Lloyd George's *War Memoirs* proudly display a nine-page Appendix of all the terms.[25] German armies were required to evacuate 'the invaded countries – Belgium, France, Luxemburg, as well as Alsace-Lorraine'; they were required not only to withdraw behind the Rhine, but to surrender the bridgeheads on the German side and to evacuate a continuous strip along the right bank from the frontier of Holland to that of Switzerland, with an Allied army of occupation moving in to monitor the position. At sea, it was much the same story. German U-boats were required to cease operations but the Allied naval blockade was to be maintained; the German High Seas Fleet was required to sit at anchor, immobilised and under supervision; and, since no neutral port would accept it, it had to do so at Scapa Flow itself, the home base of the enemy it had been constructed to challenge. As Churchill later put it: 'No one could think of any further stipulation.'[26]

Colonel House had agreed to all of this. He had been sent to Europe in mid-October, as soon as it became clear that the Germans were, in effect, putting themselves in the hands of the American President in negotiating terms. Moreover, Wilson had given House great latitude, simply trusting him to implement principles on which they were jointly agreed. Whether the terms of the Armistice fulfilled that aspiration is doubtful. But, fresh off the boat, House had given Foch and the Royal Navy more or less everything that they wanted.

Wilson had good reason to allow House a free hand since they had been working closely together on peace terms for over twelve months. It was in September 1917 that they had set up 'the Inquiry', with a small staff under House, charged with formulating the basis of a lasting settlement – the origin of the Fourteen Points. House had gone to Europe on one of his annual wartime visits (as they now seemed) in late 1917, this time as an official US representative at the Supreme War Council at Versailles, and had found Lloyd George rather a disappointment. His Foreign Secretary, Balfour, seemed more impressive, as House had already judged from his contacts earlier that year with the Balfour Mission, sent to the United States to concert joint action over issues of war and peace. House thus found Balfour a congenial successor to Grey, now in semi-retirement as the revered champion of plans for a League of Nations.

After his own return home at the end of 1917, House had also sent over his personal emissaries to report back to him from Europe. They included able younger figures, notably the lawyer Felix Frankfurter and also Ray Stannard Baker, who was drawn more closely into the Wilson circle from this point. Another progressive publicist with a bright future, Walter Lippmann, had already been recruited for the Inquiry. In this sense, House cast his net wide, trawling for talent; but he also gave key jobs on the Inquiry to his wife's brother-in-law and to their own son-in-law, thus reinforcing the impression that a 'House Party' nourished on nepotism and favouritism was outflanking the State Department, under Lansing as under Bryan.

One way or another, it was House who had to square the circle over the adumbration and implementation of the Fourteen Points. For it was he who was uniquely close both to Wilson himself and to the co-belligerents of the United States, especially the British, with whom he worked so well in Europe. 'Whenever the President gives evasive or foolish reasons – reasons I know are not the real ones, I never argue with him,' House disclosed in his diary in June 1917, confident that if Wilson were 'talking nonsense' he would thereby sense it himself.[27] A nudge here, a wink there, a significant silence: this was the House style.

In such ways, many of the bottom-line demands of the Allies had already been presciently incorporated into the public declaration of the Fourteen Points in January 1918. Thus, some eight months previously, during the Balfour Mission, the British Foreign Secretary and the Colonel had pored together over a large map of Europe. 'We took for granted that Alsace and Lorraine would go to France, and that France, Belgium, and Serbia would be restored.' At this tête-à-tête in May 1917, such common assumptions had not been a matter of secret treaties, like those that the Allies now ruefully acknowledged to exist (and were soon to be gleefully published by the Bolsheviks). Balfour made no secret to House of his embarrassment at the 1915 Treaty of London, which had brought Italy into the war, and 'spoke with great regret at the spectacle of great nations sitting down and dividing the spoils of war or, as he termed it, "dividing up the bearskin before the bear was killed"'.[28]

So nobody was going to cavil over Point 1 – 'Open covenants of peace, openly arrived at' – when the President duly proclaimed it in January 1918, any more than over Point 7 (Belgium), or Point 8 (Alsace and Lorraine), or Point 11 (Romania, Serbia and Montenegro). Point 9 (Italy) needed more finesse if it were to be rendered consistent with the Treaty of London – a fecund source of future difficulties at the peace conference. Balfour had already felt able to report back to the Foreign Office in May 1917 that the President, far from insisting on 'no transfer of territory & no indemnities', was already committed to restoring Poland – this became Point 13 – as well as Alsace and Lorraine 'and to exact compensation for Belgium & Northern France'.[29]

Wilson's evolving views were hardly concealed. It was in a Flag Day address in June 1917 that he proclaimed: 'It is plain enough how we were forced into the war.' And it was equally plain that he meant not just a naval war, conducted against the United States, but the war of 1914. 'The war was begun by the military masters of Germany, who proved to be also the masters of Austria-Hungary.' Their plan for 'a broad belt of German military power and political control across the very centre of Europe and beyond the Mediterranean into the heart of Asia' betrayed a clear geopolitical intention of the most sinister kind. 'The dream had its heart at Berlin,' Wilson explained. 'It could have had a heart nowhere else!' This was the same President who had, a year previously, playfully chided audiences to tell him what or who had started it all. Now he chided them in different terms: 'Do you not now understand the new intrigue, the intrigue for peace, and why the masters of Germany do not hesitate to use any agency that promises to effect their purpose: the deceit of the nations?'[30]

This was no careless or isolated utterance but instead represented Wilson's appeal to 'the forces of justice and of liberalism' that would put the world to rights. His scorn for the current German peace proposals was echoed in what Bryce was now telling House: 'They are not to be taken seriously till they intimate a willingness to leave Belgium as free as before the war and to compensate her.'[31] Likewise it was Lansing's view in August 1917 that 'neutral Belgium has been grievously outraged and her people impoverished', which surely merited 'full reparation' for what they had suffered from the Germans.[32] It was this demand that headed the agenda for a peace settlement, stated not in terms of revenge by the victors but of a liberal international settlement that could alone guarantee a lasting peace. In the process the guilty would be brought to justice in a lawful way.

Such concerns were really an Anglo-American preserve since establishing German guilt was hardly a problem for the French, who simply assumed all along that an indemnity would be required. Nor had the existence of a state of war suspended issues of strictly legal responsibility for injuries and damage inflicted during the hostilities. Here indeed the Americans were even more concerned than the British, for obvious reasons. Indeed the United States had been neutral for nearly three years of the war, during which it had zealously sought to uphold the rights of neutrals, especially in conducting maritime trade according to established legal principles and, most emotive of all, in safeguarding the rights of civilians on the high seas. Infringements of law, even in wartime, were thus an issue: justiciable disputes to be resolved by courts and judges according to established principles of international law.

Beyond this, however, there lurked a bigger issue. Guilt was not just a legal concept: it was a moral issue peculiarly embedded in that dominant style of Anglo-American politics, to which, albeit in different registers, Wilson and Lloyd George (and Keynes too) all subscribed. Voiced in the language of moral righteousness, guilt elevated the level of discourse – or debased it, as some came to think, into a sort of formal piety that teetered on the brink of hypocrisy. And though a judgemental preoccupation with guilt fed on emotions of moral righteousness, it simultaneously fulfilled a necessary requirement on the more mundane level of legal responsibility.

Here lay the fatal ambiguity of the justification for 'reparations'. In January 1918, Wilson's Point 7 claimed that 'Belgium, the whole world will agree, must be evacuated and restored.' Point 8 added, 'All French territory should be freed and the invaded portions restored,' which was what the Germans were to accept under the terms of the Armistice in November 1918. Moreover, they were required to return Alsace and Lorraine to France without any question of a plebiscite to determine the issue. It could be said, then, that the return of the lost provinces to France was as simple a transaction as their annexation by Germany in 1871: in either case, they went to the victors. This implicitly reinforced the French view that an indemnity was likewise appropriate.

But 'indemnities' had been ruled out not only by Wilson but also by Lloyd George. In January 1918, while the outcome of the war still hung in the balance, Lloyd George had apparently made this clear in a speech to a trade-union audience at the Caxton Hall in London. He was speaking as a Liberal, albeit one who headed a coalition with the Conservatives; and he had cleared this statement of war aims with Asquith, still undisputed for the moment as leader of the Liberal party, and with Grey. Moreover, Lloyd George's speech at this juncture, well publicised around the world in making its case for the Allies, anticipated by a few days the promulgation of Wilson's Fourteen Points – to an extent that Wilson initially thought potentially embarrassing. Like himself, Lloyd George stressed the centrality of democracy and of self-government, and – in a phrase that does not actually grace the Fourteen Points – of a 'general principle of national self-determination'.[33]

Here was a great slogan. It had been propagated by Lenin on the eve of war in 1914, in the German form: *Selbstbestimmerungsrecht*. It had done good service in the Russian cause in the revolution of 1917 and in legitimating the Bolshevik seizure of power. Moreover, it was to be easily assimilated to the Wilsonian vocabulary in the month after his Fourteen Points were proclaimed. '"Self-determination" is not a mere phrase,' Wilson explained in appropriating it. 'It is an imperative principle of action, which statesmen will henceforth ignore at their peril.'[34] True enough, it was a genie that had found its moment to be let out of its bottle.

In January 1918, then, within a few days of each other, the two great spokesmen of Anglo-American liberalism found themselves singing, almost in unison, from the same hymn-sheet – with just the odd word of difference that hardly anybody noticed at the time. Whereas Wilson talked about what needed to be 'restored', Lloyd George had used slightly different language. He claimed that 'we were forced to join in this war in self-defence, in defence of the violated public law of Europe', and the first requirement of peace was thus 'the complete restoration, political, territorial and economic, of Belgium and such reparation as can be made for the devastation of its towns and provinces'. The primacy of Belgium, stemming from the violation of its neutrality, was thus reasserted, harking back to the original purity of the Liberal government's motives in declaring war in the first place. Lloyd George explicitly ruled out a 'war indemnity such as that imposed on France by Germany in 1871', in this war at any rate: 'It is not an attempt to shift the cost of warlike operations from one belligerent to another, which may or may not be defensible.' For here the point was a recognition of a breach of public law. 'Reparation means recognition,' he explained. 'Unless international right is recognised by insistence on payment for injury done in defiance of its canons it can never be a reality.'[35]

Lloyd George's language was pregnant with unremarked implications for the peace conference. His resort to the rather archaic term 'reparation', of course, simply echoed what Grey had been saying since 1914 (which helps explain the endorsement by Asquith and Grey). It sounded well, as the sort of quasi-scriptural elevated diction that often dignified oratory in the moral populist tradition of Lincoln and Gladstone. Though not in itself a calculated ploy, it served to license later ploys, once such declarations of war aims received subsequent exegesis as the agenda for a post-war settlement. So the effect was to legitimise a concept that could subsequently be stretched, as the need arose. Thus a duty to restore could, via 'reparations', become an obligation on the guilty party to indemnify the innocent parties.

Nor was this implication confined to Lloyd George. For the identification of the German Empire as the guilty party, as we have seen, had already been made by the American President himself by the time that he proclaimed his Fourteen Points. In reassuring Wilson before he gave his address to Congress, House insisted that 'it would so smother the Lloyd George speech that it would be forgotten and that he, the President, would once more become the spokesman for the Entente, and, indeed, the spokesman for the liberals of the world'.[36] This prophecy was to be fulfilled.

As a matter of legal responsibility, the glossing of the Fourteen Points became a pressing matter for Wilson in negotiating the Armistice terms later that year. House was by then already away in Europe. In the early morning of 29 October, preparing for his talks with the Allied leaders beginning that day, House received a briefing memorandum, of which Lippmann was joint author. Point 7 (Belgium) was crucial. 'The only problem raised here is in the word "restored",' the advice read. 'Whether restoration is to be in kind or how the amount of the indemnity is to be determined is a matter of detail, not of principle.' This was so because if the initial invasion was illegitimate, all the consequences were likewise illegitimate. 'Among the consequences may be put the war debt of Belgium.'[37] The moral reason for which the British liberals had started a world war in 1914 had thus become the legal reason for an American President, speaking for the liberals of the world, to levy upon Germany a form of reparations that amounted to an indemnity, for Belgium if not for France.

These Fourteen Points had never impressed Clemenceau. But when he and Lloyd George licensed Wilson to negotiate an Armistice, all fourteen of them were quickly accepted – although not all fourteen by each of them. Thus Lloyd George, employing his habitual elasticity, accepted thirteen, all except Point 2, absolute freedom of navigation. Clemenceau only really cared for the single Point 8, Alsace and Lorraine; but also wanted some means of recovering the costs of the war. Lloyd George was ultimately appeased by House, with a tortuous formula that registered the (British) reservation on naval issues. And he and Clemenceau then secured a second formal reservation: 'that compensation will be made by Germany for all damage done to the civilian population of the Allies and to their property by the aggression of Germany by land, by sea, and from the air'.[38]

Lloyd George now had all he needed for his own peace agenda. So did Clemenceau with this commitment to 'réparation des dommages'; and, focused on the tangible advantage of securing Alsace and Lorraine at once, he swallowed all Fourteen Points, though frequently regretting that this exceeded the number specified by *le Bon Dieu*. What he and Lloyd George accepted, then, was a gloss on the Fourteen Points, as helpfully supplied to them by House. The terms on offer to Germany were formally drafted by the US State Department in the 'Lansing Note'. The Germans then put their trust in the Americans and signed up for the Armistice. The slaughter ceased at 11 a.m. on 11 November.

Thomas Woodrow Wilson's own moment of apotheosis had arrived. No serving President had ever travelled to Europe; but then, no previous President had a constituency in Europe like this one. He landed at Brest on 13 December and was to be received everywhere with a degree of adulation that would have turned anyone's head. On the transatlantic boat he had talked humbly to his junior staff members: 'Tell me what is right and I'll fight for it.'[39] After a heady initial visit to Paris, he found London even more sympathetic. He told a delegation of Free Church leaders: 'I think one would go crazy if he did not believe in Providence. It would be a maze without a clue.'[40] These earnest Nonconformists naturally hoped that their man had this clue. At last he met Edward Grey face to face, leading a deputation from the League of Nations Union. 'I feel as if I met him long ago,' Wilson commented, much as he had once said about Edward House.[41]

For Wilson had a higher conception of his mission than mere banalities about the English-speaking peoples. He cautioned one British official not to speak of Americans 'as cousins, still less as brothers: we are neither'. It was not any bond of supposed national kinship that he sought with the sympathisers, supporters and believers who now crowded around him: it was a bond of common belief. 'I have come to Europe to do the little I can, but I am under no delusion,' he affirmed. 'Without the assistance of Divine Providence no man can effect anything which is lasting, anything which is great; no man of intelligence can deny the existence of a Divine Providence.'[42] Then he returned to Paris to begin his labours as peacemaker.

The Fourteen Points in Paris: Wilson and Lloyd George

The obvious ally for Wilson to co-opt in a moral crusade based on the principle of self-determination was Lloyd George. No such alliance was formed. The fact that Lloyd George had just won a General Election in coalition with the Conservatives, annihilating the Asquithian Liberals in the process, was perhaps a warning sign. Colonel House took it as such and was equally apprehensive about the way that the French Assembly had now voted overwhelmingly to affirm the hard line taken by Clemenceau. Wilson kept his distance from both leaders on arrival in Europe, whereas Lloyd George and Clemenceau were already establishing a degree of camaraderie based on a safeguarding of key national interests. Again, there was not one agenda for the conference but three.

The President sought solace elsewhere, especially in his own household. This was initially established at the Villa Murat, a grand residence made available by the French government, though he and Edith Wilson moved to a smaller house in March. Edith was with Woodrow throughout nearly six months based in Europe. But in the days before shuttle diplomacy was facilitated by air travel, the Wilsons were absent from Paris for a month from 15 February, allowing the President to take home his draft proposals for a League of Nations to Washington, where he was to be left with only two weeks for this difficult task since he had to spend a precious week or so on each of the sea voyages.

These afforded him some relaxation, of course, which came as a relief to those who became increasingly worried about his health.

The presidential naval doctor, Cary Grayson, now luxuriating in the rank of admiral, attended him throughout and, as his diary shows, became an influential member of the coterie. It was Grayson, nearing the American coast with his distinguished patient on 22 February 1919, who was present, along with Franklin and Eleanor Roosevelt, at a small shipboard lunch when the League project was discussed. 'The failure of the United States to back it', Wilson told them, 'would break the heart of the world, for the world considers the United States as the only nation represented in this great conference whose motives are entirely unselfish.'[1]

It was also Admiral Grayson who had earlier recorded how the Wilsons preferred to spend a quiet evening. On 21 January, a week or so after the conference opened, A. G. Gardiner was invited to dinner. He was still the editor of the *Daily News* at this point (although already vulnerable in his tenure since its proprietors, the Quaker Cadbury family, while pro-League, were also even more firmly pro-Lloyd George). The editor and the President launched into a free-ranging discussion that went on until 11 p.m., which was itself unusual for the Wilsons. Conversation ranged over Robert E. Lee, Lincoln, Andrew Jackson, Grant, Theodore Roosevelt – all subjects on which Gardiner's knowledge and insights impressed the Americans present. Almost inevitably, talk turned to Gladstone and Bryce, and to Asquith's sad failure to stand his ground in the election. Wilson also explained his strategy on the League of Nations: not to disclose his own 'concrete program' in advance, which would have presented the Europeans with a fait accompli, but instead to initiate a process that 'allowed everyone to suggest plans along all lines, so that when the agreement was reached all would feel that they had equally participated'. This seems to have gone down well; Gardiner's own commitment was palpable; and Grayson celebrated his own part in bringing the event about. 'The meeting between them was a real love feast.'[2]

As an author, Gardiner remained favourite reading for the Wilson entourage, his books of essays now read aloud as often in Paris as previously in Washington. This was not just another friendly journalist, worth priming for favourable comment. Wilson left all that to House and Baker. It was long after Wilson had left the White House, as a convalescent, that he addressed 'My Dear Friend' in a rather wistful letter: 'I often wish our too brief acquaintance might ripen into something much more intimate.'[3] For Gardiner was a notably well-versed representative of the strand of Anglo-American liberal opinion that Wilson strove to represent in early 1919 – indeed he was ready to caution the President on the danger of losing touch with American opinion at this bright moment of opportunity in reshaping the world. It was wholly in character that Wilson would rather spend an evening with Gardiner than with Lloyd George, still less with Clemenceau.

Clemenceau too liked his own quiet evenings. Even when he tried to have a night off at the opera, it turned out to be Figaro here, Figaro there – just like Lloyd George, as he complained. But Clemenceau also commented: 'Mr Lloyd George annoys me less when I see him than when I don't see him.' They were both pragmatists, playing the cards that they had been dealt. This is what Churchill stressed in telling Lloyd George: 'Your strength at the present time is largely due to the fact that, whereas Wilson relies on words, you deal in facts.'[4] What Lloyd George himself later chose to emphasise was slightly different: 'Old politicians like Clemenceau, and I claim the same for myself, had been from our early youth upwards working and hunting in the most snake-infested jungles that politics can provide.'[5] They had thus acquired an immunity to the savageries of personal criticism, however rancorous, through long careers as professional politicians with a keen sense of how to get things done.

Wilson had almost no comparable experience. This was one reason why he had relied so much on House as his 'fixer' and why the Colonel's diary kept seasoning its professed admiration for Wilson as an inspiring leader and orator with rueful reflections on his lack of administrative talent. Lansing, in a key position as Secretary of State, held a similar view; and it was he who took the unusual step at the end of March of setting down on paper some of his own acute frustrations, for reasons that are worth exploring further.

Sir William Orpen, a perceptive portraitist, spent a good deal of time in Paris working on sketches for the paintings that he finally produced. These plainly show that he did not warm to the aloof Wilson (centre left), *whereas he relished the human interaction between Lloyd George and Clemenceau* (right and middle respectively).

Ten weeks had now elapsed since the start of conference proceedings, with little to show on substantive issues. For the first month, Wilson sat there conscientiously, day by day and for long hours, insisting on the League of Nations as the prime business and imprinting key documents with his peculiar stamp. One of the other four members of the official US delegation (General Tasker H. Bliss) had commented enthusiastically on the President's own draft, building on the work of the Inquiry: 'The idea of the word "COVENANT" is so good that it is suggested that it be adhered to in the subsequent phraseology, notwithstanding the repetition that will ensue.'[6] Subsequent drafts duly conformed. Here was Wilson, gathering all the voices, elevating the tone, aiming to enlist European support, striving for a consensual proposal to take back to Washington.

The real decision-making at the conference was always dominated by the heads of government of the major victorious powers. Formally these included not only the United States, Britain and France but also two others, each with specific territorial interests. Japan had entered the war as Britain's naval ally, and had adroitly seized the German concessionary area in China, on the Shandong peninsula behind the docks and breweries of Tsingtao. It was determined to keep Shandong. Italy was likewise intent on securing territorial gains: if not those specifically promised to it by the Allies in the disreputable Treaty of London, then such frontier adjustments as might be wholesomely justified by 'clearly recognizable lines of nationality' under Wilson's Point 9.

These five government leaders plus their foreign ministers constituted the Council of Ten. House was formally made the President's deputy during his four-week Washington trip, starting out on 15 February. During this ensuing month, a significant new procedure evolved. Not only Wilson but also Lloyd George was initially absent from Paris at this juncture; and Clemenceau, narrowly surviving an assassination attempt, was convalescent for a time; so more informal methods were improvised, with the result that House began working closely with Lloyd George and Clemenceau, and (episodically) with the Italian premier, Vittorio Orlando. This procedure was to become institutionalised as the Council of Four on Wilson's return in mid-March. One striking fact was that the business had actually been transacted more expeditiously in Wilson's absence; and his reappearance now signalled trouble rather than amity. It was a couple of weeks after his return that an open row between the President and Clemenceau broke out in the new Council of Four.

Hence Lansing's memorandum, retailing his own understanding of the situation:

> The report of this incident caused me to say to Colonel House that I heartily wished that the President had never come to Europe because it subjected him to such embarrassments, deprived him of the position of superior authority, and had caused him to lose steadily the exalted position which he held in the eyes of the people and to lose even more his influence with foreign statesmen.

If this was remarkably outspoken, so was the Colonel's response: 'Yes, I quite agree with you. It was a mistake for him to come at all.'[7]

Of course, the fact that Lansing and House both saw it this way reflected some of their own vanity over how well they had managed without the President. And he, for his part, had reason for some disaffection with what he had found on his return. In particular, House had not resisted French pressure as strongly as Wilson wished (as he now forthrightly made clear), especially on proposals for detaching the Rhine valley from Germany, which was a proposal lacking any sanction in the Fourteen Points of course. Edith Wilson may well have later exaggerated the bitterness of the terms in which her husband now expressed himself – 'House has given away everything I had won before we left Paris' – but she certainly became vigilant in her suspicions.

None of this helped the American cause; nor did it avert breaking the heart of the world. The US Senate, now under the influence of Henry Cabot Lodge, the Republican majority leader, had signalled a crucial lack of support for the draft Covenant. This had deliberately been made an integral part of the Treaty by the President precisely in order to ensure its approval by Congress. So Wilson's insistence that the Covenant be the first work of the peace conference now looked like taxing the patience of the world at the expense of tackling the German problem, which all the victors acknowledged as the cause of the Great War. With his American political base steadily eroding, Wilson could no longer rely upon compensating support in Europe; his second coming in March 1919 lacked the messianic impact of his advent three months previously.

Back in Paris, though House refused to acknowledge any rupture in his relations with the President, the fissures within the American camp were increasingly apparent. Ray Stannard Baker, now handling press relations, was paid to put on a good public face for the journalists. But privately he viewed the situation in a new light. It was House who had initially recruited him, but by early April Baker was confidentially writing of the Colonel as 'the dilettante' who loved the game itself: 'He gains experiences to put in his diary, makes great acquaintances, plays at getting important men together for the sheer joy of making them agree.' By contrast, Wilson 'fights a losing battle against heavy odds'. Beleaguered in the Council of Four, Wilson may seriously have contemplated quitting the conference at this stage. Yet to Baker it was this serious-minded President's sense of being *'real'* that distinguished him as 'the only great man here', compared with Clemenceau's honest but narrow focus on 'selfish ends' and Lloyd George's tendency to live for the moment and to seize on any compromise, even at the expense of the future.[8]

Conversely, Lloyd George and Clemenceau had warmed to House over long months, not least in negotiating the Armistice on a basis of give and take. Admittedly, Lloyd George's retrospective judgement on House was barbed: 'It is perhaps to his credit that he was not nearly as cunning as he thought he was.'[9] One way or another, the British and French leaders became increasingly ready to lament how much more difficult it was to work with the headstrong American President than with his more flexible henchman. Wilson sensed some conspiracy to demote the League of Nations from its prime role in the peace process.

In Washington too the President had faced widespread suspicion of what he was up to with this League of Nations scheme. He accordingly brought back with him Senate demands for revisions to the Covenant, notably a clause that specifically declared that nothing in the Covenant prejudiced the Monroe Doctrine. Wilson thus had to bargain for this concession, not only from the French, who purported not to understand how any such problem could logically arise nor therefore why it needed to be addressed, but also from the pragmatic British. Since British naval power had historically underpinned the Monroe Doctrine, the point was one that Lloyd George exploited with some cynicism in getting what he really wanted: an American undertaking not to engage in a naval race with Britain, which was something that Wilson had threatened more than once. The President duly backed down, in his single-minded commitment to saving the Covenant. Moreover, the freedom of the seas also quietly disappeared as an issue since, on reflection, it appeared to the American delegation to be inconsistent with the League's capacity to use a blockade as a sanction.

Colonel House soldiered on regardless, but his exclusion from key decisions became increasingly noticeable. Members of the Inquiry became restive, no longer flattered by a President who sought their guidance. He had once inspired awe in Europe as a distant and omnipotent figure who never actually appeared, rather like God in a medieval miracle play; but in Paris the aura of celestial magic began to give way to sly mockery, covert for the time being.

Week by week, Wilson persisted, whether stubbornly or heroically. He did not draw the conclusion that his time might have been better spent in recruiting wider support at home rather than in dissipating his political capital in Paris: a city which, as early as St Valentine's Day, had given signs of falling out of love with him. The perceptive young British diplomat Harold Nicolson, part of the Foreign Office delegation in Paris, had observed the French mood steadily souring. 'The French papers', he noted on 16 March, 'accuse Wilson of "holding up the Treaty for the sake of his Pact of the League of Nations." This most unfair.' Nicolson himself, like many British liberals, shared the internationalist viewpoint of the American officials on House's Inquiry.

True, the support for the League of Nations came disproportionately from the English-speaking world. The fact that the conference had broken diplomatic precedent by adopting English as an official language had itself affronted *amour-propre* in Paris. (In practice, it assisted Clemenceau, who would make a point of waiting for the French translation before replying to points that he had himself understood perfectly well in English.) And another precedent was the seating of a British Empire delegation, with the self-governing Dominions and India all directly represented. Given that their war dead outnumbered those of the United States itself, this had its own logic, its own sentiment and its own momentum. Their inclusion as full members of the League was now assured – though this provided further fuel for those American opponents who saw it as a dodge to give the British Empire six votes.

The two Dominion representatives with real clout were Hughes of Australia and Smuts of South Africa. 'Billy' Hughes was a street-fighter, the champion of the 'White Australia' outlook of the Labor party, his interests sharply focused on making sure that his own country's sacrifices received fitting compensation. His impact on the reparations issue was to be significant. The Canadian Prime Minister, Sir Robert Borden, playing his hand less aggressively, had been content to establish the principle of separate Dominion representation and was thereafter less prominent than Hughes – and still less than the charismatic South African leader.

Jan Christiaan Smuts, Cambridge scholar, Boer War general, radiated high-minded magnanimity. He was a much admired figure in the eyes of British liberals, not least through his early and persistent championship of a League of Nations. Though a lawyer himself, Smuts had moderated the legal emphasis characteristic of earlier American proposals, proposing a more political, power-broking structure, in accordance with the British perspective. He had provided a crucial draft that meshed with the work of the Inquiry in forming Wilson's proposals.

Smuts now worked closely with Lord Robert Cecil. An aristocratic Tory, a son of that great pragmatist Lord Salisbury and thus Balfour's cousin (and formerly his deputy at the Foreign Office), Cecil had emerged as a fervent believer in the League and served alongside Smuts as the other British Empire representative on the League Commission. Like Clemenceau, Lloyd George delegated such duties, but Smuts had his ear, having served in the imperial war cabinet for eighteen months. Wilson insisted on chairing the Commission personally and did so with a diligence in handling its complex business that impressed officials like Nicolson. It was possible, then, to counter French impatience over the League by rallying anglophone support at various levels and, of course, by appealing to all the newly enfranchised nationalities promised their due under Wilson's trademark Fourteen Points.

Like the Ten Commandments, everyone had heard of them, some could recite them, but few strictly observed all of them. The first four points had sketched aspirations for the workings of an open and liberal world order. Of these, Point 2 (freedom of the seas) had sunk under its own weight, to ill-disguised British glee; the fact that the others remained rather sketchy gave them the status of work-in-progress. Point 5 was about colonies; and here the progress on Point 14 (League of Nations) made it possible to take up the idea of 'mandates', as proposed by Smuts. He had originally been thinking of the Ottoman Empire; but South Africa eventually found that this was its means of annexing the former German colonies that it coveted in southern Africa. And Hughes too could be bought off when Australia, along with New Zealand, got hold of German colonies in the South Pacific on the same basis.

Points 6 to 11 had covered diverse national claims within Europe. Former allies were appeased to different extents – least so when Russian borders were redrawn, but then, since Point 6 had been first proclaimed, the Bolsheviks had submitted to a separate peace, virtually dictated by the Germans at Brest-Litovsk in March 1918. This and the collapse of the Habsburg Empire pre-emptively settled the future shape of much of eastern Europe. In the west, Belgium had duly been liberated, and Alsace-Lorraine transferred to France.

The demands of the Italians made a more complex story. Since they were no longer content with their promised gains under the Treaty of London and demanded also the Adriatic port of Fiume, citing the 'nationality' provision of Point 9, Wilson sought to face down Orlando. First he exploited the inconsistency in the grounds of their claim, and thereby got Britain and France to withdraw their already reluctant commitment to the malodorous Treaty; then Wilson issued his own grandiloquent appeal to the Italian people over the heads of their own government. Though this failed to elicit the popular support he had anticipated in Italy, his démarche served to legitimise his principled stand in Paris over Fiume. It was Orlando who now departed, then slunk back, and soon found himself deposed by his own people. As for Points 10 and 11, the Habsburg Empire was carved up, acknowledging the new priority of ethnic-nationalist aspirations. This left a tiny residual Austria, essentially German but forbidden to join Germany; and new or extended states were recognised for Hungarians, Czechs, Slovaks, Romanians, Serbians, Slovenes, Montenegrins, much as previously promised (or at least hinted). The Treaties of Saint-Germain with Austria in September 1919 and Trianon with Hungary in June 1920 formalised all this.

The resurrection of an independent Poland (Point 13) was notable, if messy. It came at the price of a spacious geographic cost to the old Russian Empire but with an inescapable ethnic loss for Germany, which was to find East Prussia isolated behind a 'corridor' that ran from the Silesian coalfields (provisionally assigned to Poland) to the Baltic Sea at Danzig (Gdansk). All of this persistently troubled Lloyd George, and with good reason, as creating an incipient irredentist grievance; but Wilson got his way.

In what we now call the Middle East, things were even more complicated. Whereas the Hohenzollern Empire had been cut down to the size of a German republic, and the Habsburg Empire had fallen apart anyway, and the Romanov Empire had fragmented under the Bolsheviks, the Turkish core of the Ottoman Empire (point 12) proved unexpectedly resilient. And this despite facing dismemberment in August 1920 under the terms of the Treaty of Sèvres, which a rejuvenated Turkey under the remarkable leadership of Mustafa Kemal (later Atatürk) adroitly subverted.

Here it was the British who ultimately overplayed their hand. Lloyd George repeatedly placed too much reliance on Greek power in restraining Turkey and he staked out imperial gains that looked more impressive at the time than they do in retrospect. It is difficult to know what gave most trouble in the end: the British wartime promises to France, or their (unsuccessful) attempt to repudiate these, or their wartime promises to the Arabs, or their (more successful) attempt to break these, or the Balfour Declaration, a wartime promise to the Zionists, which Lloyd George and Balfour kept, though again at the expense of defaulting on pledges to the Arabs over this 'twice-promised land'. Mandates served as smoke and mirrors in the Middle East, with Palestine and Mesopotamia for the British, Syria and Lebanon for the French. Armenian hopes of a similar mandate under the United States, in some compensation for their notorious wartime sufferings, were to be dashed by Senator Lodge; and Mustafa Kemal's success in holding virtually all of Anatolia under the new government of Turkey necessarily left the Armenians in a weaker position than ever.

On such a checklist, Wilson could eventually claim a measure of vindication for his advertised principles, albeit in a much adulterated form. (If there had been a Point 15, in homage to Gladstone, it might well have covered Ireland: a claim for recognition in Paris that Irish nationalists now noisily proclaimed but one denied them by a tight-lipped British veto and ready American acquiesecence.)

Wilson's most notable setback came in dealing not with Europe but with Asia. Japan, after all, was one of the victorious powers and, in effect, demanded at least one major triumph. Its initial proposal was for a declaration of racial equality in the Covenant of the League. This became an acute embarrassment. The British were against it, citing opposition in Australia, where Hughes personified 'White Australia'; likewise, for the great liberal hero Smuts, acceptable talk of 'racial' equality in South Africa had always meant conciliating his Boer and British constituents, not the 'kaffirs'. So Wilson connived in blocking the Japanese proposal, no doubt mindful of the fact that Chinese immigration to California was restricted and, himself an emotional Southerner, well aware that he was the President who had institutionalised a colour bar in Washington.

The only option left, at a point when the Italians had already gone home, was to appease the Japanese by handing over Shandong. 'The opinion of the world', Baker told the President privately, 'supports the Chinese claims.' Wilson replied that he knew this; also that he knew that it was especially true in the United States, with its network of missionary and educational links with China. But, Wilson mused, should the Japanese now quit Paris, 'what becomes of the League of Nations?' In Baker's view: 'He is at Gethsemane.'[10] This was on 25 April. On 4 May, when the conference's decision to approve the Japanese claim reached China, there were furious nationalist demonstrations, and an outcry duly followed in the United States. Wilson justified what he did as a necessary accommodation with political realities. More broadly, it may well be true that only by putting the League of Nations first had he been able to achieve as much as he did.

But the price was heavy. Wilson's energies had been sapped in the process. His loss of confidence in House had become apparent – Lloyd George thought the Colonel's efforts towards a backstage resolution of the Fiume crisis was a critical moment – leaving the President more isolated than ever. Above all, other pressing business had been forced to wait. After his return to Paris, Wilson had recognised the need to do more in a deteriorating situation, with political instability now manifest throughout Europe, not least in Germany itself, where it was no longer clear that there would be any government capable of signing any treaty. 'At this moment there is a veritable race between peace and anarchy, and the public is beginning to show its impatience,' he told the Council of Four on 24 March. He mentioned reparations as one key problem. 'I support President Wilson's suggestion,' said Lloyd George, 'especially regarding the question of reparations, which is the most difficult of all.'[11] At last, his own agenda and that of Clemenceau was to receive due priority.

Lloyd George had an apartment in Paris where he and Frances Stevenson could discreetly live together. The worldly, unshockable Balfour, attending the conference as British Foreign Secretary, had the apartment above. They worked together much better than Wilson and Lansing, Lloyd George a quick learner in all the arts of diplomacy as in everything else. It was a rare day when the Prime Minister, in his operatic Figaro-mode, did not relish the delights of the city. But on 5 April the Stevenson diary records him as not feeling well – with the only consolation coming from the news that Wilson had actually taken to his bed. 'Clemenceau was very pleased at Wilson's absence, & could not conceal his joy. "He is *worse* today," he said to D., & doubled up with laughter. "Do you know his doctor? Couldn't you get round him & bribe him?"' Lloyd George gaily came home that day claiming that they were now making progress – 'which means that I am getting my own way!' So they had now 'reached an agreement on reparation & indemnities & D. had got his own way, after having fought the matter for over a fortnight'.[12]

This was indeed a crucial turning point in the peace conference, belatedly confronting the issue that was subsequently to cloud its reputation. Meanwhile, Wilson's illness may have been a laughing matter for 'the Tiger': another victory for age and wisdom. But the President's (temporary) viral infection was not a good sign, given the acute stress he was undergoing in re-establishing a better grip on the Paris agenda while watching it unravel in Washington. Dr Grayson appreciated all this, later taking note of Lloyd George's relaxed comments on the political style of the President. 'I have pointed out to him in considering several questions, how he could help himself politically through certain moves,' Lloyd George observed in his worldly way, then added the reflection: 'He is not like Gladstone. Gladstone was a statesman but also a politician.'[13] Baker put it slightly differently, in the light of the Shandong dilemma: 'The League of Nations is a matter of *faith*: and the President is first of all a *man of faith*.'[14] It was now time to shift the agenda of peacemaking from the moral intentions expressed in the Fourteen Points to the economic consequences.

A Carthaginian Peace? Keynes

The most significant impact of the locomotive of war can be seen in economic terms. It may be true that nobody saw this more clearly than John Maynard Keynes, nor expressed this view with more cogency at the time, nor with more influence – in the long run at least. Yet in all this, he was simply speaking to problems that he saw in the world around him.

The war changed everything, for Britain and France, but also for the United States. Taking a long view, we now know that in Britain and France alike the total value of national capital, of all kinds, had fluctuated at around 700 per cent of national income throughout two centuries – until 1914, that is. There were differences between the two countries, of course, notably that France continued to hold a larger proportion of its national wealth in agricultural land (about 20 per cent in 1910), far more than in Britain, where housing was already more significant; and the real pre-war peculiarity of the British was that the overseas investment portfolio accounted for over a quarter of national capital. By 1920 both countries had been humbled; national capital in each of them fell to 300 per cent of national income in an unprecedented shock from which there was to be no significant recovery until the 1950s. This was quite unlike the pattern in the United States, where capital had reached 500 per cent of national income only as late as 1910 and then suffered no catastrophic decline. Above all, net overseas American investment moved from long-term deficit to surplus during and after the First World War.[1]

This is what we know today, with much greater certainty and sophistication than previously. But Keynes was not alone among his contemporaries in pointing at the time to the significant shift that was taking place. From his professional perspective within the British Treasury, the salient fact was that Britain had previously been the prime creditor nation: one with a unique ability to dictate the terms on which much of the world did its business. Hence the facility with which the international gold standard operated. The Bank of England sent out signals that other central banks picked up, ultimately requiring less fortunate beings on distant continents to make adjustments in their getting and spending; and thus the whole wonderful mechanism was brought into equilibrium, so smoothly (as it seemed to London bankers), so painlessly (as it seemed to London bankers). The illusion that, in these international transactions, it was still business as usual had been maintained until 1917, with London financing the greatest war in history while maintaining the outward forms at least of the international gold standard.

But from his privileged vantage point Keynes perceived that this had become little more than the political economy of prestidigitation. He knew this because he was now one of the conjurors. The British Treasury had progressively become engaged in a gigantic exercise in bluff, in which Britain's hand could have been called at critical moments. The most critical moment of all had actually come after the United States entered the war, bringing a multi-faceted confrontation between the various financial authorities in the summer of 1917.

This was critical for Keynes personally, as well as in terms of the fate of the British war economy. The 'authorities' in Britain comprised the Treasury and the Bank of England, working in tandem. But with his expanding responsibility for external finance at the Treasury, Keynes had come into direct conflict with the Governor of the Bank of England himself, now elevated to the peerage as Lord Cunliffe, who insisted on his own privileged access to the Prime Minister, under Lloyd George as under Asquith. Cunliffe did so explicitly with the intention of bypassing the influence of this presumptuous young Treasury official, Mr Keynes, who evidently had notions above his pay-grade. Cunliffe had got away with it under McKenna. But the Chancellor of the Exchequer in the Lloyd George coalition was now Bonar Law, the tough-minded Conservative leader, who asserted the prerogatives of the Treasury, facing the Prime Minister with the threat of his own resignation in early July 1917, which served to win the point. Keynes thus became a grateful beneficiary – he always expressed respect for Bonar Law – whereas Cunliffe became a casualty, forced out of the Governorship later that year (though evidently not disgraced in the eyes of Lloyd George, who was to recall him as a key adviser in the peace negotiations).

This seemingly petty incident was a preliminary to the great Anglo-American crisis over war finance. As US Treasury Secretary, William McAdoo was confronted with a difficult task: to raise the money for American mobilisation without compromising the finances of the Allies, who were still left to do the actual fighting in Europe until the US Army was itself fit and ready (in the judgement of Black Jack Pershing). McAdoo, moreover, had to act without offending political susceptibilities at home, continually wary of seeming to be hoodwinked by those wily British. But in launching its series of US Liberty Loans, the US Treasury naturally tapped and cultivated the patriotic instincts of American investors, thus impairing Britain's own ability to borrow in dollars, on which the parity of the pound sterling now depended.

Providing funds to support the sterling exchange rate was no part of McAdoo's brief as he saw it, looking over his shoulder at Congress. That he had to be made to see things differently, to be educated by the superior intellects of the British Treasury, was suddenly urgent. In a note from Bonar Law, drafted by Keynes, and then formally transmitted (through Balfour and Ambassador Page) to McAdoo, full substantiating detail was eventually spelled out. The stark conclusion was that, without US support, 'the whole financial fabric of the alliance will collapse' and that this would be 'a matter not of months but of days'.[2] Keynes acknowledged that this was partly a self-induced problem of confidence, a matter of perceptions, fostered by the British authorities themselves: 'We have openly attached hitherto the utmost importance to the position of the exchanges.'[3] These pleas reached Washington at the end of July 1917.

McAdoo relented, the conditions were eased, the crisis passed, the pound remained on the gold standard. It did so until 1919, courtesy of the US Treasury. Incrementally, British private borrowing on Wall Street through J. P. Morgan was to be replaced by inter-government loans. The macro-economic effect was much the same as previously: to sustain the British war economy with the dollars that were clearly necessary now that the resources of sterling were exhausted. But the political implications were quite different, making British war debts into a high-profile issue on which congressional approval continued to be essential, whether in granting the loans or in collecting the subsequent debts.

The underlying reality was that the US economy could well take the strain. In 1914 it was still in the doldrums of recession; GDP had declined by 8 per cent since the benchmark pre-war year of 1913. But the hostilities in Europe proved a fine tonic; by 1915 the US economy was growing and by 1916 it was 17 per cent bigger than two years previously. Admittedly, growth was then checked, with a slight check in 1917 that may lend some credence to the notion of a 'low-growth war economy', in years when the draft came into operation, thus taking men out of productive employment. But by the time that President Wilson sailed for Europe at the end of 1918, the US economy was 24 per cent bigger than in 1914. Moreover, unlike the European economies, it was not facing a mountainous war debt.

In France the problem was most acute, with a raucous cry for Germany to pay. The Finance Minister, Klotz, made this his signature tune; Clemenceau simply shrugged, his expressive eyebrows arched in world-weary disdain for financial issues. This was truly a matter of political economy, with the emphasis on the political.

In France the cumulative public debt had already reached nearly 100 per cent of annual national income by 1880, not least because of the impact of the 1871 indemnity to Germany; it was still around 80 per cent in 1910 – but was no higher than that in 1920. Moreover, French public assets were of much the same value as the debt, so the net internal position was roughly neutral. In Britain, by contrast, the real value of public debt had decreased through the nineteenth century from the heroic level of nearly 200 per cent of national income at the end of the Napoleonic Wars to about 30 per cent by 1910, more than matched by public assets of nearly 50 per cent. But the debt then soared to nearly 150 per cent by 1920, with public assets worth only half that sum.[4]

The relative efficiency of the British tax system is one reason for the differences. In France, and even more so in Germany, the reliance on loans was both a cause and an effect of the general assumption that a post-war indemnity would enable the victors to charge the costs of the war to the vanquished, as in 1871. In that perspective, resort to high taxes could be seen as a sort of defeatism. It is true that in Britain new levels of taxation enabled more of the internal costs of this war to be covered than in France (and still more than in Germany). The Treasury was self-consciously aware that Gladstone had covered fully half the total costs of the Crimean War by taxation. But McKenna's version of Gladstonianism introduced a novelty, 'the normal year', which meant aiming at a balanced budget for notional peacetime expenditure, even though the conditions of wartime meant borrowing about three-quarters of actual expenditure in the fiscal years 1915–18.

Keynes at the time tacitly deferred to this curious doctrine of the normal year. But when the prominence of the 'rentiers' who had possessed the resources to invest in war loans at relatively high levels of interest became a controversial political issue, Keynes was not the only economist, and not the only Liberal, to advocate a post-war capital levy. It is true that Britain faced a problem in financing its own national debt, amounting to £7,000 million by 1919. This was held primarily by its own citizens, and the consequent interest payments indeed made a heavy claim upon post-war budgets. But an altogether more combustible political issue, in domestic and foreign politics, was its official level of indebtedness in dollars to the United States.

The United States' position was totally different from that of its co-belligerents and fellow peacemakers France and Britain. The public debt of the United States had historically been exceeded by the value of the public assets that the loans had helped to create; and this remained as true in 1920, when the debt reached 50 per cent of national income, as it had been in 1910, when it was about half that. And whereas the British national debt was to continue inexorably climbing in the 1920s, the US public debt was to decline, falling to about 40 per cent of national income by 1930.⁵ Moreover, the real strength of the Americans' financial position, of course, was as the only great international creditor left standing: one that was owed, on Keynes's contemporary reckoning, about £2,000 million ($9,000 million), rather less than half of which was due from Britain.⁶

The French too had such debts. They owed the United States about £550 million and owed Britain just over £500 million. The Italians owed the Americans over £300 million and owed the British nearly £500 million. Then there were the official Russian debts, contracted before the Bolsheviks took over and repudiated them. Keynes put these at £568 million to Britain and £160 million to France, but it hardly matters what value was assigned to these scraps of paper. These were all inter-Allied government debts; but the French commitment to their former Russian alliance was also signalled by the noisy presence of perhaps a million citizens who had patriotically subscribed to the Romanov loans and accordingly flourished their scrip (or scrap).

So here was a fine game in which everyone owed some debts – except the United States. And virtually everyone had some debts that they knew were owing to them, if not legally then morally. And just as the United States was unique in being only a creditor, Britain was unique in being both creditor and debtor on a grand scale. It does not require much insight to see why the British were continually tempted to propose magnanimity in writing off everyone's debts, or why the Americans held sternly to the probity of contract in resisting such schemes. President Coolidge was subsequently to put it best: 'They hired the money, didn't they?'

How on earth had this situation arisen? When Keynes had tried to describe it back in early 1916, he had said that Britain had only France as an ally and that the rest were mercenaries; and then France too, in the course of 1916, had become a mercenary; and then in the course of 1917, Britain itself had become a mercenary – of the United States of course.

This was now the American way in warfare. In the days when it was Britain that had waged its foreign wars by using mercenaries to do the actual fighting, it had often financed them by means of 'subsidies', a term helpfully defined by the *Oxford English Dictionary*: 'A sum of money paid by one country to another for the promotion of war or the preservation of neutrality'. It is almost as useful a term as 'reparations'. It seems to cover not only the sort of advantages for which Britain paid up in previous centuries but also those enjoyed by the United States, both as a neutral and as a belligerent, during the European conflict that so enriched it between 1914 and 1918. A key difference was that Britain had never expected its subsidies to be repaid.

The expectations of President Wilson, as he outlined them on his voyage to the Old World in December 1918, were quite different. He spoke airily of the various ways in which he would enlighten the Europeans, former enemies and allies alike. Thus he would stun the French with the moral example of Château-Thierry, or would cow the British with a naval threat to outbuild them, or would outflank the European leaders by appealing to public opinion and thus inspire awe for the unique unselfishness of the United States. Above all, he would make money talk by invoking the mighty American dollar.

A financial strategy was certainly a potent option since so many of the problems of peacemaking in Europe were manifestly economic. Thus it may seem obvious in retrospect that western Europe could not be put back on its feet, on any peaceful basis, except through enlisting American economic resources in some way. Whether this happened through the action of government or through private enterprise was (we may think today) irrelevant to the macro-economic impact. What was essential was that, whether the language was that of 'subsidies' or 'reparations' or 'debts' or 'bonds', the economic system should be lubricated by the necessary transfers. When the President of the United States arrived in Paris to bring peace and prosperity to the ravaged lands of Europe, he was not thinking of this kind of Pax Americana. True, he could bring various kinds of moral force to bear, but his hands were tied in being unable to offer American concessions when it came to disentangling the skein of war debts. Here was the economic premise for the policy of reparations as actually specified in the Treaty of Versailles.

Keynes's view of Lloyd George was inevitably coloured by the Treasury spectacles that he had worn in wartime. A budding Treasury mandarin, an orthodox Cambridge economist, a disciple of the great Alfred Marshall, he had viewed the war economy rather narrowly, assuming that canons of financial prudence should prevail – the strain of small-c conservatism in Keynes's complex make-up. Personally he got on surprisingly well with the two big-C Conservatives who served as Chancellor under Lloyd George, first Bonar Law and later Austen Chamberlain, and also came to be on easy terms with the new Financial Secretary to the Treasury, Stanley Baldwin, who often deferred to his economic advice. These three men were to serve successively as leaders of the Conservative Party from 1911 to 1937; it was not any partisan animus against them but rather his complex feelings about Britain's all-conquering Prime

Minister that motivated Keynes. He went to Paris in January 1919 as Chamberlain's principal assistant, and was himself to resign in early June, in bitter disillusionment.

The Economic Consequences of the Peace, published at the end of 1919, was the result. 'A great sensation has been made here by Professor Keynes of Cambridge, who was at Versailles as an economic expert, and resigned that position and came home as a protest against the peace terms,' wrote Bernard Shaw to an Austrian friend in January 1920. 'He has now published a book in which he demonstrates that the indemnity demanded from Germany is an economic impossibility; and nobody ventures to dispute this.' True, the book suddenly catapulted Keynes to international fame; it was a bestseller on both sides of the Atlantic, used as ammunition in political debates, quoted in newspapers, in Parliament and in the United States Senate. But Shaw, with his blind spot about liberal moralism, identified the formal aim of the book rather than the reason for its wide acclaim. It was the power of its political polemic rather than the cogency of its economic analysis that generated its reputation – in a way that still remains true today when even an historian of the highest distinction will sadly shake her head and call it pernicious.

Lloyd George went to Paris as Prime Minister, backed by a huge electoral majority. His coalition supporters had been formally identified in the General Election of December 1918 through a 'coupon' issued jointly by himself and by Bonar Law, obviously acting as Conservative leader. Since Asquith was still the leader of the Liberal party, the Prime Minister's status depended simply on being Lloyd George. But though his nominal supporters won some 500 parliamentary seats, only a quarter of these were held by his own Coalition Liberals, the rest by Conservatives. Asquithian Liberals were reduced to a remnant of about thirty; Labour now had fifty-seven MPs.

The account that the Economic Consequences gave of the General Election became notorious. It was branded as 'an act of public immorality' in which 'the claims of private ambition' had driven

David Low, Solo Syndication / Associated Newspapers Ltd.

*David Low was a cartoonist capable of conveying strong political views. He had a high
regard for the arguments of Keynes, not literally in 'the rocking chair of a pundit', as Lloyd
George put it, but as rather more than an armchair critic of public policy in Britain.*

Lloyd George in basely enlisting 'the emotions of the moment'.[7] Of course, this was hardly fair. A Parliament elected in December 1910 had little authority to handle peace negotiations in 1919; Asquith's Liberal and progressive majority had fragmented; the Irish issue still remained unresolved.

Moreover, there was now a different electorate. The newly enfranchised voters comprised women over the age of thirty, with a qualification that mainly covered housewives, and younger men over twenty-one – and also all wartime servicemen, of whatever age (though relatively few actually managed to vote). Taken together, these provisions brought a small net increase in the working-class proportion of the electorate, though virtually all the new voters were the wives or sons of existing voters; so the significance of all this in improving Labour's chances can easily be exaggerated. Above all, the sheer size of the electorate had increased, from 7.7 million to 21.4 million. (Lloyd George, who had polled just over 3,000 votes in Caernarvon Boroughs in 1910, was elected with nearly 14,000 in 1918; Asquith, who had polled some 5,000 in East Fife in 1910, now got nearly 7,000, which spelled defeat.) Had Parliament not been dissolved in 1918, fully eight years since the previous election, only about a quarter of the current electorate would have actually exercised their democratic rights – a curious way of making the world safe for democracy.

'It is a moribund Parliament,' Lloyd George had said, with good reason, at the beginning of the campaign, as he later reminded everyone. He could also quote his claim that 'in the international settlement I would like to see the best traditions of Mr Gladstone's life embodied in the settlement of Europe and the affairs of the world: regard for national liberty, national rights, whether nations be great or small'.[8] In retrospect he acknowledged that this tone had not been maintained in face of strident claims for retribution against Germany, but pleaded extenuating circumstances and readily acknowledged that much stronger demands were made by many of the coalition supporters who now filled the House of Commons.

Keynes naturally sided with the Asquithian exiles. He had actually been a house guest at The Wharf, the Asquiths' country home, when he wrote in April 1918 to Florence Keynes about Lloyd George: 'We are governed by a crook and the results are natural.' Frances Stevenson quoted the published version of this letter half a century later, commenting: 'L.G., in asking Keynes to become a delegate to the Peace Conference had no idea that he was giving treachery its opportunity.' But this was hardly some retrospective revelation, given their previous clashes.

Asquithians like Keynes were now much closer to the Labour party than to the Lloyd George coalition, especially over foreign policy. Maynard's own close friend Leonard Woolf, who had laboured (with support from his wife Virginia) on an influential study propagating ideas for a league of nations, was to serve as secretary of Labour's new Advisory Committee on International Questions. When the great meeting founding the League of Nations Union, with Grey as its president, was held in October 1918, Virginia Woolf wrote of Grey in her diary (which so often punctured public pretensions): 'He said nothing but what one has read & agreed with about a League of Nations, but he said it simply, & for a "great statesman" to have sense & human feeling & no bombast does produce an odd sense of wonder & humility in me, as if human nature were worth something after all.'[9] In Bloomsbury, high hopes were invested in a Wilsonian peace: not least by Keynes as he watched three great statesmen in action, day by day, in the febrile atmosphere of Paris.

The exigencies of electioneering in late 1918 had not nurtured the Wilsonian project in Britain (nor in the United States). It was one of Lloyd George's Conservative ministers, Sir Eric Geddes, who found his moment of fame through a notorious boast about Germany. 'We will get out of her all you can squeeze out of a lemon and a bit more,' he was reported as saying. 'I will squeeze her until you can hear the pips squeak.' What gave this otherwise unremarked declaration its worldwide currency was the fact that it was to be quoted in the *Economic Consequences*.[10] And this actually came about because

Geddes happened to be the MP for Cambridge; his speech had been given in the city's Guildhall; and Florence Keynes had, as was now her custom, saved and filed the newspaper clipping for her son.

Stanley Baldwin had naturally been re-elected. His official room in the Treasury adjoined that of the permanent secretary, Sir Robert Chalmers, and when Baldwin put his nose round the door on the first day that the new Parliament assembled, he happened to find Keynes there, having tea with Chalmers. Over the tea cups, Keynes asked the minister what the new members were like. 'A lot of hard-faced men who look as if they had done well out of the war,' said Baldwin.[11] Here was another emblematic quotation that the *Economic Consequences* was to make famous.[12] And Baldwin, a wealthy ironmaster himself, certainly had the moral right to speak, as subsequently affirmed by his voluntary donation of £120,000 to the Treasury as a sort of one-man capital levy (of about £5 million in today's terms).

In many such ways, the *Economic Consequences* drew upon the author's personal viewpoint and his privileged insider status. Its wider impact was enhanced by the hands-on, real-world political context in which it was written. Keynes was fully aware of this dimension, as his concluding pages make explicit. There he invokes 'the hidden currents, flowing continually below the surface of political history, of which no one can predict the outcome. In one way only can we influence these hidden currents – by setting in motion those forces of instruction and imagination which change *opinion*.' Hence the final words of this peroration: 'To the formation of the general opinion of the future I dedicate this book.'[13]

That it lived up to this aspiration is hardly disputable. It was the polemical passion of the book, sustained by calculated artifice, that achieved this impact. In the process, a self-proclaimed analysis of economic consequences was transmuted into a tract animated by moral intentions. Bloomsbury heard much of it in early drafts. Virginia Woolf's diary shows her perusing her copy in April 1920. 'Reading Maynard too – a book that influences the world without being in the least a work of art: a work of morality, I suppose.'[14] Her artistic criteria may have been set demandingly high but her assessment of the nature of the tract's appeal is surely right, in seeing what Shaw missed: that the indictment works within a moral ambit.

In these terms, however, the *Economic Consequences* seems either inconsistent or unperceptive on at least one point. For Lloyd George is reproached not only for colluding with the hard-faced men in wanting to make the pips squeak but also for adopting a cry about 'hanging the Kaiser'. This had indeed been made during the campaign by the Labour representative in the war cabinet, George Barnes, who was subsequently appointed as one of the five official British representatives at the peace conference. Keynes pointedly cites, as two of the six points of Lloyd George's final manifesto, both a trial of the Kaiser and 'punishment of those responsible for atrocities', with the comment: 'Here is food for the cynic.' Keynes calls this a 'concoction of greed and sentiment, prejudice and deception'.[15] These proposals are depicted as some sudden and vindictive departure from the liberal norms that had hitherto distinguished British war aims.

But Lloyd George was surely right to defend himself on this point. Not only could he later affirm that he himself never used the phrase about 'hanging the Kaiser' but he could rehearse the longstanding Liberal indictment of German methods from the time of the original invasion of Belgium. In short, if the invasion of Belgium was a violation of the public law of Europe, then it was a crime. This was only what Asquith, as well as Grey, had insistently said since 1914; it was what Wilson had tacitly admitted since 1915 and openly proclaimed since 1917. As good liberals, they had all endorsed, often explicitly, the Gladstonian doctrine that there was no moral distinction between the behaviour of individuals and that of governments. In which case, it was surely necessary to identify the criminals and bring them to justice by properly establishing their guilt. It is also relevant that Asquith and Wilson both had legal careers behind them.

So, of course, had Lloyd George. 'Up to middle age I was a practising lawyer, whose business consisted largely in sifting, selecting and weighing evidence, both oral and documentary, with a view to presenting the case as a whole to trained judges and to a jury of citizens,' he wrote in the preface of his memoirs of the peace conference.[16] The former attorney then relied on contemporary documents to show why and how he succeeded in getting the peace conference to agree to putting Kaiser Wilhelm on trial. It was Lord Curzon who had first argued this to the imperial war cabinet in November 1918, after a discussion in Paris with Clemenceau, calling the Kaiser 'the arch-criminal of the world' who should be brought to justice. Lloyd George had agreed, using rather less prejudicial terms: 'I think he ought to stand his trial.'[17] Churchill demurred, as perhaps a soldier might. The matter was then referred to the law officers; and the Attorney-General, F. E. Smith, duly responded after consultation. Smith was a Conservative, a personal friend of Churchill and universally acknowledged as a highly able advocate, whom Lloyd George was well content to commend and quote at length.

Smith's argument seemed inexorable. If the Kaiser was indeed responsible for a uniquely 'daring and dangerous challenge to the principles of public law', why should he be granted impunity? Surely not simply because he was an emperor.[18] It was less easy, though, to see what offences were justiciable. If Wilhelm were charged with causing the European war, 'the trial of such a charge would involve infinite disputation'. A second count, however, was surely justified: 'charging the Kaiser with responsibility for the invasion of Belgium in breach of International Law and for all the consequent criminal acts which took place'.[19] Smith also recommended a third count, to cover unrestricted U-boat warfare. And at all events, no subordinates should be brought to trial if the Kaiser were allowed to escape. The unanimous view of the imperial war cabinet was now that 'the ex-Kaiser should be held personally responsible for his crimes against international law'.[20]

Inevitably, our reading of such matters is coloured by prosecutions of Nazi and other war criminals in a later era. The terms of the 1918 Armistice (Article VI) had made it clear that those engaged in legitimate military activity would not face prosecution; and it was not proposed that the Kaiser be charged with simply causing the war. Now whether such stipulations seem sound in a post-Nuremberg era is a good question; but they are hardly as outlandish as the *Economic Consequences* contrives to suggest. Far from his view of German culpability marking Lloyd George's sudden post-war lapse, it could be cited as evidence of his own consistency. Churchill, who was frankly bemused by the proposal, testified in 1929 that his friend was 'from the first singularly affected' by this issue and remained 'genuinely indignant' to the end.[21]

So much for retrospect. At the time, demands to put the Kaiser on trial often reflected a moralistic perspective that had informed the thinking of Liberals all along. Nor had it been simply an opportunistic invention by Asquith or Grey to justify their taking the British Empire into a war for Belgium in 1914. Even the Liberals who had been most prominently sceptical on that score accepted the moral criteria by which the Kaiser's Germany had to be judged. Though evaded in the *Economic Consequences*, this point was surely apparent at the time of its publication in December 1919.

For example, only two months previously, Lord Loreburn had published his own book, *How the War Came*. Loreburn, eminent lawyer, hammer of the Liberal Imperialists, guardian of the shrine to C-B, friend and ally of Morley, had a dual aim. He sought to establish a case against secret diplomacy (notably that of Grey in taking Britain to war) and so to call for a League of Nations that would make future wars impossible. 'Its chief Architect has been President Wilson, whose efforts in this supreme cause will place him alongside the greatest figures in history.'[22]

There could hardly be a better spokesman than Loreburn for those Liberals who had once deplored Grey's foreign policy. Yet he wrote in 1919: 'The military masters of Germany wanted war from the beginning in order to attack France and Russia, and to carry out their ambitions, but always on the condition that they could count on British neutrality, as in 1870.'[23] Though arguing that Belgium had not been crucial, because Grey had already given compromising assurances to the French, Loreburn lacked nothing in his moral commitment to the case for upholding the famous Treaty of 1839. 'We should have gone to war on behalf of Belgium if we had not already done so on behalf of France.'[24] This may seem a surprisingly narrow distinction. The origins of the war lay in the response to the Serbian crisis: 'It was Austria that began the quarrel.'[25] And it was when the Austrians found support from the Kaiser that the crisis became European in scale, with an unequivocal responsibility: 'There is something cynical and repulsive in the attempt to exculpate Germany on the ground that she would not have begun the war had she known that Great Britain would be among her enemies.'[26] Thus to Loreburn, 'the true character of German warfare has been written in letters of blood all over the face of Europe'.[27]

The stance that Lloyd George adopted was infused with like sentiments, albeit couched in his own distinctive timbre. 'The Kaiser must be prosecuted,' he claimed. 'The war was a crime. Who doubts that?'[28] The doubters were indeed hard to find, not only at the time of the election but in the succeeding months while the peace conference was deliberating. The fact that the Kaiser was not ultimately put on trial, despite provision for this in the Treaty, was because the Dutch government, as a neutral, gave him asylum. In the course of time this came to be seen as sparing the Allies an embarrassing task, perhaps one fuelled by a transitory nationalistic bloodlust. And meanwhile, the liberal moralism that had likewise infused this appeal to international law became diverted into another channel. For, belatedly but inescapably, the argument over the peace terms came to focus upon the issue of reparations.

———

When people refer, whether indulgently or indignantly, to the *Economic Consequences*, they usually turn out to mean chapter 3, 'The Conference'. In literary terms, this is fully understandable. It

contains passages as good as anything in the book that Keynes's friend
Lytton Strachey had published a year previously, *Eminent Victorians*
(which Asquith himself had hailed for its 'subtle and suggestive
art'). Austen Chamberlain, still calling himself a 'personal friend'
of his former Treasury adviser, told Keynes that 'I chortled with joy
over the conference chapter!'[29] The author remained proud of these
eighteen pages of exquisite satire, which he chose to reprint as the
first of the *Essays in Biography* that he was to publish some fourteen
years afterwards. These are indeed the most accessible, the most
quoted and the most notorious pages in his famous tract.

'Clemenceau was by far the most eminent member of the Council
of Four,' Keynes acknowledges with genuine respect. This portrait
is not a simply hostile view but one imbued with a good deal of
wry sympathy. 'One could not despise Clemenceau or dislike him,
but only take a different view as to the nature of civilised man, or
indulge, at least, a different hope.'[30] What Keynes means is that the
moralisation of both the war and the peace, which came so naturally to those brought up in the English-speaking liberal tradition,
was alien to Clemenceau's worldview, which is true enough. He
then adds, in a much more tendentious passage: 'He felt about
France what Pericles felt of Athens – unique value in her, nothing else mattering; but his theory of politics was Bismarck's.' The
key difference between the two leaders was simply in their different applications of the theory of nationalism and force. Thus
Clemenceau imputed the positive qualities to France, the negative characteristics to Germany ('though it is doubtful how far he
thought these characteristics peculiar to Germany, or whether his
candid view of some other nations was fundamentally different').
The fundamental point is that, given the politics of power, this is the
only way to operate: 'The glory of the nation you love is a desirable
end – but generally to be obtained at your neighbour's expense.'[31]
Accordingly, how Clemenceau behaved was only to be expected.
If he was in the victor's seat at the end of this further, ineluctable
Franco-German conflict then he would visit upon Germany a

heavy dose of the old Bismarckian medicine. The pessimistic view of human nature that these two statesmen allegedly shared made such reversals not only natural but necessary.

Now this is manifestly an overdrawn portrait. Lloyd George was nearer the mark in identifying Clemenceau's political antagonist, the French President, Poincaré, as the man who was 'bent on keeping Germany down'.[32] Admittedly, when at the palace of Versailles itself, Lloyd George also observed Clemenceau's 'hatred of the Germans', who in 1871 had treated France 'with an insolence which for 50 years had rankled in the heart of this fierce old patriot'.[33]

What Keynes is presenting is a stylised image of the French premier. It is one that his own observations in Paris could surely have served to qualify in all sorts of ways; but it is not so much a faithful portrait of an individual as a step in Keynes's own indictment of French policy. For this is political economy as a zero-sum game, in which the winner must prudently seize maximum advantage while the opportunity offers, lest worse befall. It is, of course, no modern innovation or principle but one already firmly rooted in the bloody wars of antiquity. Hence the natural temptation for those with a classical education to characterise the stringent terms that were now proposed in Paris as the sort of peace that Rome had once imposed upon defeated Carthage. It was a usage that Keynes picked up and propagated for a wider audience in suggesting that 'as soon as this view of the world is adopted and the other discarded, a demand for a Carthaginian peace is inevitable, to the full extent of the momentary power to impose it'.[34]

His portrait of Wilson, of course, is a study etched in disillusion. 'The President, for me, was a fallen hero,' Keynes privately admitted later.[35] Hence the tone in the *Economic Consequences*. 'The great distinction of language which had marked his famous Notes seemed to indicate a man of lofty and powerful imagination,' so Keynes acknowledges, only to ask the reader to share his disappointment about 'this blind and deaf Don Quixote'. The clue, he insists, is one that 'the ordinary Englishman' will immediately be able to decode: 'The President was like a nonconformist minister, perhaps a Presbyterian.'[36] Coming from a descendant of so many Nonconformist divines himself, but phrased as though Keynes did not know perfectly well what Wilson's own background was, this 'perhaps' is wholly disingenuous. But it prepares the reader for further digging into the President's background. Leonard Woolf, who had read a draft as early as August 1919, had urged on Keynes's efforts, assuring him that 'I expect your psychological analysis of Wilson is absolutely correct.'[37]

All three leaders come out badly to some extent. Whatever the affronted reaction in France to Keynes's half-admiring aphorisms about the world-weary cynicism of Clemenceau, or the offence created in the United States by the author's feline characterisation of Wilson as the naive Presbyterian preacher, the main impact on British public opinion came through what the book says about Lloyd George's role. Perhaps the surprise here is the keen appreciation, shown by a connoisseur of tradecraft, for the uncannily effective political artistry on display:

> To see the British Prime Minister watching the company, with six or seven senses not available to ordinary men, judging character, motive, and subconscious impulse, perceiving what each was thinking and even what each was going to say next, and compounding with telepathic instinct the argument or appeal best suited to the vanity, weakness, or self-interest of his immediate auditor, was to realise that the poor President would be playing blind man's buff in that party.[38]

With mordant disdain, Keynes goes on to attribute the puncturing of Wilson's idealistic New World innocence to the Old World wiles that ensnared him. So that in the end, when Lloyd George made a belated pitch for 'all the moderation he dared', having finally perceived the onerous effect of the Treaty's terms, he found it 'harder to debamboozle this old Presbyterian than it had been to bamboozle him' over the previous long weeks of the conference.[39]

These were phrases with a deadly sting. In this indictment of the iniquity and folly of the Treaty, Wilson could be seen as victim as much as perpetrator, Clemenceau could likewise be largely excused as a lovable rogue from central casting, but Lloyd George – precisely because of his unique gifts – was revealed as the truly culpable figure. All this, of course, played to the stereotypes of the progressive left in Britain, whether Asquithian or Labour, equally susceptible to this nicely updated dose of Gladstonian moralising. The independent Liberals put out the account of Lloyd George's role in the Coupon Election as a pamphlet; the Labour Research Department sponsored a cheap edition of the whole book for trade unionists. Keynes's rise to fame thus came at the expense of a Prime Minister whose own flaws had naturally led him into coalition with the Conservatives. In further blighting relations between these two men, all that was lacking – until *Essays in Biography* was later published – was Keynes's draft of an even more biting personal sketch of Lloyd George, omitted from the *Economic Consequences* in 1919 on prudent advice offered by the author's mother (and by Asquith too).

So much for the literary flourishes of chapter 3. In it the author indeed declares: 'My purpose in this book is to show that the Carthaginian peace is not *practically* right or possible.'[40] But that prospectus is only developed in chapter 4, 'The Treaty', and in chapter 5, 'Reparation', with more than a hundred pages of close analysis – surely less widely quoted because less widely read.

As his book's title sufficiently proclaims, it is the *economic* consequences of imposing heavy reparations on Germany that is its central message. As an economist, Keynes could see that making Germany responsible for the costs of the war was easier said than done. For this was not just a financial transaction, still less a simple question of shaking the money out of German pockets, or squeezing the Germans till the pips squeaked, or finding some stash of German gold that could handily be shipped to the Allies. The rhetoric of 'making Germany pay' confused the relative ease of running up internal debts (where debasement of the currency always offers one means of subsequent default) with the problem of inexorably meeting external payments, denominated in values fixed by the gold standard. Such extravagant claims thus lacked a grasp of the processes of the real economy, in which all transfers were ultimately made in the form of flows of goods and services, not merely through the book-keeping of financial transactions. Moreover, this was no zero-sum game, in which one country could only win if others lost, but a process in which national economies were linked organically in creating and sustaining the wealth and well-being of all.

What sums were at stake in these arguments? It was one major charge against the Treaty that it avoided stating any specified sum. Working from its detailed specifications, however, Keynes's own calculations put the total claim against Germany at £8,000 million. But because of the provisions on future interest liabilities, 'even if Germany pays £150 million annually up to 1936, she will nevertheless owe us at that date more than half as much again as she does now (£13,000 million as compared with £8,000 million)'.[41] Such sums, as we can now see, were unmatched by any comparable transfers in history, short of a Nazi-style occupation. Though there have always been some writers who stoutly maintain that Germany had a greater capacity to pay than the tender-minded Keynes alleged, his central arguments indeed remain alive and well nearly a century later: that the scale of reparations *as specified in the Treaty signed in June 1919* made demands that could not be fulfilled under peacetime conditions.

As chapter 4 tells us time and again, the problem is 'the extreme immoderation, and indeed technical impossibility, of the treaty's demands'.[42] Some international transfers, Keynes concedes, may indeed be made – not in cash but in kind. This is why he sketches, in a highly specific way, how the resources of coal and iron in the Ruhr, Upper Silesia or the Saar might be exploited. If coal was dug by German miners and exported to Denmark in return for supplies of butter (as was apparently happening) it might show 'how far modern Europe has retrograded in the direction of barter' – but then

Keynes comments on such barter exchange that under the 'extraordinary conditions of today's industry it is not without advantages as a means of stimulating production'.[43]

It is in chapter 5 that Keynes directly addresses the problem of Germany's capacity to transfer the payments required. 'The annual surplus which German labour can produce for capital improvements at home is no measure, either theoretically or practically, of the annual tribute which she can pay abroad.'[44] Any such surplus available within Germany needed to be turned into exports in order to be transferred internationally. Here Keynes obviously draws on his Treasury expertise to counter those populists who simply asserted that Germany could pay huge sums, challenging them 'to say *in what specific commodities* they intend this payment to be made, and *in what markets* the goods are to be sold'.[45] He commented ironically on the notion of generating such capacity in Germany by 'making her the greatest industrial nation in Europe, if not in the world' – a strategy that the hawks hardly had in mind.[46]

Why, though, this relentless focus on the specific industrial adjustments required to meet the level of reparations demanded? Surely the whole theory of free trade, and its financing through currency flows, notably via the gold standard, would show that such transfers could always be effected – at the right price, of course. Keynes's work at the wartime Treasury had shown his mastery of technique here. In those days, despite facing intractable immediate difficulties in meeting Britain's commitments in international finance, he had still accepted the conventional assumption that financial disciplines would always require the necessary adaptations in the real economy. Now, in framing the conclusion of his book in late 1919, he seems appalled by results that make sense only on paper.[47]

The war has ended with everyone owing everyone else immense sums of money. Germany owes a large sum to the Allies; the Allies owe a large sum to Great Britain; and Great Britain owes a large sum to the United States. The holders of war loan in every country are owed a large sum by the state; and the state in its turn is owed a large sum by these and other taxpayers. The whole position is in the highest degree artificial, misleading, and vexatious. We shall never be able to move again, unless we can free our limbs from these paper shackles.

The problem, in short, is defined as that of the system as a whole. Later economic jargon, not least through Keynesian influence, would term this macro-economic. And by adopting this model of how the system itself worked, Keynes was radically updating the sort of economic vision that he had identified, in the first chapter of the *Economic Consequences*, as that of the pre-war Garden of Eden. For in that scheme of things, the proposition that the world would always adjust, with benign flexibility, to the financial disciplines imposed from above, was still his own working assumption.

No longer. In early 1920, Keynes used the preface of the French edition of his *Economic Consequences* to challenge the way that his analysis had already been stereotyped: as pro-German and hence anti-French. This was the zero-sum mentality. In a political context where Clemenceau faced his political demise at home because of the insufficiently Carthaginian nature of the peace, Keynes insisted that the only way that France could benefit was by seeking 'the recovery and the health of Europe *as a whole*'.[48] Admittedly, his own book actually displayed as much concern with moral intentions as with economic consequences. It was this aspect that polarised its appeal in Anglo-American circles; it was this aspect that left the French cold. But its abiding significance surely lies in the new prominence given to the theme of organic interdependence, in analysing models of competitive self-interest where the actual outcome may serve only to defeat the intentions and interests of all.

Reparations and Guilt:
Lloyd George and Wilson

Ray Stannard Baker, after nearly three months in Paris, had become despondent. He wrote in his diary on 28 March 1919: 'As a matter of fact the Peace Conference is getting into deeper & deeper water – disagreeing about indemnities & reparations, both Clemenceau & Lloyd-George fearful of accepting too little lest they be turned out by their own governments. L.G. is now reaping the whirlwind of his electoral promises.'[1]

Lloyd George was indeed in a perplexing position. Whereas Clemenceau had always been sceptical of the Fourteen Points and axiomatically committed to reversing 1871 by making Germany pay, Lloyd George had to square the circle with more finesse. His Caxton Hall speech of January 1918, as he often insisted, had anticipated many of the Fourteen Points; and in particular it had renounced an indemnity like that of 1871. The Armistice terms, as he knew, had no provision for indemnities, even though 'fullest indemnities from Germany' became part of his 1918 election manifesto, just as Keynes was to remind everyone later.[2] When, with re-election in the bag, Lloyd George then raised the issue of an indemnity with Wilson, at their first meeting in London in late December 1918, he had to report to the imperial war cabinet 'that he found the President, on the whole, stiffer than on any other question'. Billy Hughes, speaking for Australia, bluntly stated that he would not be satisfied with what the Americans proposed: 'They have made no money sacrifice at all.'[3]

Of course the money was important; but so was the principle. When Grey had first formulated war aims in 1914, reparation meant the restoration of Belgium. In the course of a war subsequently fought mainly on French soil, France's similar claim for reparation came to bulk even larger. In negotiating the Armistice terms, Britain's concern for damage to other civilian property, notably at sea, was also met; so, as Keynes later insisted, 'in the case of reparations, the formula, over which (in my opinion) we have cheated, was not Wilson's but *our own*'.[4] All of this was covered by the Lansing Note, as accepted by Germany. The *Economic Consequences* offered one view of the position: 'Germany having rendered herself helpless in reliance on the contract, the honour of the Allies was peculiarly involved in fulfilling their part and, if there were ambiguities, in not using their position to take advantage of them.'[5]

This was not quite how Lloyd George saw it. His status was as 'the man who won the war', not as the man who would fastidiously refrain from exploiting a clear victory, albeit one mistakenly dressed up as a negotiated peace. Yet he was with Wilson in wanting a clear moral and legal justification for demands that he regarded as legitimate. 'If the Central Powers were not primarily responsible for the War, the basis of reparations disappears,' he argued later. He was ready to contest the view 'that war is a part of the legitimate business of States and that it cannot be treated as a tort' – that is, a fault that incurred a liability for a wrongdoer to pay compensation. 'Why should States and their responsible directors be the only corporations to escape responsibility for their injurious acts?'[6] Of course, if these arguments were to justify indemnities, they might better have been broached before the terms of the Armistice were actually agreed with Germany.

Instead the British estimates of how much Germany could pay had been developed on other lines. Keynes was involved in one early exercise when he was asked in 1916 to contribute to a paper by a colleague on the effect of an indemnity. This was clearly specified as one 'to make good damage in the territories overrun', with the role of Great Britain as that 'of a trustee, receiving wealth to be passed on', in effect to Belgium, France or Serbia.[7] Different methods of effecting this transfer were thus examined. There was no suggestion here, however, of Britain itself becoming a beneficiary, whereas at the end of 1918 that was Lloyd George's whole point, prompted by Hughes, in reopening this issue.

At this juncture Keynes was asked to prepare the Treasury's advice. His paper covered 'the indemnity payable by the enemy powers for reparation and other claims', thus employing both terms (and much of it was later reused in drafting chapter 4 of the *Economic Consequences*). The scope of reparations was taken to be that governed by the Armistice terms. 'The limit of what we can safely exact, having regard to our own selfish interest only,' Keynes summarised his advice, 'may therefore be as low as £2,000 million.' Since this fell short of the specific 'reparation' claims on Germany, a further conclusion followed: 'A claim for the general costs of the war, in addition to reparation, could not be met even in part.' Even so, the cost of this level of reparations to the German economy would greatly exceed the burden of the indemnity on France in 1871 – maybe four times heavier, so Keynes suggested.[8]

Such Treasury advice was of little interest to Lloyd George, especially with an election on his hands. He needed different advice and got it. He set up a committee that included Hughes and also Lord Cunliffe, the former Governor of the Bank of England – 'a cautious, shrewd and level-headed financier', according to Lloyd George, who subsequently claimed for himself an uncharacteristic trustfulness, which was 'completely befooled by the sequel'.[9] For the staggering level of indemnity that the committee came up with totalled £24,000 million. Maybe Lloyd George regarded this as chimerical, as he later said, but it did not stop him appointing both Cunliffe and Hughes to the Reparation Committee now set up in Paris, adding as the third British representative the eminent judge Lord Sumner, who 'so far from exerting any restraining influence upon Lord Cunliffe's strange lapse into megalomania, himself caught the infection', as Lloyd George later put it.[10] These were the hawks who sat on his shoulder.

Some reparations were squarely within the terms of the Lansing Note. They would take precedence over any transfers that could be smuggled in for indemnities. This might have taken indemnities off the table, since the scale of the devastation in northern France, partly through last-minute sabotage from the retreating Germans, came to light only after the Armistice. Keynes, having viewed the scene at first hand, said that, compared with Belgium, 'the destruction in France is on a different kind of scale altogether', which, as he always held, justified France in getting priority.[11] So reparations might have satisfied France, if paid in full with due priority for these legitimate French claims, as under the Lansing Note. But such a distribution would, in effect, have short-changed the British – and the Australians, of course, as their representative on the Reparation Committee was not likely to let anyone forget.

What emerged as the key issue, then, was the distribution of what would actually be received from Germany. At the end of March, after Wilson's return from Washington, Lloyd George became seized of the urgency of settling reparations and withdrew to Fontainebleau with key British advisers. The result was a memorandum acknowledging that what was demanded 'exceeds what, on any calculation, Germany is capable of paying' and therefore proposing that any annual payments be distributed: 50 per cent to France, 30 per cent to the British Empire and 20 per cent to others (notably Belgium and Serbia).[12]

The formula for dividing annual reparations between the British Empire and the French thus became crucial, and was to remain so for months. Rather than 50:30, the French suggested 56:25, with a later compromise at 55:25. Belgium was also accommodated. Yet how could the British Empire justify receiving its 25 per cent share of 'reparations', strictly defined? Australians had no farms or coal mines that the Germans had devastated – was Gallipoli, then, to go unrecompensed? 'How many dead had Belgium in comparison with Australia?' Lloyd George would ask at the Council of Four.[13]

By 1938 he felt able to offer a succinctly candid analysis: 'We were precluded by the Armistice terms from claiming in respect of War costs and trade losses, but the Lansing Note enabled us to demand reparation in respect of personal injuries for which we had provided compensation to the sufferers.'[14] He meant, above all, through war pensions. Maybe this was not a major consideration in France; but in the British Empire, with its pioneering welfare provisions for soldiers and their dependants, separation allowances and pensions for ex-combatants or widows were highly significant, emotionally and financially alike. Such pensions were estimated at fully twice the value of what was due to France and Belgium, thus potentially trebling the total sum demanded.

When are indemnities not indemnities? When they are reparations of course – as Lloyd George came to realise, certainly after Fontainebleau. He wrote later that he had been accompanied there by Smuts: significant if true, but logistically improbable. Now preparing to leave on a mission to revolutionary Budapest, the hallowed Smuts was indeed asked to provide an opinion on whether damage to Allied civilians, as specified in the Lansing Note, covered pensions. Working late on the night of 30–31 March, he wrote a paper arguing that 'what was or is spent on the citizen before he became a soldier, or after he has ceased to be a soldier, or at any time on his family' were all covered. Now Smuts was himself a lawyer, in rather the same sense that Jesus of Nazareth was a carpenter; but everyone knew that this was not the basis of the influence exerted by the great man. In his advice, Smuts explicitly applied a 'commonsense' yardstick, albeit in a different idiom from Hughes. Lloyd George could have found another lawyer – Lord Sumner perhaps – to try to persuade Wilson; but he could not have found another Smuts.

Two days previously Keynes had attended the Council of Four, as he did on a number of occasions. There he proposed discussions

with the Germans on their capacity to pay any final sum of reparations. This was his alternative to France's proposal to leave the sum
open-ended, which Wilson dismissed to Klotz's face as 'tantamount
to asking Germany to extend to us a blank check'. But Lloyd George,
while professing not to contradict Keynes, plainly enough did so: 'I
see great advantages in not making known today the total figure of
what Germany owes us.' He also said that 'we spoke in the Armistice
agreement only of reparation for damages'.[15] So the potential way
to reconcile all of this was, through including pensions, to inflate
the notional extent of German liability threefold, so that the British
Empire could indeed claim its share of the spoils (set at 25 per cent),
while prevaricating over any final figure on Germany's actual capacity to pay. And since it had been agreed that such annual payments
would cease after thirty years (say 1950) the effect would not in practice alter the net sum that Germany paid, but only its distribution.

For a few days Wilson refused to commit to this approach. He
said, with some deliberation, on 31 March: 'I wish to avoid, in escap-
ing certain difficulties by the adoption of a new system, to throw
ourselves into other difficulties [sic].'[16] He was under a lot of pressure from all sides. Edwin Montagu, Secretary of State for India,
was now in Paris and once more working with his old friend Keynes;
they represented the conciliatory face that Lloyd George reassur-
ingly displayed to the American delegation, with whose members
they amicably consulted and with whom they implicitly agreed that
it was best to defer the question of pensions and separation allowances. Lloyd George, however, insisted on a decision.

There are several contemporary accounts of the key meeting in
the President's library on the afternoon of 1 April. One version
is by the young lawyer John Foster Dulles (ultimately famous as
Eisenhower's Secretary of State). 'The President stated that he had
been very much impressed by a memorandum by Smuts,' Dulles
noted, though he himself warned of the 'danger that to accept
pensions would involve admitting against the enemy all war costs' –
a danger that Wilson conceded was logical.[17] Thomas Lamont, a

financial adviser from J. P. Morgan, also left an authentic contemporary record of the outcome. 'I don't give a damn for logic,' the President said, thus accepting pensions nonetheless. They all sat in a circle around him, absorbing the impact of his decision, while he seemed 'a trifle impatient of prolonged discussion'.[18] Then the advisers trooped out and reported to Montagu and Keynes that pensions were indeed now to be included. Smuts was by this time off on the night train to Budapest.

In the following days, the necessary drafting took place. The Americans explicitly agreed to a clause specifying that pensions and allowances were to be covered. There was likewise agreement on a prior clause, as finally embodied in the Treaty as Article 231, stating that 'Germany accepts the responsibility of Germany and her allies' for the relevant loss and damage to the Allies that arose as 'a consequence of the war imposed upon them by the aggression of Germany and her allies'. In the *Economic Consequences*, this is described as 'a well and carefully drafted article', meaning that Wilson could read it as an 'admission on Germany's part of moral responsibility for bringing about the war', whereas Lloyd George (and Clemenceau) only cared about its effect on financial liability for the costs of the war.[19] Keynes's description is, at best, a half-truth. In fact Lloyd George also craved the moral cover of this attribution of guilt; and Keynes's tribute to the drafting does not acknowledge his own role, notably with Dulles, in settling on this formulation, albeit doing so with a degree of embarrassment that was evident to the American officials with whom he worked.

It is likewise disingenuous to claim that the Treaty contained no 'war-guilt clause'. Whatever the legalistic distinctions that can be offered about the wording of Article 231, the fact is that it served functionally to identify the wrongdoer and to require acceptance of responsibility. It was rather more than a tort in civil law, for adjudication on the repairs needed to a few Belgian farms. Keynes in 1921, with freer access to American documents than he had had earlier, referred scornfully to 'the moral basis on which two-thirds of our claims against Germany rest'.[20] The broad scope of the financial liability specified in the Treaty indeed enlisted such feelings, perhaps generated by emotion as much as logic. Lippmann too had played his part in showing House how to draft the Armistice terms so that the Belgian war loan was covered as a further liability that stemmed from an original unlawful act by Germany. Now similar indemnities, on a much larger scale, were to be regarded as 'reparations' punitively imposed upon the guilty, and the function of Article 231 was to justify this. What was demanded of the Germans was thus much enhanced, morally and financially alike.

Why the crucial stiffening of the peace terms at this point? Like Clemenceau, Lloyd George made little secret of his sensitivity to public opinion at home; and Wilson understood the need to accommodate such political pressures rather than let three months' work go to waste, let Europe descend into chaos and let the League of Nations be aborted. True, on 8 April Lloyd George was to receive a telegram signed by 232 Conservative MPs, and obviously fomented by the newspaper baron Northcliffe, expressing alarm over any backsliding from the government's previous statements about presenting Germany with a bill for the full costs of the war. But the political signals were ambiguous. For on 29 March, in a by-election at Hull Central, an Asquithian Liberal had taken the seat from the Coalition Conservatives, and the new MP, Commander J. M. Kenworthy, was a highly prominent critic of a draconian peace. Moreover, this was the second such Asquithian gain that month, in each case with impressive swings, averaging 28 per cent since the General Election three months previously. This implies that any Conservative MP who had polled less than 78 per cent in the Coupon Election was now vulnerable to challenge from the Asquithian Liberals.

In this ambiguous situation, it was Lloyd George's own decision to cover himself by taking a tough line. The reparations settlement, with its many ambiguities, was the result. The American officials, now increasingly impatient of these British liberals, made the best of it. When they saw Wilson on 3 April, he apparently acknowledged that 'Lloyd George had nearly put it over on him', which was what the *Economic Consequences* later described as his bamboozlement. But the President authorised his own men to keep talking to Montagu and Keynes, after which a further report was made to their demonstrably demoralised chief. 'Found him in bed with a bad cold at 6:00 P.M.,' one of them recorded, 'very tired and I know discouraged.'[21]

This was the situation that Lloyd George and Clemenceau gleefully exploited a couple of days later, with Wilson still confined to bed. It was at this stage, with House once again substituting for the temporarily convalescent Wilson, that the final touches were put upon the war-guilt clause. Moreover, Lloyd George took with him to the meeting, not Keynes nor Montagu but Lord Sumner – a bad signal for the Americans. The thirty-year restriction on reparation payments was now removed, which meant that the addition of pensions indeed increased the total sum demanded of Germany, rather than just affecting its distribution between the Allies. The Colonel prided himself on knowing how to talk to Lloyd George and Clemenceau, and saw that it was now all a matter of drafting, to bring the wording into conformity with the new gloss that had been put upon the Fourteen Points and upon the Lansing Note. Wilson, on his sickbed in the adjoining room, was kept au fait with every move, though whether he retired at any point to wash his hands is not recorded. But there were others in Paris who did not have clean hands: perhaps neither Dulles nor Lippmann and certainly neither Keynes nor his ally Smuts, as they were later to encounter some difficulties in fully explaining.

It was Smuts who suggested to Keynes that he should write the *Economic Consequences*. Perhaps it is not surprising that the book has some notable silences on the way that the enhanced scale of reparations (as sanctioned in the Smuts memorandum) had generated the war-guilt clause (as drafted by Dulles and Keynes himself). So the author had excellent reason to make light of all this; but he likewise had excellent reason to know what the Germans made of it all at the time.

The diaries of Thomas Mann vividly convey the point of view of one German intellectual who wanted his own compatriots to take a liberal and democratic path. At the end of September 1918 he had talked to a friend of 'the effort Germany must make to modernize, democratize herself, sweeping away the old, romantic, imperial Germany, a task that can only proceed agonizingly and against the grain, meeting extreme resistance because the old Germany is much too deeply and firmly established in men's souls, is much too deeply identified, perhaps with Germanism itself'.[22] All this rested on fragile assumptions about the outcome of the war – 'if we can hold out in the West until the winter we will probably come out of it with no more than a black eye, aided perhaps by antagonism between England and America'. So the sudden change in the German official tone at the beginning of October, when the liberal Prince Max of Baden became Chancellor, brought some shock and was treated with some scorn: 'We now say that the enemy is in the right, admit that Germany needed to be reformed by such an enemy, and out of fear declare ourselves reformed.'[23]

Hence Mann's already jaundiced view of the Armistice negotiations in mid-October 1918. 'One must also recognize the utter comedy of the fact that an American professor, of all people, had to come along with his Fourteen Points to set the world right,' he drily observed, with the prognosis: 'Inevitable that in actual practice less will be asked of the "victors" than of the "vanquished".'[24] And a couple of days later: 'From the bottom of my heart I hope the Germans learn a profound lesson from the thorough unmasking of these virtue-mongers of democracy.'[25] Yet when the Armistice came on 11 November, the official response by the new German government was disappointing, especially 'the moral wretchedness with which it casts the guilt for the war and all guilt for what happened during the war on the German "governments and sovereigns", from whom we are now liberated, and only berates these'.[26]

And after that, from bad to worse, as reports came from Paris in February 1919 of 'Wilson's repulsively unctuous speech' about the League of Nations. 'What a swindle the whole thing is.'[27] More news came in early March 1919: 'The definitive armistice terms beyond belief. Aside from all the humiliations, annual tribute of ten to fifteen billions for thirty to fifty years, etc.' Wilson, however 'desperate and tragicomic' he now seemed, was 'still trying to seem superior while it is plain that the "Armistice" is merely a device for putting over the most arrogantly imposed peace'.[28] Mann's growing contempt, for process and outcome alike, became open after the draft treaty had been presented to the Germans in early May and he sent a telegram to the press: 'The Allied peace betrays the idiocy of the victors.'[29]

Keynes had his own German sources. One of his early responsibilities under the terms of the Armistice had been to represent the Treasury in negotiating with the Germans about the increasingly urgent problems of feeding a population already suffering from acute food shortages. The French saw the Germans' plight as largely self-inflicted; they saw the blockade as a legitimate negotiating tool under the Armistice; and they saw the release of any available German gold as a drain on what was available for reparations. This situation, then, predictably gave Anglo-American liberals qualms on humanitarian grounds, exciting some sympathy for any reasonable or cooperative German who could be found. The German spokesman, Dr Carl Melchior, was one such.

Keynes later made their personal encounter the subject of one of his finest biographical essays. Melchior, wrote Keynes, 'and he only, upheld the dignity of defeat'.[30] When Virginia Woolf heard this essay read to Bloomsbury's 'memoir club' in February 1921, she was ambivalent, impressed by the characterisation despite being bored by the politics. True, Maynard fed Bloomsbury's appetite for sexual innuendo by interpolating, into an account of how the two men had privately struck a deal, his own aside: 'In a sort of way I was in love with him.'[31] And Virginia recorded: 'I think he meant it seriously, though we laughed.'[32] The political point was that, only by taking the risk of opening an informal channel between this German banker and himself, had Keynes been able to procure German compliance over surrendering merchant ships as a prior condition for the supply of food. And in the process French intransigence was outflanked. This was the micro-politics of a nod, interpreted with keen attention, and a wink, given with sly ambiguity.

Could other equally complex but more far-reaching issues have been resolved on such a basis or through such contacts? After all, the conference in Paris was originally conceived as a preliminary meeting of the victorious powers to prepare proposals for the negotiated peace that was agreed at the Armistice. Only later did it supersede any real negotiation. Instead, draft terms formulated in copious detail were presented to the Germans, in effect on a take-it-or-leave-it basis. This was all too reminiscent of how the Germans had treated the Russians at Brest-Litovsk; and just as Trotsky had originally refused to sign, so there was real doubt about whether the equally unstable new regime in Germany would be able to produce signatories ready to go to the Hall of Mirrors.

Lloyd George had certainly been troubled on this score. As all the various parts of the draft treaty were assembled, the cumulative rigour of its provisions became increasingly apparent. In particular, the reparations claims had been ramped up through the decisions taken in the first week of April, when Lloyd George had acted like a leader bent on appeasing his own followers at home. But after a parliamentary triumph on 16 April, he knew that he had seen off the immediate parliamentary challenge from the right and became more concerned about sustaining the liberal credentials of a treaty that would last. This appeared to offer Keynes a final opportunity to shape the economic consequences of a peace still in the making, rather than to denounce the Versailles Treaty afterwards.

On 17 April Keynes told his mother about '*a grand scheme for the rehabilitation of Europe*'. The plan that had so impressed him was, of course, written by himself. It presented a financially complex plan but one with a simple aim. 'It cannot be supposed', he argued, 'that two great continents, America and Europe, the one destitute and on the point of collapse and the other overflowing with goods which it wishes to dispose of, can continue to face one another for long without attempting to frame some plan of mutual advantage.'[33] In effect, American credit would be enlisted for bonds to finance German reconstruction, which might then enable some reparations to be effected. What was not directly mentioned here was that remissions of inter-Allied debt by the United States might also follow; Keynes had put this point more directly in the previous month, with the opinion that 'I do not believe that any of these tributes will continue to be paid, at the best, for more than a few years.'[34] He was to raise the debt–reparation link again in the *Economic Consequences*. But his 'grand scheme' in late April worked towards the same objective by other means, ones that were aimed at eliciting American cooperation.

Chamberlain, as Chancellor of the Exchequer, commended the Keynes plan to Lloyd George, who then submitted it to Wilson, Clemenceau and Orlando as his own proposal. Keynes thought that the American response was soured at an early stage by leaks in the press in New York. In fact there were more intractable reasons behind its rejection, which Wilson formally conveyed to Lloyd George on 3 May: 'You have suggested that we all address ourselves to the problem of helping to put Germany on her feet, but how can your experts or ours be expected to work out a *new* plan to furnish working capital to Germany when we deliberately start out by taking away all Germany's present capital?'[35] Wilson meant, of course, through heavy reparations – part of which would then go towards repayments of British and French debts to the United States. So the circular nature of the problem, linking these two kinds of post-war transfers, was implicitly reaffirmed, from the crucially different perspective of a net creditor who simply wanted debts to be honoured by the folks who hired the money.

Keynes was not yet thirty-six. Precociously, he had become a strikingly influential British official in Paris; but it was his political masters who would shape the terms of the international settlement.

The draft terms that Wilson, Lloyd George and Clemenceau had so painfully and protractedly negotiated were presented on 7 May, in formal proceedings at the Trianon Palace Hotel, to the German representatives. Count Brockdorff-Rantzau, their leader, may have looked like a Junker, though he faithfully represented the position of the centre-left government of the German republic, and it was the brusque delivery of his speech, defiantly seated, that made a poor impression. 'Isn't it just like them?' said Wilson to Lloyd George, so the latter recalled while also personally acknowledging the force of the speech. 'We are required to admit that we alone are war-guilty,' the Count had affirmed, with good reason, and he did not seek to absolve Germany of all guilt under international law: 'Belgium has been wronged and we will make this good.'[36] The nature of his final warning was one that liberals were to echo: 'A peace, which cannot be defended in the name of justice before the whole world, would continually call forth fresh resistance.'[37] Such premonitions were to find their echo in the *Economic Consequences*: 'If we aim deliberately at the impoverishment of Central Europe, vengeance, I dare to predict, will not limp.'[38]

Lloyd George himself shared such sentiments. He had long warned about the dangers of an unjust Polish settlement in stoking irredentist nationalism in the new Germany. Brockdorff-Rantzau's reply now spurred Lloyd George to summon the whole British Empire delegation. Churchill pointed to the danger of the French position; Smuts was open in his dissent about the peace terms. 'Now that we see them as a whole we realise that they are much too stiff,' Harold Nicolson was to write on 8 June. 'They are not stern merely but actually punitive and they abound with what Smuts calls "pin pricks" as well as dagger thrusts.'

Lloyd George became seized of the need for remedial action. In recent weeks he had become less worried about the reception of the terms in Britain than about their reception in Germany. As early as 3 May Brockdorff-Rantzau's state of mind had received scrutiny from the Council of Four. Yes, 'he is completely disappointed to discover that we are in agreement', Clemenceau reported, and Wilson agreed: 'There is obviously a contrast between what the Germans hoped to find here and what they are finding in fact before them.' Lloyd George's information came from the back stairs: 'According to Mr Keynes, Mr Melchior would be a bit more optimistic than he was earlier.'[39] But a month or so later, on 9 June, with the final version of the Treaty needing to be formally presented the next week, the three leaders were in some disarray. 'One of my financial experts has just left us, because he finds the terms too hard,' Lloyd George reported, in urging last-minute concessions.[40]

Keynes had indeed quit the conference two days earlier. The rejection of his grand scheme had been his final disappointment. 'The Peace is outrageous and impossible and can bring nothing but misfortune,' he had written privately on 14 May, and he no longer blamed Lloyd George so much as the Americans – 'Wilson, of whom I've seen a good deal more lately, is the greatest fraud on earth.' The subsequent attempts to debamboozle the old Presbyterian, when Lloyd George was finally stirred to press for concessions, were doomed to fail precisely because Wilson now believed in what he had done. Keynes's final letter to the Prime Minister was surprisingly conciliatory. 'I've gone on hoping even through these last dreadful weeks that you'd find some way to make of the Treaty a just and expedient document,' he wrote on 5 June. 'But now it's apparently too late. The battle is lost.'

Wilson knew that the battle in Paris was only the preliminary to the battle in Washington. In the end the German government found a delegation ready to sign in the Hall of Mirrors on 28 June. On that same day Wilson bade farewell to Paris and to Colonel House alike; he never saw either again. He had been away from the United States (apart from a two-week visit home) for over six months. His hold over the country was now less sure, perhaps partly as a result of this absence. But his thinking rested on a belief that it was Washington that was out of touch, as the extent of resistance to the Treaty, crucially in the Senate, became undeniable during the summer.

PEACE AND FUTURE CANNON FODDER

The Tiger: "Curious! I seem to hear a child weeping!"

This emblematic cartoon, first published in May 1919, offered a powerful visual critique of the Versailles peace terms. Will Dyson captures the central figure of Clemenceau, the lofty Wilson and, almost hidden behind Orlando, an uncharacteristically shadowy Lloyd George.

Wilson's entire strategy had been founded on getting approval for the League of Nations because the Covenant was itself an integral part of a peace treaty that it was inconceivable for the Senate to repudiate. Instead, the Republican opposition, adroitly organised by Lodge, denied Wilson the opportunity of getting the Treaty without reservations over the League; and Wilson's insistence on unreserved acceptance thus sank the Treaty itself. This was to be the effect of the Senate vote on 19 November 1919.

Wilson, like Lloyd George, had lost the support of some advisers. Walter Lippmann had gone back disillusioned to the liberal journal the *New Republic*; and the young diplomat William Bullitt had made his own resignation a public issue, in the process revealing the dissensions within the US delegation. Both wanted the Senate to reject an unjust Treaty, though Lippmann's effort to get a preview from the *Economic Consequences* published in the *New Republic* before the vote took place was vetoed by Keynes.

The President himself had raised the stakes, clinging to his hope that a future Congress would approve his measures in full. He had pitched himself into a punishing round of speeches in the heat of the summer, taking his case to the people over the heads of the Senate. As so often when under stress, as we have seen, he affirmed that he believed in divine providence – 'If I did not, I would go crazy.'[41] This was said in the peroration of a speech in California on 18 September; a week later his physical collapse led to a return to Washington. On 2 October he had a stroke. He served out the remainder of his term as an invalid whose messages now reached the world through a filter, monitored by Edith Wilson. The Wilsons left the White House in March 1921 with the Treaty unratified, no American presence in the League of Nations and the rehabilitation of Europe still pending.

In the 1920 presidential election, the Democrats suffered defeat on a scale unparalleled in the twentieth century. This was the more humbling in view of the strong support for Wilson's stance offered not only by their candidate, Governor James M. Cox, but by his running mate, Franklin D. Roosevelt. Still Assistant Secretary of the

Navy at the time of the Democratic convention in July, FDR had thrown his support to Cox with the vice-presidential nomination as his reward: a considerable boost for the future prospects of a man still under forty. His later account of the visit that the two nominees made to the White House in July 1920 – the first time FDR had seen the President in ten months – spoke of his shock at Wilson's physical decline but also of the response by Cox and himself in pledging to make the League of Nations the paramount issue. 'I am very grateful,' said Wilson.[42] It was, he claimed, a battle that could still be won. But it was no longer capable of being won in his own day and would need to be fought again with different tactics and with a new generation of political leadership.

Further Economic Consequences:
Keynes and Lloyd George

Since there had been three different agenda for the Hall of Mirrors, it is not surprising that the Treaty signed there subsequently became the subject of three different national debates. To the French, it all turned on the security of France itself, especially on the status of the Rhineland and, in the event of future German aggression, on the help that could be expected – or not expected – from the United States, unbound by any League of Nations pledges, or from Britain, as ever cast in the role of Perfidious Albion. To the Americans, given the political hostility between the followers of Lodge and Wilson, the key issue had become the League of Nations itself and the extent to which joining it would compromise American foreign policy, with the result that the United States became, if not isolationist, then deeply wary in its official dealings with the British – as with European governments in general. As for the British, though support for the League of Nations was widespread, satisfaction with the Treaty proved short lived. For example, when it was debated in the House of Commons in July 1919, Commander Kenworthy, the victor of the Hull by-election, made the first of many striking parliamentary speeches, in which he offered no objection to the punishment of war criminals but challenged the cumulative impact of the economic conditions imposed on Germany. An incipient revulsion of feeling against the Treaty became increasingly focused on the form in which such issues were posed in the *Economic Consequences*.

In the process, the name of Keynes acquired its public cachet, not least as the self-appointed nemesis of Lloyd George. As Prime Minister, the latter still had some of his wartime ascendancy, buzzing around a succession of European conferences in spa towns ('casino diplomacy'), while watching first Wilson and then Clemenceau face rejection in their own countries. His turn did not come until October 1922, nominally in a crisis over whether to confront Mustafa Kemal but actually through a long-deferred revolt of Conservative backbenchers against a Prime Minister who, for all his coalitionist hankerings, was simply not one of them. So Lloyd George resigned, regained his freedom and rediscovered that he was a true Liberal, in domestic and foreign policy alike. 'Restrictions and reductions have often been imposed in Peace Treaties by triumphant nations upon their beaten foes,' he proclaimed dismissively in a speech on 20 December 1922. 'The Versailles Treaty is an example of that operation.' He now sought to follow a better path in seeking international conciliation.

This was certainly a change of tone. In another speech, six months later, on 'The Treaty of Versailles and its Critics' he observed that 'no two men who happen to profess diverse opinions as to its justice or injustice can agree upon its contents'. He referred to a recent appearance he had made in a debate at the Oxford Union, where he claimed the undergraduates were surprised to find that the League of Nations was a result of the Treaty, an impression amply confirmed by the hostile reception of his own speech because this had given scant attention to reparations. 'They honestly thought I was travelling outside the motion in giving a short summary of the other sections of the Treaty,' said Lloyd George. 'To them it is all condensed in Mr Keynes's book, and other hostile commentaries.' This was a backhanded tribute to the way that the British debate had been reshaped.

Moreover, by this time, Lloyd George was ready enough to proclaim his own views on reparations. 'The question of compelling a country to pay across its frontiers huge sums convertible into the currency of other countries is a new one,' he now acknowledged. 'At first it was too readily taken for granted that a wealth which could bear a war debt of £8,000,000,000 could surely afford to bear an indemnity of £6,000,000,000 provided that this smaller sum were made a first charge on the national revenues; and it took time for the average mind to appreciate the fundamental difference between payment inside and transmission outside a country.' So here was a problem that needed to be addressed, once 'public opinion in all the Allied countries has subsided into sanity on German Reparations, as it already has in Britain' – or so he concluded, speaking on New Year's Day 1923.

The fact that Keynes had emerged as the arch-critic of Lloyd George's peacemaking in 1919 did not, however, signal an irrevocable rupture in their personal relations. The short book that Keynes published in early 1922, *A Revision of the Treaty*, tartly acknowledges that the 'revisionists' already included Lloyd George, still British Prime Minister at that point. 'In England, opinion has nearly completed its swing,' Keynes writes sardonically, 'and the Prime Minister is making ready to win a General Election on Forbidding Germany to Pay, Employment for Everyone, and a Happier Europe for All.'[1] His satirical comment masks his serious appreciation of a uniquely gifted politician and of Lloyd George's potential capacity to lead and direct public opinion towards bold and constructive ends. It was in his memoir of Dr Melchior, written a few months previously, that Keynes had said of Lloyd George: 'He can be amazing when one agrees with him.'[2]

A Revision of the Treaty is explicitly entitled as a sequel to the *Economic Consequences*. It had initially been envisaged as little more than a series of appendices to that great bestseller and in its first six months sold less than 7,000 copies, compared with 100,000 for the *Economic Consequences* at the same stage. Yet Keynes's *Revision* is too easily overlooked, and not only as a source of updated statistics on reparations, both as envisaged in 1919 and as paid (or not paid) by 1921. For the book also shows the author speculating about the usefulness of economic analysis – in effect, asking himself what was the point of what he was doing.

Thus the opening chapter is about Keynes's conception of politics and the role of ideas. He confronts the question of whether, if 'public passions and public ignorance play a part in the world of which he who aspires to lead a democracy must take account', Lloyd George perhaps made the least bad peace under the prevailing circumstances. 'Such claims', he acknowledges, 'would be partly true and cannot be brushed away.' Here is a perennially plausible line of extenuation for what the peacemakers did in 1919: defending it as an exercise in the art of the possible, assuming that 'this is the best of which a democracy is capable – to be jockeyed, humbugged, cajoled along the right road'. And Keynes goes so far as to concede: 'A preference for truth or for sincerity *as a method* may be a prejudice based on some aesthetic or personal standard, inconsistent, in politics, with practical good.'[3]

Keynes distinguishes 'outside opinion' from 'inside opinion'. He juxtaposes 'the opinion of the public as voiced by the politicians and the newspapers, and the opinion of the politicians, the journalists and the civil servants, upstairs and backstairs and behind-stairs, expressed in limited circles'. The potential divergence between them had now crucially widened. 'Some say that Mr Gladstone was a hypocrite; yet if so, he dropped no mask in private life.' A gulf between the two kinds of opinion – three, perhaps, if the newspapers misrepresented the ordinary person – had thus become accepted, whereas the real need was for arguments to percolate from an inner circle, through another circle of opinion-formers and thence to the public at large; and it was 'the business of the modern politician to be accurately aware of all three degrees'.[4] Which could all be interpreted as justifying the obligation on a perceptive economist to tell inconvenient truths that inner opinion might already appreciate, while requiring a charismatic politician to convey the message to a wider democratic public.

Nor is this seen as simply a one-way process, rendering pure economic truths into a popular form for general consumption. His

Revision often shows Keynes working the other way around. He exhibits his grasp of the complex, technical, politically charged problems involved in reparations, just like the good civil servant he had recently been, but then also reveals his own restless temptation to theorise the issues at stake. In chapter 6, in particular, he warns that he will be speculating in this way: 'The argument is a little intricate and the reader must be patient.'[5] For what he is doing here is not simply repeating the polemical message of the *Economic Consequences*, that the demand for heavy reparations will prove self-defeating: now he is explicitly acknowledging that *in theory* such transfers could, under certain conditions, offer advantages to the country extracting them. He ruled out 'extracting at the point of a bayonet' a level of reparations 'that would never be paid voluntarily'.[6] In which case, it was a matter of market transfers, mainly through generating German exports. But, since these were closely competitive with rival British products, Germany might thus be compelled to flood and steal these markets at the expense of British workers. 'These facts, formerly overlooked, are now, perhaps, exaggerated by popular opinion,' Keynes comments, in applying his principles.[7]

In this way he reiterates his real point. 'The permanence of reparation payments on a large scale for a long period of years is, to say the least, not to be reckoned on,' he reasons. 'Who believes that the Allies will, over a period of one or two generations, exert adequate force over the German government, or that the German government can exert adequate authority over its subjects, to extract continuing fruits on a vast scale from forced labour?'[8] So the excursion into formal economic analysis yields a conclusion that could actually be reached by intuition on the basis of common sense. And much the same principles, he suggests, apply to the exaction by the United States of inter-Allied debts. For these would actually hurt the farmers of the American South and West, if their European customers were impoverished, yet it was only on Wall Street, it seemed, that this truth had sunk in.

The fact was that, with the United States now a creditor country, it would inevitably have to lend its balance of payments surplus to the rest of the world – in some form or other. This was, of course, what Britain had done in the pre-war era, thus building up its huge investments abroad. As for the United States, some postponement might notionally be gained by its importing all the gold in the world, as a vast hoard. 'But a point may even come when the United States will refuse gold, yet still demand to be paid – a new Midas vainly asking more succulent fare than the barren metal of her own contract.' This was all put as an absurdist scenario. The sober truth was that 'the project is utterly chimerical. It will not happen.'[9] Nor did it.

What actually happened was that the Americans were drawn into the economic reconstruction of Europe. Since they needed to lend and Germany needed to borrow, it might seem a match made in heaven – but it was not made on earth without a good deal of purposeful political manipulation. The Wilsonian assumption that the United States would guide the implementation of the peace settlement had been overturned by the Senate's rejection of the Treaty. But the Republican administration under President Harding (until his death in office in August 1923) was hardly isolationist in its foreign policy. Charles Evan Hughes as Secretary of State was fully conscious of the seriousness of the reparations impasse. A notable speech that he gave at Yale University at the end of December 1922 suggested that 'men of the highest authority in finance in their respective countries' might work upon the problem. Lloyd George, frustrated at losing power to act himself, instantly seized upon these words as signalling that the United States could be represented unofficially at least; and others more slowly got the message. This was the origin of the Dawes Committee as set up in late 1923, in effect putting American financial muscle behind German economic recovery.

One problem was that the Reparation Commission, as established by the Treaty, had to function without the United States as a member. American absence from the table meant that, instead of the Commission operating under the wise and dispassionate chairmanship of the United States, as envisaged by Wilson, the French claimed the chair and thus, with virtually automatic Belgian support, had a casting vote, and were able to outvote the British, even if Britain were supported by Italy. All this further delayed an eventual international agreement over the scale of reparations.

The Allies had met the Germans, for the first time since Versailles, at Spa in July 1920. There they had first settled between themselves on a division of any spoils, finally resolved as a new compromise of 52:22 between France and the British Empire. Subsequently the Dominion prime ministers agreed to splitting the Empire's share: 86.85 per cent to the United Kingdom, 4.35 per cent each to Canada and Australia, 1.75 per cent to New Zealand, 1.2 per cent to India, 0.6 per cent to South Africa, 0.1 per cent to Newfoundland (and 0.8 per cent to minor colonies).[10] So Australia's share would finally amount to less than 1 per cent of whatever sum Germany actually paid in reparations – not, perhaps, quite what Billy Hughes had once envisaged.

No settlement with Germany was reached until 1921. At that point, under an ultimatum threatening occupation of the Ruhr, yet another new German government signed up to the London Schedule of payments. Keynes commended this settlement, though with low expectations of the likely results.

His own side of the argument is set out in the *Revision*. The London Schedule of May 1921 was based on the long-anticipated report, made in the previous month, by the Reparation Commission, whose own estimate of the total implied in the Treaty was actually close to that given in the *Economic Consequences* – £6.6 billion exclusive of the Belgian war loans.[11] Yet again, no final overall figure was specified, only the scale of annual repayments. But Keynes was justified in estimating the effect of the London Schedule as about half of what the Reparation Commission had recently assessed; it was only about a quarter of what Klotz had once forecast; and it was about one-sixth of what Keynes's old adversary Lord Cunliffe had so influentially claimed possible.[12] Moreover, the London Schedule set payments in three forms: there were A bonds, to cover German arrears, and B bonds, likewise immediately effective, together totalling £2.5 billion; and also C bonds (notionally for two-thirds of all reparations). These latter were virtually worthless. 'It is probable that, sooner or later, the C bonds at any rate will be not only postponed, but cancelled.'[13] This was appreciated perfectly well at the time by 'inside opinion', whether in Britain or Germany.

'No wonder, therefore, that this settlement, so reasonable in itself compared with what had preceded it, was generally approved and widely accepted as a real and permanent solution,' Keynes wrote in his *Revision*.[14] He was now content to advise German compliance with what was asked in 1921 – a fraction of the liability specified in the Treaty in 1919. Even so, he suggested that 'at the end of the set period Germany would have paid back ten times what she took after 1870'.[15] This does not allow for the fact that the German economy was bigger than France's had been; modern estimates suggest that in 1871 the total indemnity had been less than 25 per cent of French national income, as compared with the 1921 demands totalling about 150 per cent of current German national income.

Keynes's own preference was for the British Empire to waive its share of reparations. The Empire should yield priority to France over whatever was actually transferred by Germany, but reserve some payments not only for Polish reconstruction but for the claims of a shrunken Austria, now huddled around its old imperial capital. 'The Viennese were not made for tragedy,' Keynes suggested; 'the world feels that, and there is none so bitter as to wish ill to the city of Mozart.'[16] Culturally at least, he was thus Teutonic in his sympathies. He also claimed that, in the Anglo-American sphere, there was little understanding of 'how deep a wound has been inflicted on Germany's self-respect by compelling her, not merely to perform acts, but to subscribe to beliefs which she did not in fact accept'.[17] Yet the London Schedule reiterated the provocative Article 231 as the basis of its claims.[18] So war guilt still justified reparations.

The link between the demand for reparation payments by the Allies and the demand for debt repayments by the United States had long been obvious. But it remained unmentionable in the United States; so great offence was taken there when the French had explicitly raised it. Instead, as a result of their fiscal weakness, the French had to resort to borrowing on Wall Street, on horrendous terms that were likewise the result of their fiscal weakness, in order to pay the money due in Washington. The British too drew attention to the link (the 'Balfour Note' in 1922), in proposing that the level of British reparations from Germany be limited to the amount of British international debt repayments. Since its US dollar debt was Britain's only international debt, this proposal obviously cast the United States as the villain. In fact, the schedule of British debt repayments was to be appreciably eased, by stretching these over about sixty years, in a settlement that Stanley Baldwin, as Chancellor of the Exchequer, negotiated in Washington in January 1923.

Reparations remained the intractable legacy of the peace settlement, revision or no revision. The rupture between Britain and France became increasingly obvious, especially when Poincaré, no longer President himself, returned to head an intransigent French government intent on enforcing compliance through military intervention. This had already been threatened five times in 1920–1, and implemented twice; in January 1923, the French occupation of the Ruhr began after yet another German default on reparations payments. The British prevaricated, unconvinced of the wisdom of the French action, but seeking to avoid an open breach. The occupation met passive resistance from the Germans (to whom Keynes offered sympathetic support but bad tactical advice, underestimating French resolve). Poincaré raised the stakes by encouraging the old project of an independent Rhenish republic; but deadlock prevailed. It was in this context that the Americans revived Hughes's earlier proposal of an expert committee, in which the key figure was to be the adroit Chicago banker Charles Dawes.

The great German inflation of the early 1920s had profound consequences, some of them still potent today in folk memory. Germany was not unusual in experiencing an inflationary spike in 1919–20 followed by some deflation; what was unique was the way that the double-digit inflation of 1922 spiralled, at the time of the Ruhr crisis, into the wild hyper-inflation of late 1923, with prices that had once been measured in tens of marks now measured in millions. It was this acute threat to the economy, to the authority of government, to the institutions of civil society, that first offered Adolf Hitler his political chance.

In particular, inflation had a stunning impact on the war debt inherited by the Weimar republic from imperial Germany. Denominated in marks, this debt was virtually wiped out. So, compared with Britain, where service of the national debt remained a heavy charge on the budget, German taxpayers were now spared this burden. (Of course, there were as many losers as winners in this bizarre redistribution of wealth.) What happened here served to highlight the distinction between servicing an internal debt and meeting reparations payments that involved transferring resources across the international exchanges. Germany's public debt was now disproportionately that due under Article 231 of the Versailles Treaty. In accepting the Dawes Plan, with its longer rescheduling of reparations payments (and hence a reduction of the annual amount due), the German government was permitted to repudiate this famous 'war-guilt clause'; but Hitler was not alone in refusing to forget it.

It was actually an inflow of dollars, likewise prompted by the Dawes Plan, that came to the rescue. First, a loan was made to Germany, half of it financed in the United States; and this more than covered the reparations immediately due. It was now that the economic reconstruction of post-war Germany was at last put in hand, mainly through American private investment. In a limited sense, this solved the reparations problem, at least until the slump hit the world economy in 1931–2.

Yet the result was little more than another confidence trick. Rather than German industry generating resources that were then transferred through exports, reparations payments were to be financed by dollar loans. There are good reasons why different estimates are made of the flows that took place, especially because of the difficulty in allowing for relative currency fluctuations. But there is now general agreement that foreign investment into Germany – mainly from the United States in the years 1924–9 – was substantially greater than the amount of reparations that Germany ever actually paid. Rhetorically, such transfers can be called American reparations to Germany. Much of this investment, of course, was unwise from the point of view of the optimistic speculators who put up the money and lost it in the ensuing slump and German default in 1932.

With the world economy in crisis, the link between reparations and war debts again surfaced. This seemed terribly obvious to the British, who used the one to pay the other and (privately at least) were well accustomed to talking about both in the same breath. It was President Hoover, a keen student of these interlocked issues since the time of the peace negotiations, who initiated a moratorium in the summer of 1931 on interest payments for both inter-governmental debts and reparations. The US Treasury later calculated that whereas the French war debt had been reduced by 50 per cent between 1926 and 1932 (and that of Italy by 68 per cent) the British debt had enjoyed only an 18 per cent reduction. Moreover, there was still more notionally owing to Britain than it, in turn, owed to the United States.

Such points did not escape the keen mind of Neville Chamberlain, now the British Chancellor of the Exchequer. The brother of Austen Chamberlain, Neville was less the son of the visionary Joseph than himself an accountant *manqué*. It was Neville Chamberlain, heading the British delegation at the World Economic Conference in London in June 1933, just after FDR's inauguration, who infuriated the American delegation by openly identifying war debts as a key problem. Here was scope for transatlantic bitterness at the time and for future recriminations. Though the Congress was to pass punitive legislation in 1934, directed against Britain and France for reneging on their debts, the United States was left with an outstanding total that it would never collect, any more than the Allies would ever collect German reparations. In effect, mutual cancellation thus came about, though hardly in the way that Keynes himself had so long, and so tactlessly, recommended.

———

The name Keynes is remembered today as not only a proper noun but, by extension, as an everyday economic adjective. A Keynesian approach begins with the recognition that market economies are inherently unstable and hence require corrective measures of government intervention, not just here or there (in a micro-economic way) but to address the overall performance of the system itself (in a macro-economic sense). And the most obvious way of explaining why the Keynesian revolution happened, in economic policy and theory alike, is to point to mass unemployment as the context in which the ideas were originally propounded. Specifically, in Britain it was the return to the gold standard in 1925 that entrenched unemployment as an intractable issue, as Keynes was quick to recognise. Yet there are other ways to chart the milestones on the road that he travelled.

For Maynard himself, 1925 was the year that he got married. To say that this step shocked many of his old friends would be an understatement (though several bisexual men in the Bloomsbury circle took to matrimony in the end). It was the idiosyncratic personal impression made by Lydia Lopokova, formerly the star of Diaghilev's Russian ballet, that provoked such diverse responses. We see Virginia Woolf initially mystified, her sister Vanessa Bell resolutely scornful, Florence Keynes quickly won over, Virginia more slowly – not until 1928 affectionately conceding of Lydia: 'She says very sensible things.'[19]

We soon recognise a distinctive timbre in reading Lydia's letters to Maynard. They are endowed with a capacity to triumph over mere English syntax – 'Lydiaspeak', as Maynard dubbed it. We see that she manifestly encouraged him to broaden his sympathies and make his thinking more accessible to 'outside opinion'. She was thrilled, in 1922, when this intellectually intimidating Cambridge economics don, her unlikely suitor, was now attending the international Genoa conference, part of Lloyd George's casino diplomacy, as the correspondent of Scott's *Manchester Guardian*, with articles syndicated across Europe and North America. She delighted in seeing Maynard's picture in the paper – 'quite a big photo. Very famous!' She instructed him: 'Do not speak against your articles in journalism – just think how many peoples read, understand and remember it; and when you go to bed have the feeling of the work you have done with mind and inspiration.' Keynes's *Tract on Monetary Reform* (1923) had its origins in his work for the *Manchester Guardian* – and it shows, at least in the literary style, which is certainly no longer the Strachey-like mandarin voice of some earlier writings. When Virginia Woolf read part of the *Tract* in proof, she noted that 'the process of mind there displayed is as far ahead of me as Shakespeare's'. She could not help herself from adding: 'True, I don't respect it so much.'[20]

'The deeper and the fouler the bogs into which Mr Lloyd George leads us, the more credit is his for getting us out.'[21] If Keynes already thought this when he wrote about plans for revising the Treaty in 1921, he found increasingly good reason to think so in succeeding years. 'At dinner I sat next but one to Lloyd George and talked to him a great deal,' Maynard reported to Lydia in May 1924. He told her how Lloyd George had used the occasion to make known his commendation of his former critic: 'I approve Keynes, because, whether he is right or wrong, he is always dealing with realities.'

A political rapprochement between them became increasingly evident over the next five years, raising many eyebrows in the process. By the time of the 1929 General Election, with Liberal proposals for tackling mass unemployment now a salient issue, Keynes was to co-author a striking pamphlet in support, *Can Lloyd George Do It?* To partisan contemporaries, it seemed remarkable that the author of the *Economic Consequences* should do this. As one old-fashioned Liberal put it, Lloyd George's willingness to rethink the party's policies had 'undoubtedly interested, occupied, propitiated – dare I add, bamboozled? – a large number of able Liberals who liked neither his record nor his ways'. Keynes's own line was characteristic: 'The difference between me and some other people is that I oppose Mr Lloyd George when he is wrong and support him when he is right.'

This personal détente had several dimensions. For Keynes, it indeed entailed a painful break with Asquith, whose long tenure as Liberal leader ended in 1926. Asquith and Lloyd George had worked together since 1923 in a nominally reunited party that had come together when the Conservatives, now led by Baldwin, unwisely challenged free trade – still the conventional wisdom in Britain and still a popular cry in the 1923 General Election, in which the Conservatives lost their majority. The resulting Labour government in 1924, albeit short lived and in a minority dependent on tacit Liberal support, gave Labour new credibility at Liberal expense. For left-wing Liberals like Keynes, it was Lloyd George's more conciliatory tone towards organised labour, especially in the aftermath of the General Strike of 1926, that struck the right note. Asquith, now seventy-four, was pushed aside. It was with Lloyd George's accession as leader that the Liberal party showed a renewed vitality in formulating economic and social policy, in a way not seen since the progressive legislation of the pre-war era.

Keynes's own increasing concern with the problem of unemployment thus needs to be seen in a political as well as an economic context. If we are sometimes struck by his temperamental conservatism – wearing his Treasury hat, for example – we should also recognise his fundamental intellectual radicalism. In a lecture first given at Oxford in 1924 he challenged 'the metaphysical or general principles upon which, from time to time, *laissez-faire* has been founded'. Instead he stated his own social philosophy. 'The world is *not* so governed from above that private and social interest always coincide,' he declared. 'It is *not* so managed here below that in practice they coincide. It is *not* a correct deduction from the principles of economics that enlightened self-interest always operates in the public interest.'[22]

The experience of the gold standard was indeed a further factor in shaping Keynes's outlook. Britain had been forced off it in the spring of 1919, letting sterling float against the dollar, at about $3.70 in 1920 and $3.90 in 1921, and then fluctuating in 1922–4 at around $4.40. This was about 10 per cent lower than the pre-war rate of $4.86 to the pound – the totemic 'parity' for sterling that was the only one considered. So a return to gold at this parity meant that British prices – especially of exports – would have to be squeezed down to this level. (For if the Americans had been used to paying $4.40 for a ton of coal imported from Britain, they would hardly agree to pay $4.86 once Britain went back to gold but would expect to continue paying $4.40; so the sterling proceeds from selling the exported ton of coal at $4.40, previously £1, would now be reduced to eighteen shillings – a 10 per cent reduction). Reducing British prices by about 10 per cent was thus the assigned task of the Bank of England's lending rate: set at a high level that protected the gold value of sterling on the international exchanges, with the assumption that this financial constraint would inexorably bring domestic prices into line in the real economy within Britain.

It was Churchill, now Chancellor of the Exchequer in Baldwin's Conservative government, who put Britain back on the gold standard in April 1925. But the move had long been foreseen as virtually inevitable within the Treasury, as Keynes himself had good reason to appreciate. It was while he was still at the Treasury in 1918 that the Cunliffe Committee had been set up, taking for granted that Britain would maintain the gold standard. This committee had been chaired by Lord Cunliffe, no doubt relying upon his famous sense of smell here, just as he did in producing his notorious estimate on reparations. 'The Cunliffe Report belongs to an extinct and an almost forgotten order of ideas,' Keynes wrote in the *Tract* in 1923.[23] He did not add that it was an order of ideas to which he had himself long subscribed, in sanctioning the knave-proof orthodoxies. Instead he suggested in the *Tract* that 'many conservative bankers regard it as more consonant with their cloth, and also as economising thought, to shift public discussion of financial topics off the logical on to an alleged "moral" plane, which means a realm of thought where vested interest can be triumphant over the common good without further debate'.[24]

Cunliffe had died in 1920, a few months after his labours on reparations in Paris. But the sense that Keynes was engaged in a debate with his ghost still invests what he now argued in the *Tract*: that when 'we enter the realm of State action, *everything* is to be considered and weighed on its merits'.[25] The mere assumption that Britain should go back to the pre-war gold standard ignored historical realities. Before 1914, in essence, the gold standard imposed British prices upon everyone else. After the war, in a financial world where the United States now called the shots, it was sterling's parity against the dollar that was crucial. And although Britain and the United States had each experienced a short bout of heightened inflation during 1919, the American economy then entered a path of deflation – and Britain likewise. It was necessary for the pound to follow the dollar if the pre-war parity of sterling was to be restored.

Keynes was certainly not enamoured of inflation. He had himself supported the Treasury position in raising interest rates in early 1920, as a corrective to 'inflationism' which could 'strike at the whole basis of contract, of security, and of the capitalist system generally'.[26] As he put it in the *Tract*, both deflation and inflation were 'unjust' in that they disappointed expectations. 'Of the two perhaps deflation is, if we rule out exaggerated inflations such as that of Germany, the worse,' he wrote in 1923; 'because it is worse, in an impoverished world, to provoke unemployment than to disappoint the *rentier*.'[27] The general point was that all these options needed assessing through rational arguments about their consequences, not simply by making pre-emptive moral judgements. This was why, almost alone among the experts who were consulted, Keynes opposed Britain's return to gold in 1925; and also why Churchill, with his own intellectual curiosity aroused, challenged the Treasury to meet Keynes's arguments. But orthodoxy prevailed in assuming that the 'real economy' would adjust to the financial requirements imposed upon it from above.

The effects of the return to gold were much as Keynes predicted. An over-priced pound indeed made British exports (like coal) too expensive abroad, thus making workers in the export trade (like miners) unemployed. But this was not the starting point of his advocacy of government intervention here. The fact is that it was not in 1925, but instead fully a year *before* the return to gold, that Keynes first broached his characteristic arguments about the need for an economic stimulus. He did it in an article in the Liberal weekly paper the *Nation*, under the title 'Does unemployment need drastic remedy?' He was prompted to do so, moreover, as a response to an initiative by Lloyd George in April 1924; hence the cordiality of their encounters at this juncture and of their mutual flattery.

Why, then, had Keynes decided in 1924 that Lloyd George was now on the right track? It was not because either of them, at the time, had worked out detailed proposals for job creation. Nor was it because of any sudden surge in the level of British unemployment. This was actually falling rather than rising at the time, though it was admittedly stuck at around 10 per cent of the registered labour force, as compared with a norm of about half that before the war. Yet both men now agreed that unemployment needed 'a drastic remedy', even though they were still floundering when they tried to say exactly what this might comprise.

It was in 1923, in the *Tract*, that Keynes had uttered one of his most famous phrases, endlessly repeated (and often misrepresented) ever since. Yes, he conceded, there were indeed self-righting forces in the economy, provided that market forces were allowed free play – and allowed also enough time to do their job. 'But this *long run* is a misleading guide to current affairs,' Keynes suggested. '*In the long run* we are all dead.'[28] The moral is, of course, not that irresponsible short-term policies should prevail but that the true irresponsibility is to abstain, on doctrinal grounds, from remedial action that can do good.

Chancing his arm in 1924, then, Keynes was prepared to outline an approach to policy-making that still retains its cogency. Though we can find loose ends and inconsistencies in the economic detail, we also find propositions that were to become central to his agenda, not only in economic policy but in theory too. What is central to Keynes's approach is 'the principle that *prosperity is cumulative*', and he reiterates it as the merest common sense. 'There are many examples of cumulative prosperity, both in recent and in earlier experience,' he says, citing alike the nineteenth-century British railway expansion and the French post-war reconstruction programme and the current American boom in the motor industry. The problem is thus to supply the initial impetus. 'We have stuck in a rut,' he says. 'We need an impulse, a jolt, an acceleration.' Public investment must come to the rescue when the market fails to do so. The priority is currently for 'capital developments at home'. Such a programme, Keynes asserts, 'will inspire confidence', thus reinforcing 'the stimulus which shall initiate a cumulative prosperity'.[29]

The circular nature of the argument is thus its strength – once the political courage has been shown to provide the stimulus. For there is no arbitrarily fixed limit to what the economy can produce, if stimulated by investment in new projects. Here, surely, is the line of thinking that led Keynes to endorse Lloyd George's claim, in the 1929 Liberal election manifesto *We Can Conquer Unemployment*. After four years on the gold standard, defending the ancestral parity of sterling, the effect of the high bank rate had been not to bring down prices but to create a stasis where unemployment was still at about 10 per cent. Hence Keynes's active participation in support of the Liberals' interventionist measures, writing hard-hitting partisan articles in Lord Beaverbrook's tabloid paper the *Evening Standard*. But it was also Keynes, that busy man, who at the same moment (March 1929) used the scholarly pages of the *Economic Journal* to rejoin the long-running controversy over the payment of German reparations – or non-payment usually.

Keynes was returning to an issue that had now generated an enormous literature. He began by citing the Dawes Committee in distinguishing 'the *budgetary* problem of extracting the necessary sums of money out of the pockets of the German people' to pay reparations within Germany; and, as a distinct issue, 'the *transfer* problem of converting the German money so received into foreign currency'. The budgetary problem was essentially financial, within Germany; but Keynes's point – as in the *Economic Consequences* – remained that the transfer problem involved real resources, embodied in specific exports, requiring international trade to be rebalanced. 'For the last two or three years the transfer problem has been temporarily solved, by Germany borrowing abroad for capital purposes at home,' as he readily admitted.[30] But, once this influx of dollars ceased, what then?

Keynes reiterated that Germany would be required to run a huge export surplus. Yet to increase its share of foreign markets, its prices would have to become more competitive, as priced in gold, which necessarily required a reduction of earnings in Germany – in addition to any increase of reparation taxes. This was necessary if Germany were to remit its reparations to the Allies, thus requiring the real economy to fulfil these financial demands and paper commitments, and to do so in the short run. As Keynes put it, 'we are trying to fix the volume of foreign remittance and compel the balance of trade to adjust itself thereto'. And then he added a comment that now struck him as obvious: 'Those who see no difficulty in this – like those who saw no difficulty in Great Britain's return to the gold standard – are applying the theory of liquids to what is if not a solid, at least a sticky mass with strong internal resistances.'[31]

In framing his analysis in this way, Keynes revealed how far he had travelled in the years since 1914. Maybe it showed, as Lloyd George had put it, that he dealt in realities. It showed how the analysis in the *Economic Consequences* pointed to the mature formulation of a Keynesian perspective on economic policy. And it showed that

Keynes now knew that there could be no return to the Garden of Eden, the gates of which had irrevocably closed after 1914.

The cover of Lloyd George's 1929 manifesto, *We Can Conquer Unemployment*, depicts an heroic image of himself. He stands, the bold and confident leader, with both arms outstretched. His right arm points to an image of well-equipped troops, with what must be a munitions factory in the background; the caption is 'We Mobilised for War'. Lloyd George's left arm gestures towards a scene of happy house-builders and smoking factory chimneys – 'Let us Mobilise for Prosperity'. The reference to the experience of the Great War was perhaps to be expected from a man whose leadership qualities were emphasised in current Liberal propaganda. But the juxtaposition of the two images should have caused some rueful introspection on the part of one former wartime Treasury official who had once derided plans for stimulating the economy to such feats of mass mobilisation.

For Lloyd George's current political proposals did not simply draw upon Keynes's economic ideas but actually provoked their gestation. In 1929, amid the day-to-day pressures of an election campaign, Keynes was led to identify the central flaw in the Treasury argument that government spending always displaces equivalent private resources. 'The orthodox theory *assumes* that everyone is employed,' Keynes contended in March 1929. 'If this were so, a stimulus in one direction would be at the expense of production in others. But when there is a large surplus of *unused* productive resources, as at present, the case is totally different.'[32] Here was his knock-down argument against the conventional Treasury View; as he put it a couple of months later, it 'would be correct *if everyone were employed already*, but is only correct *on that assumption*'.[33]

Moreover, in 1924 he had already developed the argument that, since prosperity is cumulative, an initial stimulus can produce a dynamic impact upon the economy. Put these two concepts together

WE CAN CONQUER UNEMPLOYMENT

We Mobilised for War   Let us Mobilise for Prosperity

EXTRAVAGANCE
INFLATION
BANKRUPTCY

6D.   CASSELL AND COMPANY LTD.   **6**D.
NET   LONDON, E.C.4.   NET

Here is Lloyd George in the 1929 General Election campaign, promising to mobilise the under-employed resources of the country, just as he had in the First World War. This is reproduced from the official copy held in the Treasury, hence the scrawled comments.

and the implications have an abiding significance. For here, surely, was the explanation why Lloyd George had shown more insight than the Treasury on the capacity of the wartime economy.

In 1929, the question of whether Lloyd George could 'do it' was never put to the test. The Liberal revival failed to deliver enough seats to put him into government. The moment passed for future collaboration between himself and Keynes and their future relations were to be distinguished instead by retrospective controversy.

In March 1933 a new book by Keynes appeared. This was no economic treatise but his much more popular *Essays in Biography*, many of them previously published, including that on the 'Council of Four', reprinted from the *Economic Consequences*. But Keynes then disinterred the additional half-dozen pages that he had originally composed on Lloyd George, suppressed in 1919 on the advice of his mother and Asquith. Admittedly, Keynes still refrained from publishing one comment from the 1919 draft, referring to 'those methods of untruthful, indeed shameless, intrigue which must lead to ultimate ruin any cause entrusted to him', which would certainly have read differently after 1929. But the rest of the 1919 draft was published in the *Essays* as 'a fragment', with a footnote explaining that, although the author still felt 'some compunction' over what had been written 'in the heat of the moment', he now took a different view about publication – 'These matters belong now to history.'[34]

Lloyd George initially took a similarly lofty view. Keynes's new book had hit the headlines in such papers as the Conservative *Daily Mail*, naturally sensing a partisan opportunity to stoke the quarrels of two prominent Liberals. Lloyd George at first scornfully told a reporter that all this had been written in 1919; but then he evidently read the expanded version in print. The phrase that the press seized on was the image of 'this syren', with its dictionary derivation from Greek and Latin myth as one who 'charms, allures or deceives', which was hardly likely to inspire political trust. 'Lloyd George is rooted in nothing; he is void and without content,' Keynes's fragment continued, in a vein that was damaging, not because such things had not been said often before, but mainly because they now came from an ostensible supporter.[35]

The real offence lay elsewhere. Keynes's development of his image – 'this goat-footed bard, this half-human visitor to our age from the hag-ridden magic and enchanted woods of Celtic antiquity' – had the timbre not of any classical allusion so much as an ethnic slur. There followed other phrases, identifying 'that flavour of final purposelessness, inner irresponsibility' and his 'cunning, remorselessness, love of power', that were more politically charged. But it was surely Lloyd George's alleged 'existence outside or away from our Saxon good and evil' that again slyly reverted to the stereotype of a Welsh outsider, conveyed with a sneer of over-educated English condescension.[36] It was the culture clash of the wartime Treasury arguments all over again.

How could Keynes not have foreseen the public impact of such words? He found out soon enough when, in November 1933, the first volume of Lloyd George's *War Memoirs* was published. His dispute with the Treasury over war finance was inevitably discussed. Lloyd George did not minimise the role of Keynes, who had been 'for the first time lifted by the Chancellor of the Exchequer into the rocking chair of a pundit', but had proved 'much too mercurial and impulsive a counsellor for a great emergency'. Lloyd George made the most of his privileged opportunity to quote a 1915 memorandum by 'the volatile soothsayer who was responsible for this presage of misfortune'.[37] He duly mocked Keynes's prophecies of doom. True, the fact that Keynes was officially forbidden to quote from the same memorandum led him to complain in *The Times* of sharp practice; but Lloyd George was surely entitled to defend his own record and his own honour, as Keynes eventually conceded.

Yet a highly significant point was missed in these personal polemics. For the real reason why Lloyd George had been proved right by events in supposing that Britain could survive the strains imposed on it in 1915–17 was that the full capacity of the economy had been crucially under estimated by the Treasury mandarins. In this perspective, some of the gratuitous gibes in Lloyd George's *War Memoirs* read very ironically.

Keynes is described as 'an entertaining economist whose bright but shallow dissertations on finance and political economy, when not taken too seriously, always provide a source of merriment for his readers'.[38] Thus Lloyd George scored his point against Keynes in 1933 by implicitly siding with the financial orthodoxy that he had long scorned.

Lloyd George had one further score to settle. *The Truth about the Peace Treaties* (1938) was the opportunity for his lengthy apologia, published at a time when the rise of Hitler gave the Germans a far less sympathetic image in Britain. Lloyd George stressed the multifarious achievements of the Treaty, in an imperfect world, but obviously could not ignore reparations. Here his line, as would be expected, was to stress his own role in moderating the demands actually made. But, in showing that an indemnity of some kind was already envisaged well before the end of the war, Lloyd George exhumed the document to which Keynes had contributed in 1916, with its brief to advise on the potential economic effects. He thus accused Keynes (and his co-author) of inspiring 'the inflated estimates of Lord Cunliffe and Lord Sumner'.[39] Moreover, since the option of a method of payment over a considerable period of years had also been explored, there was a further charge: 'Mr Keynes is the sole patentee and promoter of that method of extraction.'[40]

All this created a splash on publication in October 1938. As in 1933, Lloyd George had quoted, on his privileged terms as former Prime Minister, a document that Keynes was unable to cite in any reply. He had to be content with a sarcastic letter to the press: 'It was indeed a bold, though scarcely a bright, idea on the part of Mr Lloyd George, in all the circumstances of which he is well aware, to attempt to represent my influence as having been the opposite of what he knows it to have been.'[41] That this was well justified is attested by the fact that no subsequent historian, however critical of Keynes's role over the Treaty, has ever attempted to resuscitate this particular allegation by Lloyd George. But it was a sad note on which to terminate a relationship that itself had such fruitful economic consequences.

Second Chances:
Churchill, Roosevelt, Keynes

In October 1919, when Colonel House finally departed for home, he had been fêted in Paris. Clemenceau had declared warm affection. But when House reached the United States, he found that he was denied access to the White House, where Edith Wilson, along with Dr Grayson, kept the invalid President sequestered while purporting to relay his wishes to the outside world. In November Ray Stannard Baker visited House in New York, and here the two men talked freely. House maintained that 'the ability to play upon men's vanity' was a politician's chief asset – 'Roosevelt had this gift: but Wilson has it not.' Indeed, said House, 'he simply does not know the modern Machiavellianism'.[1] Of course, House was referring to Theodore Roosevelt, recently deceased; but TR's blend of easy charm with purposeful flattery evidently ran in the family, as FDR's selection as vice-presidential candidate was shortly to indicate. FDR's future political career was to turn upon his personal charisma and his extraordinary capacity to project key issues in a way that swayed outside opinion, with an intuition as keen as that of Lloyd George in sensing how inside opinion might thus be made operational in democratic politics.

With hindsight, it can be said that FDR became the standard-bearer for the fulfilment of great causes where Wilson's efforts finally proved insufficient. And the sense that the younger man might adopt such a role was already immanent when Wilson thanked the two Democratic candidates in the 1920 election for continuing to campaign for the

League – a battle, so they all purported to believe, that could still be won. It was FDR who, from 1921, led the fund-raising for the Woodrow Wilson Foundation, still active in Washington today. Moreover, with FDR himself in the White House from 1933, those who worked closely with him perceived not only a sense of legacy over the Wilsonian agenda but also this President's abiding consciousness of the political calamity of 1919–20. Robert Sherwood, alert as a playwright to the dramatic possibilities of the situation, was to put it most vividly in describing how FDR's fireside chat of 29 December 1941, invoking the United States as 'the great arsenal of democracy', was composed. 'As Roosevelt sat at the end of the long table in the Cabinet Room working on that speech and other speeches during the war years, he would look at the portrait of Woodrow Wilson, over the mantel piece,' was how Sherwood set the scene. 'The tragedy of Wilson was always somewhere within the rim of his consciousness.'

Twenty years earlier, the debonair Roosevelt had confronted the spectre of a personal tragedy that might well have precluded such career prospects. His sudden affliction with poliomyelitis in August 1921 was a stunning blow. It happened in Canada, after typically strenuous sea-bathing and a run with his boys at their summer retreat at Campobello; the diagnosis was initially uncertain but, after two weeks, the verdict was ineluctable. Infantile paralysis was the common name at the time for this condition; and the paralysis of FDR's legs was to be almost total. As one of his doctors put it, he was 'a goner below the waist', though he was not rendered permanently incontinent nor sexually impotent. He was discreetly smuggled back to New York in a private railcar which avoided the main station; only gradually was news released, always minimising his disabilities. He struggled to beat the disease, erecting a structure of wooden bars to help him walk at Hyde Park, and exercising there with a dogged determination. Some improvement was indeed effected over time; he had hopes, as late as 1928, that some new regime might enable him to stand (literally) as a candidate, perhaps for the Governorship of New York in 1932. In the end he had to compensate for his intractable medical condition through his upper-body strength – and through subterfuge. In that era the media connived in never showing him in a wheelchair.

FDR's recovery testified both to his remarkable resilience and to his stubborn political ambition. It was stage-managed, enlisting his sons to help him return, step by painful step, to the political platform, notably at the 1924 Democratic convention in New York City and at the 1928 convention in Houston. This was national exposure on a make-or-break basis. What the party faithful observed with some awe, and what the voters saw in the newspapers or on the news-reels, was a triumph for force of personality over any handicap, with FDR's characteristic flashing smile and his diverting patter of trivial bonhomie stealing the scene. At both conventions, he commended his longstanding New York rival, Al Smith, as the 'happy warrior' who could take the White House: speeches that were more raptur-ously received than those of the candidate himself. In 1924 Smith had failed to receive the Democratic nomination; but so had William McAdoo, the Wilsonian insider, who was now tainted with finan-cial scandal; and, against an uninspiring compromise candidate, the Republicans were to romp home in the presidential election with an ease that FDR had not expected. He had anticipated, so he told Eleanor, that 'even if Coolidge is elected we shall be so darned sick of the conservatism of the old money-controlled crowd in four years time that we get a real progressive landslide in 1928!'[2]

Smith meanwhile remained a formidable figure as Governor of New York. A Catholic, he enjoyed strong support in the city, where machine politics had always mobilised the immigrant vote. But though he ran successfully on a reform ticket in New York state politics, he was thwarted in his attempts to extend his appeal to more conservative voters nationally. In 1928, seizing the Democratic presidential nomination at last, Smith was to find that carrying the big cities was not enough. But, optimistic in his campaign strategy for the Presidency, he now beseeched FDR to run in his place for the Governorship of New York, which the latter narrowly won, partly by trading on the Roosevelt name in upstate New York. Smith, by contrast, found his career virtually over after he suffered the loss of the presidential contest to Herbert Hoover.

The name Roosevelt was, of course, already familiar to New York voters. In 1924, it had been TR's son, inevitably named Theodore Roosevelt Junior, who lost the Governorship contest to Smith – the occasion if not the cause of the great feud between the Oyster Bay and Hyde Park branches of the family. Eleanor Roosevelt, by campaigning aggressively against her own first cousin, made this breach highly personal; and the family vendetta was stoked up, especially by Alice Longworth, TR's daughter, over the ensuing four decades. Eleanor increasingly led her own life, now building a separate cottage at Hyde Park, and living with close women companions. She also became increasingly active in politics in her own right, running the League of Women Voters in New York, and in 1928 supporting Smith's presidential campaign as strongly as FDR's gubernatorial bid. Eleanor Roosevelt thus emerged as a powerful independent voice on the progressive left of the Democratic party. This was a relationship that suited her husband well enough, successively as Governor and as President, offering him an inbuilt deniability over her political interventions, which often enabled him to test the water before committing himself.

The dynastic nature of the Roosevelt entourage was apparent in many ways. There was the financial support that the family could muster in sustaining FDR's own heroic return to the political stage; there was, too, the physical aid of sixteen-year-old James in getting FDR on crutches to the podium in 1924, and of young Elliott in taking his brother's place in 1928, literally at his father's elbow, now without crutches, just a cane. There was also the network of influential political supporters among other members of the Hudson River squirearchy, notably Henry Morgenthau Junior, later to become FDR's Treasury Secretary. At Hyde Park itself, Sara Roosevelt still controlled the purse-strings, helping to support her son in his activities at the well-publicised polio-treatment facilities established at Warm Springs, Georgia, where swimming in the natural spring waters proved highly beneficial for many fellow sufferers under FDR's sponsorship. Here he invested two-thirds of the substantial sum he himself inherited in 1927 on the death of his half-brother, 'Rosy', who left him $100,000 (worth about $1.3 million today).

After his defeat on the Democratic ticket in the 1920 presidential election, FDR had taken steps to attend to his own finances. His salary as Assistant Secretary of the Navy had been only $5,000 a year; and he had five children to educate, aged from five to fifteen. He now landed a job representing an insurance company in New York City, paying $25,000 a year (about $330,000 today) – and requiring his services only for half-days at that. In effect, this came as a political favour engineered through powerful figures in the New York Democratic establishment, less for FDR to exercise any legal skills than to hustle for business on the strength of his name, charm and connections. He also clearly hoped to gain more independence from his own omnipresent mother.

This hope was, within months, blighted by polio. But he retained his business connection, even though in 1926–8 he was to spend fully half of each year at Warm Springs. Everyone made allowances; Al Smith, in enticing FDR to stand for the Governorship, assured him that he could spend nine months a year at Warm Springs (naturally with Smith's people proposing to run New York, as previously). Rosy's legacy to FDR was certainly useful, even though Sara's support at Hyde Park now proved as indispensable as ever. So the invalid FDR could well afford to cultivate his hobbies. Golf, which he had loved, was never even spoken of again; likewise he never visited Campobello, with its painful memories – until he succeeded in becoming President in 1933. Meanwhile there was a new passion for stamp-collecting. Another hobby that he tried in these years of recuperation was writing: a project for a history of the United States – lightly taken up, lightly abandoned. Politics remained his vocation.

For Winston Spencer Churchill, writing was no hobby. It was, as he often said, his profession: one that sustained his political career. The pivotal work in the 1920s was his *World Crisis*, originally projected in two volumes, though progressively extended. In the original edition, his first volume begins its narrative in 1911 and gets only as far as the end of 1914, leaving 1915 to be covered in a second volume; both were published during 1923. True, Churchill was by now out of ministerial office, having abruptly lost his cabinet post (and salary) when the Lloyd George coalition was overthrown in October 1922; and since, in the General Election that immediately followed, he also lost his parliamentary seat at Dundee, standing as a 'National Liberal', he was unexpectedly liberated from day-to-day political obligations. But what enabled a couple of fat, detailed, heavily documented volumes of the *World Crisis* to be published within twelve months was the fact that Churchill had already been working on them for nearly three years while serving as a cabinet minister. Moreover, the two further volumes that continued the narrative of the war to 1918 were published (in 1927) while Churchill was again in office as Chancellor of the Exchequer, as was a fifth volume, *The Aftermath* (1929), with a sixth volume belatedly added on the eastern front.

The Prime Minister, Stanley Baldwin, was not the only one to acknowledge how remarkably impressive it was that a leading cabinet minister could find the time and energy to do this. But Churchill had two remarkably pressing motives: money and vindication. The advances from the *World Crisis* assured him of £27,000 (worth at least £750,000 today) and additional volumes brought more. The money was badly needed to support the lifestyle of a family with four growing children and a capacious country house at Chartwell in Kent. But political vindication was as strong a motive, at a time when Churchill, turning fifty in 1924, remaking his career as a Conservative, needed to face down the persistent calls: 'What about the Dardanelles?' Cries in Australia pointedly rephrased the question: 'What about Gallipoli?' The second volume of the *World Crisis* is entirely devoted to addressing this issue. It does not blench from quoting the verdict already published in the Australian official history, composed with personal feeling by the journalist Charles Bean, who had been there: 'So through a Churchill's excess of imagination, a layman's ignorance of artillery, and the fatal power of a young enthusiasm to convince older and slower brains, the tragedy of Gallipoli was born.'[3]

It was not so much the military failure itself that dogged Churchill as the allegations about its causes. Critics pointed to a man with disabling personal flaws. His lack of judgement became the crux; it was the old mantra, that this undoubtedly brilliant but demonstrably wayward man simply could not be trusted. Here was the paradigm against which all his future projects and promises were to be measured. So his own literary artifice was summoned, not only to make out his own case in bold and striking terms but also to bury the issue in a morass of corroborative detail and selective documentation.

By the time that the first two volumes of the *World Crisis* were published in 1923, the public mood about the war was already sombre. Armistice Day was celebrated annually with acute awareness that the British Empire had lost nearly a million men, mainly on the western front. It is central to Churchill's case in the *World Crisis* that, by the close of 1914, a coherent alternative strategy had been available. 'The initiative had passed to Britain – the Great Amphibian,' he writes. (Indeed he had wanted to call his book *The Great Amphibian* until his British and American publishers joined forces to talk him out of it.) The strategic choice at this juncture is expounded in the broadest terms, deploying the present tense to dramatise the options now open: 'Shall we use our reinforced fleets and great new armies of 1915, either to turn the Teutonic right in the Baltic or their left in the Black Sea and the Balkans? Or shall we hurl our manhood against sandbags, wire and concrete in frontal attack upon the German fortified lines in France?'[4] He tellingly quotes his own plea to Asquith at the end of December 1914: 'Are there not other alternatives than sending our armies to chew barbed wire in Flanders?'[5]

It was the naval superiority of the Allies that needed to be mobilised. 'Although the Central Powers were working on interior lines, this advantage did not countervail the superior mobility of sea power,' Churchill argues.[6] At any time Britain could send troops more quickly than the enemy to any point in the Mediterranean, even to the straits that gave access to the Black Sea. But Churchill's initial plan here, of course, was to force the Dardanelles through naval power alone. His argument depends on the decisive impact this would have upon the balance between the Ottoman Empire, Germany's ally, and beleaguered Russia, Britain's ally. He quotes at length from what he told the British commander about 'the supreme moral effect of a British fleet with sufficient fuel and ammunition entering the Sea of Marmora', confidently predicting 'the political effect of the arrival of the fleet before Constantinople, which is incalculable, and may well be absolutely decisive'.[7]

It could have worked, Churchill argues, if only the navy had pressed on despite initial losses. Yet he also defends the shift from a purely naval operation in the Dardanelles to the military landings on the Gallipoli peninsula. He does not minimise the awful costs of establishing lodgements on the five beaches in the Anglo-French sector, where 9,000 British troops were landed. 'Of these at least 3,000 were killed or wounded, and the remainder were clinging precariously to their dear-bought footholds and around the rim of the Peninsula.'[8] Meanwhile, the ANZAC troops, in their own assault on a small bay further north ('Anzac Cove'), faced equally shocking odds, though 'the power did not exist in the Turkish Empire to shake from its soil the grip of the Antipodes'.[9] He quotes what he had written at the time of 'a great army hanging on by its eyelids to a rocky beach' in an exhortation he had sent to Admiral Fisher on 11 May 1915.[10]

By this date, of course, Churchill's own position as First Lord of the Admiralty had come under threat. But, even after being forced out of the Admiralty, as he makes clear, he continued to argue for persevering at Gallipoli, making continual reference to the western front as a bleak alternative. 'We should be ill-advised to squander our new armies in frantic and sterile efforts to pierce the German lines,' he had told the Dardanelles Committee on 1 June 1915. 'To do so is to play the German game.'[11] He had starkly informed them on 18 June: 'Out of approximately 19,500 square miles of France and Belgium in German hands we have recovered about 8.'[12] These privileged citations from contemporary documents corroborate the unrepentant claim that 'I pointed continuously to victory at the Dardanelles as the sole and supreme remedy open to us for the evils of our situation.'[13]

'Anzac is the greatest word in the history of Australasia,' he had written at the time. 'Is it for ever to carry to future generations of Australians and New Zealanders memories of forlorn heroism and of sacrifices made in vain?. . .'[14] It was the tragically premature ending of the Dardanelles campaign, so the *World Crisis* reasons, that left the outcome on the western front to be decided in a 'war of exhaustion', with 'frontal attacks by valiant flesh and blood against wire and machine guns, "killing Germans" while Germans killed Allies twice as often' – until the belated achievement of a victory that 'proved only less ruinous to the victor than to the vanquished'.[15]

There is little triumphalism here. And when Churchill added his volume, *The Aftermath*, to the *World Crisis* in 1929, he developed his theme about the peace. One striking point is how far he now endorsed the analysis of Keynes, 'a man of clairvoyant intelligence', who had shown with 'unanswerable good sense the monstrous character of the financial and economic clauses'.[16] Indeed Churchill's own lucid exposition of the impracticability of these clauses showed his own talent – of long standing but often underestimated – in mastering the economic arguments. (He was in due course to admit that Keynes's warnings about the return to the gold standard in 1925 proved better founded than the advice of Treasury officials.) In reciprocal admiration, when Keynes reviewed *The Aftermath*, he fulsomely acknowledged Churchill's 'energies of mind and his intense absorption of intellectual interest and elemental emotion in what is for the moment the matter in hand', whatever that might be.[17]

They were in agreement too about Wilson's role at the peace conference. By the time that *The Aftermath* was written, the literature on the peace conference was already huge, and one of the incontestable merits of Churchill's book is that he had mastered so much of it. He saluted not only the six volumes of documents edited by the Cambridge diplomatic historian Harold Temperley but also the cogent and unforgiving analysis published by André Tardieu, who had served as one of the French delegates. *The Intimate Papers of Colonel House* was the title given to the four volumes, based on House's personal archive, that the Yale historian Charles Seymour edited for publication, the first two volumes appearing only a couple of years after Wilson had died. Lloyd George was to dub this 'treachery'.[18] But Churchill, an historian always grateful for a good source, had written of their 'peculiar interest' in disclosing 'a revelation of the President'.[19]

Churchill preferred House's account to the official Wilsonian apologia. For in 1922, with the full cooperation of both Woodrow and Edith Wilson, Ray Stannard Baker had published *Woodrow Wilson and the World Settlement* in three volumes, which were now subjected to scathing comment from Churchill. He dwelt mordantly on the 'Hollywood' style of Baker's scenario. 'For this purpose the President is represented as a stainless Sir Galahad championing the superior ideals of the American people and brought to infinite distress by contact with the awful depravity of Europe and its statesmen.' Deploying heavy irony, Churchill satirises the pervasive tone of American moral exceptionalism. He declines to accept that European immigrants to the United States 'took away with them all the virtues and left behind them all the vices of the races from which they had sprung' or that they had become 'an order of beings definitely superior in morals, in culture, and in humanity to their prototypes in Europe'.[20]

Throughout his career, Churchill often manifested a worldly realism in taking the world as he found it. Yet, with his blood up, he now goes on for pages in relentlessly identifying a double standard of morality. 'The American thesis after the United States entered the war', he points out with undisguised scorn, 'was that the Germans represented the most violent form of military aggression recorded by history.' Yet how could this be reconciled with Baker's account? 'If the United States had entered the war – a war, as they subsequently described it, of right and justice against unspeakable wrong and tyranny – on the 4th of August, the world would never have come into this plight.' Churchill reserves a special disdain for Wilsonian humbug over the secret treaties that the hard-pressed Allies had made during the war, represented by Baker as 'the inherent cynical wickedness and materialism of old-world diplomacy'. Here Churchill finds his patience stretched by Baker's 'film tableau' – 'The President had never heard of their existence,' he writes with caustic incredulity.[21]

On a wider canvas, too, the American position plainly left the Chancellor of the Exchequer unimpressed. He now depicted the outcome of a war in which 'Europe was to be left to scramble out of the world disaster as best she could; and the United States, which had lost but 125,000 lives in the whole struggle, was to settle down upon the basis of receiving through one channel or another four-fifths of the reparations paid by Germany to the countries she had devastated or whose manhood she had slain.'[22] The subject of war debts was admittedly seldom off the agenda in the British Treasury at this time. But if Churchill currrently harboured ambitions of moving to the Foreign Office, perhaps we can understand his wife's private warning in late 1928 that 'I am afraid your known hostility to America might stand in the way.'

Churchill was to be spared potential embarrassment in dealing with the Americans by the political outcome in 1929. The Baldwin government lost the General Election; Lloyd George's campaign failed to give the Liberals sufficient leverage; and, although in a minority again, it was to be a Labour government that (not for the last time) had the dubious privilege of confronting a world slump. Out of office, Churchill's own reputation still dogged him. It proved easy to exclude him from the so-called National Government formed in August 1931 during the financial crisis.

A book published in July of that year, *The Tragedy of Winston Churchill*, illustrates its subject's continuing difficulties. This was written by Victor Wallace Germains, well known at the time as a defender of Kitchener's reputation (and the author in 1913 of a book with the pregnant title *The Gathering Storm*). '*The World Crisis* is a brilliantly written and powerfully reasoned work,' Germains conceded, but this showed exactly why its case was meretricious. 'Churchill the writer is the specialist successful in his own sphere; Churchill, the military leader, is the amateur who blundered.' So that was the secret of how this man was now garlanded with literary plaudits for explaining away his military failures! Hence too Germains's soldierly conclusion that 'at the present time when the Empire is going through the most terrible economic crisis known to history, the facile phrases, glittering hopes, and unbalanced enthusiasm, which issued in the Tragedy of the Dardanelles, are a little out of place – they may too easily eventuate in consequences irreparable, disastrous, and appalling'.

The *World Crisis*, then, may not have silenced the military critics, but it impressed the literati. Moreover, the publication of *My Early Life* in 1930, offering its ironic gloss upon Churchill's supposed militarism, achieved high sales in Britain (though not in the United States). Here was a winning account of the congenial comradeship this emotionally needy young subaltern had found in the army, so unlike his unhappy schooldays. Readers were told how he had made many friends, of whom just three or four 'still survive' – men presumably now in their fifties, like the author himself. 'As for the rest, they are gone,' Churchill explains. 'The South African War accounted for a large proportion not only of my friends but of my company; and the Great War killed almost all the others.'[23] He portrays these young subalterns as poignantly innocent of their own vulnerability, complaining only about the dearth of calls to active service. 'This complaint was destined to be cured, and all our requirements were to be met to the fullest extent.'[24] Here too the tone is hardly triumphalist.

The battle of the books, in which Churchill himself freely participated, was also conducted vicariously. He extended cooperation in the publication of a popular biography: *Winston Churchill* by 'Ephesian', first published in 1927, with a second edition in 1928. The author, Carl Bechhofer Roberts, had a background that surely commended itself to Churchill: a self-taught adventurer who had gone to India in his youth, fought in the 9th Lancers and then worked as a jobbing journalist and war correspondent before finding a niche as private secretary to Churchill's friend F. E. Smith, whose biography by 'Ephesian' had recently been published.

This quick-witted author later qualified as a barrister, and already showed aptitude in defending clients in a strategically adroit manner, as his biography of Churchill shows. 'I do not propose to recapitulate the familiar and tragic story of the Dardanelles,' Roberts states in the middle of his chapter 8 (out of ten), after briskly declaring: 'Had Churchill been given a free hand the Dardanelles would surely have been forced.' But instead, 'the War was prolonged for three more years'; and so Roberts's narrative quickly moves on. In the final chapter, turning to Churchill's literary career, there is a tribute of another kind: 'he has won immortality as a writer'. In the first edition this remark was explicitly tied to the success of the *World Crisis*, citing reviews by such well-known authors of the day as Arnold Bennett and John Masefield; but by the time that Roberts published his third edition in 1936, he stretched the tribute to cover Churchill's multi-volume biography of the first Duke of Marlborough, then in progress. By 1936, too, Roberts found the course of events more favourable to his biography's high claims. The book's final words now read: 'The day may well come when the Pitt in Churchill will be called in to restore the Empire's affairs after a disaster or in another supreme crisis like that of 1914.'

Yet it took the experience of the later 1930s to accomplish the remaking of Churchill's career in Britain. For it was the rise of Hitler that came to dominate both Churchill's own political outlook and the way in which he was perceived. With his own soldierly refusal to dwell on war guilt, and with his open record of urging concessions to Weimar Germany over the flaws of the Versailles settlement, it was nonetheless

Churchill who presciently and persistently warned that the Nazi menace was something different. And, through their common perception of its significance, this increasingly well-focused commitment was to herald his future partnership with President Roosevelt – in ways that would previously have been unthinkable on either side.

———

The loss of innocence is a timeless literary trope. The Anglo-American dimension, inimitably explored in the work of Henry James, has a special resonance in depicting the ingenuous, well-meaning openness of the New World characters, duly confronted by the stratagems and sophistries of the Old World. In their contrasting ways, this is how both John Maynard Keynes and Ray Stannard Baker told the story of how the war to end war ended instead in disillusionment. But it also seems that this kind of innocence, unlike virginity, is susceptible of being lost more than once, in different ways, in different contexts, in different generations.

Churchill touched on such themes in a notable public lecture at Oxford in June 1930. No longer the responsible minister at the Treasury, he now had the luxury of reflecting discursively upon the onset of the great depression, and in a mood less optimistic than that in which he had written *The Aftermath*. He clung to the conventional faith, in which he had been brought up, that 'the best way of governing states is by talking'. But he openly wondered how far the great talking-shop of Parliament was up to the job when confronted with new economic problems, where the inadequacy of the conventional wisdom was now suddenly exposed. The classical doctrines of the knave-proof fiscal constitution – free trade, retrenchment, unfettered private enterprise and all – had been hallowed for a century. Churchill simply said of these maxims that 'we can clearly see that they do not correspond to what is going on now'.

For Churchill this was a far-reaching admission. True, everyone knew that he had changed parties twice in his career; it was often said that he lacked principles; but during the thirty years of his political career the imperialism of free trade had been his ideological bedrock. In meetings of the war cabinet during the Second World War, he still interspersed discussions of post-war economic policy with nostalgic remarks on the 'beautiful precision' with which free trade and the gold standard had once regulated such matters – 'not in this disastrous century but in the last'. And this was what he bleakly bemoaned in 1930, only twelve years after the Armistice. 'The grand and victorious summits which the British Empire won in that war are being lost,' he told his audience at Oxford. 'The compass has been damaged. The charts are out of date.'

Where Churchill identified a problem, Keynes believed that he himself now offered a solution. Many of the specifics were set out in 1931 in his *Essays in Persuasion*, which he called 'the croakings of a Cassandra who could never influence the course of events in time'.[25] Yet, writing in November 1931, just after Britain had been forced off the gold standard, he also offered a less gloomy prognosis. 'The main point is that we have regained our freedom of choice,' he declared. 'Scarcely any one in England now believes in the Treaty of Versailles or in the pre-war gold standard or in the policy of deflation.'[26] He claimed too much here, since the policy of the Conservative-dominated government that was to hold power in Britain until the Second World War was far from receptive to his own analysis – which is one reason why Keynes's own hopes came to be pinned on the United States in the New Deal era.

Keynes's temperamental optimism was often buoyed up by his visceral relish for public engagement. He enjoyed having all the answers in debate. In private, he could reveal a more reflective capacity, as close friends like Virginia Woolf observed. She recorded a discussion on morality, which took place at the dinner table along with T. S. Eliot in 1934. Keynes said of Christianity that 'he would be inclined not to demolish Xty if it were proved that without it morality is impossible' – plainly adopting a condescending, teasing tone since the famous poet was now a declared Anglican. Then

Keynes added: 'I begin to see that our generation – yours & mine V., owed a great deal to our fathers' religion.' He thought this a contrast with the young people in their circle, who had never been brought up as believers. 'We had the best of both worlds,' he told Virginia. 'We destroyed Xty & yet had its benefits.'[27]

Four years later, Woolf was to hear Keynes formally develop such self-scrutiny. He chose to talk on the theme of 'My Early Beliefs' to Bloomsbury's memoir club in September 1938. 'Maynard read a very packed profound & impressive paper so far as I could follow,' Woolf recorded, 'about Cambridge youth; their philosophy; its consequences; Moore; what it lacked; what it gave. I was impressed by M. & felt a little flittery & stupid.'[28] This was indeed an evocative performance, taking liberties with mere accuracy in some of its statements, and one given under the shadow of the pressing crisis in Czechoslovakia.

Keynes thus spoke with implicit reference to an acute threat of impending war. Looking back on Edwardian Cambridge, he maintained that he and his friends had 'repudiated all versions of the doctrine of original sin, of there being insane and irrational springs of wickedness in most men'. They had failed to understand that 'civilisation was a thin and precarious crust erected by the personality and the will of a very few, and only maintained by rules and conventions skilfully put across and guilefully preserved'. Clearly this is a pointedly retrospective view, lending poignancy to the conclusion that, 'as the years wore on towards 1914', more complex views of human nature and civilisation forcibly intruded.[29] Keynes spoke at the memoir club on Sunday 11 September. It was two days later that Neville Chamberlain, a Prime Minister who had never been in an aeroplane, sent a telegram to Hitler offering to fly to Germany, in a chain of events that led to the Munich agreement.

There has never been much talk of an idyllic, sunlit world plunging unexpectedly into shadow in 1939. Instead, the prospect of a further war haunted Europe by the late 1930s; in which case, as many Americans saw it, the problem was for their own country to keep out of it this time. On 30 January 1933, Adolf Hitler had been appointed Chancellor of Germany; on 4 March Franklin Roosevelt had been sworn in as President of the United States. Both were to remain in office until their respective deaths, Roosevelt at Warm Springs, Georgia, on 12 April 1945 and Hitler in his bunker in Berlin on 30 April. The symmetries in their careers were not entirely accidental.

Like Hitler, Roosevelt was a political beneficiary of the economic slump. He was Governor of New York when Wall Street crashed in 1929; but few held him responsible. Herbert Hoover, once hailed by progressives for his resourceful efforts at feeding wartime Belgium and post-war Germany, was now the hapless Republican President in Washington, in years that saw incumbents throughout the capitalist world blamed for a world slump spiralling beyond their control. Already the favoured son of the progressives as the next Democratic nominee, Roosevelt found the prospects for victory in the 1932 presidential election unexpectedly bright. All he had to do was to shed some political baggage that now threatened to embarrass him. Had he once spoken of forgiving Allied debts to the United States? No longer. Had he once pledged that the League of Nations was a battle that could still be won? It was an issue that the Hearst newspaper chain now raised, putting FDR under the same kind of pressure that the Northcliffe press had applied to Lloyd George in 1919. And the response in each case was to look for political cover through adroit, pragmatic manoeuvring.

Edward House had been purposefully drawn into the Roosevelt campaign. This too had been a matter of seeking mutual accommodation; it gratified the old man's political hankerings while enhancing Roosevelt's status as the Wilsonian standard-bearer. House was shown the text of FDR's speech repudiating American membership of the League of Nations in February 1932; first he was shocked, then he was cajoled. He had to accept FDR's formulation that 'the League of Nations today is not the League conceived by

Woodrow Wilson'. This was indeed a blow to Wilsonian idealists; Eleanor Roosevelt refused to speak to her husband for four days. But the path to the nomination was duly paved and FDR, in addressing the Democratic convention in Chicago, naturally made sure that Wilson's 'great, indomitable, unquenchable, progressive soul' was duly saluted. He also pledged himself to bring 'a new deal for the American people'. On this ticket – whatever it meant – Roosevelt was to win forty-two states, Hoover only six.

It subsequently became tempting to cite the New Deal as Keynesian economics in action. It is certainly true that Keynes himself became a prominent advocate of some of the New Deal's measures, notably those that used the federal budget to stimulate economic growth. But although economics had been FDR's major at Harvard, and his library at Hyde Park still holds the books to prove it, he was ill at ease in discussing economic concepts, as a personal encounter with Keynes at the White House in 1934 sufficiently illustrated. Frances Perkins, the Secretary of Labor, who had engineered the meeting, observed later that Keynes had been ready enough to speak to her in terms of homely examples, but she wrote: 'I wish he had been as concrete when he talked to Roosevelt, instead of treating him as though he belonged to the higher echelon of economic knowledge.' The irony was that it was FDR's ability to cast his message in striking terms – 'we have nothing to fear but fear itself', as he had proclaimed at his inauguration – that so impressed Keynes. It may even have helped alert the author of the *General Theory* to the crucial, self-sustaining role of confidence in economic growth.

Churchill's only previous meeting with Roosevelt had been in 1918. The Assistant Secretary of the Navy, on his wartime visit to London, had not taken kindly to the haughty manner of the British cabinet minister. But when, in 1934, Churchill wrote about the first two years of the new President, his tone was very different: 'it is certain that Franklin Roosevelt will rank among the greatest of men who have occupied that proud position'.[30] Although this expression

THE FIRST JOB FOR THE NEW ENGINEER   By HUTTON

FDR took office as President in March 1933, faced with the challenge of bringing his 'New Deal' to the aid of a stricken economy. Here he is, now aboard the locomotive – but it took the coming of the Second World War to get the job done.

of faith was mainly grounded on the impact of the New Deal, Roosevelt's increasing concern with foreign policy further stimulated Churchill's admiration in the late 1930s, the two men now united in their apprehensions about the rise of Hitler.

The inescapable fact was that, by the late 1930s, the prospect of a renewal of hostilities in Europe had become real. The response in the US Congress was the Neutrality Acts, designed to pre-empt any repetition of what had happened in 1917 by prohibiting Wall Street from financing European belligerents or the American mercantile marine from supplying them. Provisions were thus in force, not with the grand Wilsonian aim to outlaw war but instead to outlaw American participation. For Roosevelt, however tactically constrained in his actions, this was hardly good enough. He found the outlook of Chamberlain as 'businesslike' as that of Congress, and as frustrating. But when the Chamberlain government actually declared war on Germany in September 1939, and Churchill was taken back into the cabinet as First Lord of the Admiralty, Roosevelt saw his opportunity. Only a week later he began an extraordinary personal correspondence with Churchill that ultimately ran to over 2,000 messages.

In the crisis of May 1940, Churchill became Prime Minister. When a fourth edition of the biography by 'Ephesian' was published in that summer of 1940, the author quoted his prediction in the 1936 edition about a crisis that might summon a new Pitt and simply added: 'I was right.' Here was a political revolution, testing the resilience of democracy under extreme pressure. A coalition government, including the Labour and Liberal parties, was formed. For Keynes, though now a man who had to watch his health, the door of the Treasury swung open again; in August he was given his own office there, which he occupied for the rest of his life.

The 'Keynes Plan' for financing the war was already well publicised in Britain. It had been published as a pamphlet, *How to Pay for the War*, in February 1940, and met with political difficulties, notably from Labour, before a modified version was eventually implemented by the British government in 1941. Just before joining the Treasury himself, Keynes had taken the opportunity to explain his proposals for an American readership in the *New Republic* in July 1940; and he did so in a way that stimulated him to digress on the broader impact of war upon the economic analysis that he offered.

The fact that the war effort itself served to expand the economy was fundamental (albeit a point that Keynes himself had been slow to recognise during the First World War). So the problem, as he now saw it, was that higher wages and profits might simply fuel inflation, given an insufficient supply of consumer goods. Wage-earners would thus be cheated of their reward, while 'the profit-earning class' would be able to tuck away their gains by buying war debt – 'this is exactly what happened in the last war'. Keynes's plan thus had a double aspect. The first aim was to prevent the workers from wasting their inflationary paper gains by instead restraining wartime demand through compulsory savings, with this deferred pay made available to wage-earners after the war. And their employers? 'In the case of the richer classes the greater part of their contribution was to be withheld permanently as a tax,' Keynes explained.[31]

The United States, of course, was not at war in 1940. But the British Keynes Plan, so American readers were told, was 'merely a particular example of a way of thinking about public finance which is of universal application'. It was thus relevant to understanding the chronic unemployment that both countries had recently faced. In the 1930s, with an insufficiency of demand, the remedy now seemed obvious – 'More investment *and* more consumption'. But in wartime the scale of investment was so vast that, under these conditions, private spending would need restraint if it were not to feed into pure inflation. The capacity of the economy to expand on the supply side was thus the crucial constraint. There had hitherto been too little appreciation of the sheer scale of what could be done; and this, Keynes now argued, helped explain 'the comparative failure of New Deal expenditure out of borrowed funds to produce even an approach to full employment in the United States'.[32]

Conversely, 'the gigantic powers of production, far exceeding any previous experience, of a modern industrial economy', now stood revealed. How to measure this capacity? In the days when national-income accounting was in its infancy, Keynes merely speculated that 'the full industrial and agricultural capacity of the United

States' – what we would now call gross domestic product – might well in 1940 'exceed 1929 by as much as, or even more than, 1929 exceeded 1914'.[33] We now know, with the benefit of modern statistics, that he was wrong on the historical experience, since the real GDP of the United States in 1940 exceeded 1929 by only 20 per cent, whereas 1929 had exceeded 1914 by 77 per cent – with one-third of these gains during the First World War. But Keynes was right to sense the potential for further expansion in the current American economy, under the stimulus of another European war which it had not yet entered itself. By 1945 the GDP of the United States was to exceed the 1940 level by no less than 75 per cent in real terms.

What conclusion can be drawn? Keynes wrote at the time: 'It is, it seems, politically impossible for a capitalistic democracy to organize expenditure on the scale necessary to make the grand experiments which would prove my case – except in war conditions.' He could only hope that 'good may come out of evil'. For it was through the production of armaments on the vast scale necessary to save civilisation from the Nazis, he suggested, that the United States 'will learn its strength – learn it as it can never learn it otherwise; learn a lesson that can be turned to account afterward to reconstruct a world which will understand the first principles governing the production of wealth and which can endeavour – a harder task – to put it to good use'. Keynes added his own rueful reflection in 1940: 'In the sphere of economics and politics, the mass of men believe nothing which they have not seen, and have no teacher but experience.'[34] Like most Anglo-American liberals, Keynes remained reluctant to acknowledge that war may be the locomotive of history. As for Trotsky, he would have been appalled by examples of the ability of capitalism to reform itself under pressure, reducing historic inequalities in the process.

The Legacies of War in the Long Run

I WAR GUILT REVISITED

Arguments about the origins of the First World War continue to reverberate today. Each of the countries involved has naturally sustained a point of view that not only reflects its own role but also reflects well upon it. The conventional British view has always been that Germany was responsible for the war and thus guilty of starting it. Moreover, as we have seen in earlier chapters, although the United States remained neutral in 1914, Americans were not quite as 'impartial in thought as well as in action' as their President had initially enjoined; and by 1917 Wilson himself had not just committed his country to fighting Germany but had endorsed virtually every point on which the British had grounded their case. Nonetheless, the common-sense British perception that the rise of Germany was functionally responsible for the war and *therefore* that the Germans were morally guilty of causing it, when we pause to examine it, actually collapses two arguments, which really ought to be distinguished.

That the traditional British interpretation is still prevalent was sufficiently demonstrated during the centenary of August 1914. It remains a popular view, in both senses of that term. Oh those Germans! Need we look further than their role in starting not one but two world wars? What a contrast to Britain's record as a peace-loving trading nation! Here is a powerful set of underlying assumptions that still needs to be scrutinised before we can reach slightly more subtle conclusions about the historical reality of the Anglo-German antagonism.

First, it has to be conceded that Britain was also involved in both world wars; moreover, that the British military record since 1900, when it is given even cursory examination, chronicles more than a few other relevant episodes. The Boer War of 1899–1902, as we have seen, was in some ways a dress rehearsal for Armageddon. And soon after the Armistice, in May 1919, Britain's Third Afghan War showed that the Raj was back to business as usual (though failing, as usual, to pacify Afghanistan in any permanent fashion) and with further 'police action' in India and Burma. On examination, 'police action' turns out to be quite an elastic term. It covered other British military involvement: in Palestine, Iraq, Egypt, the Sudan, Cyprus, Aden, Somaliland, Jamaica and the Yangtze River, to confine the roll-call simply to the period between the two world wars.

In the Second World War, of course, Britain (but not Germany) was engaged in bloody fighting in Asia too – in defence of the British Empire, as usual. Nor did the post-war dissolution of the Empire mark the end of British military excursions. These were not all 'imperialist' (except perhaps in the eyes of the Russian and Chinese Communists) and indeed the Korean War (1950–3) was wholesomely conducted by British forces under the flag of the United Nations. Not so in 1956, however, when they fought to retake the Suez Canal, with an official clarification that this was not 'war' but 'armed conflict' – a distinction that did not stop this action being perceived as unjustified not only by the Arabs and the Americans, but also memorably by the Canadians, indispensable allies of the British in two world wars.

In the period 1945–77, under both Conservative and Labour governments, British troops were kept busy. They were sent far away, to French Indo-China and the Netherlands East Indies; they intervened somewhat nearer to home, in Greece, Palestine, Jordan,

Cyprus, Aden, Kuwait and Oman; those with a taste for African adventure had the chance of seeing the Cameroons, Kenya, Uganda, Tanganyika, Rhodesia, Swaziland, Mozambique and Zanzibar; when the Caribbean called, others were sent off to British Guiana, Belize, Jamaica, Anguilla, the Cayman Islands and Bermuda; British troops were despatched to Malaya, to Borneo, to Hong Kong, and even, when it could be located on the map, to the New Hebrides.

But were these really 'wars'? In fact, these forty-odd operations were usually called 'emergencies'. Then came Margaret Thatcher, a Prime Minister who was never afraid to call a war a war. It was she who mobilised British forces halfway round the world in 1982 to recapture a barren group of islands in the South Atlantic, which the Argentinians tiresomely refer to as the Malvinas. And after the Iron Lady? Further British intervention – now alongside the Americans, in contrast to Suez – came in the Gulf War in 1990 under the Conservatives, and in Kosovo in 1999 under Labour. Tony Blair was peculiarly responsible, of course, for sending British forces in support of the American invasion of Iraq in 2003 – as he had been, two years earlier, for promptly committing British troops to fight in Afghanistan. Was this, then, Britain's Fourth Afghan War? And in this single case of Afghanistan, *German* troops were also involved; it was their First Afghan War, fought now by these notorious warmongers on the same side as the battle-scarred British regiments.

There is no need to dismiss all these engagements as unjustifiable. Admittedly, in several cases, there was acute difficulty in justifying them to a sceptical public in a democratic country: a process which sometimes brought the curtailment of the operations. I am not seeking to replace kneejerk responses about German militarism with a mirror-image that is equally simplistic. The point is that, merits aside, it is difficult to ignore Britain's persistent readiness to go to war – say sixty times in the twentieth century. So why all the continuing fuss about 1914?

What seemed novel and shocking at the time was that this particular war began in Europe. And not just in the Balkans, where such conflicts seemed to be endemic, but, crucially for Britain, in Belgium.

EPILOGUE

Not only was it near at hand (the big guns could soon be heard on the white cliffs of Dover) but Belgium was a neutral country whose status was protected by a longstanding treaty, to which all the relevant great powers had subscribed. This was the famous 'scrap of paper', as the German Chancellor dubbed it, over which the British Empire went to war. The Germans were as mystified by this quixotic decision as they were irritated at the fact that the Belgians actually resisted overwhelming German might, asserted under the rationale of 'military necessity'. Perhaps it is true that imperial Germany did not speak the same language when it came to international law; but it is also significant that the country of Bismarck did not speak the same *political* language as the country of Gladstone. In this respect, the English-speaking peoples really did have a common vocabulary of liberal moralism to draw upon – for better or for worse.

Whether this shows that Germany was guilty of starting the First World War, however, is another matter. For guilt, as we have seen, depends on intention, which is often difficult to prove. Indeed the debate about the origins of the war, a debate reignited in Germany itself fifty years ago, seems now to have foundered in the end, largely because of failure to establish clear evidence about the prior intentions of the German hierarchy. Instead of an intentionalist reading of German war guilt, perhaps we should be content with a functionalist analysis of the rise of Germany as the dynamic factor that precipitated a catastrophic breakdown of the European peace.

For it was surely the growing economic and political power of the united German Empire that disturbed the status quo in international affairs. Great Britain and France, as satisfied powers with great empires, had particular difficulty in adapting to the natural ambitions of the Germans, who came late to the game in building an empire and thus found themselves constrained in their ambitions. An escalating (English) vocabulary described German power as growing, as expansionist, as aggressive, as threatening, as intolerable and finally as wicked. To Germans, it all seemed natural and legitimate, only asking for what the British, in particular, already enjoyed.

Unfortunately, this included an empire and – much more intractably – a fleet. Now much the same demands were currently being made upon the international system by another rising power: the United States, of course. Here the British effected a rapprochement based on adroit appeasement, not least in ceding American territorial demands in longstanding diplomatic disputes in the western hemisphere. (Thus Canada lost land but gained imperial security.) What made such a strategy inappropriate as a means of dealing with the German Empire was not so much British resistance to German colonial acquisitions as the German insistence, after Bismarck, on building a navy that challenged the Pax Britannica and thus undercut the imperialism of free trade. Since Britain was dependent for its very sustenance on the sea lanes to North America and the Antipodes, the existence of the new German High Seas Fleet in the North Sea was a threat that neither Conservative nor Liberal governments could ignore (though in recent years many historians have tried hard to ignore it). Moreover, the coming of the dreadnought class of battleship raised the stakes, by largely cancelling Britain's historic advantage.

This is surely adequate reason to identify the rise of Germany, *in a functional sense*, as the cause of a new fragility in the international system. Though the system survived crises like that over Agadir in 1911 and over the Balkans in 1912–13, it proved incapable of meeting the challenge posed by a further Balkan crisis in 1914. In that context, the rival alliances constructed across Europe indeed enticed the sleepwalkers to stumble towards the abyss.

What pushed Britain itself over the brink, however, was a late – and largely unforeseen – development in that escalating crisis, when the Schlieffen Plan was put into effect. It turned out that Plan A was predicated on a fundamental violation of Belgian integrity, as guaranteed by the international treaty, with no Plan B, but with cataclysmic effect upon Belgium itself. At this point, moreover, the perceived significance of the 'scrap of paper' became wholly different in the eyes of the impatient imperial regime in Germany from its status in the eyes of the bewildered Liberal government in Britain. The moral chords that were struck suddenly revived the politics of virtuous passion with a force not seen since the death of Gladstone. It was the moral indictment of Germany for causing the European war that then led ineluctably, step by step, to the indictment of Germany for war guilt, even though actual German intentions may not have borne this construction. The presence of a dead body is no proof that anyone is guilty of murder; but a war that left its many millions of dead bodies gave rise to sharply conflicting inferences about where guilt rested in causing it.

2 CARTHAGE REVISITED

It was, then, the moralisation of the origins of the war that led to the moralisation of the peace terms, as ultimately negotiated between the victorious Allies in Paris. The victors' demands, duly garbed in self-righteousness, were simply imposed upon Germany, which was required to assent in short order. In the process, the 'reparation' of Belgium, step by step, had become the rationale for the exaction of an indemnity from Germany, under the cover of a verbal ploy about 'reparations', which in turn required justification under a war-guilt clause.

In retrospect, the fatal flaw in this process was surely its hypocrisy, conscious or unconscious. Such a treaty could not have the legitimacy it claimed; its terms were not negotiated, except between the victors themselves; the German signatures were obtained under duress, with no real assent. Yet the paradox is that, when the provisions of the Treaty are actually examined, this could only be termed a 'Carthaginian' peace in contrast with the elevated pretensions of its justifying rhetoric. Had all this been imposed as a victors' peace, after an acknowledged defeat of Germany and a formal capitulation, such terms might well have seemed relatively moderate or at least bearable. But in the event they were seen – not only by the Germans but by many Anglo-American liberals – as a fraudulent outcome that violated the preconditions of the Armistice, creating an obvious injustice made all the more galling by the Wilsonian language in which it was framed. In exposing such flaws, one might say, German propaganda did not limp.

From a German perspective, the charge of 'war guilt' provided an important impetus for the 'innocence campaign' that was speedily launched. The crux of the debate was already apparent by May 1919, when the official German response to the peace terms was given in Paris by Brockdorff-Rantzau. The work of the German foreign office (AA, Auswärtiges Amt) in sustaining this campaign made it a highly effective propaganda exercise, playing upon the bad consciences of Anglo-American liberals, and it was successful on a scale disguised for many years only by the necessary subterfuges that had to be adopted. One coup was the swift publication of German pre-war documents, as far back as Bismarck, in an adroitly edited and sanitised form. This pre-emptively focused subsequent historical debate, despite the belated publication of official documents on the Allied side. We now know that the AA specifically targeted American historians in the process, with the result that ostensibly dispassionate academic studies of the origins of the war, sympathetic to the German plea of not guilty, were published under the auspices of prestigious imprints.

We can also see how the popular literature on the war reinforced scepticism about the role of Allied propaganda as conducted during hostilities. In retrospect, the efficiency of British efforts during the war in influencing American opinion appeared as just another wily dodge to fool the over-trustful Yanks. It was not explicit pro-German sentiment that increasingly took hold but, certainly in the United States, renewed scepticism about entanglement in European affairs, or, in Europe itself, a mood of pacifism bred by revulsion against the horrors of Armageddon.

The period 1928–9 was some kind of watershed. It was in 1928 that the politically influential book *Falsehood in Wartime* was published in Britain by Arthur Ponsonby, now a prominent and well-connected Labour MP and longstanding pacifist. His short tract purported to expose the fabrications of British propaganda but, as modern research has demonstrated, itself made many unfounded allegations, uncritically rehearsing themes from German propaganda. The citation of one notorious trail of crude anti-German stories, supposedly as published in wartime Allied newspapers, was promptly reproduced verbatim in the bestseller by the war poet Robert Graves, *Goodbye to All That*, published the next year. (This recital concerned increasingly far-fetched accounts of the enforced ringing of the church bells after the German capture of Amiens, with monks hung upside-down inside them by the Huns, et cetera.) Neither the fact that Graves's (undisclosed) source was Ponsonby, nor that Ponsonby's (undisclosed) source turned out to be a German propaganda invention, inhibited the credence given to such accounts at the time.

The greatest bestseller, of course, was itself German. Erich Maria Remarque's *All Quiet on the Western Front* was published early in 1929 – with a readership and impact vastly greater than another book published at almost the same time: Winston Churchill's volume *The Aftermath*. It is their tone and perspective upon the horrors of modern warfare that proves surprisingly congruent. Remarque's anti-militarist message, reinforced by the release of a Hollywood film version in the next year, was to provoke a ban by the Nazis; but the film was acclaimed by Lloyd George, heralding a shift in viewpoint that was to be reflected in his *War Memoirs*, now in gestation, alleging that nobody willed a war that everybody slithered into. 'The last thing the vainglorious Kaiser wanted was a European war,' Lloyd George now proclaimed of a man whom he had once proposed to put on trial as a war criminal.[1]

One way or another, the war and the peace alike came to be seen in terms more sympathetic to Germany than had been the case in 1918–19. The arguments to which Keynes had given canonical expression in publishing his *Economic Consequences* inevitably fed the 'innocence campaign', as did some of his personal actions in collaborating with German liberals to mount resistance to any real fulfilment of the reparations provisions. In this sense, the suddenly famous economist might be called a fellow-traveller of his German friends like Melchior; more cynically, Lenin's term 'useful idiot' could be applied to the young Keynes; and he has even been characterised in some quarters, albeit by shuffling the chronology somewhat, as an apologist for the rise of the Nazis. Certainly his role was controversial at the time and has remained so whenever these historical issues have been revisited.

The classic critique of the *Economic Consequences* came during the Second World War and was written from a quintessentially French perspective. Étienne Mantoux, the son of Clemenceau's interpreter during the Paris negotiations, had a tragically shortened life, killed on active service in Bavaria barely a week before VE Day in 1945. *The Carthaginian Peace: or the economic consequences of Mr Keynes* was published in the following year, from a final draft completed in the summer of 1944. The circumstances of the book's composition and publication obviously command sympathy and respect for a highly intelligent, bilingual young man who died in the struggle for the liberation of Europe. For Mantoux, it had always been axiomatic that the Germans, if allowed to do so, would prepare for a further war. His inbred sympathy for the position taken by Clemenceau was shaken by nothing he saw in the world around him up to the time of his own death.

Mantoux's book, alas, has to serve as his monument; but it remains indispensable. Many recent publications on the same topic simply demonstrate that its ideas are alive and well, seventy years later. Its case for the viability of the policy of reparations under the Versailles Treaty depends largely on the author's ability to demonstrate two central points, each of which deserves some comment.

Mantoux's first theme was that Germany's capacity to pay had been greatly underestimated in the *Economic Consequences*. Instead, he cited statistics on the performance of the German economy in the 1920s and 1930s to show what was actually achieved. Some of this economic growth was under the impact of the Dawes Plan, which had even seen some payment of reparations. Hence his verdict: 'The Dawes Plan worked to perfection.'[2] Admittedly, this had been financed in the main by American loans, but Mantoux evidently supposed he had made his key point.

Now it is true that in 1919 Keynes had hardly expected this. And the contention that the scale of payments proposed in the London Schedule of 1921 was manageable by Germany may well be valid in its own terms. But, whatever the merits of his econometric assessment here, Mantoux simply bypassed the central point: that the case mounted in the *Economic Consequences* was squarely directed against the demands made *in the Treaty of 1919*. And on this score, in making quantitative estimates of what the Treaty itself had implied, Mantoux honourably went out of his way (twice) to endorse the correctness of Keynes's own calculations.[3]

Mantoux's second point, however, was really the crux. He returned time and again to contesting Keynes's claim that the international transfer of reparations on the scale proposed was impossible, instead insisting that if 'Germany *did* not' comply, this was no 'proof that she *could* not'; so if 'Germany *did not*' achieve the set targets, this proved nothing: 'Whether she *could* have done so is of course another question.'[4] Much scorn was poured on the reality of any 'transfer problem'. Numerous examples were supplied of international transfers that exceeded the scale of those envisaged under the Treaty (anticipating many such exercises in the later literature on this topic). Mantoux even cited the current programme of Lend-Lease, by which the United States was indeed providing the external economic support necessary for the British war effort at the time he wrote.[5] But Lend-Lease was, in effect, the Dawes Plan writ large – it was financed by US dollars that were never repaid in the end.

Mantoux's somewhat literal interpretation of what was meant by 'impossible' trivialised the real issue – whether the Germans would actually pay up. It should never be forgotten that Keynes was writing in the context of 1919, Mantoux in the context of 1944. Thus it was the brute experience of the Second World War that not only infused this patriotic young Frenchman's analysis with its polemical power but also supplied a viewpoint drastically different from the presuppositions of 1919. Time and again, Mantoux cited the example of the Nazi armaments-based economy in exceeding the sort of economic estimates that Keynes had supposed feasible, back in 1919.[6] And in challenging the appropriateness of the description 'Carthaginian' for the stipulations of the Versailles Treaty, Mantoux likewise imported the norms manifested by wartime Nazi policy in exacting tribute from the countries of occupied Europe. Mantoux's case thus rested on the object lesson of the Nazi occupation of France, in particular, to show just how effective this was in extracting economic advantages for Germany.[7] Evidently, nothing was 'impossible' when the jackboot was on the other foot.

Here is the premise from which Mantoux naturally worked. He wrote his powerful tract as a child of the era in which Hitler scorned the naive liberal nostrums of his predecessors. Keynes, by contrast, sharing the assumptions of the Anglo-American peacemakers in 1919, had explicitly ruled out a permanent occupation of Germany as a means of exacting tribute. This was a fundamental premise of the *Economic Consequences*. Two years later, his *Revision of the Treaty* simply reiterated – almost in passing because it was so obvious – that the idea of 'extracting at the point of a bayonet' a level of reparations 'that would never be paid voluntarily' was unthinkable.[8] It was unthinkable, that is, before Hitler changed all the rules.

3 TROTSKY REVISITED

This book has repeatedly suggested that two different vocabularies have often been used in talking about war. One is that of economic consequences, which was essentially the way that Trotsky analysed the impact of war in speaking of it as the locomotive of history. But an alternative vocabulary is that of moral intentions, in an idiom that Anglo-American liberals shared. This found notable expression in the (endlessly retailed and recycled) utterances of Gladstone at various historical junctures. So there is a clear analytical distinction between these two types of discourse. But history is a messy business, in the course of which a lot of things get muddled up, in different times and places, sometimes by accident and sometimes by design.

To illustrate this we need look no further than the writings of John Maynard Keynes, which have already been cited so often in this book. In his famous critique of the Versailles Treaty, he had claimed to write about the economic consequences but in fact often presented a moral case, in which intentions necessarily played an important role; hence his charge of hypocrisy when piously declared intentions were belied by an inconsistent outcome. Given that he was not only an economist by vocation but also himself a liberal, and one responsible for some notorious polemics against a Liberal Prime Minister for betraying liberalism, this may be understandable.

Even so, Keynes's *Economic Consequences of the Peace* had surely been wrong on some significant counts, which retrospect casts in a different light. Thus in 1919, when mounting its case against Lloyd George, it influentially conflated the (allegedly despicable) call to 'make Germany pay' with the (equally deplorable) cry to 'hang the Kaiser'. Yet though the proposal to impose an indemnity could indeed be treated in terms of its economic consequences, by assessing Germany's ability to pay and the impact of its doing so, it was surely another matter to propose putting the Kaiser on trial (which was all that Lloyd George himself had asked). Such proposals were entirely congruent with the Anglo-American liberals' moral case about the war, which turned on German intentions and actions from the time of the Belgian invasion onward. True, the two issues could be rolled up together on the common basis of war guilt. But the fact that they were separable was later to be demonstrated in the ending of the Second World War, when, after some hesitations, Anglo-American policy abjured the exaction of indemnities and, when Roosevelt prevailed over Churchill on this point, moved expeditiously to bring Nazi war criminals to justice at Nuremberg.

Our tendency to accept the Second World War as 'the good war' inevitably colours many of our perceptions of the First. This is often cursorily slighted as a bad war in which hapless armies were doomed to countless, pointless deaths. In British eyes, it naturally remains shocking that over 700,000 British troops died – a million if we count the whole of the British Empire. The war dead of the Canadians at Vimy Ridge, or the Australians at Gallipoli, became the focus of purposeful forms of commemoration in which the facts of these engagements were subsequently subordinated to the imperatives of nation-building in their home countries. This was, as we have seen, an imperialist war at one level for the British. But the Dominions too were willing accomplices, rallied by the morality of the cause, and it was in this way that a European war had been transformed into a world war.

The leaders of Britain and the United States in the Second World War were clearly influenced by their own experience of the First World War. For Churchill there would be no more Gallipolis, no more occasions when he would stake his political future on outguessing the advice of his key military advisers, however long into the night he might argue with them. Equally, there would be no premature commitment to mounting a cross-Channel invasion, however much the Americans wanted this, given Churchill's aversion to opening a new western front, with men chewing on barbed wire in France.

For Roosevelt, playing to different demons from the recent past, there would be caution about any premature military commitment in Europe and dissimulation about his covert support for the British war effort – until he found himself unshackled by the Japanese attack on Pearl Harbor. Thus December 1941 could conceivably be termed FDR's 'Edward Grey moment', in that, to adopt the idiom of the old Gladstonian liberal J. L. Hammond, Grey 'was really doing for Britain what Franklin Roosevelt was to do later for the United States, breaking down a tradition of isolation that had become a dangerous weakness'. Moreover, in translating war policy into peace aims, Roosevelt took immense care in broaching any plans to revive the dream of a League of Nations, with the term 'United Nations' initially applied by him to the ever-widening military alliance that he determinedly mobilised.

FDR insisted too on 'unconditional surrender' by Nazi Germany, initially to Churchill's scepticism. At the time, this step was taken in the face of arguments that such a declaration might prolong the war, or consolidate support for Hitler, or suggest vindictive peace terms. In fact, the ambiguity of the 1918 Armistice was avoided and unconditional surrender became the stern precondition for a peace that was then made consistent with Churchill's maxim of magnanimity in victory. Thereafter, Churchill's own country hardly benefited from anything that could be termed an indemnity from Germany and instead turned for succour to the North American allies that had aided Britain in wartime. Admittedly, it was claimed by one reputable British newspaper (the *Sunday Times*) that 'as victors we are being asked to pay reparations', meaning that the terms of the North American loan of 1946 amounted to this. But while it is true that this big loan (from the United States and Canada) was not finally paid off until 2006, it could equally well be said that the United States also paid its own reparations in Europe (in the form of Marshall Aid). Such were some of the economic consequences of the peace after 1945.

For Keynes, too, this new war had been a second chance. He took full advantage of his extraordinary role in overseeing Treasury policy not just in Britain but, crucially, in its dealings with the United States. Already hailed in Anglo-American circles as the man who had transformed the study of economics through the publication of his *General Theory* in 1936, this philosopher-king had his chance to return to many of the issues that he had first confronted a quarter of a century previously. The crucial difference was that his own experience had meanwhile taught him that it was no longer a matter of imposing top-down financial imperatives, requiring adjustments in the real economy of a kind that were unlikely to prove feasible.

Instead, a Keynesian macro-economic policy gave government a key role in managing the output of the economy as a whole, directing resources accordingly.

If this marked the reception of the mature Keynesian policy agenda, it rested also upon a revolution in economic theory. Now it has always seemed plausible to link this intellectual breakthrough with the stimulus provided by the practical problems of unemployment that Britain experienced in the 1920s and with the onset of the world slump that was triggered from 1929 onwards. This remains a valid interpretation in many ways; but it now seems to me that Keynes's ideas had been much more powerfully influenced by the impact of the Great War and its aftermath than has usually been recognised.

In that case, the *Economic Consequences of the Peace* is an even more important book than perhaps we have supposed. For it already shows us the fallacy of a zero-sum model of economic relations, whereby one party can only benefit at the expense of another – a fallacy that can be identified equally in the behaviour of individuals and in that of nations. Thus after the Second World War the European economic recovery, powerfully aided by assistance from the United States, indeed set the continent upon a path that generated growth upon a hitherto unexampled scale. Moreover, wealth was to be more equally distributed than ever before – or ever again, as we now sadly realise half a century later. This was, in short, a liberal or social-democratic post-war consensus, showing that 'reformist' policies could be creatively developed within a framework that Marxists continued to disparage as 'bourgeois democracy'.

Hence the contrast with Trotsky's perspective. Yet he too still surely merits a hearing, in identifying the locomotive of war as such a powerful historical force. His own assumption always remained that, sooner or later, a Communist-led revolution was indeed the inevitable destination at the end of the line. Right to the end of his life, even after his later exile at Stalin's hands, Trotsky had clung to this belief. At the close of 1939, he suggested that the test for Marxist analysis was whether the outbreak of this Second World War would ultimately lead to proletarian revolution in the west. Within months, on Stalin's orders, Trotsky was assassinated and thus deprived of the opportunity to observe the fate of his own challenging hypothesis. Twice in the twentieth century the locomotive of war offered, to revolutionists and liberal reformists alike, crucial challenges of a new kind; but the point is to seize such historical opportunities.

And today? It is not only remarkable but also paradoxical that the Germans became notable beneficiaries of the locomotive of war. In the long run, they did so not as military victors, extracting their gains by putting the jackboot on the windpipe of others, but actually by prospering as a vanquished people, replacing their machine guns with machine tools. It was the post-war settlement that allowed them to achieve through their economic endeavours the sort of mastery of Europe that they had twice failed to achieve through military means. Whether this has evoked magnanimity in economic victory is now perhaps less evident when we observe contemporary Germany, seemingly intent upon visiting the self-defeating disciplines of 'austerity' upon others, as though the zero-sum game could reward German victors only if others lost. In the long run, maybe the author of the *Economic Consequences of the Peace*, so frequently taunted as pro-German in his own lifetime, posthumously deserves to find more readers for his writings in Germany itself.

NOTES

ABBREVIATIONS

JMK   D. E. Moggridge (ed. with Sir Austin Robinson), *The Collected Writings of John Maynard Keynes*, 30 vols (Cambridge, 1971–89)

PWW   Arthur S. Link (ed.), *The Papers of Woodrow Wilson*, 69 vols (Princeton, 1966–94)

PROLOGUE: A TRAIN OF THOUGHT

1 Winston S. Churchill, *Liberalism and the Social Problem* (London, 1909), p. 67.
2 Thomas Piketty, *Capital in the Twenty-First Century*, trans. Arthur Goldhammer (London, 2014), p. 33.
3 Ibid., p. 20.
4 Ibid., p. 41.
5 Ibid., p. 118.
6 Ibid., p. 350.
7 Ibid., p. 471.
8 Ibid., p. 261.
9 Ibid., pp. 316–17.
10 Ibid., p. 514.
11 H. C. G. Matthew (ed. and intro.), *The Gladstone Diaries*, vols 9–11 (Oxford, 1986–90), vol. 9, p. 181.
12 Ibid., pp. 373–4.
13 Ibid., p. 471.
14 PWW, vol. 45, p. 536.
15 Ibid., pp. 538–9.

CHAPTER 1: THE DISCIPLE AS PROPHET

1 PWW, vol. 53, p. 534.
2 Ray Stannard Baker, *Woodrow Wilson: Life and Letters*, 8 vols. (New York, 1928–39), vol. 1, p. 48.
3 Ibid., p. 68.
4 PWW, vol. 63, p. 350.
5 Baker, *Woodrow Wilson*, vol. 1, pp. 66–7.

6 PWW, vol. 1, pp. 43–6.

7 Baker, *Woodrow Wilson*, vol. 1, p. 57.

8 Ibid., p. 88.

9 PWW, vol. 18, p. 631.

10 Baker, *Woodrow Wilson*, vol. 1, p. 80.

11 Ibid., p. 89.

12 PWW, vol. 2, p. 79.

13 Ibid., vol. 1, p. 274.

14 Baker, *Woodrow Wilson*, vol. 1, p. 93.

15 Ibid., pp. 139–40.

16 PWW, vol. 1, p. 374.

17 Ibid., vol. 2, pp. 350, 352.

18 Ibid., pp. 499–505.

19 Ibid., vol. 4, p. 118.

20 Ibid., vol. 10, pp. 86–7.

21 Ibid., vol. 1, p. 352.

22 Ibid., p. 609.

23 Ibid., pp. 610, 612.

24 Ibid., pp. 615, 618.

25 Ibid., vol. 18, p. 641.

26 Ibid., vol. 1, p. 625.

27 Ibid., p. 642.

28 Ibid., p. 633.

29 Ibid., p. 626.

30 Ibid., pp. 626–7.

31 Ibid., p. 629.

32 Ibid., pp. 635–6.

33 Ibid., pp. 637–9.

34 Ibid., p. 628.

35 Ibid., vol. 6, p. 327.

36 Ibid., pp. 646–9 (italics in original).

37 Ibid., vol. 12, p. 140.

38 Ibid., vol. 18, p. 645.

39 Ibid., vol. 19, p. 33.

40 Ibid., pp. 42–3.

41 Ibid., p. 46.

42 Ibid., p. 35.

43 Ibid., vol. 9, p. 521.

44 Ibid., p. 533.

45 Ibid., pp. 521–2.

46 Ibid., vol. 11, p. 155.
47 Ibid., p. 184.
48 Ibid., p. 186.
49 Ibid., vol. 14, p. 269.
50 Ibid., vol. 18, p. 402.
51 Ibid., vol. 11, p. 298.
52 Ibid., p. 573.
53 Ibid., p. 532.
54 Ibid., vol. 18, p. 401.
55 Baker, *Woodrow Wilson*, vol. 2, p. 348.

CHAPTER 2: A MAN OF THE PEOPLE

1   David Lloyd George, *War Memoirs*, 2 vols, continuous pagination (London, 1938; first published in 6 vols, 1933–6), vol. 1, p. vii.
2   David Lloyd George, *The Truth about the Peace Treaties*, 2 vols, continuous pagination (London, 1938), vol. 1, p. 5.
3   Lloyd George, *War Memoirs*, vol. 1, p. 621.
4   Ibid., p. 148.
5   Frances Stevenson, *Lloyd George: A Diary*, ed. A. J. P. Taylor (London, 1971), pp. 68–9.
6   Lloyd George, *War Memoirs*, vol. 1, p. 1.
7   Ibid., p. 2.
8   Ibid., p. 3.
9   Ibid., p. 4.
10 Winston S. Churchill, *The World Crisis, 1911–18*, 2 vols, continuous pagination (London, 1938; first published in 5 vols, 1923–7), vol. 1, p. 20.
11 Lloyd George, *War Memoirs*, vol. 1, p. 7.
12 Lord Loreburn, *How the War Came* (London, 1919), p. 5.
13 Lloyd George, *War Memoirs*, vol. 1, p. 15.
14 Stevenson, *Lloyd George*, p. 10.
15 Lloyd George, *War Memoirs*, vol. 1, pp. 23–4.
16 Churchill, *The World Crisis*, vol. 1, p. 31.
17 Ibid., p. 34.
18 Loreburn, *How the War Came*, p. 81.
19 Lloyd George, *War Memoirs*, vol. 1, p. 28.

CHAPTER 3: ARISTOCRAT AND SOLDIER

1   Winston S. Churchill, *My Early Life* (London, 1930; Fontana edn, 1959), p. 96.

2 Piketty, *Capital in the Twenty-First Century*, pp. 316, 319.

3 Churchill, *The World Crisis*, vols., 1923–7), vol. 1, p. 32.

4 Churchill, *My Early Life*, p. 117.

5 Michael and Eleanor Brock (eds), *H. H. Asquith: Letters to Venetia Stanley* (Oxford, 1982), p. 508.

6 Martin Gilbert (ed.), Companion Volumes to Randolph S. Churchill and Martin Gilbert, *Winston S. Churchill*, 8 vols (London, 1966–88), vol. 2, p. 2.

7 Ibid., p. 22.

8 Churchill, *My Early Life*, p. 373.

9 Ibid., p. 139.

10 Ibid., pp. 70–1.

11 Ibid., p. 72.

12 Ibid., pp. 72–3.

13 Ibid., p. 73.

14 Ibid., pp. 200–1.

15 Ibid., p. 191.

16 Ibid., p. 187.

17 Gilbert (ed.), Companion Volumes, vol. 2, p. 63.

18 Churchill, *My Early Life*, p. 378.

19 Churchill, *Liberalism and the Social Problem*, p. xv.

20 Gilbert (ed.), Companion Volumes, vol. 2, pp. 755–6.

21 Ibid., p. 863.

22 Churchill, *Liberalism and the Social Problem*, pp. 345–6.

23 Gilbert (ed.), Companion Volumes, vol. 2, p. 863.

24 Churchill, *Liberalism and the Social Problem*, pp. 122–3.

25 Churchill, *The World Crisis*, vol. 1, p. 49.

26 Ibid.

27 Ibid., p. 21.

28 Gilbert (ed.), Companion Volumes, vol. 2, pp. 64–5.

29 Ibid., p. 943.

30 Churchill, *The World Crisis*, vol. 1, p. 24.

31 Ibid., pp. 91–2.

32 Churchill, *My Early Life*, p. 74.

33 Churchill, *The World Crisis*, vol. 1, p. 73.

34 Ibid., p. 53.

35 Ibid., p. 94.

36 Ibid., pp. 95–6.

37 Ibid., p. 97.

38 Ibid., p. 100.

39 Ibid., p. 102.
40 Ibid., p. 76.
41 Ibid., p. 33.

CHAPTER 4: HOW THE LIBERALS STARTED A WORLD WAR

1 Churchill, *The World Crisis*, vol. 1, p. 143.
2 Brock and Brock (eds), *H. H. Asquith*, p. 45.
3 Ibid., p. 55.
4 Ibid., p. 93.
5 Ibid., pp. 122–3.
6 Ibid., p. 146.
7 Lloyd George, *War Memoirs*, vol. 1, p. 130.
8 John Morley, *Memorandum on Resignation: August 1914*, ed. F. W. Hirst (London, 1928), p. 20.
9 Lloyd George, *War Memoirs*, vol. 1, p. 32.
10 Churchill, *The World Crisis*, vol. 1, p. 155.
11 Ibid., p. 161.
12 Winston S. Churchill, *The Aftermath: The World Crisis, 1918–28* (New York, 1929), p. 470.
13 Lloyd George, *War Memoirs*, vol. 1, p. 58.
14 Morley, *Memorandum on Resignation*, p. 16.
15 Churchill, *The World Crisis*, vol. 1, p. 175.
16 Brock and Brock (eds), *H. H. Asquith*, p. 140.
17 Lloyd George, *War Memoirs*, vol. 1, p. 39.
18 Brock and Brock (eds), *H. H. Asquith*, p. 150.
19 Gilbert (ed.), Companion Volumes, vol. 2, pp. 1996–7.
20 Lloyd George, *War Memoirs*, vol. 1, p. 40.
21 Brock and Brock (eds), *H. H. Asquith*, p. 148.
22 Churchill, *The World Crisis*, vol. 1, p. 177.
23 Morley, *Memorandum on Resignation*, p. 23.
24 Lloyd George, *War Memoirs*, vol. 1, p. 40.
25 Brock and Brock (eds), *H. H. Asquith*, p. 148.
26 Churchill, *My Early Life*, pp. 88–9.
27 Cited in Morley, *Memorandum on Resignation*, p. 31; but see Notes on Sources.
28 Stevenson, *Lloyd George*, p. 38.
29 Lloyd George, *War Memoirs*, vol. 1, pp. 41–2.
30 Stevenson, *Lloyd George*, p. 3.
31 Ibid., p. 2.

CHAPTER 5: GOODBYE TO THE GARDEN OF EDEN

1 JMK, vol. 10, p. 446.
2 Ibid.
3 Ibid., p. 196.
4 Churchill, *My Early Life*, p. 96.
5 JMK, vol. 2, pp. 6–7.
6 Ibid., p. 7.
7 JMK, vol. 11, p. 254.
8 Lloyd George, *War Memoirs*, vol. 1, p. 62.
9 Ibid., p. 69.
10 JMK, vol. 11, p. 278.
11 JMK, vol. 16, p. 10.
12 JMK, vol. 11, p. 259.
13 JMK, vol. 16, p. 7.
14 Ibid., pp. 11, 13.
15 Ibid.
16 Ibid., p. 16.
17 Lloyd George, *War Memoirs*, vol. 1, p. 64.
18 JMK, vol. 11, p. 279.
19 Lloyd George, *War Memoirs*, vol. 1, p. 65.
20 Ibid., p. 71.
21 Ibid., p. 74.

CHAPTER 6: KNIGHT-ERRANT OF PROGRESSIVISM

1 Henry Adams, *The Education of Henry Adams: An Autobiography* (Boston, MA, 1918), p. 19.
2 Ibid., p. 54.
3 Ibid., p. 69.
4 Ibid., p. 64.
5 Ibid., p. 321.
6 Ibid., p. 106.
7 Ibid., p. 332.
8 Ibid., p. 362.
9 Elliott Roosevelt (ed.), *Roosevelt Letters, 1887–1945, being the personal correspondence of Franklin Delano Roosevelt*, 3 vols (London, 1949–52), vol. 1, p. 311.
10 Ibid., vol. 2, p. 82.
11 Ibid., vol. 1, p. 427.
12 Ibid., vol. 2, p. 82.
13 Ibid., p. 315.

14 Ibid., pp. 199–200.
15 Ibid., p. 206.
16 Adams, *The Education of Henry Adams*, p. 419.

CHAPTER 7: THE BRITISH WAR EFFORT
1 Churchill, *The World Crisis*, vol. 2, p. 1128.
2 Lloyd George, *War Memoirs*, vol. 1, p. 78.
3 Ibid., p. 185.
4 Ibid., p. 83.
5 Ibid., pp. 91–2.
6 Ibid., pp. 173–4.
7 Ibid., p. 101.
8 Churchill, *The World Crisis*, vol. 1, p. 297.
9 Ibid., p. 363.
10 Stevenson, *Lloyd George*, p. 41.
11 Churchill, *The World Crisis*, vol. 1, p. 551.
12 Ibid., p. 661.
13 Ibid., p. 688.
14 Ibid., vol. 2, p. 786.
15 Ibid., p. 798.
16 Winston S. Churchill, *Great Contemporaries* (London, 1937; Fontana edn, 1959), pp. 122–3.
17 Stevenson, *Lloyd George*, p. 53.
18 Lloyd George, *War Memoirs*, vol. 1, pp. 140–1.
19 Brock and Brock (eds), *H. H. Asquith*, p. 593.
20 Ibid., p. 425.
21 JMK, vol. 16, p. 210.
22 Ibid., pp. 299–300.
23 Lloyd George, *War Memoirs*, vol. 1, pp. 408–9.
24 Ibid., p. 410.
25 JMK, vol. 16, p. 187.
26 Ibid., p. 124.
27 Ibid., pp. 197–8.
28 Churchill, *Great Contemporaries*, p. 123.
29 JMK, vol. 16, p. 211.
30 Lloyd George, *War Memoirs*, vol. 1, p. 130.
31 JMK, vol. 16, p. 180.
32 Ibid., p. 183.
33 Ibid., p. 178.
34 Ibid., p. 114.

35 Ibid., p. 212.
36 Ibid., p. 247 (italics in original).
37 Ibid., vol. 2, p. 172.

CHAPTER 8: THE AMERICAN WAY IN WARFARE

1 PWW, vol. 30, p. 214.
2 Ibid., p. 253.
3 Ibid., p. 258.
4 Ibid., p. 324.
5 Ibid., p. 336.
6 Ibid., p. 352.
7 Ibid., p. 390.
8 Ibid., p. 458.
9 Ibid., p. 462.
10 Ibid., vol. 31, pp. 33–4.
11 Ibid., vol. 30, p. 394.
12 Ibid., vol. 32, p. 60.
13 Ibid., vol. 30, p. 403.
14 Ibid., vol. 31, pp. 21–2.
15 Ibid., p. 45.
16 Ibid., p. 58.
17 Ibid., pp. 60–1.
18 Ibid., pp. 385–6.
19 Ibid., vol. 32, p. 44.
20 Churchill, *The World Crisis*, vol. 2, p. 1123.
21 Ibid., p. 1126.
22 PWW, vol. 31, pp. 13–14.
23 Ibid., vol. 32, p. 61.
24 Ibid., p. 207.
25 Ibid., p. 267.
26 Ibid., p. 277.
27 Ibid., vol. 33, p. 134.
28 Ibid., pp. 147–9.
29 Ibid., p. 127.
30 Ibid., p. 129.
31 Ibid., pp. 146–7.
32 Ibid., pp. 449–52.
33 Ibid., vol. 37, p. 57.
34 Ibid., vol. 38, p. 89.
35 Ibid., vol. 40, pp. 62–3.

36 Ibid., pp. 533–9.
37 Ibid., vol. 36, p. 320.
38 Ibid., pp. 379–80.
39 Roosevelt (ed.), *Roosevelt Letters*, vol. 2, p. 212.
40 PWW, vol. 41, pp. 519–27.
41 Ibid., pp. 529–30.
42 Ibid., vol. 38, p. 538.
43 Ibid., vol. 46, p. 324.
44 Ibid., vol. 38, p. 538.
45 Ibid., vol. 33, p. 147.

CHAPTER 9: AGENDA FOR THE HALL OF MIRRORS

1   Roosevelt (ed.), *Roosevelt Letters*, vol. 2, pp. 327–8.
2   Churchill, *Great Contemporaries*, p. 254.
3   Ibid., p. 256.
4   Matthew (ed. and intro.), *Gladstone Diaries*, vol. 10, p. 404.
5   JMK, vol. 10, p. 32.
6   Roosevelt (ed.), *Roosevelt Letters*, vol. 2, p. 328.
7   Ibid., pp. 313–14.
8   Ibid., p. 331.
9   Ibid., p. 335.
10 Ibid., pp. 365–6.
11 Lloyd George, *War Memoirs*, vol. 1, p. 229.
12 Ibid., p. 289.
13 Stevenson, *Lloyd George*, pp. 121–2.
14 Ibid., p. 147.
15 Ibid., pp. 138–9.
16 Ibid., p. 147.
17 Ibid., p. 157.
18 Lloyd George, *War Memoirs*, vol. 2, p. 2038.
19 Ibid., p. 1826.
20 Ibid., p. 1825.
21 Gilbert (ed.), Companion Volumes, vol. 4, p. 364.
22 Churchill, *The World Crisis*, vol. 2, p. 1365.
23 Lloyd George, *War Memoirs*, vol. 2, p. 1870.
24 PWW, vol. 53, p. 352.
25 Lloyd George, *War Memoirs*, vol. 2, pp. 2044–53.
26 Churchill, *The World Crisis*, vol. 2, p. 1399.
27 PWW, vol. 43, p. 290.
28 Ibid., vol. 42, pp. 155–6.

29 Ibid., p. 385.
30 Ibid., pp. 499–503.
31 Ibid., vol. 43, p. 498.
32 Ibid., pp. 523–4.
33 Lloyd George, *War Memoirs*, vol. 2, p. 1515.
34 PWW, vol. 46, p. 321.
35 Lloyd George, *War Memoirs*, vol. 2, pp. 1511–13.
36 PWW, vol. 45, pp. 556–7.
37 Ibid., vol. 53, pp. 499–500.
38 JMK, vol. 2, p. 37.
39 PWW, vol. 53, p. 352.
40 Ibid., p. 530.
41 Ibid., p. 531.
42 Ibid., pp. 574–6.

CHAPTER 10: THE FOURTEEN POINTS IN PARIS

 1 PWW, vol. 55, p. 224.
 2 Ibid., vol. 54, pp. 175–8.
 3 Ibid., vol. 68, p. 287.
 4 Gilbert (ed.), Companion Volumes, vol. 4, p. 496.
 5 Lloyd George, *The Truth about the Peace Treaties*, vol. 1, p. 236.
 6 PWW, vol. 54, pp. 84–8.
 7 Ibid., vol. 56, p. 352.
 8 Ibid., p. 578.
 9 Lloyd George, *The Truth about the Peace Treaties*, vol. 1, p. 246.
10 PWW, vol. 58, p. 143.
11 Ibid., vol. 56, pp. 208–9.
12 Stevenson, *Lloyd George*, p. 178.
13 PWW, vol. 60, p. 303.
14 Ibid., vol. 58, p. 270.

CHAPTER 11: A CARTHAGINIAN PEACE?

 1 Piketty, *Capital*, pp. 116–17, 151.
 2 JMK, vol. 16, p. 250.
 3 Ibid., p. 261.
 4 Piketty, *Capital*, pp. 126–7.
 5 Ibid., p. 153.
 6 JMK, vol. 16, p. 172.
 7 Ibid., vol. 2, p. 86.

8 Lloyd George, *The Truth about the Peace Treaties*, vol. 1, pp. 158–9.

9 Virginia Woolf, *The Diary of Virginia Woolf*, ed. Anne Olivier Bell, 5 vols (London, 1977–84; Penguin edn, 1979–85), vol. 1, p. 201.

10 JMK, vol. 2, p. 89.

11 Ibid., vol. 17, p. 15.

12 Ibid., vol. 2, p. 91 ('very well' in this version).

13 Ibid., pp. 188–9.

14 Woolf, *Diary of Virginia Woolf*, vol. 2, p. 33.

15 JMK, vol. 2, p. 90.

16 Lloyd George, *The Truth about the Peace Treaties*, vol. 1, p. 5.

17 Ibid., pp. 97–8.

18 Ibid., pp. 103–4.

19 Ibid., pp. 109–10.

20 Ibid., p. 114.

21 Churchill, *The Aftermath*, pp. 29, 160.

22 Loreburn, *How the War Came*, p. 317.

23 Ibid., p. 216.

24 Ibid., p. 243.

25 Ibid., p. 118.

26 Ibid., p. 178.

27 Ibid., p. 4.

28 Lloyd George, *The Truth about the Peace Treaties*, vol. 1, p. 178.

29 JMK, vol. 17, p. 12.

30 Ibid., vol. 2, p. 18.

31 Ibid., p. 20.

32 Lloyd George, *The Truth about the Peace Treaties*, vol. 1, p. 252.

33 Lloyd George, *War Memoirs*, vol. 2, p. 1606.

34 JMK, vol. 2, p. 22.

35 Ibid., vol. 17, p. 42.

36 Ibid., vol. 2, p. 26.

37 Ibid., vol. 17, p. 4.

38 Ibid., vol. 2, p. 26.

39 Ibid., p. 34.

40 Ibid., p. 23.

41 Ibid., p. 104.

42 Ibid., p. 51.

43 Ibid., p. 60.

44 Ibid., p. 131.

45 Ibid., p. 127.

46 Ibid., p. 128.

47 Ibid., p. 178.

48 Ibid., p. xx.

CHAPTER 12: REPARATIONS AND GUILT

1   PWW, vol. 56, p. 354.

2   JMK, vol. 2, p. 90.

3   Lloyd George, *The Truth about the Peace Treaties*, vol. 1, pp. 192–5.

4   JMK, vol. 17, p. 12.

5   Ibid., vol. 2, pp. 37–8.

6   Lloyd George, *The Truth about the Peace Treaties*, vol. 1, pp. 436–7.

7   JMK, vol. 16, p. 333.

8   Ibid., pp. 381–3.

9   Lloyd George, *The Truth about the Peace Treaties*, vol. 1, pp. 459–60.

10 Ibid., pp. 473–4.

11 JMK, vol. 2, pp. 75–9.

12 Lloyd George, *The Truth about the Peace Treaties*, vol. 1, p. 415.

13 JMK, vol. 10, p. 30.

14 Lloyd George, *The Truth about the Peace Treaties*, vol. 1, p. 492.

15 PWW, vol. 56, pp. 357–8.

16 Ibid., p. 449.

17 Ibid., pp. 498–9.

18 Ibid., p. 502.

19 JMK, vol. 2, pp. 96–7.

20 Ibid., vol. 3, p. 104.

21 PWW, vol. 56, pp. 579–80.

22 Thomas Mann, *Diaries, 1918–1939*, trans. Richard and Clara Winston (New York, 1982), p. 9.

23 Ibid., p. 11.

24 Ibid., p. 13.

25 Ibid., p. 14.

26 Ibid., p. 22.

27 Ibid., p. 33.

28 Ibid., p. 40.

29 Ibid., p. 56.

30 JMK, vol. 10, p. 403.

31 Ibid., p. 415.

32 Woolf, *Diary of Virginia Woolf*, vol. 2, p. 90.

33 JMK, vol. 17, p. 436.

34 Ibid., p. 428.

35 Ibid., p. 441.

36 Lloyd George, *The Truth about the Peace Treaties*, vol. 1, pp. 676–8.
37 Ibid., p. 682.
38 JMK, vol. 2, p. 170.
39 PWW, vol. 58, p. 399.
40 Ibid., vol. 60, p. 315.
41 Ibid., vol. 63, p. 350.
42 Ibid., vol. 65, p. 521.

CHAPTER 13: FURTHER ECONOMIC CONSEQUENCES

  1 JMK, vol. 3, p. 115.
  2 Ibid., vol. 10, p. 419.
  3 JMK, vol. 3, pp. 1–2.
  4 Ibid., pp. 3–4.
  5 Ibid., p. 105.
  6 Ibid., p. 129.
  7 Ibid., p. 108.
  8 Ibid., p. 109.
  9 Ibid., p. 113.
 10 Ibid., p. 89.
 11 Ibid., p. 24.
 12 Ibid., p. 46.
 13 Ibid., p. 43.
 14 Ibid., p. 47.
 15 Ibid., p. 130.
 16 Ibid., p. 123.
 17 Ibid., p. 27.
 18 Ibid., p. 143.
 19 Woolf, *Diary of Virginia Woolf*, vol. 3, p. 181.
 20 Ibid., vol. 2, p. 266.
 21 JMK, vol. 3, p. 115.
 22 Ibid., vol. 9, pp. 287–8.
 23 Ibid., vol. 4, p. 153.
 24 Ibid., p. 56.
 25 Ibid., pp. 56–7.
 26 Ibid., vol. 17, p. 184.
 27 Ibid., vol. 4, p. 36.
 28 Ibid., p. 65.
 29 Ibid., vol. 19, pp. 219–23.
 30 Ibid., vol. 11, pp. 451, 453–4.
 31 Ibid., p. 458.

32 Ibid., vol. 19, p. 807.

33 Ibid., p. 823.

34 Ibid., vol. 10, pp. 20–1.

35 Ibid., p. 24.

36 Ibid., p. 23.

37 Lloyd George, *War Memoirs*, vol. 1, pp. 409–10.

38 Ibid., p. 410.

39 Lloyd George, *The Truth about the Peace Treaties*, vol. 1, p. 446.

40 Ibid., p. 448.

41 JMK, vol. 16, p. 335.

CHAPTER 14: SECOND CHANCES

 1 PWW, vol. 64, pp. 61–2.

 2 Roosevelt (ed.), *Roosevelt Letters*, vol. 2, p. 446.

 3 Churchill, *The World Crisis*, vol. 1, p. 553.

 4 Ibid., pp. 456–7.

 5 Ibid., p. 484.

 6 Ibid., p. 474.

 7 Ibid., pp. 649, 652.

 8 Ibid., vol. 2, p. 757.

 9 Ibid., p. 762.

10 Ibid., p. 779.

11 Ibid., p. 818.

12 Ibid., p. 833.

13 Ibid., p. 840.

14 Ibid., p. 905.

15 Ibid., p. 929.

16 Churchill, *The Aftermath*, p. 156.

17 JMK, vol. 10, p. 57.

18 Lloyd George, *The Truth about the Peace Treaties*, vol. 1, p. 248.

19 Churchill, *The World Crisis*, vol. 2, p. 1123.

20 Churchill, *The Aftermath*, pp. 118–19.

21 Ibid., pp. 126–8.

22 Ibid., p. 124.

23 Churchill, *My Early Life*, p. 67.

24 Ibid., p. 83.

25 JMK, vol. 9, p. xvii.

26 Ibid., p. xix.

27 Woolf, *Diary of Virginia Woolf*, vol. 4, p. 208.

28 Ibid., pp. 168–9.

29 JMK, vol. 10, pp. 447–9.
30 Churchill, *Great Contemporaries*, p. 311.
31 JMK, vol. 22, pp. 145–6.
32 Ibid., pp. 147–8.
33 Ibid., p. 149.
34 Ibid., pp. 149–50.

EPILOGUE: THE LEGACIES OF WAR IN THE LONG RUN

1 Lloyd George, *War Memoirs*, vol. 1, p. 34.
2 Étienne Mantoux, *The Carthaginian Peace: Or the Economic Consequences of Mr Keynes* (Oxford, 1946), p.146; see also pp. 162–3.
3 Ibid., pp. 107, 160.
4 Ibid., pp. 87, 119.
5 Ibid., pp. 131–2.
6 Ibid., pp. 115–17, 123–4, 163.
7 Ibid., pp. 125–6.
8 JMK, vol. 3, p. 129.

BIBLIOGRAPHY

Adam, George, *The Tiger: Georges Clemenceau, 1841–1929* (London, 1930)

Adams, Henry, *The Education of Henry Adams: An Autobiography* (Boston, MA, 1918)

Addison, Paul, *Churchill on the Home Front, 1900–1955* (London, 1992)

—, *Churchill: The Unexpected Hero* (Oxford, 2005)

Asquith, Earl of Oxford and, *Memories and Reflections, 1852–1927*, 2 vols (London, 1928)

Badger, Anthony J., *The New Deal: The Depression Years, 1933–40* (London, 1987)

Bailey, Thomas A., *A Diplomatic History of the American People*, 5th edn (New York, 1955)

Baker, Ray Stannard, *American Chronicle* (New York, 1945)

—, *Woodrow Wilson and World Settlement*, 3 vols (New York, 1922)

—, *Woodrow Wilson: Life and Letters*, 8 vols (New York, 1928–39)

Bateman, Bradley W., *Keynes's Uncertain Revolution* (Ann Arbor, 1996)

Beaverbrook, Lord, *Politicians and the War, 1914–16* (London, 1928; 1959 edn)

Belich, James, *Replenishing the Earth: The Settler Revolution and the Rise of the Anglo-world, 1783–1939* (Oxford, 2009)

Bell, Christopher M., *Churchill and Sea Power* (Oxford, 2013)

Berg, A. Scott, *Wilson* (New York, 2013)

Biagini, Eugenio, *Liberty, Retrenchment and Reform: Popular Liberalism in the Age of Gladstone, 1860–1880* (Cambridge, 1992)

—, 'The Third Home Bill in British history', in Gabriel Doherty (ed.), *The Home Rule Crisis, 1912–14* (Cork, 2014), pp. 412–42

Black, Conrad, *Franklin Delano Roosevelt: Champion of Freedom* (New York, 2003)

Blum, John Morton, *Woodrow Wilson and the Politics of Morality* (Boston, MA, 1956)

Bonham Carter, Mark and Mark Pottle (eds), *Lantern Slides: The Diaries and Letters of Violet Bonham Carter, 1904–14* (London, 1996)

Bonham Carter, Violet, *Winston Churchill As I Knew Him* (London, 1965)

Bradley, Ian, *The Optimists: Themes and Personalities in Victorian Liberalism* (London, 1980)

Broadberry, Stephen and Mark Harrison, *The Economics of World War I* (Cambridge, 2005), esp. for the editors' intro., pp. 3–40, and Albrecht Ritschl, 'The pity of peace: Germany's economy at war, 1914–18 and beyond', pp. 41–76

Brock, Michael and Eleanor (eds), *H. H. Asquith: Letters to Venetia Stanley* (Oxford, 1982)

—, *Margot Asquith's Great War Diary, 1914–16,* (Oxford, 2014), with intro. by M. Brock, pp. xxxi–cxlvii

Brown, Judith M. and Wm Roger Louis (eds), *The Oxford History of the British Empire*, vol. 4: *The Twentieth Century* (Oxford, 1999), esp. Robert Holland, 'The British Empire and the Great War, 1914–18', pp. 114–37 and Anthony Clayton, 'Imperial Defence and Security, 1900–68', pp. 280–305

Brown, Neville, *Dissenting Forbears: The Maternal Ancestors of J. M. Keynes* (Chichester, 1988)

Burk, Kathleen, *Britain, America and the Sinews of War, 1914–18* (London, 1985)

Cain, P. J. and A. G. Hopkins, *British Imperialism: Innovation and Expansion, 1688–1914*; and *British Imperialism: Crisis and Deconstruction, 1914–1990* (London, 1993)

Campbell, John, *Lloyd George: The Goat in the Wilderness, 1922–31* (London, 1977)

Cannadine, David, *The Decline and Fall of the British Aristocracy* (New Haven and London, 1990)

Carter, Miranda, *George, Nicholas and Wilhelm: Three Royal Cousins and the Road to World War I* (New York, 2010)

Churchill, Winston S., *The Aftermath: The World Crisis, 1918–28* (New York, 1929)

—, *Great Contemporaries* (London, 1937; Fontana edn, 1959)

—, *Liberalism and the Social Problem* (London, 1909)

—, *My Early Life* (London, 1930; Fontana edn, 1959)

—, *The People's Rights* (1909), intro. Cameron Hazlehurst (London, 1970)

—, *The Second World War*, 6 vols (London, 1948–54)

—, *Thoughts and Adventures* (London, 1932; 1947 edn)

—, *Victory: War Speeches*, ed. Charles Eade (London, 1946)

—, *The World Crisis, 1911–18*, 2 vols, continuous pagination (London, 1938; first published in 5 vols., 1923–7)

Clark, Christopher, *The Sleepwalkers: How Europe Went to War in 1914* (London, 2012; Penguin edn, 2013)

Clarke, Peter, 'The English-speaking peoples before Churchill', *Britain and the World*, 4(2):199–231 (2011)

—, *Keynes: The Twentieth Century's Most Influential Economist* (London and New York, 2009)

—, *The Keynesian Revolution in the Making, 1924–36* (Oxford, 1988)

—, *Lancashire and the New Liberalism* (Cambridge, 1971)

—, *The Last Thousand Days of the British Empire: The Demise of a Superpower, 1944–47* (London and New York, 2007; Penguin edn, 2008)

—, *Liberals and Social Democrats* (Cambridge, 1978)

—, *Mr Churchill's Profession: Statesman, Orator, Writer* (London and New York, 2013)

—, *A Question of Leadership: Gladstone to Blair*, 2nd edn (London, 1999)

Clavin, Patricia, *Securing the World Economy: The Reinvention of the League of Nations, 1920–46* (Oxford, 2013)

Collini, Stefan, *Liberalism and Sociology: L. T. Hobhouse and Political Argument in England, 1880–1914* (Cambridge, 1979)

—, *Public Moralists: Political Thought and Intellectual Life in Britain, 1850–1930* (Oxford, 1991)

Collini, Stefan, Donald Winch and John Burrow, *That Noble Science of Politics: A Study in Nineteenth-Century Intellectual History* (Cambridge, 1983)

Conyne, G. R., *Woodrow Wilson: British Perspectives, 1912–21* (London, 1992)

Cooper, John Milton, *The Warrior and the Priest: Woodrow Wilson and Theodore Roosevelt* (Cambridge, MA, 1983)

—, *Woodrow Wilson: A Biography* (New York, 2009)

Craig, F. W. S. (ed.), *British Electoral Facts, 1885–1975* (London, 1976)

—, *British Parliamentary Election Results, 1885–1918* (London, 1974)

—, *British Parliamentary Election Results, 1918–1949* (Glasgow, 1969)

Dangerfield, George, *The Strange Death of Liberal England, 1910–14* (New York, 1935; Capricorn edn, 1961)

Daniels, Jonathan, *Washington Quadrille* (New York, 1968)

Darwin, John, *The Empire Project: The Rise and Fall of the British World System, 1830–1970* (Cambridge, 2009)

—, *Unfinished Empire: The Global Expansion of Britain* (London, 2012)

Daunton, Martin, *Just Taxes: The Politics of Taxation in Britain, 1914–79* (Cambridge, 2002)

—, *Trusting Leviathan: The Politics of Taxation in Britain, 1799–1914* (Cambridge, 2001)

Davenport-Hines, Richard, *Universal Man: The Seven Lives of John Maynard Keynes* (London, 2015)

David, Edward (ed.), *Inside Asquith's Cabinet: From the Diaries of Charles Hobhouse* (London, 1977)

Davis, Kenneth S., *FDR: The New York Years, 1928–1933* (New York, 1985)

—, *FDR: The New Deal Years, 1933–1937* (New York, 1986)

Deutscher, Isaac, *The Prophet Armed: Trotsky, 1879–1921*; *The Prophet Unarmed: Trotsky, 1921–29*; *The Prophet Outcast: Trotsky, 1929–40* (Oxford, 1954–63)

Devlin, Patrick, *Too Proud to Fight: Woodrow Wilson's Neutrality* (Oxford, 1974)

Ducray, Camille, *Clemenceau* (London, 1919)

Edgerton, David, *Warfare State: Britain 1920–70* (Cambridge, 2006)

Eichengreen, Barry, *Golden Fetters: The Gold Standard and the Great Depression, 1919–39* (Oxford, 1992)

Ferguson, Niall, *The Cash Nexus: Money and Power in the Modern World, 1700–2000* (London, 2001)

—, *Paper and Iron: Hamburg Business and German Politics in the Era of Inflation, 1897–1927* (Cambridge, 1995)

—, *The Pity of War* (London, 1998)

Floud, Roderick, Kenneth Wachter and Annabel Gregory, *Height, Health and History* (Cambridge, 1990)

Forcey, Charles B., *The Crossroads of Liberalism: Croly, Weyl, Lippmann and the Progressive Era, 1900–25* (New York, 1961)

Freud, Sigmund and Bullitt, William C., *Thomas Woodrow Wilson: A Psychological Study* (London, 1967)

Friedel, Frank, *Franklin D. Roosevelt*, 4 vols (Cambridge, MA, 1952–73)

Fusfield, Daniel, *The Economic Thought of Franklin Roosevelt and the Origins of the New Deal* (New York, 1956)

Fussell, Paul, *The Great War and Modern Memory* (Oxford, 1975)

Gallagher, J. and R. E. Robinson, 'The imperialism of free trade', *Economic History Review*, 2nd ser., 6:1–15 (1953)

Gardiner, A. G., *The Pillars of Society* (London, 1914; popular edn, London, 1916)

—, *Prophets, Priests and Kings* (London, 1908)

—, *The War Lords* (London, 1915)

George, William, *My Brother and I* (London, 1958)

Germains, Victor Wallace, *The Tragedy of Winston Churchill* (London, 1931)

Gilbert, Bentley Brinkerhoff, *David Lloyd George, a Political Life: The Architect of Change, 1863–1912* (Columbus, OH, 1987)

Gilbert, Martin (ed.), Companion Volumes to Randolph S. Churchill and Martin Gilbert, *Winston S. Churchill*, 8 vols (London, 1966–88)

Gough, Barry, *Pax Britannica: Ruling the Waves and Keeping the Peace before Armageddon* (London, 2014)

Graves, Robert, *Goodbye to All That* (London, 1929; UK Penguin edn, 1960; US Doubleday Anchor edn, 1957)

Gregory, Adrian, *The Last Great War: British Society and the First World War* (Cambridge, 2008)

Grigg, John, *The Young Lloyd George* (London, 1973); *Lloyd George: the people's champion, 1902–11* (1978); *Lloyd George: from peace to war, 1912–16* (1985); *Lloyd George: war leader, 1916–18* (2002)

Groenewegen, Peter, *A Soaring Eagle: Alfred Marshall, 1842–1924* (Aldershot, 1995)

Gunther, John, *Roosevelt in Retrospect: A Profile in History* (London, 1950)

Haig, Douglas, *War Diaries*, ed. Gary Sheffield and John Bourne (London, 2005)

Hammond, J. L., *C. P. Scott of the Manchester Guardian* (London, 1934)

—, *Gladstone and the Irish Nation* (London, 1938)

—, 'Gladstone and the League of Nations mind', in J. A. K. Thomson and A. J. Toynbee (eds), *Essays in Honour of Gilbert Murray* (London, 1936), pp. 95–118

Hancock, W. K., *Smuts: The Sanguine Years, 1870–1919* (Cambridge, 1962)

Hancock, W. K. and Jean Van Der Poel (eds), *Selections from the Smuts Papers*, vol. 4 (Cambridge, 1966)

Hanks, Robert K., 'Georges Clemenceau and the English', *Historical Journal*, 45:53–77 (2002)

Harrod, Roy, *The Life of John Maynard Keynes* (London, 1951)

Hazlehurst, Cameron, *Politicians at War, August 1914 to May 1915: A Prologue to the Triumph of Lloyd George* (London, 1971)

Hicks, Ursula K., *British Public Finances: Their Structure and Development, 1880–1952* (London, 1954)

Hill, Polly and Richard Keynes (eds), *Lydia and Maynard: Letters Between Lydia Lopokova and John Maynard Keynes* (London, 1989)

Hirst, F. W., *In the Golden Days* (London, 1947)

Hobhouse, L. T., *Democracy and Reaction* (1904), ed. and intro. P. F. Clarke (Brighton, 1972)

—, *Liberalism* (London, 1911)

—, 'The new spirit in America', *Contemporary Review*, 50:1–10 (1911)

Hofstadter, Richard, *The Age of Reform: From Bryan to F.D.R.* (New York, 1955)

—, *The American Political Tradition* (New York, 1948; Vintage edn, 1954)

Holroyd, Michael, *Lytton Strachey: A Biography* (revised Penguin edn, London, 1979; first published in 2 vols, 1967–8)

Hölscher, Jens and Matthias Klaes, *Keynes's Economic Consequences of the Peace: A Reappraisal* (London, 2014)

Howard, Michael, *The Continental Commitment: The Dilemma of British Defence Policy in the Era of the Two World Wars* (London, 1972; Penguin edn, 1974)

Hull, Isabel V., *A Scrap of Paper: Breaking and Making International Law during the Great War* (Ithaca, NY, 2014)

Hyndman, H. M., *Clemenceau: The Man and his Time* (London, 1919)

Jeffery, Keith, *1916: A Global History* (London, 2015)

Jenkins, Roy, *Asquith* (London, 1964)

Johnston, Louis and Samuel H. Williamson, 'What was the US GDP then?', MeasuringWorth website, 2015

Jones, Thomas, *Lloyd George* (Oxford, 1951)

Judt, Tony, *Postwar: A History of Europe since 1945* (London, 2005)

Kennedy, Paul, *The Rise and Fall of the Great Powers: Economic Change and Military Conflict from 1500 to 2000* (London, 1988; Fontana edn, 1989)

Kimball, Warren F., *Forged in War: Roosevelt, Churchill and the Second World War* (New York, 1997)

Koch, H. W. (ed.), *The Origins of the First World War: Great Power Rivalry and German War Aims* (London, 1972), esp. for James Joll, '1914: the unspoken assumptions', pp. 307–28

Koss, Stephen, *Asquith* (London, 1976)

—, *Fleet Street Radical: A. G. Gardiner and the Daily News* (London, 1973)

—, *The Rise and Fall of the Political Press in Britain*, vol. 2: *The Twentieth Century* (London, 1984)

Lentin, A., *Guilt at Versailles: Lloyd George and the Pre-history of Appeasement* (London, 1985)

Levin, N. Gordon, *Woodrow Wilson and World Politics* (Oxford, 1968)

Liddell Hart, B. H., *The British Way in Warfare* (London, 1932)

—, *History of the First World War* (London, 1930; Pan edn, 1972)

Link, Arthur S. (ed.), *The Papers of Woodrow Wilson*, 69 vols (Princeton, 1966–94)

Lloyd George, David, *Is It Peace?* (London, 1923)

—, *The Truth about the Peace Treaties*, 2 vols, continuous pagination (London, 1938)

—, *War Memoirs*, 2 vols, continuous pagination (London, 1938; first published in 6 vols, 1933–6)

Loreburn, Lord, *How the War Came* (London, 1919)

Losurdo, Domenico, *Liberalism: A Counter-History* (London, 2011)

Lough, David, *No More Champagne: Churchill and his Money* (London and New York, 2015)

Louis, Wm Roger, *The Ends of British Imperialism: Collected Essays* (London, 2006)

McCallum, R. B., *Public Opinion and the Last Peace* (London, 1944)

McKibbin, Ross, *Parties and People: England, 1914–1951* (Oxford, 2010)

—, 'Political sociology in the guise of economics: J. M. Keynes and the rentier', *English Historical Review*, 128: 78–106 (2013)

MacMillan, Margaret, *Peacemakers: The Paris Conference of 1919 and its Attempt to End War* (London, 2001)

—, *The War that Ended Peace* (London, 2013)

Mallet, Charles, *Mr Lloyd George: A Study* (London, 1930)

Mann, Thomas, *Diaries, 1918–1939*, trans. Richard and Clara Winston (New York, 1982)

Mantoux, Étienne, *The Carthaginian Peace: Or the Economic Consequences of Mr Keynes* (Oxford, 1946)

Martel, Gordon, *The Month that Changed the World: July 1914* (Oxford, 2014)

Martet, Jean, *Le Silence de M. Clemenceau* (Paris, 1929)

—, *Le Tigre* (Paris, 1930)

Matthew, H. C. G. (ed. and intro.), *The Gladstone Diaries*, vols 9–11 (Oxford, 1986–90)

Mazower, Mark, *Governing the World: The History of an Idea* (London, 2012; Penguin edn, 2013)

Miller, David, *The Drafting of the Covenant*, 2 vols (London and New York, 1928)

Mitchell, B. R., *British Historical Statistics* (Cambridge, 1988)

Moe, Richard, *Roosevelt's Second Act: The Election of 1940 and the Politics of War* New York, 2013).

Moggridge, D. E., *British Monetary Policy, 1924–31: The Norman Conquest of $4.86* (Cambridge, 1972)

— (ed. with Sir Austin Robinson), *The Collected Writings of John Maynard Keynes*, 30 vols. (Cambridge, 1971–89)

—, *Maynard Keynes: An Economist's Biography* (London, 1992)

Morgan, Kenneth O., 'The future at work: Anglo-American progressivism, 1890–1917', in H. C. Allen and Roger Thompson (eds), *Contrast and Connection: Bicentennial Essays in Anglo-American History* (London, 1976), pp. 245–71

— (ed.), *Lloyd George: Family Letters, 1885–1936* (Cardiff and London, 1973)

Morley, John, *The Life of William Ewart Gladstone*, 2 vols (London, 1905; first published in 3 vols., 1903)

—, *Memorandum on Resignation: August 1914*, ed. F. W. Hirst (London, 1928)

Mowat, Charles Loch, *Britain between the Wars, 1918–40* (London, 1955)

Neu, Charles E., *Colonel House: A Biography of Woodrow Wilson's Silent Partner* (New York, 2015)

Newton, Douglas, *The Darkest Days: The Truth Behind Britain's Rush to War, 1914* (London and New York, 2014)

Nicolson, Harold, *Peacemaking 1919* (London, 1933; University Paperback edn, 1964)

Offer, Avner, *The First World War: An Agrarian Interpretation* (Oxford, 1989)

Owen, Frank, *Tempestuous Journey: Lloyd George, his Life and Times* (London, 1954)

Parker, R. A. C., *Churchill and Appeasement* (London, 2000)

Peacock, Alan T. and Jack Wiseman, *The Growth of Public Expenditure in the United Kingdom* (London, 1961)

Pelling, Henry, *America and the British Left: From Bright to Bevan* (London, 1956)

Perkins, Frances, *The Roosevelt I Knew* (London, 1947)

Philpott, William, *Attrition: Fighting the First World War* (London, 2014)

Piketty, Thomas, *Capital in the Twenty-First Century*, trans. Arthur Goldhammer (London, 2014)

Pimlott, Ben (ed.), *The Second World War Diary of Hugh Dalton, 1940–45* (London, 1986)

Prior, Robin, *Churchill's 'World Crisis' as History* (London and Canberra, 1983)

Reynolds, David, *The Long Shadow: The Great War and the Twentieth Century* (London, 2013)

Robbins, Keith, *Sir Edward Grey: A Biography* (London, 1971)

Roberts, Carl Bechhofer ('Ephesian'), *Winston Churchill* (London, 1927; 2nd edn, 1928; 3rd edn, 1936; 4th edn, 1940)

Roberts, Richard, *Saving the City: The Great Financial Crisis of 1914* (Oxford, 2013)

Robinson, E. A. G., 'John Maynard Keynes, 1883–1946', *Economic Journal*, 57:1–68 (1947)

Rodgers, Daniel T., *Atlantic Crossings: Social Politics in a Progressive Age* (Cambridge, MA, 1998)

Roosevelt, Elliott (ed.), *The Roosevelt Letters, 1887–1945, being the personal correspondence of Franklin Delano Roosevelt*, 3 vols (London, 1949–52)

Runciman, David, *The Confidence Trap: A History of Democracy in Crisis from World War I to the Present* (Princeton, 2013)

Russell, Bertrand, *Autobiography*, 3 vols (London, 1967–9)

Schriftgiesser, Karl, *The Amazing Roosevelt Family* (New York, 1942)

Searle, Geoffrey, *A New England: Peace and War, 1886–1918* (Oxford, 2004)

Service, Robert, *Trotsky: A Biography* (London, 2009)

Seymour, Charles, *The Intimate Papers of Colonel House*, 4 vols (Boston, MA, 1926–8)

Shannon, Richard, *Gladstone and the Bulgarian Agitation, 1876* (London, 1963), *Gladstone: God and politics* (London, 2008)

Shaw, Bernard, *Collected Letters*, ed. Dan H. Laurence, *1898–1910* (London, 1972) and *1911–1925* (London, 1985)

Sherwood, Robert E., *Roosevelt and Hopkins: An Intimate History* (New York, 1948)

Skidelsky, Robert, *John Maynard Keynes*, 3 vols (London, 1983–2000)

Soames, Mary (ed.), *Speaking for Themselves: The Personal Letters of Winston and Clementine Churchill* (London and Toronto, 1998)

Spender, J. A. and Cyril Asquith, *Life of Herbert Henry Asquith, Lord Oxford and Asquith*, 2 vols (London, 1932)

Steinberg, Jonathan, *Bismarck: A Life* (Oxford, 2011)

Steiner, Zara, *The Lights that Failed: European International History, 1919–33* (Oxford, 2005)

Steiner, Zara S. and Keith Neilson, *Britain and the Origins of the First World War* (London, 1977)

Stevenson, Frances, *Lloyd George: A Diary*, ed. A. J. P. Taylor (London, 1971)

—, *The Years that are Past* (London, 1967)

Strachan, Hew, *The First World War*, vol. 1 (Oxford, 2001)

Sylvester, A. J., *Life with Lloyd George: The Sylvester Diary, 1931–45*, ed. Colin Cross (London, 1975)

Tanner, Duncan, *Political Change and the Labour Party, 1900–1918* (Cambridge, 1990)

Tardieu, André, *The Truth about the Treaty* (Indianapolis, 1921)

Taylor, A. J. P. (ed.), *My Darling Pussy: The Letters of Lloyd George and Frances Stevenson, 1913–41* (London, 1975)

—, *Politics in Wartime* (London, 1964)

—, *The Struggle for Mastery in Europe, 1848–1918* (Oxford, 1954)

—, *The Trouble Makers: Dissent over Foreign Policy, 1792–1939* (London, 1957; Panther edn, 1969)

Thompson, F. M. L., *English Landed Society in the Nineteenth Century* (London, 1963)

Thompson, John A., *Reformers and War: American Progressive Publicists and the First World War* (Cambridge, 1987)

—, *A Sense of Power: The Roots of America's Global Role* (Ithaca, NY, 2015)

—, *Woodrow Wilson* (London, 2002)

—, 'Woodrow Wilson and a world governed by evolving law', *Journal of Policy History*, 20:113–25 (2008)

Tooze, Adam, *The Deluge: The Great War and the Remaking of Global Order, 1916–31* (London 2014; Penguin edn, 2015)

Toye, Richard, *Churchill's Empire: The World that Made Him and the World He Made* (London, 2010)

—, *The Labour Party and the Planned Economy, 1931–51* (Woodbridge and Rochester, NY, 2003)

—, *Lloyd George and Churchill: Rivals for Greatness* (London, 2007)

Trentmann, Frank, *Free Trade Nation: Commerce, Consumption and Civil Society in Modern Britain* (Oxford, 2008)

Trevelyan, G. M., *Grey of Fallodon* (London, 1937)

Trotsky, Leon, *Report on the Communist International* (December 1922), Leon Trotsky Internet Archive (www.marxists.org, 2002)

Watson, David Robin, *Georges Clemenceau: A Political Biography* (London, 1974)

Weaver, Stewart A., *The Hammonds: A Marriage in History* (Stanford, 1997)

Weber, Max, 'Politics as a vocation', trans. and ed. H. H. Gerth and C. Wright Mills, *From Max Weber: Essays in Sociology* (London, 1948), pp. 77–128

Wilson, Keith M., *The Policy of the Entente: Essays on the Determinants of British Foreign Policy, 1904–1914* (Cambridge, 1985)

Wilson, Trevor, *The Myriad Faces of War: Britain and the Great War* (Cambridge, 1986)

— (ed.), *The Political Diaries of C. P. Scott, 1911–28* (London, 1970)

Winter, Jay (ed.), *The Cambridge History of the First World War*, 3 vols (Cambridge, 2014), esp. Barry Supple, 'War economies', vol. 2, pp. 295–324

Winter, Jay and Blaine Baggett, *1914–18: The Great War and the Shaping of the Twentieth Century* (London, 1996)

Woolf, Virginia, *The Diary of Virginia Woolf*, ed. Anne Olivier Bell, 5 vols (London, 1977–84; Penguin edn, 1979–85)

Young, John W., 'Conservative leaders, coalition and Britain's decision for war in 1914', *Diplomacy & Statecraft*, 25:214–19 (2014)

NOTES ON SOURCES

PROLOGUE: A TRAIN OF THOUGHT

Robert Service's excellent *Trotsky* is now the authority. But the classic (partisan) biography in three volumes by Isaac Deutscher is still well worth reading; see his *The Prophet Armed*, pp. 155–6, 255–7 for the rapprochement with Lenin in 1917 and *The Prophet Unarmed*, p. 61, for 'the skein of history'. I quote the famous speech from the Trotsky Internet Archive, www.marxists.org. Some of my general themes are addressed in two fairly recent books: David Runciman, *The Confidence Trap* and David Edgerton, *Warfare State*. On the European empires and their demise, see Miranda Carter, *George, Nicholas and Wilhelm*, which supplies telling human detail. On the British Empire and the 'anglo-world', I am much indebted to the work of two ground-breaking historians: James Belich for *Replenishing the Earth*, and John Darwin for *The Empire Project* and also for his *Unfinished Empire*, from which (p. 7) my quotation about 'the default mode' is taken.

Empirical research now challenges some axioms about democratic government (allegedly entailing more equal distribution or budget deficits) that economists as distinguished as Simon Kuznets and James M. Buchanan lent their names in propagating. My debt to the work of Piketty is obvious in my citation of it as a text. Other economic statistics come from the excellent website MeasuringWorth, here citing the work of Samuel H. Williamson (2015), with which the figures given in Stephen Broadberry and Mark Harrison's useful volume, *The Economics of World War I*, are broadly consistent (though their table 1.4, p. 12, unfortunately transposes the columns for the UK and the USA). On the franchise in Britain, I now follow the authoritative work of the late Duncan Tanner, *Political Change and the Labour Party*, esp. pp. 4–5, 387–9. Tony Judt's brave book *Postwar* gives an overview on European developments (though least good on Britain).

On American progressivism, we still ignore Richard Hofstadter's work at our peril; my quotation is from his *Age of Reform*, p. 272. On Gladstone, the work of Colin Matthew is fundamental, not least in editing and commenting on the diaries. I am sympathetic to the interpretation of Eugenio Biagini in his important book *Liberty, Retrenchment and Reform*; this in turn extended some insights first developed by Richard Shannon on the Bulgarian campaign, though later rather exaggerated in Shannon's revised biography, *Gladstone: God and Politics*. J. L. Hammond's essay 'Gladstone and the League of Nations mind' is an interesting perspective from 1936 in a festschrift for his friend Gilbert Murray, the presiding spirit of the League of Nations Union.

I am recapitulating some points from my book *Liberals and Social Democrats*, especially pp. 7–8 on Gladstone, and p. 87 for Shaw on Liberal reform. My essay on Gladstone in *A Question of Leadership* developed this interpretation, with the context for Gladstone's utterance on 'the masses against the classes' at pp. 34–5 (and, on p. 348, a suggestion about Blair that is now corroborated in recent biographies of him). The quotation from Max Weber is from his seminal essay 'Politics as a vocation'. W. T. Stead is quoted from Ian Bradley, *The Optimists*, p. 113. On Morley, both as biographer and Gladstonian standard-bearer, see the memoir by his devoted research assistant F. W. Hirst, *In the Golden Days*, especially pp. 174, 184; and Stefan Collini's fine study *Public Moralists*. On Scott, Morley and Hobhouse at the time of the great 1899 meeting in the Free Trade Hall see my *Lancashire and the New Liberalism*, pp. 177–80; and Hobhouse is quoted from his books *Democracy and Reaction*, pp. 191–2, and *Liberalism*, p. 135.

CHAPTER I: THE DISCIPLE AS PROPHET

I begin my account with the mediating role of Ray Stannard Baker, who also published under the name David Grayson, and wrote an interesting autobiography, *American Chronicle*. His three volumes, *Woodrow Wilson and World Settlement*, were composed in collaboration with Wilson as an apologia for the President's role in the peace negotiations; the eight volumes of *Woodrow Wilson: Life and Letters* were published after Wilson's death, covering his life before Paris in great detail, some of it telling. Nowadays, all this is supplemented but not superseded by the work of the great Wilson scholar Arthur S. Link, notably as editor of sixty-nine volumes of *The Papers of Woodrow Wilson* [PWW]; hence my copious quotation from them. The portrait of Gladstone is reproduced in PWW 30, following p. 299, along with those of the Rev. Isaac Stockton Axson and the Rev. Joseph Ruggles Wilson.

I have greatly benefited from the work of John Milton Cooper, both *The Warrior and the Priest*, on Wilson and TR, and especially *Woodrow Wilson: A Biography* (to which the recent biography of Wilson by A. Scott Berg does not greatly add). My greatest debt is to John Thompson's *Woodrow Wilson* as a concise survey and interpretation of the career, from which I differ on some points with due diffidence. Unfashionably, I also benefited from some earlier studies, notably John Morton Blum, *Woodrow Wilson and the Politics of Morality* and, more controversially, Sigmund Freud and William C. Bullitt, *Thomas Woodrow Wilson: A Psychological Study*. Admittedly, the great psychologist is rather reductive in his interpretation, and his junior collaborator somewhat evasive about the authorship of a book not published until after Edith Wilson's death; but Bullitt knew Wilson, first as an admirer and later as a critic, and sometimes brings real insight to bear from his own (jaundiced) perspective.

CHAPTER 2: A MAN OF THE PEOPLE

Lloyd George's own memoirs are today much underestimated but as a literary tour de force fully equal those of Churchill. The story of their original commission is told in Frank Owen, *Tempestuous Journey*, a biography by a journalist who had the backing of Lord Beaverbrook, who then owned the Lloyd George papers; and there are insights on the writing of the memoirs in *Life with Lloyd George*, the diaries of A. J. Sylvester, who was Lloyd George's secretary at the time. In the original edition, the first two volumes were published in September and October 1933; volumes 3 and 4 a year later; and volumes 5 and 6 in September and November 1936. The two-volume edition of 1938, which I cite, reprints the full text. *The Truth about the Peace Treaties* followed in September 1938.

The great modern biography of Lloyd George is by John Grigg, and his first volume, *The Young Lloyd George*, is particularly good. But the four volumes that Grigg completed before his death only reached as far as 1918; and the biography by Bentley Brinkerhoff Gilbert only as far as 1916. A. J. P. Taylor played a notable part in giving a fuller understanding of Lloyd George, not least by editing Frances Stevenson's diary after she herself had published her memoirs, *The Years that are Past*. Taylor also later edited the letters between the couple, published as *My Darling Pussy*. Another valuable scholarly contribution came from Kenneth O. Morgan in editing *Lloyd George: Family Letters*, many of which are helpfully translated from the original Welsh. And these can be supplemented with the memoirs of William George, *My Brother and I*. I quote from all these sources.

Just as Lloyd George's reputation has risen in the historiography of recent years, so Asquith's has commensurately declined – to such an extent that today we need reminding what a formidable figure he was in his prime. Roy Jenkins's *Asquith*, when published to great acclaim in 1964, inevitably suggested some affinities between author and subject; and its great coup was to reveal the full extent of the correspondence with Venetia Stanley. Twelve years later, Stephen Koss's biography cast a more dispassionate eye, with an insight on the social nuances of Asquith's career, well captured in the chapter title 'From Herbert to

Henry' – the significance of which has obviously been missed by all the distinguished historians today who propagate the usage 'Herbert Asquith'.

Churchill's tribute to Lloyd George, delivered after his death to the House of Commons, is in the volume *Victory: War Speeches*, pp. 113–16. All electoral statistics in this and later chapters are taken from F. W. S. Craig's authoritative compilation, *British Parliamentary Election Results*. In remarking on Lloyd George's height, I turned for comparative statistics to the exacting study by Roderick Floud and his co-authors, *Height, Health and History*, pp. 322–3. And in commenting on the difference between radical non-interventionism and the Gladstonian tradition, I am remembering apt distinctions that A. J. P. Taylor made as long ago as 1954 in *The Struggle for Mastery in Europe* and then developed in his seminal Ford Lectures, published in 1957 as *The Trouble Makers*. The fact that Taylor intuitively understood this tradition in Liberal thinking, having been steeped in it in his youth, means that we now neglect some of his insights at our own loss.

CHAPTER 3: ARISTOCRAT AND SOLDIER

Violet Bonham Carter's *Winston Churchill As I Knew Him* is by no means without merit; my point is that it cannot be taken literally. The publication of her own diary edited by her son Mark and by Mark Pottle, *Lantern Slides*, can be read as a useful corrective and is the source of my quotations. Setting Churchill's impressions alongside Piketty's findings helps build a fairly consistent picture about the British elite, on which Michael Thompson's *English Landed Society in the Nineteenth Century* remains a classic study, its findings reinforced by the deep research beguilingly presented in David Cannadine's *Decline and Fall of the British Aristocracy*. Many of my statistics come from that authoritative source, Brian Mitchell's *British Historical Statistics*; and on tax issues I rely on Martin Daunton's two volumes, *Trusting Leviathan* and *Just Taxes*. Churchill's own defence of the People's Budget can be traced in the speeches reprinted in his tract *The People's Rights*, from which I quote. Gardiner's subtly changing view of him is shown by essays in his two volumes, *Prophets, Priests and Kings* (1908) and *The Pillars of Society* (1914); the latter is quoted. And here, as later, I quote Churchill's contemporary views from Martin Gilbert's invaluable Companion Volumes to the official biography.

I have made use of Churchill's own copious apologia, *The World Crisis*, using the two-volume edition, which substantially reprints what became volumes 1–4 (the first couple published during 1923 and the second couple in March 1927). Then *The Aftermath* was added (in 1929), separately cited here; and a sixth volume on the eastern front eventually concluded the whole work. It will be apparent, then, that it was only after laboriously composing the first five volumes of the *World Crisis* that Churchill turned, in an altogether lighter vein, to writing his memoir *My Early Life*. Its status as an imaginative reconstruction is one reason for scrutinising it critically; I cite the modern paperback, with its wide circulation, for ease of reference, and likewise his *Great Contemporaries*. Modern research, of course, supplies other perspectives, notably in Richard Toye's fine study, *Churchill's Empire*. In dealing with Churchill's early political career in Oldham and Manchester, I rediscovered my own early research for *Lancashire and the New Liberalism*; and for his work as a social reformer I gained much from Paul Addison's *Churchill on the Home Front*.

'The imperialism of free trade' was the title of a seminal article by that legendary pair Robinson and Gallagher back in 1953; and the concept is like a vintage car that may need some servicing from time to time but keeps on running. Thus I mean it as a compliment to say that the work of Peter Cain and Tony Hopkins is in this tradition, with their two important volumes, *British Imperialism*. James Belich's *Replenishing the Earth* is now also highly pertinent. And the crucial work tying the peculiarities of the British Empire to the world crisis is Avner Offer's thought-provoking study *The First World War: An Agrarian Interpretation*, from which the quotation from Haldane comes. The important book by Frank Trentmann, *Free Trade Nation*, is also germane.

It seems to be currently unfashionable among historians to dwell on *Flottenpolitik*. But this dimension is well explored in recent work by Barry Gough in his *Pax Britannica* and Christopher M. Bell, *Churchill and Sea Power*. This helpfully takes us back to the perspectives developed in Paul Kennedy's *The Rise and Fall of the Great Powers*. The quotation from the Kaiser comes from Miranda Carter's *George, Nicholas and Wilhelm*. On Tirpitz's ambitions, compare the assessment in Hew Strachan's scrupulous synthesis of mainstream scholarship, *The First World War*, with the revisionist treatment in Christopher Clark's *The Sleepwalkers*. The impact of heavy government investment in new military technologies is the theme of David Edgerton's challenging book, *Warfare State*, nominally beginning its treatment in 1920 but with an analysis already relevant earlier.

CHAPTER 4: HOW THE LIBERALS STARTED A WORLD WAR

The long-running debate about the origins of the war has taken on a new lease of life as a response to the centenary. The most notable achievement is clearly that of Christopher Clark's *The Sleepwalkers* in reorientating the focus towards the Balkans; his originality is to establish the deep complicity of Serbs at many levels of society in furthering the irredentist political ambition for a 'Greater Serbia'. The Sarajevo assassination was no random, isolated incident but one that understandably stimulated Austrian concern, suspicion and pride alike, super-charging an international crisis that then slipped out of anyone's control in provoking a major European war. From my perspective, however, this fails to give adequate attention to the role of the Belgian issue in persuading a Liberal government to commit the British Empire to a war that thereby became world-wide in scope. Thus the cogent account in Zara Steiner's *Britain and the Origins of the First World War* remains broadly persuasive to me, as it clearly does to Margaret MacMillan in *The War that Ended Peace*. I am also closely in tune with Michael Brock's coverage of British decision-making in his 115 pages of introduction to the recent edition of *Margot Asquith's Great War Diary*. Another welcome addition to the literature is Gordon Martel, *The Month that Changed the World*, with its very clear chronology of the key developments.

On Asquith, of course, the irresistible source these days is the edition by Michael and Eleanor Brock, *H. H. Asquith: Letters to Venetia Stanley*. This gives the original text of letters first published (in sanitised form) by Asquith himself as *Memories and Reflections* in 1928: the same year that F. W. Hirst, after Morley's death, published his old mentor's *Memorandum on Resignation: August 1914*, which naturally created a great stir at the time in reinforcing the 'revisionist' case that Britain's decision for war was morally spurious. I quote Morley's letter of 3 August to Asquith, with a reference at note 27 to the *Memorandum*, p. 31, but in fact I follow the original wording in the facsimile printed in *Memories and Reflections*, pp. 11–14. This also prints some of Asquith's cabinet letters, though I have taken the text of those I quote from Spender and Asquith, *Life of Herbert Henry Asquith*. Lord Beaverbrook's *Politicians and the War*, also first published in 1928, was responsible for linking Churchill's name to coalition-gossip; Cameron Hazlehurst's mighty labours in diverse political archives, as presented in *Politicians at War*, later revived this theme; and John Young has recently speculated along similar lines in 'Conservative leaders, coalition and Britain's decision for war in 1914'. Personally, I have often consulted F. W. S. Craig's authoritative edition of *British Electoral Facts*, and would recommend the same to any historian who writes airily about the option of a Conservative-based coalition in 1914.

On Lloyd George, the third volume of Grigg's biography is useful; also Kenneth Morgan's edition of the family letters, from which I quote. My quotation from Morley's *Gladstone* is from Book VI, chapter 5, in either of the pre-war editions; cabinet ministers at the time could well have afforded the three-volume set but my own copy, acquired when I was doing A-Level History, is the two-volume reprint. On Morley's 'views of a lifetime' the source that I quote is Edward David's useful edition of the diary of Charles Hobhouse, *Inside*

Asquith's Cabinet. On London at the time of the August bank holiday, I follow the convincing treatment in Adrian Gregory, *The Last Great War* (also authoritative on the German atrocities in Belgium).

The cabinet notes between Lloyd George and Asquith are printed in Gilbert's relevant Companion Volume, pp. 1996–7. 'Would you commit yourself in public *now* to war,' Lloyd George is quoted as asking Churchill, with the date 1 August appended. But that was *Saturday*, with no Belgian issue in sight; and nor can it be Monday 3 August, when Belgium was already under a German ultimatum. Hence my redating as fitting (exactly) what was happening on Sunday 2 August; and Churchill thus replies 'No' – but on Monday would obviously have replied 'Yes'. So all of these exchanges must surely date from Sunday 2 August. Churchill's later gung-ho letter to his wife is from Mary Soames's excellent edition of their correspondence, *Speaking for Themselves*.

On Grey, the biography by Keith Robbins, *Sir Edward Grey*, is a model of modern academic scholarship but the official life by G. M. Trevelyan, *Grey of Fallodon*, which embodies more research in the relevant documents than is apparent on the page, benefits in unique ways from its closeness to its subject, not least on the great speech of 3 August 1914, on which I take the text from the official Hansard website, cited as HC Deb 03 August 1914 vol 65 cc1809–32.

On the impact of the decision for war on Liberal intellectuals, I went back to research of my own that I had almost forgotten from forty years ago; and I turned with even greater profit to Stefan Collini's sensitive analysis of L. T. Hobhouse, *Liberalism and Sociology*, with an apt quotation from p. 86 on Morley's significance. If Churchill tried to drag Lloyd George into the war, C. P. Scott tried to keep him out. Trevor Wilson's edition of *The Political Diaries of C. P. Scott* is invaluable and quoted in my text; as is J. L. Hammond, *C. P. Scott of the Manchester Guardian*. This biographer's own biography by Stewart Weaver, *The Hammonds*, rightly covering Barbara Hammond too, has a good account (pp. 119–23) of the impact of the Belgian crisis, not least upon the Hammonds' relations with Arthur Ponsonby, previously their closest friend but henceforth treading a pacifist line, as noted below in chapter 14. Shaw's letter (to Webb) is from his *Collected Letters, 1911–1925*, ed. Dan H. Laurence; it seems as emblematic in its way as the letter from Leonard to Emily Hobhouse, which I quote from my *Liberals and Social Democrats*, p. 168 (and see pp. 164–72 for other quotations).

My personal sense that such perspectives are still valid was enormously boosted just after I had completed this chapter when a new book came into my hands: Isabel Hull's impressive and original study *A Scrap of Paper*, documenting in chapter 1 the role of the Belgian Treaty in international law. Her conclusion on 'the unique salience and multi-determined quality of this one issue' is one that I endorse with great respect; but since this complements from a legal stand-point what I am arguing within a moral ambit, I felt it better not to change my own text but to let others read both congruent accounts.

It may be obvious, then, why I am unpersuaded by the hard-nosed, dismissive treatment of the Belgian issue in Keith Wilson, *The Policy of the Entente*, despite its close scholarship; and the more impassioned version of the same story in Douglas Newton's *The Darkest Days: The Truth Behind Britain's Rush to War, 1914*, though well researched in the relevant archives, likewise fails to move me. Nor is the due importance of Belgium adequately captured in Niall Ferguson, *The Pity of War*, despite its attractive sweep of argument and its acknowledge-ment of the extra-European dimension. The role of the Empire in making this into a world war is brought out well in two important volumes, each entitled *The First World War*: one by Avner Offer and the other by Hew Strachan, both already cited. This dimension is also one of the strengths of James Belich's *Replenishing the Earth*, which is the source of some of my statistics, along with Rob Holland's useful chapter in volume 4 of *The Oxford History of the British Empire*, edited by Brown and Louis.

CHAPTER 5: GOODBYE TO THE GARDEN OF EDEN

The incomparable source on Keynes is, of course, the Royal Economic Society's edition of *The Collected Writings*, with Austin Robinson and Donald Moggridge as managing editors [JMK]. Here I quote especially from JMK 2, *The Economic Consequences of the Peace* (1919); JMK 10, *Essays in Biography*, for 'Marshall' and 'My Early Beliefs'; JMK 11 for academic articles; JMK 16 for wartime Treasury papers. Keynes has also been lucky in his biographers. Roy Harrod, *The Life of John Maynard Keynes*, though bound by discretion in its day, was a great achievement; see pp. 192–3 for 'the presuppositions of Harvey Road', and it also saw the first use of the Blackett diary, from which I quote. Richard Davenport-Hines's candid treatment, *Universal Man*, reflects the mores of our own era and is good on this period. The two outstanding modern biog-raphies are Donald Moggridge's fat volume, *Maynard Keynes: An Economist's Biography*, packed with relevant documentation, and Robert Skidelsky's three volumes, *John Maynard Keynes*, of which the first dwells most on the private life (creating some shock when first published). In *Keynes: The Twentieth Century's Most Influential Economist* I have myself attempted a concise treatment, though saying far less there than I do here about the impact of the First World War. And on Keynes's intellectual orientation see Bradley Bateman's thought-provoking study, *Keynes's Uncertain Revolution*.

I quote freely from the first volume of Bertrand Russell's evocative *Autobiography*. For the intellectual milieu in which economics sprang from the moral sciences see Stefan Collini, Donald Winch and John Burrow, *That Noble Science of Politics*, chapters 10 and 11; and on Marshall, see Peter Groenewegen, *A Soaring Eagle*, from which I quote Neville Keynes on the fiscal controversy. Austin Robinson's shrewd assessment is quoted from his evocative obituary notice on Keynes in the *Economic Journal*; for chapter and verse, see Neville Brown's family memoir, *Dissenting Forbears*.

The letters in *Lydia and Maynard*, edited by Polly Hill and Richard Keynes, throw a lot of light on their relationship; see p. 256 for the quoted comments on Montagu. The crisis of 1914 has now found its historian in Richard Roberts, whose well-researched book *Saving the City* is invaluable. As usual I rely on Brian Mitchell, *British Historical Statistics*, not only for the trade figures but for public expenditure; see pp. 590–1 for the public expenditure series (out-turn of government budgets) and p. 836 for Charles Feinstein's estimates of GDP – both given at current prices, which yield my own calculations. Slightly different estimates were made in Alan Peacock and Jack Wiseman's pioneering work, *The Growth of Public Expenditure in the United Kingdom*, table A-5; this is clearly because they used total public expenditure, not just central government. But puzzlingly lower calculations for the share of UK government spending in GDP are given in Stephen Broadberry and Mark Harrison, *The Economics of World War I*, table 1.5, p. 15, and (with slightly different figures) table 7.5, p. 210. For changes in the various budgets and their effects see Martin Daunton's second volume, *Just Taxes*; and the concise survey by Ursula K. Hicks, *British Public Finances* remains a good introduction. The broad point remains that, whatever the methodological differences in producing exact figures, the sheer scale of the impact of the war is incontestable.

CHAPTER 6: KNIGHT-ERRANT OF PROGRESSIVISM
There is a clear and factually reliable account of the development of British–American relations in Thomas A. Bailey's *Diplomatic History of the American People*; and another older book that usefully surveys the ground is Henry Pelling's *America and the British Left*. Kenneth Morgan shrewdly focused on the progressive theme in his article 'The future at work: Anglo-American progressivism, 1890–1917', and Daniel T. Rodgers later extended the sweep of such comparisons in *Atlantic Crossings*. My own quotations are from L. T. Hobhouse's report of his visit in 1910, published in the following year as 'The new spirit in America'.

Ray Stannard Baker's account of his own odyssey is quoted from his autobiography, *American Chronicle*. John Thompson's *Reformers and War* is the indispensable study of how progressive publicists responded; and the 1916 quotation from the *New Republic* is taken from Charles B. Forcey's interesting study of Croly, Weyl and Lippmann, *The Crossroads of Liberalism*. I quote A. G. Gardiner from his 1915 essay on Wilson in his collection *The War Lords*. G. R. Conyne collected some similar material in his *Woodrow Wilson: British Perspectives*.

The Education of Henry Adams was published in 1918 but written before the war: a beguiling picture from a privileged viewpoint which seemed to me highly relevant to the implicit assumptions of the Roosevelts – *The Amazing Roosevelt Family* as an early author, Karl Schriftgiesser, called them in his 1942 book, which has some relevant financial and other information. From the 1920s the two branches of the family sustained a notorious feud, vigorously fuelled by TR's daughter Alice Longworth, who assured me, on my meeting her at Harvard in 1974, that 'we are the Roosevelts of Oyster Bay' (pronounced as in 'rue') whereas 'they are the Roosevelts of Hyde Park' (pronounced as in 'roe'). Only the spite seems genuine here and I accept the authority of Professor John Milton Cooper's private advice to me: 'It wasn't a matter of family accents but rather the patois of the northeastern, particularly New York, upper crust.'

The Roosevelt Letters, 1887–1945, which Elliott Roosevelt edited under the supervision of Eleanor Roosevelt in the late 1940s, is very much a work of family piety but the text seems to be authentic. The four volumes of the authorised biography by Frank Friedel were written with some constraint, though I liked his phrase 'unsnubbable stock'; and there is much to be said for the unconstrained work of Conrad Black in his volume *Franklin Delano Roosevelt: Champion of Freedom*, which gives a candid but not prurient account of the Lucy Mercer story, on which see also the comments in Jonathan Daniels, *Washington Quadrille*.

CHAPTER 7: THE BRITISH WAR EFFORT

This is another huge subject, yet I have often focused on peculiarly personal aspects, so the literature is both general and particular. The work of Basil Liddell Hart cannot be ignored: neither his *History of the First World War*, first published in 1930, nor his subsequent – and influential – analysis of what he called *The British Way in Warfare*; I quote from p. 36 on 'our traditional grand strategy'. Two works are heroic in their own coverage of Britain's role: Trevor Wilson's *The Myriad Faces of War* and Geoffrey Searle's volume in the Oxford History, *A New England: Peace and War, 1886–1918*. And I would select Adrian Gregory's *The Last Great War: British Society and the First World War* as perhaps the most stimulating recent work, particularly good on recruitment issues. But Alan Taylor's *Politics in Wartime* can still be read with profit; it was the author himself who once told me about Lloyd George's fine disregard for flatulence.

Paul Addison's *Churchill: The Unexpected Hero* is a welcome expansion of the author's authoritative contribution to the *Oxford Dictionary of National Biography* and reinforced my own reading of the significance of Gallipoli: on which I also benefited from the shrewd first chapter in Keith Jeffery, *1916: A Global History*. Much of my later treatment focuses closely on Keynes, e.g. the story about 'Mr Keynes and another gentleman' is taken from the revised edition of Michael Holroyd's *Lytton Strachey*, p. 598. On the wartime Treasury, Donald Moggridge's biography of Keynes is so weighty because the author had previously been immersed in the preparation of the relevant volumes of the JMK edition on which I draw. Despite my debt to Kathleen Burk, *Britain, America and the Sinews of War*, there are times when I prefer to follow Moggridge on war finance; and I likewise prefer him over Skidelsky's first volume on the 'conscientious' issue. Nonetheless, I find Skidelsky interestingly suggestive on why Lloyd George at times guessed better than Keynes about the performance of the economy; and for the statistics here I have calculated GDP growth from Feinstein's estimates in Brian Mitchell, *British Historical Statistics*, p. 836, checked against the figures given on the MeasuringWorth website (both already cited).

CHAPTER 8: THE AMERICAN WAY IN WARFARE

The documentary spine of this chapter, of course, is again Link's edition of PWW, spreading over volumes 30–41 for this period. As a source, this obviously supersedes the earlier publication of a selection, under the inevitably partisan editorship of Baker. But, in view of the centrality of Edward House and his diary, it might be wondered why I do not cite *The Intimate Papers of Colonel House*, as edited, with admirable restraint, by the historian Charles Seymour. My reason is that, while this was indeed a landmark contribution to historical understanding in the 1920s, so much of the documentation it offered, notably House's diary, is reproduced in Link's scholarly edition. The recent publication of the long-awaited biography by Charles E. Neu, *Colonel House*, with its scrupulous specification of its sources, appreciably eased my own labours. And I continue to rely on the guidance of John Thompson, not only in the war chapters of his *Woodrow Wilson* but also the suggestions in his subsequent article 'Woodrow Wilson and a world governed by evolving law'. On the legal theme, the expert guidance of Patrick Devlin, *Too Proud to Fight*, can now be supplemented by Isabel Hull's *A Scrap of Paper*.

Mark Mazower offers a useful overview of internationalist thinking in *Governing the World: The History of an Idea*. With a closer focus, the biography of A. G. Gardiner by Stephen Koss, *Fleet Street Radical*, offers essential context. Trevor Wilson is the best authority on the Bryce Report; I quote the *New York*

Tribune from his *Myriad Faces of War*, p. 190; and Adrian Gregory corroborates much of this on atrocities in *The Last Great War*. My final section alludes (rather subversively) to the way that the concept of a 'universal class' is developed in *Towards the Critique of Hegel's Philosophy of Law*, written by Marx in 1843, which I think has lasted rather better than the sort of Marxist analysis widely deployed in the 1960s, of which a prime example is N. Gordon Levin, *Woodrow Wilson and World Politics*.

CHAPTER 9: AGENDA FOR THE HALL OF MIRRORS

For the opening of the conference, I quote the speeches of Wilson and Lloyd George from Camille Ducray's contemporary account, *Clemenceau* (1919), pp. 169–70, and see Clemenceau's rambling but telling reminiscences from the two volumes published by his secretary, Jean Martet, *Le Silence de M. Clemenceau* and *Le Tigre*, quotation at p. 306. I learned a lot from the well-focused article by Robert K. Hanks, 'Georges Clemenceau and the English'; and this encouraged me to trust the account by H. M. Hyndman, *Clemenceau: The Man and his Time*, published during 1919, and quoted from pp. 33–4. A reliable and sympathetic modern biography is David Robin Watson, *Georges Clemenceau*. For the meeting with Gladstone, I took my quotation of the *Daily News*, 12 February 1883, from the version that reached eager readers in New Zealand in the *Waikato Times*, 5 May 1883 (available on the web). FDR's encounter with Clemenceau and his own visit to Château-Thierry are documented in his diary as cited; the 1936 speech is quoted from David Reynolds's perceptive study, *The Long Shadow*, p. 239.

John Grigg's fourth volume, *Lloyd George: War Leader, 1916–18*, is again very good (and tragically his last), inevitably sympathetic to his hero but by no means uncritical. And for Haig's side of the story, his *War Diaries* as edited and introduced by Gary Sheffield and John Bourne are likewise indispensable (quoted here by date). For the big picture on war strategy, the classic account from the perspective of 1930 by Basil Liddell Hart, *History of the First World War*, can be supplemented by the modern scholarship of Trevor Wilson in *The Myriad Faces of War*, though of course it is a pity that Hew Strachan's formidable volume *The First World War* stops short of the later struggles.

I am in sympathy with the incisive view of the German perspective given by Albrecht Ritschl in commenting that the invisibility of defeat to the man-in-the-German-street led to the Allies' making 'a desperate attempt to achieve an ersatz victory by economic means' (Broadberry and Harrison (eds), *The Economics of World War I*, pp. 66–8). The role of Colonel House in the Inquiry and then in the Armistice negotiations is well treated in Charles Neu's biography. On issues in international law, as previously, I defer to the legal expertise of Patrick

Devlin and the recent scholarship of Isabel Hull; but the *moral* ambit is more my own concern. The insights and research of Anthony Lentin's acute analysis in *Guilt at Versailles* seem to me to have lacked due appreciation in the subsequent historiography, perhaps because his book evidently had such a curious publishing history. And I was surprised to find that, while everyone knows about the importance of reparations in the Treaty, the history of the concept had, so far as I could see, received so little attention in the subsequent historical literature.

CHAPTER 10: THE FOURTEEN POINTS IN PARIS

The conference has generated, over nearly a century, an enormous and impassioned literature. What is surprising is that so many of the older books, like David Miller, *The Drafting of the Covenant*, published in 1928, and Harold Nicolson's *Peacemaking 1919*, published in 1933, retain their value. This is reinforced by the fact that both those authors were participants in the process, and Nicolson's diary entries, printed in the second part of his account, are particularly useful. In the modern historiography, the prize-winning book by Margaret MacMillan, *Peacemakers*, has a special place (though personally I regret that this clever, allusive title was changed in the North American edition to *Paris 1919*) and it is the most influential restatement of the 'pragmatic' defence of the politics of the settlement. But for due attention to the economic themes as well, we are all now indebted to the magnificent conspectus by Zara Steiner, *The Lights that Failed*, which is so good that it might well have overawed others venturing into this field – but happily did not deter Adam Tooze from offering his own impressive synthesis of the political and economic forces at play (or at work) in *The Deluge: The Great War and the Remaking of Global Order*.

I have already saluted the scholarly work of two old friends: that of the late Stephen Koss on A. G. Gardiner continues to be relevant here and I also found his formidable second volume of *The Rise and Fall of the Political Press in Britain* illuminating on the journalistic background, at a time when the 'cocoa press' was brewing almost as much trouble for the Liberals as the interventions of the megalomaniac Northcliffe. Second, the synthesis that John Thompson offers in *Woodrow Wilson* goes far beyond biography; though I am perhaps less charitable than either Thompson or John Milton Cooper in reviewing the Wilsonian case on 'breaking the heart of the world'. On House's role, Charles Neu's compendious biography remained a great support and supplied some of my quotations, e.g. Edith Wilson's view of the malign influence of the Colonel. For 'mandates', and the role of G. L. Beer in fostering a concept too easily attributed to Smuts himself, see Wm Roger Louis, *The Ends of British Imperialism: Collected Essays*, pp. 226–8.

CHAPTER 11: A CARTHAGINIAN PEACE?

My debt to the work of Thomas Piketty is again obvious. Another general debt is to Barry Eichengreen's *Golden Fetters: The Gold Standard and the Great Depression*. Specifically on Keynes and war finance, I supplemented the outline in Kathleen Burk, *Britain, America and the Sinews of War*, chapter 9, by reference to the big biographies of Keynes: not only the earlier insights in Skidelsky's first volume, chapters 15 and 16, but, above all, the exact scholarship of Donald Moggridge's chapter 12 and, of course, his editorship of JMK, vols 16 and 17 on the Treasury period. The GDP figures are taken from the MeasuringWorth website (2015), Louis Johnston and Samuel H. Williamson, 'What was the US GDP then?', showing the US real GDP (measured in 2009 dollars) for 1914 as $598 million and for 1918 as $744 million, thus 24 per cent higher; a lower estimate of 12 per cent had been given in table 1.4 of Broadberry and Harrison, *The Economics of World War I*. Either way, I distance myself from describing the whole period from 1914 as a 'low-growth war economy', as identified *only for the period of American hostilities from 1917* in Adam Tooze, *The Deluge*, pp. 216–17, which uses earlier GNP estimates. The 'normal year' was a concept exhumed by the pioneering research of Dr Mary Short, as acknowledged in Martin Daunton's *Just Taxes*, chapter 2. On Keynes and the 'rentier' rhetoric, see the deft treatment in the article by Ross McKibbin, 'Political sociology in the guise of economics'.

On the *Economic Consequences* [JMK 2], Shaw is quoted from his *Collected Letters, 1911–25*, edited by Dan H. Laurence, and the epithet 'pernicious' is Zara Steiner's. For interpretation of the 1918 General Election, the great authority is the book by the late Duncan Tanner, *Political Change and the Labour Party*, chapter 13, which, on the actual impact of the franchise changes, certainly modifies views that used to be held by myself and (albeit in a different sense) by Ross McKibbin, whose persuasive Ford Lectures, *Parties and People*, now deal with this aspect pp. 194–5. On Keynes and Lloyd George, Frances Stevenson is quoted from her memoirs, published in 1967, *The Years that are Past*, p. 142. Anne Olivier Bell's excellent edition of *The Diary of Virginia Woolf* is such a fine source on Keynes precisely because their relationship has so often been distorted in the secondary literature on Bloomsbury. Likewise, Loreburn is worth quoting directly as an antidote to much trite stereotyping of 'Radicals' and 'Liberal Imperialists'. And my bigger point, of course, is about the widespread Liberal moralisation of such issues, turning on guilt; on this point David Reynolds, *The Long Shadow*, pp. 289–91, also has some pertinent comments. This is one reason why it is still worth consulting R. B. McCallum's book *Public Opinion and the Last Peace*, especially pp. 46–52, published by an historian who had lived through these events and was familiar with the different stripes of Liberal commitment.

On Keynes's *Economic Consequences* itself, my comment that 'his central arguments indeed remain alive and well nearly a century later' picks up the gauntlet thrown down in 1998 by Niall Ferguson, *The Pity of War*, especially the scornful comment, p. 408: 'These are Keynes's arguments, alive and well eighty years on.' (See also my notes to chapter 13 below on this point.) Conversely, the abiding relevance of Keynes's analysis for contemporary problems that are similarly European-wide is brought out in the volume edited by Jens Hölscher and Matthias Klaes, *Keynes's Economic Consequences of the Peace*, notably in a persuasive essay by Anna Carabelli and Mario Cedrini on the broader methodological implications.

CHAPTER 12: REPARATIONS AND GUILT

In following these two linked themes, I again find myself more in tune with Anthony Lentin's *Guilt at Versailles* than with any other account of the peace settlement. Zara Steiner, *The Lights that Failed*, is as lucid as ever on the economic issues at the conference and afterwards. The title of Lloyd George's copious two volumes, *The Truth about the Peace Treaties*, should not, of course, be taken too literally; but the book prints a good deal of useful documentation which can be offset against that in the Keynes edition [especially JMK 16 and 17]. Similarly, Keith Hancock does not suppress material damaging to his hero either in *Smuts: The Sanguine Years*, pp. 514–16, 539–42, or in his edition with Jean Van Der Poel of *Selections from the Smuts Papers*, vol. 4, pp. 96–8, from which I quote the crucial memorandum justifying the inclusion of pensions. PWW reprints cognate diary entries from Dulles, Lamont and others.

The voting figures in the by-elections (taken from Fred Craig's compendium, as usual) show an anti-government swing of 24.7 per cent at Leyton West on 1 March 1919 and 32.9 per cent at Hull Central on 29 March, in each case in straight fights between (Asquithian) Liberals and Coalition Conservatives, compared with the December 1918 result. At Aberdeenshire and Kincardineshire Central on 16 April, Labour intervened, polling 26.4 per cent, taking 16.5 per cent from the poll of the 1918 Coalition Conservatives and 9.9 per cent from the vote of the Liberals, who thus gained the seat only narrowly (whereas, in a straight fight, they would have walked home comfortably). So it is equally true to say that the two straight fights had flattered the Liberals or that the move from a two-party to a three-party system cushioned the Conservatives. Lloyd George had to ponder all this.

I found the scrupulous edition by Richard and Clara Winston of Thomas Mann's diaries illuminating about what an educated, liberal German took for granted, as well as of personal interest about a great writer. For Melchior, the sympathetic portrait by Keynes in his *Essays in Biography* [JMK 10] should be supplemented with the acerbic view of their relationship taken by Niall Ferguson, who makes some fair (as well as unfair) hits, not only in *Pity of War* but in his earlier monograph *Paper and Iron*. Harold Nicolson's diary in *Peacemaking* is again useful. Keynes's letter of 14 May 1919 is given fully in both Moggridge's *Keynes*, pp. 311–12 and Skidelsky, vol. 1, pp. 370–1. On Lippmann, see John Thompson, *Reformers and War*, pp. 236–9; and for William Bullitt, see the book on Wilson that he composed with Sigmund Freud, printing Bullitt's resignation letter at pp. 234–5.

CHAPTER 13: FURTHER ECONOMIC CONSEQUENCES

For Kenworthy, see R. B. McCallum, *Public Opinion and the Last Peace*, pp. 58–60; and there is good supporting context on this period in Charles Mowat, *Britain between the Wars*, which is too little consulted today. David Lloyd George, *Is It Peace?*, reprints his speeches of these years; I quote from p. 3 (on the treaty), p. 213 (on Keynes) and p. 50 (on the Hughes initiative). Keynes's *Revision of the Treaty* [JMK 3] is not only a polemic but a quarry of relevant documentation on these negotiations.

On the tangled diplomatic history, Zara Steiner's *The Lights that Failed* is again indispensable. So is Barry Eichengreen, *Golden Fetters* on the economic context, and specifically his table, p. 278, on the debts position at the time of the Hoover moratorium; and see *Securing the World Economy*, Patricia Clavin's deeply researched study of the ghostly presence of the League of Nations in international economic relations, especially pp. 97, 117–22, for the tensions exposed between European and American conceptions of what was at stake. On inflation and the German debt, Adam Tooze provides a cogent exposition in *The Deluge*, summed up in his table 11, p. 444. For various estimates on the burden of reparations on the German economy, see Moggridge's *Keynes*, pp. 342–5; also Eichengreen, pp. 131–2, and his helpful note (p. 129) explaining methodological difficulties and questioning some of the inferences underlying Stephen Schuker's notion of 'American reparations to Germany'. Modern theoretical analysis, as Albrecht Ritschl pithily puts it, 'has emphasised the dominance of willingness-to-pay constraints over capacity-to-pay constraints in sovereign country debt' (Broadberry and Harrison (eds), *Economics of World War I*, p. 71).

The estimates of reparations tabulated in Niall Ferguson's formidably researched monograph, *Paper and Iron*, p. 477, are duly replicated as a graph in his subsequent work, *Pity of War*, p. 416. This later book (1998) comments on the London Schedule (p. 414): 'Nor can it credibly be maintained that the reparation total set in 1921 constituted an intolerable burden' – thus silently countering his earlier conclusion (*Paper and Iron*, 1995, p. 315) drawn from the same evidence: 'Reparations, as envisaged in 1921, *were* therefore excessive – as the German government claimed' (italics original). Ferguson (1995 vintage) thus seems more Keynesian than Keynes himself, whose real fire, of course, had been directed against the scale of reparations as envisaged in 1919.

In identifying a 'Keynesian' approach to economic policy in the 1920s, I happily find myself in agreement with Skidelsky's second volume, especially pp. 20, 147, 173. Harrod's biography was of much the same mind; and Moggridge's chapters 15 and 16 are also highly germane. The edition by Polly Hill and Richard Keynes, *Lydia and Maynard*, again comes into its own here; the letters at the time of the Genoa conference in 1922 at p. 36, the Lloyd George dinner at p. 205. Charles Mallet, *Mr Lloyd George*, p. 306 is my source for 'bamboozled' and Thomas Jones, *Lloyd George*, p. 229 for 'when he is right/ wrong'. John Campbell's study *Lloyd George: The Goat in the Wilderness, 1922– 31* is shrewd and helpful; and I provide further political detail with full references in my article on Lloyd George and Keynes in the Lloyd George Sesquicentenary edition of the *Journal of Liberal History*, 77:46–53 (Winter 2012–13).

On the return to gold, the great authority is Donald Moggridge, *British Monetary Policy, 1924–31*; see pp. 17–21 for the Cunliffe Report. Keynes's reflections in his *Tract on Monetary Reform* [JMK 4] are buttressed by more ephemeral writings on the end of reparations [JMK 18], including correspondence with Melchior, and on the (mainly British) aspects of the gold standard and unemployment policy [JMK 19 and 20], as well as some of the writings reprinted in *Essays in Persuasion* [JMK 9]. To my mind the cited article on the German transfer problem in JMK 11 establishes the link with reparations in a highly pertinent way. The cover of *We Can Conquer Unemployment* makes my point in visual terms; it can be found reproduced as the frontispiece of my book, *The Keynesian Revolution in the Making*. For the quoted exchanges between Keynes and Lloyd George in 1933 see Harrod, *Keynes*, pp. 440–1, and the 1938 letter is cited in the text from JMK 16 because it pertains to the 1916 documents, also reproduced in that volume.

CHAPTER 14: SECOND CHANCES

Conrad Black's accessible biography, *Franklin Delano Roosevelt*, is particularly good on the onset of polio; and Kenneth S. Davis's second volume *FDR: The New York Years* offers a detailed treatment of this period. Two well-informed older books have a compelling sense of immediacy: Robert Sherwood, *Roosevelt and Hopkins*, from which I quote at p. 227; and John Gunther's *Roosevelt in Retrospect*, with the doctor quoted at p. 247. On finances, I take some details from Karl Schriftgiesser, *The Amazing Roosevelt Family*.

On Churchill's finances, we now have the exhaustive analysis by David Lough, *No More Champagne*; and on his literary career in the inter-war years, see my own book, *Mr Churchill's Profession*. Robin Prior, *Churchill's 'World Crisis' as History*, is a close scholarly study, particularly good on the early volumes. I quote Victor Wallace Germains, *The Tragedy of Winston Churchill*, pp. 47, 81 and 280. Clementine's comment is from Mary Soames's useful edition of her parents' letters, *Speaking for Themselves*, p. 332. On the changing public mood in the 1920s, there is a perceptive analysis in David Reynolds, *The Long Shadow*. For the career of Carl Bechhofer Roberts, I rely on the obituary in *The Times*, 16 December 1949; his biography of Churchill, writing as 'Ephesian', is quoted from the four editions as specified in my bibliography, with the main changes apparent between the 1928 and 1936 editions.

Churchill's Romanes Lecture at Oxford in 1930, 'Parliamentary government and the economic problem', is quoted from his collection *Thoughts and Adventures*, at pp. 172, 176, 177, 183. His nostalgic comment on the financial Garden of Eden is in the excellent edition by Ben Pimlott, *The Second World War Diary of Hugh Dalton*, p. 578. Keynes's paper to the memoir club, 'My Early Beliefs', is now available as an addendum to the collected edition of *Essays in Biography* [JMK 10]. His words have often been taken at face value – a problem of literary artifice that Keynes stored up for himself and which I explore in my chapter, 'A religion and no morals', in *Keynes* (2013), pp. 21–52: a book which also explores the relationship of Keynes to the New Deal.

On the Roosevelt Presidency, as well as Kenneth Davis's third volume, *FDR: The New Deal Years*, and material on House from the biography by Charles Neu, there is a useful general account in Tony Badger's *The New Deal: The Depression Years*. Daniel Fusfield's *The Economic Thought of Franklin Roosevelt* shows that, at best, FDR had no excuse for not acquiring a more sophisticated economic understanding. I quote the shrewd account by Frances Perkins in *The Roosevelt I Knew*, p. 183, on the ill-starred personal encounter with Keynes. Churchill's essay on Roosevelt did not appear in the first edition of *Great Contemporaries* (1937), which went through five impressions that year; it was added (along with three other essays) in the revised edition, published in October 1938, with the statement, 'written in 1934' (p. 381n.), which seems to be accurate. Given the wartime correspondence between the two men, Warren F. Kimball has a rich subject, and makes the most of it, in his excellent analysis *Forged in War: Roosevelt, Churchill and the Second World War*. I have also benefited from an early sight of John Thompson's magisterial overview on the development of an American world role in *A Sense of Power*.

Finally, we return – sadder and wiser perhaps – to the theme of the actual impact of the locomotive of war upon capitalism. 'How to Pay for the War' was Keynes's way of posing the immediate problem, one issue authoritatively explored in the work of Richard Toye, *The Labour Party and the Planned Economy*. JMK 22 prints not only Keynes's highly significant article from the *New Republic* but also much other relevant documentation. In seeking to assess Keynes's back-of-an-envelope speculations on the economic statistics, I turned again to the invaluable MeasuringWorth website, in particular Louis Johnston and Samuel H. Williamson, 'What was the US GDP then?'

EPILOGUE: THE LEGACIES OF WAR IN THE LONG RUN

There is a Punch-and-Judy dimension to the whole issue of Anglo-German relations in the past century, and perhaps my own sketch partakes of this. For the military involvement in protecting the British Empire, see Anthony Clayton, '"Deceptive Might": imperial defence and security, 1900–68', in Brown and Louis (eds), *The Oxford History of the British Empire*, vol. 4, pp. 280–305, with its useful maps 12.1 and 12.2 on 'police action' and 'emergencies'. The historiographical ghost in this section, of course, is that of the late Fritz Fischer; see H. W. Koch's useful collection of essays, *The Origins of the First World War: Great Power Rivalry and German War Aims*, in order to recapture some of the perspectives of forty years ago.

I am indebted to the scrupulous research of Isabel Hull, *A Scrap of Paper*, especially pp. 6–12 on the 'innocence campaign', and to the study of the role of propaganda in Adrian Gregory, *The Last Great War*, especially pp. 41–4; much of this confirmed in David Reynolds, *The Long Shadow*, pp. 199–204. In Graves's *Goodbye to All That* the replication of the Ponsonby canard is simply prefaced: 'Recently I saw the following contemporary newspaper cuttings put in chronological sequence' – see the British Penguin edition (1960), pp. 60–1, or the American Doubleday Anchor edition, pp. 67–8. Gregory's comment on the propensity of Ponsonby's book to 'disappear' was borne out when I tried to consult it in the admirably comprehensive holdings of the Cambridge University Library. The only available copy was an American paperback reprint (Torrance, CA, 1980) applauding its 'admission' of British lies and deploring the fact that the (allegedly similar) 'Holocaust charade' in the Second World War had not been exposed owing to 'the power of Zionism' over the American media.

Mantoux's *Carthaginian Peace* is accorded due prominence here, not as a straw man but because there are many points on which it remains a key source. Its rigorous treatment certainly convicted Keynes of particular errors, for example on the Silesian coalfields. I am also sympathetic to its comments on 'the disastrous consequences of the ambiguity' over 'the moral foundations of the Treaty of Versailles', with the consequence that the 'war guilt' agitation 'was to poison the moral life of Europe for the next twenty years' (pp. 100–1). As Albrecht Ritschl nicely puts it, because the peace process was 'too lax and too strict at the same time', the Treaty 'strengthened the elements aimed at revenge instead of promoting change and modernisation' (Broadberry and Harrison (eds), *The Economics of World War I*, pp. 66, 72). In a sense, I accept Mantoux's conclusion: 'Reparations were not paid because Germany, as was quite natural, did not want to pay them, and – which was perhaps not *quite* so natural – the Allies showed themselves incapable or unwilling to take jointly the necessary measures which could have made Germany pay' (p. 156). But surely *either* that means no Allied occupation *or* it simply takes us back to the flawed moral ambiguities of the Treaty.

On the impact of the Second World War, and the sense in which some lessons were learned from the First, my own understanding of the British perspective was conveyed in my book *The Last Thousand Days of the British Empire: The Demise of a Superpower* – with an explanatory subtitle for the paperback edition that I wish I had thought of earlier; the quotation on 'reparations' is from p. 403, citing the *Sunday Times*, 16 December 1945. And for the American perspective I am much influenced by John Thompson's *A Sense of Power: The Roots of America's Global Role*. The quotation from J. L. Hammond is from the weekly paper the *Listener*, 13 February 1947, still faithful to his own sudden epiphany on Monday 3 August 1914.

ACKNOWLEDGEMENTS

The rich and blessedly accessible resources of the University Library in Cambridge are too easily taken for granted by those of us who live here. And I have become increasingly conscious not only of support through my continuing membership of St John's College and of Trinity Hall, but of the intellectual stimulus I have received through a web of personal contacts in Cambridge over many years. In writing this book, I see again that the influence of early teachers – the late Ronald Robinson and Harry Hinsley, the indefatigable Jonathan Steinberg and Zara Steiner – remains with me. I appreciate too the stimulation of (sometimes wayward) exchanges over many years with erstwhile colleagues: Derek Beales, Martin Daunton, Niall Ferguson, Adrian Gregory, Sue Howson, Peter Mandler, Don Moggridge, David Reynolds, Barry Supple, Simon Szreter, Robert Tombs, Adam Tooze and Jay Winter. More still is owed to those who read primitive drafts of this book, especially when they pointed to any lack of coherence in the story I was trying to tell: Eugenio Biagini, Chris Clark, Stefan Collini, John Thompson and Richard Toye.

Bloomsbury, in both London and New York, have again proved to be admirably patient, perceptive and proficient publishers. This book was finally commissioned from London, under the benign aegis of Nigel Newton; it was Michael Fishwick who deftly suggested how its strategic focus might be shifted and sharpened and his assistant Marigold Atkey who subsequently aided my efforts. The

ACKNOWLEDGEMENTS

hands-on editorial assistance of Anna Simpson has been invaluable in conquering so many problems of presentation with versatility and flair. Peter James copy-edited the text with formidable acuity, gracefully applied; and I thank Catherine Best for reading the proofs and David Atkinson for the index. Beyond this, of course, my heaviest debt of all is that to Maria Tippett, whose green fingers found scholarly employment in nurturing this sapling as it germinated, sprouted and grew.

Peter Clarke

INDEX

INDEX

ALSO AVAILABLE BY PETER CLARKE

KEYNES

THE TWENTIETH CENTURY'S MOST INFLUENTIAL ECONOMIST

In the midst of the economic crisis, we peered anxiously into an uncertain future and tried to put things in perspective by looking to the past. One name above all kept on cropping up: John Maynard Keynes, who first came to public attention on both sides of the Atlantic in the early 1920s, when the depression in Britain engaged his attention. And then came the great meltdown of 2008, which caused the ideas of the economist to be rediscovered and rehabilitated.

Engaging and authoritative, *Keynes* explores the often misunderstood man in the context of his own life and times, and explores the significance of his groundbreaking ideas today.

'A wonderfully lucid exposition of complicated ideas ... required reading'
GUARDIAN

'Clarke's prose sparkles, and his book is the place to begin if you want to understand the economist's personality and charisma'
NEW YORK TIMES

'Makes the case for Keynes's continued relevance by combining an absorbing narrative of his life with perceptive comments on how that life shaped his views'
ECONOMIST

ORDER YOUR COPY:

BY PHONE: +44 (0) 1256 302 699; **BY EMAIL**: DIRECT@MACMILLAN.CO.UK
DELIVERY IS USUALLY 3–5 WORKING DAYS. FREE POSTAGE AND PACKAGING FOR ORDERS OVER £20.
ONLINE: WWW.BLOOMSBURY.COM/BOOKSHOP
PRICES AND AVAILABILITY SUBJECT TO CHANGE WITHOUT NOTICE.

WWW.BLOOMSBURY.COM/AUTHOR/PETER-CLARKE

BLOOMSBURY

MR CHURCHILL'S PROFESSION

STATESMAN, ORATOR, WRITER

In 1953, Winston Churchill received the Nobel Prize for Literature. In fact, Churchill was a professional writer before he was a politician. Now historian Peter Clarke traces the writing of the magisterial work that occupied Churchill for a quarter century: his four-volume *History of the English-Speaking Peoples*.

The magnum opus was to be delivered in 1939, but in that year, history overtook history-writing. The book would indeed be written and become a bestseller, after Churchill left public life. In these pages, Peter Clarke follows Churchill's monumental quest to chronicle the English-Speaking Peoples – a quest that helped to define the enduring 'special relationship' between Britain and America.

'Brilliant ... *Mr Churchill's Profession* is a pleasure in itself'
TIMES LITERARY SUPPLEMENT

'Fascinating, erudite and witty'
GUARDIAN

'It is a tribute to his protean personality, and to Clarke's diligent scholarship and elegant narration, that every aspect of [Churchill's] life remains eternally fascinating'
SUNDAY TELEGRAPH

ORDER YOUR COPY:

BY PHONE: +44 (0) 1256 302 699; **BY EMAIL:** DIRECT@MACMILLAN.CO.UK
DELIVERY IS USUALLY 3–5 WORKING DAYS. FREE POSTAGE AND PACKAGING FOR ORDERS OVER £20.
ONLINE: WWW.BLOOMSBURY.COM/BOOKSHOP
PRICES AND AVAILABILITY SUBJECT TO CHANGE WITHOUT NOTICE.

WWW.BLOOMSBURY.COM/AUTHOR/PETER-CLARKE

BLOOMSBURY